THE LITERATURE OF THE
ANCIENT EGYPTIANS

THE LITERATURE
OF THE
ANCIENT EGYPTIANS

POEMS, NARRATIVES, AND MANUALS OF INSTRUCTION, FROM THE THIRD AND SECOND MILLENNIA B.C.

BY

ADOLF ERMAN 1854-1937.

TRANSLATED INTO ENGLISH BY

AYLWARD M. BLACKMAN

BENJAMIN  BLOM, INC.

First Published 1927
Reissued 1971 by
Benjamin Blom, Inc., New York, N.Y. 10025

Library of Congress Catalog Card Number 68-56522

Printed in the United States of America

TRANSLATOR'S PREFACE

WHEN I undertook to prepare the English edition of Professor Erman's *Die Literatur der Aegypter*, I intended to carry out my task in the manner indicated in my review of the book in the *Journal of Egyptian Archæology*, vol. x. pp. 193 ff. This meant that a fuller use was to be made of Dr. Gardiner's *Notes on the Story of Sinuhe*, that full advantage was to be taken of that scholar's brilliant translation of the *Complaints of the Peasant*, recently published in the *Journal of Egyptian Archæology*, vol. ix. pp. 5 ff., and that various corrections, many of them noted in my review, were to be made in the translations of other texts. Shortly after I had begun the work, I received a letter from Professor Erman urgently requesting me not to make any alterations in his translations, or, if I felt compelled to do so, to content myself with inserting them in footnotes. In deference to his wishes I abandoned my original project, but at the same time decided that the suggestion with regard to footnotes was not feasible, for I realized that if I adopted it, they would in many instances occupy more than half the page. This would have been not only most disfiguring to the book, but highly distracting to the reader.

I felt it to be imperative, however, that the English renderings of the Egyptian texts appearing in this volume should not be merely translations of translations. They have, accordingly, in every instance been made directly from the Egyptian, though strictly in accordance with Professor Erman's interpretation, as set forth in his own German translations. Only on the very rarest occasions have I ventured to diverge from his interpretation of a passage or rendering of a word, and then solely on the strength of statements, almost indisputably correct, to be found in Battiscombe Gunn's *Studies in Egyptian Syntax*, or in philological articles by Dr. Gardiner and other authorities—all of which have appeared since Professor Erman's book was published.

I should now like to take this opportunity of thanking Professor Erman for the great pleasure I have derived from translating this delightful book of his. I hope he will regard my undertaking as a tribute from one of the younger Egyptologists to the great scholar, who inaugurated those exhaustive and systematic researches, which, during the last thirty years, have so vastly increased our knowledge of Egyptian grammar and syntax, and of Egyptian philology as a whole.

When this book was already in print, an interesting article by Battiscombe Gunn on King Snefru appeared in the *Journal of Egyptian Archæology*, vol. xii. pp. 250 f. ; it ought certainly to be read in connexion with the narratives and other compositions appearing on pp. 38 ff., 67, and 112 ff.

AYLWARD M. BLACKMAN

OXFORD, 1927

AUTHOR'S PREFACE

MY object in writing this book has been to make accessible to lovers of Antiquity the extensive remains of Egyptian literature which have been brought to light by the labours of Egyptologists. Most of this material has hitherto been known to none but a very limited circle of specialists, as it has been published in books and periodicals that are only available to a few. Yet this literature deserves to be known, not only because it is the oldest secular literature that has grown up in the world, but because it affords us an insight into an active, intellectual life, and into a poetry, which may well hold place beside the achievements of the Egyptians in the artistic and technical spheres. In any case, no one, if he is not acquainted with their literature, ought to pass judgment on the Egyptians and on the period in human development to which they belong.

I planned this book many years ago, and did a great deal of preliminary work for it ; but it was not until I began seriously to carry out my project that I realized upon what a hazardous undertaking I had embarked. I have stated below (p. xlii) what the position is with regard to our translations. A great deal is still entirely unintelligible to us ; and though, indeed, we know the approximate meaning of other passages, yet the exact significance of the words still escapes us, or the relationship of the sentences remains doubtful. In such cases one would prefer to give up all attempts at translating.

Still, if we would wait until all this uncertainty were removed, we should have to wait a long time—in the case of many texts this will never happen—and in the long run it is really more important that the whole should be made accessible together, than that every subsidiary detail and every individual sentence should be rendered with absolute accuracy.

At the same time a translator should, of course, retail to the reader nothing as certain that is not so. I have tried to attain this object by the omission of what is unintelligible, by special type where there is uncertainty, and by a liberal use of notes of interrogation. On the other hand, I have had to resist the desire to give my reasons for the choice of any particular translation in cases of doubt, and to enter into other scientific discussions. For—and I should like expressly to emphasize this—I have not written this book for the limited circle of Egyptologists,[1] but for the many who are interested in the ancient world, yet to whom admittance to the field of Egyptian literature has hitherto been denied. I must request them, however, not to make a wrong use of the book, nor to wish to infer from it more than it is in a position to give. It sets out to acquaint the reader with the texts as a whole, and so I would ask the student, who is desirous of investigating particular points, to consult also the works of those Egyptologists to which I have referred in dealing with each individual composition. I have, as a rule, only mentioned two of my predecessors, the one who first recognized the content of the text, and the one whose work thereon is at present to be regarded as the best and most exhaustive. From them can be seen all that is satisfactory and unsatisfactory in what has previously been written about the texts in question, and what other translations have been proposed for particular passages. Many of these texts have been edited as much as sixty years ago, and a full understanding of them has only been arrived at gradually—from the first gropings and guesses to a grammatical elucidation, and from that again to an appreciation of the style. The

---

[1] Most of my fellow-specialists may well experience the same sensation as I did : they will be astonished at the great number of literary texts which have already been got together. Also an Egyptian work affects one quite differently, when read as a whole, than when, as is customary with us, it is laboriously translated sentence for sentence

scholars who have devoted themselves to this problem are not few, and if I mention here the names of Chabas, Dévaud, Gardiner, Golénischeff, Goodwin, Griffith, Lange, Maspero, W. Max Müller, de Rougé, and Vogelsang, the list is not by any means complete. I myself also have participated in this opening up of the literary texts, more indeed than is to be seen from my printed works. It was my task to prepare most of these writings for the *Lexicon* which the German Universities have in hand, and it was my privilege, moreover, to expound them for a period of more than forty years in my lectures. That in these lectures I was not always the giver, but also obtained many good ideas from my pupils, is to be taken for granted, although I can no longer give a detailed acknowledgment of them. But all these pupils have my thanks now as I write this, and especially those four of our company, to whom this book is dedicated, and whom my thanks can no longer reach.

I could have greatly extended the scope of my book. I could also have included the demotic writings of the Græco-Roman epoch ; but they assuredly belong to another world, and so I have preferred to call a halt at the end of the late New Kingdom, where, moreover, the great break occurs in the life of the Egyptian people. It will be better to form a separate collection of the demotic literary texts. The same holds good for the medical and mathematical works ; both indeed belong, as is now even more evident, to the great achievements of the Egyptians, but they demand a special kind of treatment, and accordingly a book to themselves. From the endless multitude of religious texts I have taken only isolated examples, less on account of their contents than with a view to giving the reader an idea of their form.[1] I have acted also with similar restraint, towards the innumerable inscriptions, even when they are couched in poetic language ; for it was my business

---

[1] The student desiring more of them will find good translations in ROEDER, *Urkunden zur Religion des alten Ägyptens*, Jena, 1915 ; EDV. LEHMANN, *Textbuch zur Religionsgeschichte*, Leipzig, 1912 (translated by Grapow) ; SCHARFF, *Ägyptische Sonnenlieder*, Berlin, 1920.

to see that the remains of the actual literature were not hidden by what is unessential.[1]

I should like to have spared the reader the explanatory and introductory notes, and have permitted the Egyptians to speak for themselves ; but the world into which I am leading him is so peculiar, that he would not be able to find his way about in it entirely unaided, and still less would he notice the niceties which an Egyptian author is so fond of inserting into his work. However, I have in these respects limited myself as far as possible, and in particular I have not gone more deeply into the questions of the religion, history, and geography than was necessary for the proper understanding of the passages concerned.

A translation is always an unsatisfactory thing, and no one has ever yet succeeded in bringing out the external features of the foreign original, and at the same time producing an intelligible translation of its contents in straightforward language. I have endeavoured not to deviate too far from the Egyptian text, although I have often allowed myself to stress the relationship of the sentences with one another, and have, where it could safely be done, interpolated particles which denote this relationship in our languages. On the other hand, I would often have liked to make the arrangement of words and sentences conform more closely to our own, but I could not do this if I wished to avoid concealing the indications of versification (see below p. xxxi, note 2).

With regard to titles and all kinds of technical terms, I have often had to content myself with inexact translations, and always so in the case of those antiquated names of peoples and countries, which the Egyptians preserved from the earliest period of their history, and which they themselves employed quite vaguely. Accordingly, when Nubian, negro, Asiatic, Bedouin, Palestine, or Syria are encountered in my translation, it would be well, before too much is inferred therefrom, to

---

[1] I have therefore also in the case of the actual literary texts not accepted every unimportant or meaningless fragment.

examine the original so as to see which of these ominous words is used there. A serious difficulty is presented also by the names of persons, gods, and Egyptian localities, of which we only know the consonants. To make them pronounceable I have merely adopted the customary practice of the present day. Where, however, there exists any tradition, or even just a generally recognized usage, in the rendering of a name, I have naturally availed myself of it. The reader must not, therefore, be surprised if side by side with monstrous forms such as Khekheperre-sonbu, are to be found Græcized forms such as Amenōphis, or pure Greek forms such as Heliopolis, Arabic forms such as Siut, or modern European forms such as Luxor and Thebes ; this cannot be avoided, and in the end no great harm is done.

In my translations I have indicated free renderings of passages and other interpolations by italics ; brackets denote restorations. The gaps which I have been obliged to leave in the translation I could naturally not reproduce in their full length, which is often considerable. I have been content to distinguish between two kinds of such omissions : . . . means that a single word is omitted, while – – – – indicates that a sentence, or a longer passage, is missing.

Herr Grapow, before the printing was begun, undertook the tedious task of comparing my translations once more with the originals, whereby various omissions and mistakes have been avoided. I thank him here once more for this friendly service.

ADOLF ERMAN

PFORTA, *January* 1, 1923

[1] An *e* is quite arbitrarily inserted throughout, and, moreover, the so-called weak consonants *alef, ayin, w*, and *y* are rendered by *a, u*, and *i*. Still, in the use of many oft-recurring names, one allows oneself the privilege of acting differently.

CONTENTS

I. FROM THE OLDEST POETRY

xiii

II. FROM THE OLDER PERIOD

III. FROM THE NEW KINGDOM

OUTLINE OF EGYPTIAN HISTORY

THE customary division into "Kingdoms" and "Dynasties" must, in view of our defective knowledge of Egyptian history, be retained. The dates given here are, from *circa* 2000 B.C. onwards, approximately correct. The lower figures have been adopted for the time of the Old Kingdom, the various estimates for which still differ by centuries.

OLD KINGDOM.

> Dynasty 3 : 3000–2900 B.C.
> > A period still almost entirely unknown to us (pp. 37, 66).
>
> Dynasty 4 : 2900–2750 B.C.
> > King Snefru (pp. 38, 111), and the builders of the great pyramids—Kheops (p. 36), Khephrēn (p. 36), and Mykerinos.
>
> Dynasty 5 : 2750–2625 B.C.
> > Flourishing period for the art and possibly also for the literature (p. 54).
>
> Dynasty 6 : From 2625 onwards.
> > About 2500 a political collapse (see p. 93) ; Egypt sinks into obscurity.

PERIOD BETWEEN THE OLD AND MIDDLE KINGDOMS.

Egypt has broken up into separate states. About 2360 B.C. Akhthoes (p. 81) founds the kingdom of Herakleopolis (pp. xxiv, 75, 116), and under him the languishing civilization once more revives. The coexistent Eleventh Dynasty in Thebes gains the upper hand after prolonged struggles (pp. 79, 82).

MIDDLE KINGDOM.

> Dynasty 12 : 1995–1790 B.C., a period of high attainment both in political power and in general culture.
> > Its founder, Amenemhēt I (1995–1965) puts an end to the disorders (pp. 15, 72 ff., 111 ff.).

His son Sesōstris I (1975–1934 ; see pp. 15, 49) and King Sesōstris III (1882–1845 ; see p. 134), extend their dominion over the neighbouring countries. Amenemhēt III (1844–1797 ; see p. 84) turns the Fayyûm into cultivable land.

Dynasty 13 : from *circa* 1790 B.C. ; downfall of the realm. Egypt is overthrown by a barbarous people from Asia, the Hyksōs, who bear rule from their capital Avaris (on the north-eastern frontier of the Delta). From among their vassals the princes of Thebes become independent (see pp. 52, 165), and one of these, King Amōsis (*circa* 1580 B.C.), succeeds in expelling the Hyksōs.

NEW KINGDOM.

Dynasty 18 : Period of the highest attainment in general culture and in political power. Thebes becomes the capital, and its god Amūn the chief of the gods. Thutmōsis I (*circa* 1555–1501) and his son Thutmōsis III (*circa* 1478–1447) create an empire that extends from the Sudân to the Euphrates (see pp. 167, 254).

Amenōphis III (*circa* 1415–1380 B.C.) ; a long, brilliant reign, in which, however, there are already signs of a revolution. This comes to pass under his son Amenōphis IV (from 1380 B.C.), who strives to bring about a religious reformation associated with pure sun-worship (pp. 288–292). On meeting with opposition, he deserts Thebes and founds a new capital at El-Amarnah, in Middle Egypt ; the art also takes on a new character and the old literary language is replaced by the colloquial (p. xxvi). The king henceforth calls himself Ikhenaton. The later history of this heretical period is quite obscure ; all we know is that the old faith finally triumphed (pp. 293 ff., 309).

Dynasty 19 : *circa* 1350–1200 B.C.

The centre of gravity of the realm lies henceforth in the Delta, though Thebes remains the sacred city, which is adorned with the enormous temples of Karnak, Luxor, etc.

Sēthos I (*circa* 1320–1300) fights against the Bedouins of Palestine. His son, Ramesses II (*circa* 1300–1234), wages a long war with the Hittite empire in Asia Minor for the possession of Palestine (pp. 261–270), and founds the new Residence, House-of-Ramesses (pp. 206, 270 ff.). The power of the empire declines. Under his son, Merneptah, a war against the Libyans, and battles in Palestine against, among other peoples, the tribe of Israel (pp. 274–278). Then a period of internal disorders.

Dynasty 20 : Reign of Ramesses III (*circa* 1200–1169 B.C.), a period of revival ; then under his successors, all bearing the name Ramesses, the complete downfall.

Dynasty 21 : *circa* 1090–945 B.C.
The high-priest of Amūn, Hrihōr, becomes king in Thebes, and there are other princes in other cities, *e.g.* Smendes, in Tanis (p. 175).

THE END.

Dynasty 22 : One of the Libyan princes, who had long been settled in the country, Sheshonk, makes himself king about 945 B.C. His family reigns in different princedoms.

Then follow : *circa* 712 B.C., the conquest by the Ethiopians ; *circa* 670, the conquest by the Assyrians. Under the family of Psammetikhos I (663–525 B.C.) the unhappy country enjoys a period of revival, but the Persians put an end to this (525 B.C.). Egypt becomes again independent at intervals, until it at last falls to Alexander (332 B.C.).

BY WAY OF INTRODUCTION

1. THE DEVELOPMENT OF THE LITERATURE

THE Egyptian people became known to our European world only in their dotage, when they had expended their last energies in unsuccessful struggles against foreign oppressors. They clung tenaciously at that time to the beliefs and the outworn practices of the past, as if by so doing they could still maintain their position among the nations of the earth. The Greeks viewed with a mixture of disdain and reverence this survival from a remote past, so utterly out of keeping with their own enlightened world. Thus the Egyptians have lived on in the conception of Europeans as the Chinese, so to speak, of antiquity, and, despite all the discoveries of our time, they still bear the reputation of having been a strange people, ossified and without any proper development.

And yet in the earlier millennia of their history the Egyptians were the exact antithesis to this popular conception—a gifted people, intellectually alert, and already awake when other nations still slumbered ; indeed, their outlook on the world was as lively and adventurous as was that of the Greeks thousands of years later. That is plainly to be seen in their vast technical achievements, and still more so in their plastic art, which reproduces life so joyously and with so sure a touch.

It is not to be wondered at that so gifted a people took a pleasure in giving a richer and more artistic shape to their songs and their tales, and that in other respects also an intellectual life developed among them—a world of thought extending beyond the things of every day and the sphere of religion. And since the Egyptians had also invented a system of writing, there grew up among them at an early date a body of writings of a varied kind, which they cultivated and esteemed consciously, and to which we do not ascribe too much honour if we speak of it as their literature. But while the works preserved from the plastic art of the Egyptians are so many, that we have by now gained a conception of it which could not be greatly modified, our position with regard to the literature is unfortunately very different; for of this we possess comparatively little. And how could it be otherwise, seeing that the preservation of a literary work depends upon an unlikely chance making it possible for a fragile sheet of papyrus to last for three or four thousand years ! Accordingly, out of a once undoubtedly large mass of writings, only isolatèd fragments have been made known to us, and every new discovery adds some new feature to the picture which we have painted for ourselves of Egyptian literature. And on the whole this picture is now a fairly correct one, for it possesses an intrinsic probability. Each of the large chronological divisions, into which it falls, displays a special uniform character, and this character harmonizes with what we otherwise know about the period in question.

As far back as we can trace it, the Egyptian language displays signs of being carefully fostered. It is rich in metaphors and figures of speech, a " cultured language " which " composes and thinks " for the person who writes. One at least of the old books of proverbs [1] may even have been composed during the Old Kingdom, in the time of the Fifth Dynasty (*circa* 2700 B.C. or earlier), which is known to us as an age in which the plastic art was at a particularly high level. But the full development of the literature appears only to have been reached in the dark period which separates the Old from the Middle Kingdom,[2] and in the famous Twelfth Dynasty (1995–1790

[1] See what is said with regard to the *Proverbs of Ptahhotep* on p. 54, below.

[2] Three of the most important books of the older literature—the *Instruction for King Merikerē*, the *Instruction of Duauf*, and the *Complaints of the Peasant*—will have been written under the kings who then ruled from Herakleopolis over Middle Egypt and the Delta. We know very little of them, and therefore ordinarily assume that they played an unimportant rôle in the development of the Egyptian people. Yet it may well be possible that it was at their court that the literature blossomed forth. This is also suggested by Blackman, who draws attention to the remarkably high level of the art of that period as displayed in the tombs of Meir (see *Discovery*, iii. pp. 35 ff. ; *Journ. of Egypt. Archæology*, xi. pp. 213 f. ; *Luxor and its Temples*, p. 42).

B.C.). It is the writings of this age that were read in the schools five hundred years later, and from their language and style no one dared venture to deviate. The feature which, from an external standpoint, gives its character to this classical literature —it cannot be called by any other name—is a delight in choice, not to say far-fetched, expressions. " To speak well in good sooth " is regarded as a high art, to attain to which an effort must be made. That this was really the tendency of this epoch is to be seen also from its inscriptions, which, so far as they originate from educated people, are composed in the same elaborated style. However, it would not be correct to maintain that the real achievement of the classical period is to be seen in this stylistic art. Be it rather said that its writers venture upon very diverse and remarkable topics, and do not recoil from even the more profound questions.

On the other hand, the actual religion falls into the background in this body of writings, and hardly anything is said in these books about all the divinities, with the worship of whom, according to current conception, the Egyptians were so much occupied. It might be supposed that, for an educated person of this period, the old faith was just an inheritance which he outwardly cherished ; in his world of thought he contented himself with the indefinite idea of " God."

We have no intention of blinding our eyes to the fact that a great deal must be lost of precisely this old literature ; we cannot well suppose that there were no 'love-poems at that time, or that collections of proverbs were much more frequent than hymns to the king. To this phenomenon there apparently contributed, besides blind chance, a special circumstance, which gives to what is scholastic in the literature a prominence beyond its due. Our papyri are derived mostly from tombs, and it would be natural enough for a boy to have his exercise-books placed with him in the grave, whereas books of another character were retained for the living.

However that may be, in the second period of the literature also, that of the later New Kingdom (since about 1350 B.C.) the schools are no less to the fore.

This later literature grew up in opposition to the old tradition. Until then, through all the centuries, the language of the classical literature had been retained as the literary language, and at most it had permitted itself to approach the actual colloquial language in documents of everyday life or in popular tales.[1] Finally, however, the difference between both languages became so great, that the classical language could scarcely be understood by ordinary people.[2] In the great revolution at the end of the Eighteenth Dynasty, which we associate with the name of Amenōphis IV, these shackles also were broken. Men began to write poetry in the actual language of the day, and in it is composed the beautiful hymn to the sun, the manifesto of the reformed religion. But whereas the other innovations of the heretical *régime* disappeared after its collapse, this particular one survived, doubtless because the conditions hitherto existing had become impossible. Under the Nineteenth and Twentieth Dynasties there burst forth into flower a vigorous literature, written in the new language, which we call New Egyptian, and to which belong almost all the writings contained in the second half of our book.

In the New Egyptian epoch also the schools thrust themselves into prominence, but their productions have now a more lively tone than they had in the old epoch. And this liveliness is, moreover, characteristic of the literature of this period ; men saw the world as it is and took a pleasure in it. On that account, indeed, so far as our knowledge goes, the profounder thoughts are wanting ; though actually a new discovery may correct our judgment in this respect.

New Egyptian literature, which, as we might suppose, had set out to be really popular, did not long pursue this course, and soon the same striving after refinement of expression, which characterized the older literature, is active in it also. The language of the educated person was again adorned with far-fetched words and phrases, and he delights in embellishing it with foreign words. For something like five centuries this later literature appears to have been cultivated, and then its language also became a dead one, which the boys at school had to learn ; and with that the literary life in decadent Egypt seems to have expired. It was not till several centuries later, perhaps only

---

[1] See, *e.g.*, below, the *Story of King Kheops and the Magicians* ; the reader will notice the simplicity of its language even in translation.

[2] If the writing, which omits all vowels, did not gloss over a considerable part of the deviations, the difference would seem as great to us as that separating Old High German from modern German, or Italian from Latin.

in the Greek period, that a new literature appears, the so-called demotic, which does not come within the scope of this book.

I have spoken above of the foreign words, of which the writings of the later New Kingdom are full. They are almost all borrowed from the inhabitants of Palestine, and show, as is known to us from other sources, in what close relationship Egypt and Palestine then stood. We may therefore suppose that Canaan was also influenced by Egypt in the sphere of literature, just as it was in that of sculpture. We should certainly encounter Egyptian influence in the literature of the Phœnicians, were that preserved ; but in Hebrew literature also, which belongs to so much later a period, there are a number of features that strikingly remind one of the body of Egyptian writings—namely, in the wisdom-literature of the Hebrews, in the Psalms,[1] and in the Song of Songs. It might be supposed that similarities of this sort are to be traced, at least indirectly, to Egyptian prototypes. That being so, then even we ourselves must, without suspecting it, have all along been under the influence of the intellectual life of Egypt.

2. THE LEARNED SCRIBES

I have spoken in the preceding paragraphs of the cultured classes as the upholders of the older and later literature, and possibly this expression may strike many as being too modern. And yet it is correct. Through the Egyptian people from the earliest period there ran a deep cleavage, which separated him who had enjoyed a higher education from the common mass. It came into existence when the Egyptians had invented their writing, for he who mastered it, however humble his position might outwardly be, at once gained a superiority over his fellows. Without the assistance of his scribes even the ruler was now of no account, and it was not without good reason that the high officials of the Old Kingdom were so fond of having themselves represented in writing posture ; for that was the occupation to which they owed their rank and their power. The road to every office lay open to him who had learnt writing and knew how to express himself in well

[1] See the essay by BLACKMAN in SIMPSON, *The Psalmists*, Oxford, 1926, pp. 177 ff.

chosen terms, and all other professions were literally under his control. There thus developed among the scribes a pride and a caste-consciousness, that are very evident in the old literature which they created (more so in fact than accords with our taste), and that also distinguish all their inscriptions. Still we ought not to condemn this mandarinism, for it did set up an ideal of the official, which possesses some elements of greatness. The official is to be impartial, one who protects the insignificant against the powerful ; the clever person, who knows a way out even in the midst of the greatest difficulties ; the humble one, who never thrusts himself forward, and yet whose opinion is heard in the council. His every writing and utterance, too, must be distinct from the vulgar. In this spirit generation after generation of scribes did their work, and they brought up the younger members of their class on the same principle. And in the New Kingdom, likewise, the tendency of the bureaucracy and its schools [1] remained the same, and, despite all external differences, the preceptors' letters preach nothing but what the old wisdom-books had preached, except that their teaching is clothed in a wittier garb, and that the arrogance of their outlook is, if possible, more strongly evinced in them than ever.

3. SINGERS AND STORY-TELLERS

The educated " scribes," it is true, created Egyptian literature, but there existed before them, and in addition to them, persons who practised a less sophisticated art—an art that exercised an influence, moreover, on the literature.

Whoever is closely acquainted with modern Egypt will carry about with him a recollection of the singing of the *fellâhîn* and boatmen, whose monotonous songs resound continually over the green fields and over the yellow Nile. I do not know if the peculiar nasal drawl of this singing, which strikes us as so peculiar, is to be claimed as an inheritance from ancient times, but the joy in singing certainly is. The peasant and craftsman of Ancient Egypt also accompanied their work with their unpretentious singing, which so obviously formed part

---

[1] Particulars as to the schools of the New Kingdom are to be found in the introduction to the section concerned with that subject.

of the task in hand, that the sculptor, when depicting this, also added the song to the representation. Such songs from the different periods I give below in the appropriate sections. What the beauties of the *harîm* sing in their lord's presence is unfortunately not included in the representations of them. We see only that one body of girls sings in accompaniment to the dance, which the other executes ; what they are singing will scarcely have been so naïve and innocent as the songs of the workpeople ! At all times we meet with blind men as singers,[1] and it cannot be doubted that these unfortunates were professional musicians. There were certainly also professional female singers, and at the end of the New Kingdom, in the *Voyage of Unamūn*, we shall actually encounter an " Egyptian female singer " in Syria, where she, in her way, will have spread Egyptian civilization.

If the male and female singers have thus found admission into the series of tomb-scenes, we nevertheless search there in vain for the other representative of popular art, the storyteller. That is not to be wondered at, for he plied his trade, not in the house of the noble lord, nor yet in his fields, but recited his stories only to the common people in the street, and street-life is not depicted in the tombs. And yet the storyteller in ancient times certainly entertained his simple-minded audience just as he does in Egypt at the present day ; for from all periods of Egyptian history we possess popular narratives, whose tone and contents indicate such an origin. If the tales of the modern story-tellers are preferably made to revolve round some historical personality, the Sultan Bibars, or the Khalif Harūn, those older stories are also connected with figures famous in history. From the Christian period in Egypt we have a tale of Cambyses, and from the Greek period one about Nektanebus ; Herodotus has preserved to us among others the delightful story of Rhampsinitus, and in demotic papyri we read of King Petubastis and of the high priest Khamoes. Then from the end of the New Kingdom we have the stories of King Thutmōsis III, and of the Hyksōs king Apōphis, and from the end of the Middle Kingdom those of Kheops.

The same naïve, and at times burlesque, tone is displayed in much of what Egypt has bequeathed to us as mythology— legends of Isis and Osiris, of the old sun-god and his drunken

---

[1] See, *e.g.*, BLACKMAN, *Rock Tombs of Meir*, ii. Pl. III. pp. 12 f.

messenger (p. 47), and of the goddess who would not return to Egypt again.[1] These stories look as though they had been transmitted by people who took into account the taste of the masses. That they finally also attained religious currency in this popular form does not speak against such an origin.

4. THE FORMS OF THE POETRY

All that the Egyptian writes in elevated language falls into short lines of approximately equal length, and although we know nothing about their sound, we are none the less inclined to regard these lines [2] as verse, *i.e.* to ascribe to them some sort of metrical structure. This is in many cases undoubtedly correct, positively certain in those where invariably, as the meaning shows, a fixed number of lines—generally there are three or four—belong together :

> Thou embarkest on thy ship of cedar-wood,
> That is manned from bow to stern,
> And thou arrivest at this thy fair mansion,
> Which thou hast builded for thyself.

> Thy mouth is full of wine and beer,
> Of bread, and meat, and cakes ;
> Oxen are slain and wine-jars opened,
> And pleasant singing is before thee.

> Thy chief anointer anointeth with kemi-unguent,
> Thy water-bailiff beareth garlands,
> Thine overseer of the country folk presenteth fowl,
> And thy fisherman presenteth fish.[3]

These are indubitable verses.

Many such poems show, in addition, the peculiarity of all their stanzas having the same opening word. Thus in the *Dispute with his Soul of one who is tired of Life*, the eight stanzas of the first song all begin with " Lo ! my name is

---

[1] One may also compare the *Tale of the Two Brothers*.

[2] The scribes of the New Kingdom divide them up mostly by means of red dots, which they also employ, however, in purely prose texts as stops.

[3] See below, p. 212.

abhorred," those of the second with "To whom do I speak to-day?" etc.[1]

In the hymn on the victory of Thutmōsis III the connection is, as a matter of fact, a double one, for the third lines of the stanzas have also the same beginnings; the first lines begin with "I have come that I may cause thee to tread down . . .," the third with "I show them thy majesty . . ."; the second and fourth have optional beginnings.

But these initial similarities are to be found also in texts, the sections in which are of varying length, and display no regularity with regard to the number of lines. Such irregular sections are also to be recognized as stanzas, only of a freer structure. And there will naturally have been such freer stanzas in poems, in which they are not revealed by the similarity of the opening words. It can be seen that we are here still groping almost entirely in the dark,[2] and shall probably always be doing so, since the question, upon which everything depends,—what metre did Egyptian verses have?—remains an unanswered one for us.

As to this question, we can at most venture on a supposition. If we assumed, what on the ground of grammatical considerations is probable, that every virtual word in the language—substantive, adjective, verb, etc.—had only one strongly accented vowel, then every Egyptian line of verse would have had two to four accentuations, with optional depressions between; we should thus have verses in a free rhythm and not in a rigid metre. The fact that the Egyptians of the Christian epoch, the Copts, actually constructed their verses in the same free manner would well agree with this supposition :

> Ershan-uróme bók epshmó
> tef-er-urómpe shaf-któf epef-éy
> a-Archellítes bók etanséf
> is-uméshe enhóu epináu epef-hó.

> Another mán who goés abroad
> Tarries a yeár and retúrns to his hoúse.
> But Archellíte to schóol he hath góne,
> And how mány the dáys till I loók on his fáce!

---

[1] In New Egyptian poetry the custom of lines having the same beginning no longer exists.

[2] I have therefore in my translations avoided breaking up the printed text into verse-lines, apart from a few instances of absolute certainty.

The Ancient Egyptian quatrains must have sounded something like this Coptic one.

Such free rhythm is also vouched for by yet another circumstance : when a verse, for example, is repeated, a longer expression can be interpolated in place of a single name, and instead of the " Osiris awaketh in peace " of the first stanza, there can be sung in the second " The ever enduring, the lord of victuals, that giveth sustenance to him whom he loveth, awaketh in peace."

But in this discussion I have so far not touched upon the feature which lends all this poetry and semi-poetry its special character, the extraordinary custom which we are wont to call " parallelism of the members." It is not enough to express an idea once, it must be done twice, so that two short sentences, of the same or similar purport, always follow one another. Thus, for example : " The judge awaketh, Thōth lifteth himself up," or : " Then spake these friends of the king, and they made answer before their god," where in both instances the second sentence is quite superfluous. Or again : " They that enter into this tomb, they that behold what is in it," where the repetition does introduce something new. It is the delight in fine speeches that has been responsible for this peculiar mode of expression ; the speaker feels that he could have employed, for what he has just said, yet a second no less telling phrase, and he cannot resist the temptation to utter it once again in this version. In process of time it became an established fashion, that will have been regarded as the natural ornamentation of dignified speech. The Old Testament has accustomed us to this strange mode of expression—for it prevailed just as much among the Hebrews and Babylonians—and so in Egyptian texts it does not surprise us as much as it should. But its absurdity is fully appreciated so soon as a piece of other poetry is rendered in this style. The fifth book of the *Odyssey*, which begins :

" Now the Dawn arose from her couch, from the side of the lordly. Tithonus, to bear light to the immortals and to mortal men. And lo, the gods were gathering to session, and among them Zeus, that thundereth on high, whose might is above all " ;

would read somewhat like this in the Egyptian style :

The Dawn raised her up from the bed of Tithonus,
And the Red Glow of Morning arose from her resting-place,
That she might shine for the immortals,
And bring light to mankind.
Now the gods were going to the assembly,
And the immortals sat them down to take council.
In their midst was seated Zeus the thunderer,
And the king of gods was enthroned at their head,
He whose strength is great,
And his might surpasseth all.

That all this is narrated in a pleasing manner may be true enough, but such a method waters down the narrative far too much.

However, this parallelism was never consolidated into an established form for poetry, but remained always just a decoration, which was employed, to be sure, without stint, whenever it was desired to express oneself in dignified language.

The pleasure taken in varying an expression led also to the habit of referring to the person, extolled in a song, under repeatedly new names and designations. To this is attributable, for example, the *Morning Hymn* translated below on p. 12, the single verse of which is varied in this manner *ad infinitum*—monotonous to our ears, but only because we cannot appreciate the subtleties of all the carefully chosen appellations. It is also responsible for the peculiar style of the hymns of praise, so characteristic of Egypt. They begin with the name of the recipient of the eulogy, preceded, possibly, by an additional acclamation, such as, " Be thou praised ! " or " Adoration to thee ! " Then follow, virtually as attributes to this name, pure adjectives, substantives, participles, and relative sentences, which describe the qualities of the object of eulogy or call to mind his achievements [1]—endlessly and confusedly, the more so as the poet attaches no value to a consecutive arrangement of the many things which he calls to mind. Egyptian poetry, therefore, possesses, on the whole, no meaning, and he who reads the lamentations of the prophet of the *Admonitions*, depicting the misery of his time, is surprised to find that this

---

[1] Examples of such hymns of praise are to be found below among the religious poems of the older period.

c

poet has made no attempt to keep what is homogeneous more or less together. His heart is full of the country's distress, and he now bursts forth with this complaint and now with that. So it can at least be understood. However, on closer examination, a different impression is gained. The man is improvising, and accordingly any word, which he has used in the last verse, leads him on purely extraneous grounds to a new idea, which he immediately expresses. Thus he says once that all are sated with life, even little children. At the mention of children it occurs to him that the children are killed and thrown on to the high-desert ground. And the high-desert ground brings him again to the mummies, which are there torn from the tombs and cast on to it.

Lastly, mention must be made of two more artifices with which the Egyptians liked to ornament their discourses, though they are not to be numbered among the distinctive marks of poetry—paronomasia and alliteration.

Paronomasia was always a favourite device, and there is, for example, a very ancient ritual for the presentation of offerings, in which a pun is made on the name of every article of food. Punning is regularly employed also in two poems of the New Kingdom, which are given below,[1] though naturally this cannot be reproduced in the translation.

In the times with which we are concerned, cases of alliteration can only now and then be instanced, e.g. in the two following lines of verse, which refer to Amenōphis III : " His club contends against Naharina, his bow bends down the negroes." [2]

But alliterative poems must have existed at that date, for where else can the Egyptians of the Greek period, who were not given to making new discoveries, have obtained the pattern for their alliterative poetry, for which they show such a marked predilection in their temple inscriptions ? The priests of that period take delight in presenting to us one and the same sentence with ever new alliterations. Thus they say of the inundation : " The Nile neareth thy nether lands," " the water welleth up over thy wold," " the flood floweth to thy fields," etc. The employment of similar artifices may also be postulated for the New Kingdom.

---

[1] A love-song and the poem on the war-chariot.
[2] *Mém. de la Mission*, xv. 15, 2.

5. WRITING AND BOOKS

We must at least make some brief mention here of that invention of the Egyptians, without which their intellectual life would never have been able to expand, namely, writing. It began as a system of picture-writing, such as other peoples also have devised—a very inadequate expedient, that serves well enough to recall something to one's own mind, but from which another will have difficulty in discovering the idea that it is desired to express. Thus, to take a purely imaginary example, if two people agree that the one is to supply an ox in three months' time, in return for which the other will pay five jars of honey, pictures of the moon, the ox, the bee, and the jar, in addition to some small strokes indicating the numbers, suffice as tokens for them both, but a third person would never be able to explain these signs with certainty. This preliminary structure must therefore undergo considerable development. Individual peoples have proceeded on very different lines, and have thereby arrived at all sorts of writings of words and syllables. The Egyptians alone were destined to adopt a remarkable method, following which they attained to the highest form of writing, the alphabet.

The method was fundamentally very simple. It was desired to write words which it would have been difficult or impossible to draw, and so the idea was arrived at of substituting for such a word another, that could easily be drawn and that had a similar sound. The reader then recognized from the context what was really meant, especially when the usage had become stereotyped and every one was accustomed to think, in the case of the swallow ⟷ *wr*, of *wr* "great," and, in the case of the beetle 🪲 *khpr*, of *khpr*, "to become." Since in Egyptian, as in the related languages, the meaning of a word is attached to its consonants, whereas the vowels decide its grammatical form, regard was only paid to the fact that the word which had been substituted for another had the same consonants as it, while the vowels were disregarded. It was as if—to take an English example—"heed" were written with the picture of a "head," and broad with that of a loaf of "bread."

Many signs, which were thus employed, were in process of time transferred to so many words, that they were scarcely any longer used for special ones ; and they became purely phonetic signs. Thus the swallow is used not only, as in the first instance, for *wr* " great," but also to write the consonants *w* and *r* in words like *ḥwr*, *śwr*, *wrś*, *wrryt*, etc. Thereby the writing obtained phonetic signs of two consonants.

Other peoples have also arrived thus far by a similar process, but the Egyptians now went one step further, and employed especially short words, which consisted of not more than one consonant, for the writing of this one consonant. Thus ⬭ *ro* " mouth " was taken for *r*, ⬭ *zt* " snake " (-*t* is the feminine termination) for *z*, ⬭ *shy* " lake " for *sh*. The result was an alphabet of twenty-four consonants, which later on, upon Canaanite soil, became the prototype of our own.

With this alphabet were now written single short words, such as ⬭ *r* " to," ⬭ *m* " in," ⬭ *iw* " be," or grammatical endings were thereby expressed : ⬭ *khpr·f* " he becomes." What was no less important, it facilitated the reading of word-signs. In the case of ⬭, the draughts-board, or ⬭, the hoe, it was in itself possible to think of other words for draughts-board and hoe than *mn* and *mr* ; but if their final consonants *n* and *r* were added to them : ⬭, the reader saw at once that *mn* and *mr* were intended.

Several longer words also were only written with alphabetic signs, such, for example, as ⬭ *byn* " bad " and ⬭ *nht* " sycomore," though the system remained on the whole a mixed one, consisting of word-signs in their original or transferred meaning, and of alphabetic signs tacked on to them.

In the course of further development yet a third element was introduced, the so-called determinative. To the single word one more sign was added, which guided the reader to its meaning ; *nht* " the sycomore " received, *e.g.*, a tree ⬭, *nfr* " good " a papyrus roll to indicate the abstract ⬭, and so forth.

The writing, which had thus developed, could be read by an Egyptian with ease and with certainty; so much can be seen from the fact that no attempt was ever made to simplify the system and to make way for a purely alphabetic writing. But it certainly had its deficiencies, from which we who are not Egyptians, and yet want to understand Egyptian books, suffer severely. I return to that point again.

We are accustomed, in accordance with Greek precedent, to call Egyptian writing " sacred signs," hieroglyphs, and to speak in addition of a special " hieratic " script. Both names [1] have been adopted into our language, and no one will therefore be ready to discard them, though they are both somewhat absurd, particularly the latter. For this " hieratic," in which almost all that is translated in this book is written, is not a special script at all; it is just the cursive form of hieroglyphic writing, and to distinguish the one from the other is as if we were to explain our own handwriting as something different from our printed type.

Egyptian literature found great assistance in the excellent material with which its scribes worked. They had not, like their colleagues in Babylonia, to imprint their signs on clay, a proceeding which has produced the ugly shapes of cuneiform ; they could really " write," as our world has learnt to do from them. They had a black ink of indestructible permanence, which they ground on a wooden palette ; they had a reed, the tip of which they fashioned into a brush ; and they had above all else an admirable smooth paper, which they manufactured from the pith of papyrus-stalks. All this was of assistance in writing, and in a good manuscript it can still be seen with what pleasure the writer has drawn his round, firm signs.

Papyrus made it possible for books to be made of any length, by gumming separate sheets together ; and there are magnificent manuscripts measuring twenty and forty metres.

---

[1] They date from the latest phase of Egyptian history, when the old writing was only the property of the priests and therefore something " sacred."

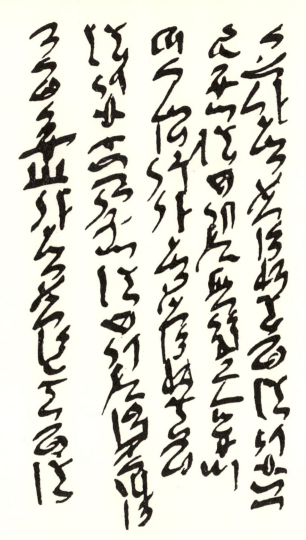

FROM THE "DISPUTE WITH HIS SOUL OF ONE WHO IS TIRED OF
LIFE."
(Manuscript of the Middle Kingdom.)
HIERATIC WRITING.

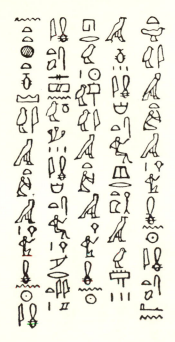

·t. *iw mt m-ḫr·i min, my šty 'n-
tyw, my ḥmśt ḫr ḫt;w
ḥrw t;w. iw mt m-ḫr·i myn
my šty sšnw, my ḥmśt ḥr mryt
nt tḫt . iw mt m-ḫr·i myn my*

TRANSLITERATION

TRANSCRIPTION INTO HIEROGLYPHS

Death is before me to-day
As the odour of myr/rh,
As when one sitteth under the sail/
    On a windy day.

Death is before me to-day/
As the odour of lotus flowers,
As when one sitteth on the shore/
    Of drunkenness.

Death is before me to-day
As . . .

ENGLISH TRANSLATION

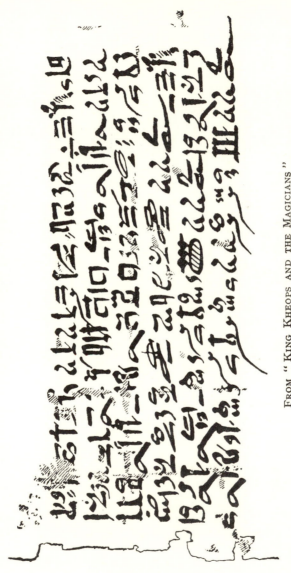

FROM "KING KHEOPS AND THE MAGICIANS"
(Manuscript dating from the beginning of the New Kingdom)
HIERATIC WRITING

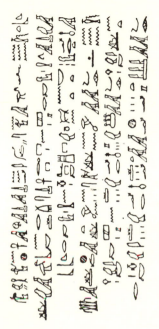

TRANSCRIPTION INTO HIEROGLYPHS

ḳbt, n gmꞏnꞏï sy ḏdꞏïn wꞏf ḏiḏꞏꞏmꞏ'nẖ : ḥwy
'wḏ; ḥmꞏk r šy n prꞏ'; ('nẖ wḏ; snb), 'pr wꞏk biw
m nfrt nt ẖnw Ꞌẖꞏk . ïb n ḥmꞏk r ḳbb
n mꞋ; ḥnwꞏśn ẖnt m ẖd m ẖnt
ïwꞏk ḥr mꞋ; ššw nfrw n šyꞏk, ïwꞏk ḥr
mꞋ; šẖtꞏf ẖfꞋꞏtꞏf nfrw ïw ïbꞏk r

TRANSLITERATION

" . . . a diversion, but I could find none." And Zazamonkh said unto him : " If / thy majesty would but betake thee to the lake of the Great House ! Man thee a boat / with all fair damsels from the inner apartments of thy palace. Then will the heart of thy majesty be diverted, / when thou shalt see how they row to and fro. / Then as thou viewest the pleasant nesting-places of thy lake, and / viewest its fields and its pleasant banks, thine heart will . . .

ENGLISH TRANSLATION

Properly only one side of a roll was written on, that upon which the fibres run horizontally and where the pen consequently met with least resistance. But not everybody could afford such extravagance, and we meet with remarkable instances of thrift. The man to whom we are indebted for the, to us, most interesting *Papyrus Harris*, No. 500, supplied himself with paper by taking an old volume and washing off the ink ; he then wrote on its *recto* three collections of love-songs and the old drinking-song. Later on, another person used also the *verso* of the papyrus, to make himself a copy of two stories. A different procedure was adopted by the writer of the two Leningrad papyri, which have preserved to us the *Instruction for King Merikerē* and the *Prophecy of Neferrohu*. He was a scribe of accounts, and he simply took documents of his department, gummed them together, and copied out the two works on their empty reverse side as a goodly possession for himself and for a " dear trusty brother."

For him who could not acquire paper there existed that cheap substitute, which we have acquired the habit of calling by the high-sounding name of " ostracon." This is either the sherd of a largish pot, or merely a smooth flake of limestone —either of which may be found lying about anywhere in Egypt. Since these ostraca were naturally used by schoolboys for their exercises, much of what is translated in this book is obtained from them.

6. OUR UNDERSTANDING OF EGYPTIAN TEXTS

The student who compares the older translations of a difficult text with our modern version, may well at times ask whether it is really the same passage that both renderings are reproducing. To explain such a difference, it is not enough to refer in general terms to the progress of our science ; rather there must be some special reason to account for such different interpretations. This reason is the defective system of writing, to which reference has already been made above on p. xxxvii. No vowels are written, and consequently the most diverse grammatical forms look the same. *Szm* can just as well mean " to hear," as " hears," " is heard," " may hear," " hearing," " heard," etc., and we are thrown back on guessing from the context what form is meant in the case in question. That is not so difficult when we have to do with straightforward texts, for there we are helped by the context and by what are to us well-known usages. Far otherwise is it with writings which contain unusual ideas and unusual phrases ; a conscientious translator will then only too often have to give in altogether, or anyhow confess that various other, and as likely, renderings could have been adopted.

The reader must not be surprised that we have left so much still untranslated, but rather that, in spite of everything, we now stand on firm ground even when dealing with difficult texts.

Besides the obstacles presented by this ambiguous system of writing, yet another, laughable may be, but for us only too serious, is to be found in the levity and ignorance of the scribes. That manuscripts swarm with mistakes is unfortunately no unusual thing elsewhere, but in hardly any other script are mistakes in writing so fatal as in hieroglyphic. It is often sufficient for the scribe to add a false determinative to a word, to change it into something entirely different, and an error of this kind, when once it has crept in—and this, in view of the otherwise ambiguous nature of the writing, may easily happen—leads to a false interpretation of the whole passage. Anyhow, that is how it affects us ; the Egyptians themselves will have been less disturbed than we by such mistakes, for they knew approximately what ought to be there, and will therefore have more readily emended the text while reading. We must suppose this to have been so, for otherwise it would be incredible that persons, who copied out a book for their own use, could have put up with so inexpressibly many mistakes.

And now for the products of the schoolboys of the New Kingdom—those papyri and ostraca, on which, certainly not always willingly, they had to write out the daily task which their teacher assigned them ! The mess they made of the texts which they copied absolutely beggars belief ! Even a straightforward text in the language of the day does not escape this fate, and a good part of the great poem on the battle of Kadesh would remain unintelligible to us, if we had to depend only upon the copy of Pentawēre, and had not also the inscriptions, which enable us to correct his innumerable mistakes. But when the schoolboy had to make a copy of a work, the understanding of which was made difficult for him by old linguistic forms, it was often changed under his hands into what is obviously nonsense, and we must be thankful if we can still here and there conjecture what is the subject under discussion.   It is a pity that so interesting a work as the *Instruction of Duauf* should have fallen a victim to these schoolboys of the Nineteenth Dynasty, and it is no consolation to us that, some centuries later, the schoolboys of the Twenty-Second Dynasty should on their part have in like manner misused the writings of the Late Egyptian literature.   We owe our thanks to the Egyptian schools for having rescued for us so much of the literature, but the thanks of him who undertakes to translate such scribblings will always be mixed with less friendly feelings.

THE LITERATURE OF THE ANCIENT EGYPTIANS

I. EXAMPLES OF THE OLDEST POETRY

IT must be taken for granted that songs and hymns and well-ordered discourses were not lacking even in that very early period, when the Egyptians were gradually developing their civilization ; indeed, in the poetic forms and in the language of the historic age there is much that harks back to that remote epoch. Of this old poetry, however, but little survives, and then not that which reveals it in its pristine freshness, for we possess only formulæ and hymns of religious content. Yet the student, who knows how to read them, can gain from them some conception of what the corresponding secular poetry would have been like—something very different to what the later classical literature of Egypt with its rhythmical cadences would lead us to expect.   The vivacity and power of expression, the *naiveté* of simile, the play of thoughts, and the unexpected change of personal pronouns—all these have something fresh and youthful about them ; and he who can overlook the rawness and strangeness of the contents of these old formulæ will some-times [1] detect a breath of wild poetry, which is lacking in the productions of a more refined period.

I. FROM THE PYRAMID TEXTS

The so-called Pyramid Texts are collections of very ancient formulæ, concerned with the destiny of the blessed dead—dead kings in particular—and preserved to us in five pyramids dating from the end of the Old Kingdom (*circa* 2600 B.C. or earlier).   In

---

[1] Naturally only sometimes, for most of them are quite uninteresting and have nothing to do with poetry.

I

the first instance, these formulæ were for the most part quite short, but later on several were often combined and mixed up with one another, even when they were mutually incompatible.

The Pyramid Texts are mainly concerned with the desire of the august dead to avoid leading a gloomy existence in the underworld—the fate of ordinary dead mortals—and to dwell in the sky like the gods. There he might voyage with the sun-god in his ship, or dwell in the Fields of the Blessed, the Field of Food-Offerings, or the Field of Iaru. He might himself become a god, and the fancy of the poets strives to depict the king in this new rôle. No longer is he a man whom the gods graciously receive into heaven, but a conqueror who seizes heaven from them.

Intermingled with these conceptions are others that have to do with the god Osiris,[1] the prototype of all dead persons. He was once murdered, but was recalled to life and became the ruler of the dead. In that capacity the Pyramid Texts conceive of him as now dwelling in the sky.

The language of the Pyramid Texts is extremely archaic, and the understanding of it, therefore, still presents great difficulties.

(a) The deceased's journey to the sky [2]

He that flieth flieth! He flieth away from you, ye men. He is no longer on earth, he is in the sky.

Thou his city-god, his ka [3] is at thy side (?).

He rusheth at the sky as a heron, he hath kissed the sky as a hawk, he hath leapt skyward as a grasshopper.[4]

(b) The same [5]

How happy are they that behold him, crowned with the head-dress of Rē! His apron is upon him as that of Hathor,[6]

---

[1] For particulars as to Osiris and his legend in the religious hymns of the earlier period, see pp. 140 ff.

[2] From Utterance 467.

[3] His vital force, which dwells in him as a separate entity, and which he is supposed to retain in death. (For further views as to the nature of the " ka " see *Cambridge Ancient History*, i. pp. 334–337; *Proceedings of the Society of Biblical Archæology*, xxxvii. pp. 257–260.)

[4] This naïve simile is preserved in two of the pyramids, but it offended the taste of the learned editor who prepared the texts for the pyramid of Phiops, and he substituted " as Harakhti," *i.e.* the sun-god. This spoilt the sense, but for the king of a civilized people was more suitable than a comparison with a grasshopper.

[5] Utterance 335.

[6] Meaning one such as the goddess weaves for the sun-god ?

and his plumage is as the plumage of a hawk. He ascendeth into the sky among his brethren, the gods.

(c) THE SAME [1]

Thou hast thine heart, Osiris; thou hast thy feet, Osiris; thou hast thine arm, Osiris. He hath his own heart; he hath his own feet; he hath his own arm.[2]

A ramp to the sky is built for him, that he may go up to the sky thereon.[3]

He goeth up upon the smoke of the great exhalation.[4]

He flieth as a bird, and he settleth as a beetle on an empty seat that is in the ship of Rē: "Stand up, get thee forth, thou without . . . , that he may sit in thy seat." [5]

He roweth in the sky in thy ship, O Rē, and he cometh to land in thy ship, O Rē.

When thou ascendest out of the horizon, he is there with his staff in his hand, the navigator of thy ship, O Rē.

Thou mountest up to the sky and art far from the earth – – – –.

(d) THE SAME [6]

Wake up, judge! [7] Thōth, arise! Awake, sleepers! Bestir you, ye that are in Kenset! [8] before the great bittern that hath risen up out of the Nile, and the jackal-god that hath come forth from the tamarisk.[9]

His mouth is purified, the Double Ennead of gods hath censed him; pure is this tongue which is in his mouth. He loatheth dung, and he rejecteth urine; [10] he loatheth that he loatheth. He loatheth this, and he eateth not this – – – –.

[1] Utterance 267.

[2] As nothing was missing from the body of Osiris, so too with the deceased.

[3] Where we should erect wooden scaffolding, in Egypt, where wood is scarce, high sloping ramps were built of brick.

[4] On the smoke of incense.

[5] He voyages as an oarsman in the ship of the sun, and in his favour Rē ejects some other god from his place.

[6] Utterance 210.

[7] Name of the moon-god Thōth, who settled the dispute of the gods.

[8] Northern Nubia, but here probably conceived of as in heaven.

[9] The dead appears unexpectedly, as a bird flies up and as a jackal steals forth.

[10] The primitive Egyptian had a horror of being driven through want to eat excrement after death.

Ye twain (?), that voyage over the sky, Rē and Thōth,[1] take him unto you to be with you, that he may eat of that whereof ye eat ; that he may drink of that whereof ye drink ; that he may live on that whereon ye live ; that he may dwell there where ye dwell ; that he may be strong in that wherein ye are strong ; that he may voyage there where ye voyage.

His booth is set up in the Field of Iaru, and his refreshment is in the Field of Food-offerings. His victuals are with you, ye gods, and his water is as wine, like that of Rē.

He compasseth the sky like Rē, he traverseth the sky like Thōth.

(e) THE SAME [2]

He is Satis,[3] that seizeth the Two Lands, the burning one, that taketh possession of her Two River-banks.

He hath gone up into the sky and hath found Rē, who standeth up when he draweth nigh unto him. He sitteth down beside him, for Rē suffereth him not to seat himself on the ground, knowing that he (the deceased) is greater than he (Rē).

He is more glorified than the Glorified Ones,[4] more excellent than the Excellent Ones, more enduring than the Enduring Ones. His hall (?) is a mistress of food-offerings.

He hath taken his stand with him [5] in the northern part of the sky, and hath seized the Two Lands [6] like a king.

(f) THE DECEASED CONQUERS THE SKY [7]

" There is strife in heaven, we see a new thing," say they, the primordial gods.[8]

The Ennead [9] of Horus is dazzled (?), the Lords of Forms

---

[1] Sun and moon.   [2] Utterance 439.

[3] Goddess of the Cataract-region. The dead as a new god is mighty like her.

[4] Who live in the sky as stars.   [5] Rē.

[6] Egypt ; here probably to be regarded as the entire world.

[7] Utterance 257.   [8] Who view the conflict.

[9] Ennead (*pśdt* in Egyptian) is the designation of the sun-god and the Eight Gods, who, according to the usually accepted legend, are his children, grandchildren, and great-grandchildren : Shu and Tefnet, Kēb and Nut, and the brothers and sisters, Osiris, Sēth, Isis, and Nephthys. Besides this Great Ennead there was also a Lesser Ennead, with Horus at its head see, *e.g.*, immediately below and also above in *d*, where the "Double Ennead," *i.e.* the two Enneads combined, is mentioned.)

are in terror of him. The entire Double Ennead serveth him, and he sitteth on the throne of the Lord of All.

He seizeth the sky, he cleaveth its metal.[1] He is led along the road to Khepre, he setteth alive in the west, the dwellers in the nether world [2] follow him, and he riseth renewed in the east.

He that adjudged the quarrel [3] cometh to him, making obeisance. The gods are afraid of him, for he is older than the Great One. He it is that hath power over his seat. He layeth hold on Command,[4] Eternity is brought to him. Discernment [5] is placed for him at his feet.

Cry aloud to him in joy, he hath captured the horizon.

(g) THE DECEASED DEVOURS THE GODS [6]

The sky is overclouded, the stars rain down (?) ; the Bows are moved, the bones of the earth-god tremble [7] – – – –, when they see how he appeareth and is animated,[8] as a god that liveth on his fathers, that feedeth on his mothers.

He is the Lord of . . ., whose name his mother knoweth not.[9]

His glory is in the sky, his power in the horizon, like Atum his father that begat him—he begat him, but he (the dead king) is stronger than he.

His kas are about him, his qualities are under his feet ; his gods are upon him, his serpents are on his brow, his guiding-snake [10] is on his forehead, – – – –, his powers protect him.

---

[1] Of which the sky is formed. What follows describes how he accomplishes the daily course of the sun-god.

[2] The underworld or nether sky.

[3] Thōth, the counsellor of the sun-god ; see p. 3, note 7.

[4] Egyptian *Ḥw* ; the personification of " that aspect of the royal power which is manifested in the words that fall from the lips of a king " (see A. H. GARDINER, *Proceedings of the Society of Biblical Archæology*, xxxviii. p. 49).

[5] The wisdom which is required for ruling. See also A. H. GARDINER, *op. cit.* xxxviii. pp. 43–54, 63–95.

[6] Utterance 273–274. Translated by J. H. BREASTED, *Development of Religion and Thought in Ancient Egypt*, pp. 127–129 ; R. O. FAULKNER, *Journ. of Egypt. Archæology*, x. pp. 97–103.

[7] The whole world is in confusion from fear ; the Bows are a part of the sky.

[8] Or perhaps " appeareth in manifest form " ; see A. H GARDINER, *op. cit.* xxxvii. p. 258.

[9] Because he is a divinity of higher standing than she

[10] The so-called uræus-snake, the king's diadem which was supposed to burn up his foes.

He is the Bull of the Sky, with his heart bent on thrusting (?), that liveth on the being of every god, that eateth their . . . limbs, when (?) they have filled their bellies with magic on the island of Nesisi [1] – – – –.

He appeareth as this Great One, the lord of (divine) ministers (?). He sitteth down with his back to Kēb,[2] and he it is that executeth judgment together with him whose name is hidden, on this day of slaying the Eldest.[3]

He is the lord of food-offerings, that knotteth the cord,[4] that prepareth his own meal.

He it is that eateth men, that liveth on gods, that possesseth carriers, and despatcheth messages.[5]

The Grasper-of-Horns, that is in . . ., he seizeth them for him.[6] The serpent Splendid-Head (?), he watcheth them for him and driveth them to him (?). Heri-terut, he bindeth them for him. The Runner-with-all-Knives (?), he strangleth them for him ; he draweth out for him their entrails, he the messenger, whom he sendeth to . . . He-of-the-Winepress, he cutteth them up for him, cooking for him a portion of them in his evening cooking-pots.

He it is that eateth their magic and swalloweth their lordliness. Their great ones are for his morning meal, their middle-sized ones for his evening meal, and their little ones for his night meal. Their old men and their old women are assigned for his fumigation.[7] The Great Ones who are in the north of the sky, they place for him the fire to the kettles, that which is under them being the thighs of their eldest ones.[8] The sky-dwellers serve him, and the cooking-pots are wiped out (?) for him with the legs of their women.

He hath encircled the two entire skies, he hath traversed the Two River-banks. He is the Great Mighty One that hath

[1] It is a well-known belief of cannibals that with the flesh of their enemies they also assimilate their strength. The island of Nesisi, or Neserser, is often mentioned in the myths.

[2] The earth-god.   [3] Those whom the court has condemned ?

[4] Probably that of the lasso, with which he caught his victims.

[5] He has his servants, who are enumerated under their strange names in the following passage. They will probably have been constellations.

[6] The victims were captured with the lasso like oxen. The following description corresponds exactly to the scenes of slaughtering in the ancient tomb-chapels.

[7] *I.e.* they were burnt as incense.

[8] *I.e.* they were used as fuel.

power over the mighty ones – – – –. Him that he encountereth on his way, he eateth him up quite raw (?).

His place is at the head of the nobles that are in the horizon.
He is a god older than the Eldest. Thousands serve him,
hundreds make offering to him. A deed of appointment as
Great Mighty One is given him by Orion, the father of the gods.[1]
He is crowned anew in the sky, and weareth the crown as lord
of the horizon.

He hath broken up the backbones and the spinal marrow,
he hath taken away the hearts of the gods. He hath eaten the
Red Crown, he hath swallowed the Green One. He feedeth
on the lungs of the Wise Ones; he is satisfied with living on
hearts and their magic; he rejoiceth (?) when he devoureth
the . . . which are in the Red Crown.[2] He flourisheth, and
their magic is in his belly, his dignities are not taken from him.
He hath swallowed the understanding of every god.

His duration is eternity and his boundary everlastingness,
in this his dignity of " If he will, he doeth it; if he will not,
he doeth it not,"—one that is within the boundary of the
horizon for ever and ever.

Lo, their soul is in his belly, their lordliness is with him.
His superfluity of food is more than that of the gods, and what
is burnt for him is their bones. Their souls are with him, and
their shadows are with their companions.[3]

He is this that ascendeth, ascendeth, is hidden, hidden
– – – –. The place of his choosing [4] is among the living in this
land for ever and ever.

(h) To a constellation, which is to announce the arrival of the deceased in the sky [5]

If thou desirest to live, O Horus, that is upon his . . .
of Truth,[6] then do thou shut the doors of the sky – – – –,
when thou takest his ka to this sky,[7] unto the august ones of
the god,[8] unto the beloved of the god, who lean upon their

---

[1] It is characteristic how the bureaucracy obtrudes itself, even in the
midst of this extreme savagery. Even a cannibal god needs a deed of
appointment!

[2] The crowns possess supernatural powers.   [3] Meaning ?

[4] The tomb, in which he appears to dwell.

[5] Utterance 440.   [6] A constellation.

[7] No one will be able to rob him of this power, whereby he lives.

[8] Divinities or the blessed dead.

sceptres, who keep watch over Upper Egypt, who are clothed in red linen, who live on figs, who drink wine, who are anointed with fine oil.

Let him speak of (?) him to the great god, let him lead him up to the great god.[1]

(i) The deceased comes as messenger to Osiris [2]

An appeal is addressed to a ferryman in the sky to transport the deceased to where Osiris dwells.

O ferryman of the Field of Food-offerings, bring me this![3] It is he, hasten! It is he, come! He, the son of the morning bark, to whom she (the morning-bark of the sun-god personified) gave birth over against the earth—his unblemished birth (?), whereby the Two Lands live.

He is the harbinger[4] of the year, O Osiris. See, he cometh with a message from thy father Kēb: "A fortunate year's yield, how fortunate is the year's yield! The year's yield is good, how good is the year's yield!"

He hath gone down with the double Ennead into the Cool Water,[5] he that is the builder for the double Ennead, the founder of the Field of Food-Offerings.[6] He found the gods waiting, wrapped (?) in their garments, their white sandals on their feet. Then threw they their white sandals to the ground, then cast they off their garments:[7] "Our heart was not at ease until thou camest," said they – – – –.

(k) The goddesses suckle the deceased [8]

He that ascendeth ascendeth! He ascendeth.

The mistress of Buto rejoiceth, and the heart of her that

---

[1] The constellation is to announce him to the sun-god.

[2] Utterance 518.

[3] See K. Sethe, *Zeitsch. für ägypt. Sprache*, liv. p. 2.

[4] Presumably the one who renders a report to his master on the result of the harvest; as such he brings to Osiris a cheering message from the earth-god Kēb.

[5] Name of the heavenly river.

[6] A god must have created this resort of the gods and the blessed, and with him the deceased is compared.

[7] Tokens of joy, or of homage?

[8] Utterance 508; probably recited at the making of a milk-libation.

dwelleth in El-Kâb [1] is dilated (?), on that day when he ascendeth at the place of Rē. [2]

He hath trampled for himself these thy rays into a ramp beneath his feet, [3] that he may go up thereon unto his mother, the living snake that is upon Rē. [4] She hath compassion on him, she giveth him her breast, that he may suck it : " My son, O king, take to thee this my breast and suck it, O king. How is it that thou hast not come on every one of thy days ? '

At the end of this long Utterance we read :

It is Kēb [5] that taketh hold of his hand and leadeth him through the portals of the sky. The god is on his throne, well is it that the god is on his throne.

Satis [6] hath washed him with her four pitchers in Elephantine.

" Ho ! Whither art thou come, my son, O king ? " He is come unto the Ennead that is in the sky, that he may eat of its bread.

" Ho ! Whither art thou come, my son, O king ? " He is come unto the Ennead that is on earth, that he may eat of its bread – – – –.

" Ho ! Whither art thou come, my son, O king ? " He is come to these his two mothers, the two vultures, [7] they of the long hair and the pendulous (?) breasts, that are upon the hill of Sehseh. They draw their breasts to his mouth, and never more do they wean him.

(*l*) THE FATE OF THE ENEMIES OF THE DECEASED

From a long Utterance ; [8] *it is concerned with enemies who would rob him of his food and breath.*

---

[1] The goddesses of the old capitals of Upper and Lower Egypt.

[2] The place where the sun has risen. (But Professor Sethe would read here not *m śt* R' " at the place of Rē," but *m śty R'* " as the representative of Rē." [Translator].)

[3] As a ramp was trampled out of Nile mud, so the deceased trampled one out of the sunbeams.

[4] The fire-spitting serpent which encircles the sun and fights his foes. Here she also has to suckle the deceased.

[5] The earth-god.

[6] The Cataract-goddess of Elephantine (Aswân), where the water of the Nile, according to the ancient belief, gushes forth from the underworld.

[7] The same goddesses as those discussed above in note 1. Since the Upper Egyptian goddess has the form of a vulture, both are here, as often, conceived of as vultures. That they are here simultaneously conceived of as women is poetic licence.

[8] Utterance 254.

He is stronger than they, when he appeareth upon his river-bank. Their hearts fall to (?) his fingers.[1] They of the sky have their entrails, they of the earth [2] their red blood.

Poverty hath their inheritances, the past their dwellings, a high Nile their gates.[3]

(But) he is glad of heart, glad of heart, he, the Sole One, the Bull of the Sky. He hath put them to flight that did this unto him, he hath destroyed their survivors.

(m) Joy over the Inundation [4]

From a somewhat long Utterance of doubtful purport.

They tremble, that behold the Nile in full flood. The fields laugh and the river-banks are overflowed. The god's offerings descend,[5] the visage of men is bright, and the heart of the gods rejoiceth.

2. TO THE CROWNS

The different crowns of the king, and the serpent which he wore as a diadem, were regarded as goddesses, who fought for him. They were therefore from the earliest times regularly called upon to succour the monarch.

(a) To the Crown of Lower Egypt [6]

O Net-crown, O In-crown, O Great Crown, O Sorceress, O Serpent! Let the slaughter that he maketh be as the slaughter that thou makest! Let the fear of him be as the fear of thee! — — — —

Let the love of him be as the love of thee!

Let his sceptre be at the head of the living, let his staff be at the head of the Glorified![7] Let his knife be firm against his foes!

---

[1] He tears them out ?
[2] Birds and beasts of prey.
[3] A high Nile washes them away.
[4] From Utterance 581.
[5] Even the gods will now receive more food.
[6] From the *Pyramid Texts*, Utterance 221.
[7] Since the king was regarded as the ruler of the dwellers in the sky, the blessed dead are introduced here as his subjects. In the original form of the address " men " or the like would have occurred here.

(b) To the Crown of Upper Egypt [1]

Praise to thee, thou Eye of Horus,[2] white, great, over whose beauty the Ennead of gods rejoices, when it (the eye of Horus) riseth in the eastern horizon.

They that are in what Shu [3] upholdeth adore thee, and they that descend in the western horizon, when thou art revealed to them that are in the nether world.

Grant that (king N.) conquer the Two Lands through thee, and have power over them.

Grant that the (foreign countries) [4] come to him making obeisance, even to (king N.). Thou art the mistress of brightness.

(c) The Same [5]

Praise to thee, O Eye of Horus, that didst cut off the heads of the followers of Sēth.[6]

She trod them down (?), she spat at the (foes) [7] with that which came forth from her—in her name of "Mistress of the Atef-crown." [8]

Her might is greater than that of her foes—in her name of "Mistress of Might." [8]

The fear of her is instilled into them that defame her—in her name of "Mistress of Fear." [8]

O (king N.), thou hast set her on thine head, that through her thou mayest be great, that through her thou mayest be lofty, that through her thy might may be great among (men).[9]

Thou abidest on the head of (king N.), and shinest forth on his brow—in this thy name of "Sorceress."

(Men) [9] fear thee, the foreign peoples fall down before thee upon their faces, and the Nine Bows [10] bow their heads to thee because of thy slaughtering, O Sorceress.

[1] From a collection of ancient hymns of this kind. The manuscript was written for the temple of Sobk in the Fayyûm, in the Hyksōs period or thereabout. Since the gods were regarded as kings, they also had their crowns. See Erman, *Hymnen an das Diadem*, p. 23 (*Abh. Berl. Akad.*, 1911).

[2] The crown is identified with the eye of Horus, *i.e.* originally the sun.

[3] The sky, which Shu, the god of the atmosphere, supports.

[4] The MS. reads "the gods."

[5] Erman, *op. cit.* p. 47.   [6] When he fought against Sēth.

[7] The MS. reads "the gods."   [8] Paronomasia.

[9] MS. "The gods."

[10] Ancient designation of the nine neighbouring peoples of Egypt.

Thou holdest in bondage for (king N.) the hearts of all foreign countries, the southern and northern, the western and eastern, all together.

Thou beneficent one, that protecteth her father,[1] protect thou (king N.) from his foes, thou Upper Egyptian Sorceress !

3. MORNING HYMNS [2]

The gods in the temples were greeted in the morning with a hymn, consisting mainly of the constantly repeated summons " Awake in peace," followed each time by a different name of the divinity. Accordingly, it was assumed that the gods were also thus awakened in heaven, and, moreover, by goddesses, a circumstance which enables us to conjecture what this hymn originally was : the song with which the women in earliest Egypt awakened their sovereign in the morning.

One may suppose that such words as " Thou king, thou lord of Egypt, thou lord of the palace," took the place of the divine names in the original version of the hymn, and that in this form it will have been chanted by the women in front of the dwelling of the primitive king, monotonously and endlessly, as long as suitable names occurred to the singer.

(a) TO THE SUN-GOD [3]

Awake in peace, thou Cleansed One,[4] in peace !
Awake in peace, thou Eastern Horus, in peace !
Awake in peace, thou Eastern Soul, in peace !
Awake in peace, Harakhti, in peace !
Thou sleepest in the bark of the evening,
Thou awakest in the bark of the morning,
For thou art he that overlooketh the gods, there is no god
  that overlooketh thee !

(b) TO THE ROYAL SERPENT [5]

Awake in peace ! Great Queen, awake in peace ; thine awakening is peaceful.

Awake in peace ! Snake that is on the brow of (king N.), awake in peace ; thine awakening is peaceful.

---

[1] The sun-god.   [2] Cf. ERMAN, *op. cit.* pp. 15 ff.
[3] *Pyramid Texts*, Utterance 573.
[4] The sun washes himself on rising out of the darkness.
[5] *Hymnen an das Diadem*, p. 34.

Awake in peace ! Upper Egyptian snake, awake in peace, thine awakening is peaceful.

Awake in peace ! Lower Egyptian snake, awake in peace ; thine awakening is peaceful.

Awake in peace ! Renenutet, awake in peace ; thine awakening is peaceful.

Awake in peace ! Uto with splendid . . ., awake in peace ; thine awakening is peaceful.

Awake in peace ! Thou with head erect, with wide neck,[1] awake in peace ; thine awakening is peaceful.

etc. etc.

[1] The angered snake which raises itself erect and puffs out its throat ; the royal serpent is always thus depicted.

II. FROM THE OLDER PERIOD

A. NARRATIVES

MATERIAL of a very varied sort has been brought together in this section. The stories of *King Kheops and the Magician,* and that of the *Deliverance of Mankind,* are of an entirely unsophisticated character ; the *Tale of the Shipwrecked Sailor,* as indeed its high-flown language shows, lays claim to being a more serious work, and in the *Story of Sinuhe* there is absolutely nothing that is unsophisticated. The last named is, in fact, the finished product of a poet who was less concerned with the contents than with the form of his work. The *Founding of a Temple* illustrates the style of an official account of a solemnity.

1. THE STORY OF SINUHE [1]

If among the accidentally preserved fragments of Egyptian literature we encounter the same work over and over again, if we know of three manuscripts of the Middle Kingdom,[2] and a papyrus, and at least ten ostraca, of the New Kingdom,[3] then we can be sure that we have before us a masterpiece of Egyptian poetry, the admiration for which not even the passage of five hundred years could dim.[4]

---

[1] Brought to notice by Chabas in 1863. Most recent edition, that of A. H. GARDINER, *Notes on the Story of Sinuhe,* Paris, 1916.

[2] Thus dating from the age in which the work was composed and in which the events described took place. The two most important MSS. are in the Berlin Museum.

[3] They contain, for the most part, the beginning or the end of the work ; four are in Berlin.

[4] Quotations from it are to be found in inscriptions of the New Kingdom. The dwellers in the incense-country say to the sailors of Queen Hatshepsut as they draw near : " Wherefore, pray, are ye come hither ? " employing the very words with which the barbarous prince greets Sinuhe. In the biography of the general Amenemheb the death of Thutmōsis III is described in the same words as that of Amenemhēt, and into a list of

Wherein lay the attraction of this book for the Egyptian reader ? Certainly only to a lesser degree in its matter, which could actually be related in a few sentences. It is full of unusual expressions, which strike us as highly artificial, but which will have greatly taken the fancy of the Egyptians.[1] Another attraction we, too, are still able to appreciate—the art displayed in telling the story. It does not occur to this poet to relate to us in detail the life of his hero, although he could have furnished his readers with all sorts of interesting facts about foreign countries ; he only picks out single episodes, which he depicts minutely, and then cleverly and not ungracefully strings together. The humour also which he displays in treating of the contrast between the elegant courtier and his new friends with their dirt and their bellowing, still has the same effect upon us as it will once have had upon Egyptian readers.

Sinuhe lived during the Middle Kingdom under the famous king Amenemhēt I (1995–1965 B.C.) and under his son Sesōstris I.

The prince and count, administrator of the domains of the sovereign in the lands of the Asiatics, the true acquaintance of the king, whom he loveth, the henchman Sinuhe. He saith : I was a henchman who followed his lord, and a servant of the king's harîm waiting on the princess, the greatly praised, the Royal Consort of Sesōstris, the Royal Daughter of Amenemhēt in the Pyramid-town of Ka-nefru, even Nefru the revered.

In the year 30, on the ninth day of the third month of Inundation, the god entered his horizon.[2] King Amenemhēt flew away to heaven and was united with the sun, and the god's body was merged with his creator.[3] The Residence was hushed, hearts were filled with mourning, the Two Great Portals [4] were shut, the courtiers sat head on knees, and the people grieved.

Palestinian localities, dating from the reign of Thutmōsis III, are incorporated the countries of Yaa and Kedemi, about which we otherwise possess no information.

[1] So, *e.g.*, "to give a road to the feet" for "to go"; "to take the crouching posture" for "to bow oneself down"; "to unite with the place" for "to arrive" at it, etc. In translating I had to eliminate this for the most part, if I wished to be intelligible.

[2] What I have, according to usage, translated "horizon" is in the first instance the dwelling of the sun-god in the sky, and is then used of the places where the sun rises and sets. Since the king is the earthly counterpart of the sun-god, his palace and his tomb are also designated his "horizon." Here the tomb is meant.

[3] He journeys to the sky and becomes again a part of the sun, from which he had issued.

[4] At the entrance to the palace.

Now his majesty had sent forth an army to the land of the Temehu,[1] and his eldest son was captain thereof, the good god Sesōstris ; and even now he was returning, having carried away captives of the Tehenu [2] and all manner of cattle without count.

And the Chamberlains of the Royal Palace sent to the western border (of the Delta) to inform the king's son of the event that had befallen at the Court. And the messengers met him on the road and reached him at eventide. Not a moment did he tarry ; the hawk [3] flew away with his henchmen, and did not make it known unto his army. Howbeit, a message had been sent [4] unto the king's children that were with him in this army, and one of them had been summoned. And lo, I stood and heard his voice as he spake,[5] being a little way off (?).

Then was mine heart distraught, mine arms sank, and trembling fell on all my limbs.[6] I betook me thence leaping, to seek me a hiding-place ; I placed me between two bushes so as to sunder the road from its traveller.[7]

I set out southward, yet did I not purpose to reach the Residence, for I thought that strife would arise, and I was not minded to live after him. I crossed the waters of Maaty,[8] hard by the Sycamore,[8] and came to the island of Snefru,[8] and tarried there in a plot of ground (?). I was afoot early, and when it was day I met a man who stood in my path ; he shrank from me and was afraid. The time of the evening meal came, and I drew nigh to Ox-town.[9] I crossed over in a barge [10]

[1] A Libyan people on the west of the Delta, who regularly raided it.

[2] Another Libyan people.   [3] The new king Sesōstris I.

[4] *I.e.* by another faction ; there was a plot to set up a rival king. Sinuhe purposely passes lightly over this affair.

[5] Probably the prince who had been " summoned."

[6] What so terrifies Sinuhe is probably the prospect of domestic war ; yet he must have special grounds for fear besides, which he later invariably hides under excuses.

[7] *I.e.* in order to separate myself from the road, to be well away from the beaten track ?

[8] Unknown locality.

[9] Unknown : from what follows it must be looked for in the region of Cairo. Sinuhe has fled along the western edge of the Delta to this place, where the Nile does not yet branch apart and so is most easily crossed.

[10] What is meant is a broad vessel such as was used for the transport of stone ; he finds it lying alongside of the bank and the wind drives him over the stream.

without a rudder, with the aid of the breath of the west wind, and passed on east of the quarry, in the region (?) of the Mistress of the Red Mountain.[1] I gave a road to my feet northwards, and attained the Wall of the Prince,[2] which was made to repel the Asiatics. I bowed me down in a thicket for fear lest the watcher for the day on the wall should espy me.

At eventide I passed on, and when day dawned I reached Peten and halted on the island of Kemwer.[3] There it o'ertook me that I fell down for thirst, I was parched, my throat burned, and I said : "This is the taste of death." Then lifted I up mine heart and gathered up my body, for I heard the sound of the lowing of cattle and descried Bedouins. The sheikh among them, who had been in Egypt, recognized me.[4] He gave me water and cooked milk for me, and I went with him to his tribe, and they entreated me kindly.

Land gave me to land.[5] I set forth from Byblos and drew near to Kedemi and spent half a year there. Nenshi the son of Amu, the prince of Upper Retenu,[6] took me and said unto me : "Thou farest well with me, for thou hearest the speech of Egypt." This said he, for he had become aware of my qualities, and had heard of my wisdom ; Egyptians that dwelt with him had testified to him concerning me.

He said unto me : "Why art thou come hither ? Hath aught befallen at the Residence ?" And I said unto him : "King Sehetepibrē [7] hath gone to the horizon, and none knoweth what hath happened in the matter." And I said again, dissembling: "I came from the expedition to the land of the Temehu,

---

[1] A mountain east of Cairo, in which is to be found that reddish brown sandstone which the Egyptians were so fond of using for their statues. It is called "the Red Mountain" even at the present day, and the quarries are still worked. The "Mistress of the Red Mountain" is the goddess worshipped there.

[2] An oft-mentioned fortification intended to keep off the Bedouins ; see below, p. 115, note 8.

[3] Name of the lakes on the Isthmus of Suez.

[4] Sinuhe was thus a personage whom every one in Egypt knew.

[5] The poet does not trouble the reader with all the lands through which Sinuhe wandered and which he naturally did not know himself. He only introduces Byblos, the universally known port at the foot of Lebanon, whence the Egyptians imported their wood, and Kedemi, which probably lay in the east.

[6] Upper Retenu later stands for what we designate Palestine.

[7] The official name of the old king.

2

and report was made unto me, and mine heart trembled and mine heart was no longer in my body. It carried me away upon the pathways of the wastes. Yet none had gossiped about me, none had spat in my face ; I had heard no reviling word, and my name had not been heard in the mouth of the herald.[1] I know not what brought me to this land ; it was like the dispensation of God." [2] Then said he unto me : " How will yon land fare without him, that beneficent god, the fear of whom was throughout the lands like that of Sekhmet [3] in a year of plague ? " But I said unto him answering him : " Nay, but his son hath entered into the palace and hath taken the inheritance of his father, he, the god without peer, whom none surpasseth, a lord of prudence, excellent in counsel, efficacious in giving orders. Going out [4] and coming in are at his command. He it was that subdued the foreign lands, while his father sat within in his palace, that he might report to him that what had been commanded him had been done (?).

" He is the strong one that achieveth with his mighty arm, the champion without peer.

He is seen charging down on the foe (?), attacking the warriors (?).

It is he that curbeth the horn [5] and maketh weak the hands, and his foes cannot marshal their ranks.

It is he that venteth his wrath and smasheth the foreheads, and none can stand in his neighbourhood.

It is he that is wide of stride when he shooteth the fugitive, and there is no end (to flight) for him that turneth on him his back.

Steadfast of heart is he at the moment of a repulse ; he is the repeller and turneth not his back.

Stout of heart is he when he seeth a multitude ; he alloweth his heart no rest (?).

Bold is he, when he falleth upon the Easterners ; his delight it is to take captive the enemy (?).

He seizeth his buckler, he trampleth under foot ; he repeateth not (his blow) in order to kill.

---

[1] He thus stresses the fact that there was no charge against him ; how far this account was " dissembling " escapes us.

[2] A supernatural intervention.   [3] The dreadful lion-headed goddess.

[4] From Egypt to the war.   [5] *I.e.* of the enemy.

There is none that hath turned his shaft, there is none that hath bent his bow.

The People-of-the-Bow flee before him, as before the might of the Great Goddess.[1]

He fighteth without end, he . . . eth not, and there is no remnant.

He is a master of grace, rich in sweetness, and through love hath he conquered.

His city loveth him more than itself, and they (*i.e.* the citizens) rejoice over him more than over their god.

Men and women pass by [2] and exult over him.

He is a king, and he conquered while yet in the womb ; [3] on that [4] was he set ever since he was born.

He it is that multiplieth them that were born with him ; [5] he is unique, god-given.

How this land which he ruleth rejoiceth ! It is he that extendeth the borders.

He will conquer the southern lands, but (as yet) he payeth no heed to the northern lands.

(Still) he was created to smite the Bedouins, to crush the sand-farers.

Send to him, let him know thy name, utter no curse against his majesty. He faileth not to do good to a land that will be loyal to him."

Then said he unto me : " Verily Egypt is happy, for it knoweth that he [6] flourisheth. But see, thou art here and shalt abide with me, and I will entreat thee kindly."

And he placed me at the head of his children, and mated me with his eldest daughter. He caused me to choose for myself of his country, of the best of what belonged to him on his border to another country. It was a goodly land called Yaa. There were figs in it and vines, and it had more wine than water. Plentiful was its honey, abundant its oil, and all fruits were on its trees. There was barley in it and wheat, and countless cattle of all kinds. Great too was that which accrued to me

---

[1] The serpent on the brow of the sun-god, that burns up his foes.

[2] Paying him homage in front of the palace ?

[3] Lit. " while yet in the egg."   [4] Conquest.

[5] The people increase under him.

[6] The new king ; the barbarian does not attempt to emulate Sinuhe's song of praise and admonition, and replies in arid prose.

by reason of the love bestowed upon me [1] (?).   He made me ruler
of a tribe of the best of his country.   Bread was made for me
for my daily fare, wine for my daily drink, cooked meat and
roast fowl, over and above the wild game of the desert ; for
that men hunted for me and laid it before me, besides the spoils
of my hounds.   And many . . . were made for me, and milk
prepared in every way.

I spent many years, and my children grew up to be mighty
men, each one having his tribe in subjection.   The envoy who
went north or south to the Residence [2] tarried with me.   I
made all men to tarry.   I gave water to the thirsty, set upon
the road him that had strayed, and rescued him that had been
plundered.   When the Bedouins began to wax bold and to
withstand the chieftains of the lands, I counselled (?) their
movements.[3]   This prince of Retenu caused me to pass many
years as the captain of his host, and every country against
which I marched, when I had made my attack, it was driven
from its pastures and its wells.   I plundered its cattle and
carried off its people and took away their food.   I slew people
in it by my strong arm, my bow, my marchings, and my excellent
counsels.   That found favour with him and he loved me ; he
marked how brave I was, and placed me at the head of his
children, for he saw how my hands prevailed.

There came a mighty man of Retenu, that he might challenge
me in my camp.   He was a champion without peer, and had
subdued the whole of Retenu.   He vowed that he would fight
with me, he planned to rob me, he plotted to take my cattle
as a spoil, by the counsel of his tribe.   That prince communed
with me and I said : " I know him not ; forsooth, I am no con-
federate of his, that I should stride about his encampment.
Or have I ever opened his door (?) or overthrown his fence ?
Nay, it is envy (?), because he seeth me doing thy behest.[4]
Assuredly I am like a bull of the cattle in the midst of a strange
herd, and the steer of the kine attacketh him, the long-horned
bull chargeth (?) him.   *I am even so a foreigner whom none
loveth, any more than a Bedouin would be loved in the Delta.   But
if that man* is a bull and loveth combat, *I also am a fighting bull*

---

[1] The gifts which he received as chieftain of the tribe.
[2] Of the Egyptian king.
[3] Meaning probably that he led the military expeditions of the prince.
[4] Meaning probably : it is only envy and jealousy of me, the foreigner.

and am not afraid to try conclusions with him.   If his heart be set on fighting, let him speak his will.   Doth God not know what is ordained for him – – – – ? " [1]

At night-time I strung my bow and shot my arrows.[2]   I drew out (?) my dagger and burnished my weapons.   At dawn when Retenu came, it had stirred up (?) its tribes, it had assembled the countries of a half of it, and it had planned this combat.   Every heart burned for me ; the men's wives jabbered, and every heart was sore for me.   They said : " Is there another mighty man who can fight against him [3] ? "

Then his shield, his axe, and his armful of javelins. . . . But after I had drawn out his weapons, I caused his arrows to pass by me, uselessly sped.[4]   As one approached the other, he charged me, and I shot him, mine arrow sticking in his neck.[5] He cried out and fell on his nose.   I laid him low with his own axe, and raised my shout of victory on his back.   Every Asiatic bellowed.[6]   I offered praise to Month,[7] and his following mourned for him.   This prince Nenshi, the son of Amu, took me to his embrace.

Then carried I off his goods and spoiled his cattle.   That which he had devised to do to me I did to him.   I seized what was in his tent and plundered his encampment.   I became great thereby, wide in my riches, abundant in mine herds.

And (this) hath God [8] done, in order to be gracious to one that had trespassed (?) against him, that had fled away unto another land.   To-day his heart is again glad.

> Once a fugitive fled in his season—
> now the report of me is in the Residence.
> Once a laggard lagged because of hunger—
> now give I bread to my neighbour.
> Once a man left his country because of nakedness—
> now am I shining white in raiment and linen.

[1] Meaning probably : the issue is ordained by fate.
[2] To test the bow ?
[3] Sinuhe's opponent.
[4] The whole passage is probably corrupt and the translation dubious.
[5] Accordingly the opponent must have fled.
[6] The word which is used of the bellowing of cattle.
[7] The war-god.
[8] The king is probably meant, to whose divine might Sinuhe ascribes even his present success in the affray.

Once a man sped for lack of one to send—
now have I slaves in plenty.
Fair is my house, wide my dwelling-place,
and I am remembered in the palace.

O God, whosoever thou art, that didst ordain this flight, be merciful and bring me again to the Residence. Peradventure thou wilt suffer me to see the place wherein mine heart dwelleth. What is a greater matter than that my corpse should be buried in the land wherein I was born ? Come to mine aid ! May good befall, may God show me mercy – – – –, in order to make good the end of him whom he hath afflicted (?), his heart being compassionate on him whom he *hath compelled* to live abroad. Is he in truth appeased to-day ? Then may he hearken to the prayer of one that is afar off, – – – –.

O may the king of Egypt show me mercy, that I may live by his mercy. May I ask the Lady of the Land that is in his palace what her will is. May I hear the behests of her children.

O may my body grow young again, for now hath old age befallen, and weakness hath overtaken me. Mine eyes are heavy, mine arms are weak, and my legs have ceased to follow. Mine heart is weary, and death draweth nigh unto me. May they bring me to the cities of Eternity.[1] May I serve the Sovereign Lady ; O may she speak well to me of her children ; may she spend eternity over (?) me.[2]

Now it had been told unto the majesty of King Kheperkerē [3] concerning this state in which I was.[4] Thereupon his majesty sent to me with presents of the royal bounty, to gladden the heart of the servant there,[5] as it had been the prince of any foreign country. And the royal children in his palace caused me to hear their behests.[6]

---

[1] *I.e.* the tombs in Egypt.

[2] His old mistress, Queen Nefru, is to take him again into her service and assign him a grave beside her own.

[3] The official name of Sesōstris I.

[4] Who undertook this negotiation is left purposely obscure. The reader will naturally think of the envoys who, as above related, passed by Sinuhe on their missions, and whom he was in the habit of entertaining.

[5] Usual polite expression for " I. "

[6] *I.e.* they wrote to me also.

COPY OF THE DECREE WHICH WAS BROUGHT TO THE
SERVANT THERE CONCERNING HIS RETURN TO EGYPT

Horus, Life-of-Births, Two Crown-Goddesses, Life-of-Births,
King of Upper and Lower Egypt, Kheperkerē, Son of Rē,
Sesōstris, that liveth for ever and ever.[1]

A royal decree unto the henchman Sinuhe. Behold, this
decree of the King is brought to thee to instruct thee as here
followeth : Thou hast traversed the foreign lands and art come
forth from Kedemi to Retenu, and land gave thee to land, by
the counsel of thine own heart. What hast thou done that
aught should be done against thee ? Thou didst not curse,
that thy speech should be reproved, and thou didst not so speak
in the council of the magistrates, that thine utterances should
be thwarted. (Only) this thought, it carried away thine
heart – – – –. *But* this thine heaven,[2] that is in the palace,
yet abideth and prospereth to-day ; *she hath her part* in the
kingdom of the land, and her children are in the council-chamber.
Thou wilt long subsist on the good things which they give thee,[3]
thou wilt live on their bounty. Come back to Egypt, that thou
mayest see the Residence wherein thou didst grow up, that
thou mayest kiss the earth at the Two Great Portals, and mingle
with the Chamberlains.

Even to-day thou hast begun to be old, thou hast lost thy
manhood, and hast bethought thee of the day of burial, the
passing to honour.[4] An (?) evening is devoted (?) to thee with
cedar-oil and with bandages from the hand of Tait.[5] A funeral
procession is made for thee on the day of burial ; the mummy-
shell is of gold, with head of lapis lazuli ; the heaven [6] is above
thee, and thou art placed upon a sledge.[7] Oxen drag thee,
and singers go before thee, and the dance of the Muu is per-

[1] The official titulary of the king ; the beginning of the decree is
couched quite in official form.

[2] The queen.

[3] The victuals which they will send thee when thou livest once more at
Court.

[4] *I.e.* his coming among the honoured dead. In the subsequent passages embalming and burial are described.

[5] The goddess of weaving.

[6] The lid of the sarcophagus ? The lid of the coffin was conceived of
as symbolizing the sky-goddess Nut.

[7] The Egyptians of the earlier period employed sledges for the transport of all loads and therefore also of corpses.

formed for thee at the door of thy tomb. The Requirements of the Offering-Table are recited for thee, and victims are slain at thine offering-stones. Thy pillars [1] are wrought of white stone in the midst of (the tombs of) the royal children. Thus shalt thou not die abroad, nor shall the Asiatics bury thee. Thou shalt not be placed in a sheep-skin, – – – –. *Wherefore* bethink thee (?) of thy corpse and return.

This decree reached me as I stood in the midst of my tribe. It was read to me, and I threw myself on my belly ; I touched the dust and strewed it on my hair. I strode about my encampment rejoicing and saying : " How should such things be done to a servant, whom his heart led astray to barbarous lands ? Yea, good indeed is the Benevolent One that delivereth me from death. Thy ka [2] will suffer me to bring my life to an end in the Residence.

COPY OF THE ACKNOWLEDGMENT OF THIS DECREE

The servant of the palace Sinuhe saith : In very beautiful peace ! [3] Ascertained is this flight, which the servant there made unwillingly, by thy ka, thou Good God, Lord of the Two Lands,[4] beloved of Rē, praised of Month, lord of Thebes. Amūn, lord of Karnak, Sobk, Rē, Horus, Hathor, Atum with his Ennead of gods, Sopdu-Neferbau-Semseru the Eastern Horus,[5] the Mistress of Buto that resteth on thy head,[6] the Conclave on the Waters, Min-Horus that is in the foreign countries, Wereret mistress of Punt,[7] Nut, Haruēris-Rē, the gods of Egypt and of the islands of the sea,[8]—may they all give life and happiness to thy nose, may they endue thee with their gifts, may they give thee eternity without limit, everlastingness without end !

Men tell of the fear of thee in the plains and hill-countries ; what the sun encircleth hast thou subdued. This prayer of

---

[1] The pillars of thy tomb.

[2] The often-mentioned " ka " is the force in a man that keeps him alive and at the same time also the sustenance which produces it. Furthermore, the ka is the actual personality which feels and perceives, and finally " thy ka," as here, is nothing more than a choice expression for " thou."

[3] Mayest thou read this writing.

[4] The usual expression for Upper and Lower Egypt.

[5] The god through whose district Sinuhe fled.

[6] The royal serpent, the diadem.

[7] The incense-producing countries.   [8] The Greek islands.

the servant there to his lord that rescueth from the West,[1]— the lord of Perception, that perceiveth men, he perceived it in the majesty of the Palace.[2] The servant there feared to say it, (for) it is a grave matter to repeat it, *but* the great god, who is like unto Rē, giveth discretion even unto him that serveth him [3] – – – –. Thy majesty is the victorious Horus and thine arms are strong against all lands.

Now let thy majesty command that Meki be brought from Kedemi, Khentiuiaush from Khentkeshu, and Menus from the lands of the Fenekhu. They are princes and . . . witnesses, that have grown up in love of thee—without my making mention of Retenu, for that is thine, as it were thy dogs.[4]

This flight, which the servant there made, I planned it not, it was not in mine heart, and I had not conceived it. I know not what sundered me from my place. It was after the manner of a dream, as if a man of the Delta should see himself suddenly in Elephantine, or a man of the marshes in Nubia. I had nought to fear, none had persecuted me, I had heard no reviling speech, my name had not been heard in the mouth of the herald. Only this befell, that my body quivered (?), my feet quaked (?), mine heart led me on, and the god that ordained the flight drew me away. And yet I was not presumptuous aforetime (?),[5] and a man that knoweth his land is afraid, for Rē hath put the fear of thee throughout the land, the dread of thee in every foreign country. Whether I am in the Residence or in this place, it is (ever) thou that obscurest this horizon,[6] and the sun ariseth at thy pleasure ; the water in the river is drunk when thou willest, and the air in heaven is breathed when thou biddest.

The servant there will hand over my viziership, which the servant there hath exercised in this place.[7]

Thereupon men came to the servant there—thy majesty wilt do as he pleaseth ; [8] men live on the breath which thou

---

[1] The realm of the dead.

[2] Thou hast surmised my wish without my expressing it.

[3] Thou givest me courage and wisdom to speak to thee.

[4] He wishes to show the king that he lives in a well-disposed country the princes mentioned, who will be known at the Court, can testify for him, and over the loyalty of his own land he need not waste words.

[5] I did not run away through brazen insolence.

[6] *I.e.* probably : thou canst plunge us into night.

[7] He regards himself as being the king's viceroy.

[8] He thereby expresses his acquiescence to the king's command.

givest. May Rē, Horus, and Hathor love this thine august nose [1] which Month, lord of Thebes, willeth shall live for ever.

I was suffered to spend a day in Yaa, and handed over my substance to my children, so that my eldest son had charge of my tribe and all my substance was in his hand, my serfs, all my cattle, my fruits, and every pleasant tree of mine.

Then the servant there came southwards and I halted at Paths-of-Horus.[2] The commander there, who was in charge of the patrol, sent a message to the Residence to bear tidings. And his majesty despatched a trusty overseer of the peasants of the royal domain, having with him ships laden with presents of the royal bounty for the Bedouins that had followed me and had conducted me to Paths-of-Horus. And I named each one of them with his name.[3]

Every cook was at his task, and I set out and sailed; and men kneaded and brewed beside me, until I reached the town of Conqueress-of-the-Two-Lands.[4] And at daybreak, very early, they came to summon me; ten men came and ten men went and conducted me to the palace.

I touched the ground between the sphinxes [5] with my forehead, and the royal children stood in the gateway and received (?) me, and the Chamberlains, that conduct to the hall, set me on the way to the Privy Chamber. I found his majesty on his great throne in the golden gateway. When I had stretched myself on my belly, my wits forsook me in his presence, albeit this god addressed me kindly. I was as a man that is carried off in the dusk, my soul fled, my body quaked (?), mine heart was no longer in my body, and I wist not whether I were alive or dead.

Then said his majesty to one of these Chamberlains : " Raise him up, let him speak to me." And his majesty said : " See, thou art returned, after thou hast trodden the foreign lands — — —. Eld assaileth thee and thou hast reached old age.

---

[1] The nose is the seat of life.

[2] On the borders of Egypt on the Pelusiac arm of the Nile, from whence the Egyptian armies were accustomed to start on their campaigns.

[3] He paid the barbarians the compliment of introducing them to the Egyptian officials.

[4] Name of the capital at that time, situated on the site of the modern Lisht, some way south of the later Memphis.

[5] Or " statues."

It is no small matter (?) that thy body be laid in the ground, and that the barbarians bury thee not. But be not silent, be not silent ; speak, thy name is pronounced [1] _ _ _ _."

I answered thereto with the answer of one that is afraid : " What saith my lord unto me ? Would that I might answer it, *but I cannot.* It is as it were the hand of God, it is a dread ; it is in my body, as it were that which (once) caused that destined flight. Behold, I am in thy presence. Thine is life, and thy majesty will do as it pleaseth thee."

Then the royal children were caused to be ushered in. Said his majesty to the Queen : " See, this is Sinuhe, who hath come back as an Asiatic, a creature (?) of the Bedouins." She uttered an exceeding loud cry, and the royal children shrieked out altogether. They said unto his majesty : " It is not he in sooth, O king, my lord." His majesty said : " It is he in sooth." [2] Now they had brought with them their necklaces, their rattles, and their sistra. And they held them out to his majesty : [3] " Thy hands be on the Beauteous One, O long-living King, on the ornament of the Lady of Heaven. May the Golden One [4] give life to thy nose, and the Mistress of the Stars [4] join herself to thee. May the Upper Egyptian crown go down stream, and the Lower Egyptian crown go up stream, [5] and be joined both together in the mouth of thy majesty. [6] May the serpent [7] be set on thy brow. Thou hast delivered the poor from evil. May Rē be gracious unto thee, O Lord of the Two Lands ! Hail to thee as to the Mistress of All. Loose thine horn [8] and pull out thine arrow ; give breath to him that

[1] Thou art now received in audience.

[2] They do not recognize the elegant courtier in the wild Bedouin.

[3] The rattles and sistra with which the women make music, and their large necklaces, are the attributes of their goddess Hathor. When they hold them out to anyone during the dance, they thereby present him with the blessing of the goddess (see also BLACKMAN, *Rock Tombs of Meir*, i. pp. 24 f.). What follows is the song with which they accompany their action.

[4] Name of Hathor.

[5] The crown of either of the two ancient kingdoms is to take possession of the other.

[6] Meaning : both divisions of Egypt are subject to thee, and thou issuest commands to them.

[7] The king's diadem which he wears, like his prototype, the sun-god (see p. 9, note 4).

[8] The king is conceived of as a bull, and he is to set free him who has been pierced with his horn.

is stifled, and bestow on us as our goodly festival-gift (?) this sheikh, the son of the Goddess of the North,[1] the barbarian born in Egypt. He fled through fear of thee ; he left the land through dread of thee. But a face that hath seen thy majesty shall no more blench (?), and an eye that hath regarded thee shall not fear." [2]

Then said his majesty : " He shall not fear, he shall not dread. He shall be a Chamberlain among the magistrates, and be placed in the midst of the courtiers. Get you gone to the Chamber of Adoration (?) in order to make [3] . . ."

So when I was gone forth from the Privy Chamber, the royal children giving me their hands, we then went to the Two Great Portals.[4] And I was placed in the house of a king's son, in which there was noble equipment, and a bath was therein and – – – –. Precious things of the Treasury were in it, garments of royal linen, myrrh, and fine oil of the king. Counsellors whom he loveth were in every chamber, and every serving man was at his task. Years were made to pass away from my body, I was shaved (?), and my hair was combed (?). A load (of dirt) was given over to the desert, and the (filthy) clothes to the Sand-farers. And I was arrayed in finest linen and anointed with the best oil. I slept on a bed, and gave up the sand to them that be in it, and the oil of wood to him that smeareth himself therewith.

And I was given the house of a . . ., such as appertaineth (?) to a Chamberlain. Many artificers built it, and all its wood-work was new appointed.

And meals were brought me from the palace, three times and four times a day, over and above that which the royal children gave, without cessation at any time.

And there was constructed for me a pyramid out of stone within the precinct of the pyramids.[5] The chief architect began the building of it (?), the painter designed in it, the master-

---

[1] Paronomasia ; Sinuhe means " Son of the (sacred) sycomore," now as a barbarian he must be called after the Goddess of the North, Si-mehyt.

[2] Meaning : he is only anxious because he does not yet know thy goodness as we do.

[3] What is probably meant is that they should assist Sinuhe in his highly necessary toilet (see also BLACKMAN, *Journ. of Egypt. Archæology*, v. pp. 148 ff.).

[4] Thus out of the palace.

[5] The members of his court are buried around the king's grave.

sculptor carved in it, the master-builders of the necropolis busied themselves with it.[1] All the glistening gear that is placed in a tomb-shaft,[2] its (the tomb's) needs were supplied therefrom. And funerary priests were given me, and there was made for me a sepulchral garden, in which were fields, over against the abode (?), even as is done for a chief Chamberlain. And my statue [3] was overlaid with gold and its apron was of fine gold. It was his majesty who caused it to be made. There is no humble man for whom the like had been done.

And so live I, rewarded by the king, until the day of my death cometh.

2. THE STORY OF THE SHIPWRECKED SAILOR [4]

This is actually a tale of the simplest character, but in the form preserved to us, it has been adapted to suit the taste of the educated reader, as its carefully chosen phraseology plainly shows. Hence, too, the remarkable dressing-up which it has undergone : an Egyptian of high rank [5] has been sent South by the king, but on this voyage has met with little success. He is now in grave anxiety as to the reception awaiting him. But one of his comrades speaks to him and exhorts him to face his sovereign with more confidence. He will then fare just as well in the king's presence as he himself did on a similar occasion. He now gives an account of this voyage of his, namely, our tale.—Into this tale a second has been incorporated, but in the Leningrad manuscript it is abbreviated to a few sentences.

A noteworthy feature of this book is the fact that it leaves the reader to form his own ideas as to the characters and their circumstances. It might, therefore, be supposed that we have here only an extract from a longer chain of stories, and that other travelling

---

[1] What is meant is that the best craftsmen who work on the royal pryamid are also employed on that of Sinuhe.

[2] The numerous offerings which a well-equipped tomb of this period must contain.

[3] Which was erected in the tomb.

[4] In a Middle Kingdom papyrus acquired by Golénischeff, and now in Leningrad. See my article (transcription, commentary, and translation) in *Zeitschr. für ägypt. Sprache*, xliii. pp. 1 ff. ; GOLÉNISCHEFF, *Le conte du naufragé* (Cairo, 1912). See also DÉVAUD, *Le conte du naufragé*, in *Receuil de travaux*, xxxviii. pp. 188 ff. ; A. H. GARDINER, *Notes on the Tale of the Shipwrecked Sailor*, in *Zeitschr. für ägypt. Sprache*, xlv. pp. 60 ff.

[5] Probably a prince of Elephantine, whose duties included expeditions such as this.

companions had previously recounted to the prince other narratives, in order to console him in his affliction.

A worthy henchman said : Be of good cheer, Prince, behold, we have reached the Residence.[1] The mallet hath been taken, the mooring-post driven in, and the bow-rope run along the ground. There is praising and thanksgiving to God, and every one embraceth his fellow. Our crew hath come home safe and sound, and our soldiers have suffered no loss. We have reached the end of Wawat and have passed by Senmet. See, we have returned in peace and have reached our own land. Hearken to me, Prince ; I am one that is free from exaggeration. Wash thyself and pour water on thy fingers. Answer when thou art greeted, speak to the king having thy wits about thee, and answer without faltering. It is a man's mouth that saveth him, and his speech maketh men forbearing towards him. Thou wilt do as thou willst ; to speak [2] to thee is irksome (to thee).

Yet I will relate to thee something like thereunto, that was experienced by me myself, when I had set out for the mines of the Sovereign [3] and gone down to the sea in a ship of an hundred and twenty cubits in length and forty cubits in breadth ; [4] and therein were an hundred and twenty sailors of the pick of Egypt. They scanned the sky, they scanned the earth, and their hearts were more . . . than those of lions. They foretold a storm or ever it came, and a tempest when as yet it was not.

A storm burst while we were yet at sea, before we had reached land. We flew before the wind [5] and it made a . . ., and a wave eight cubits high was within it. It was a piece of wood that . . . it to me.

[1] The henchman wakes up his lord in the morning on board ship and announces that they are once more in Egypt ; they have passed the frontier-island of Senmet (the modern Bigeh, near Philæ), and the ship is already alongside of the quay. Accordingly " the Residence " must here mean Elephantine, thus possibly the residence of the prince himself. But he has still to continue his voyage northward to the king, in order to make report to him.

[2] Thus attempts to encourage him have already been vainly made on previous days.

[3] He sails from a harbour on the Red Sea for the mines of the Sinaitic peninsula.

[4] *I.e.* 60 by 20 metres ; thus a very large ship.

[5] The whole account of the storm is unintelligible to us ; it occurs again below in identically the same words.

Then the ship perished, and of them that were in it not one survived. And I was cast on to an island by a wave of the sea, and I spent three days alone with mine heart (only) as my companion. I slept under the shelter of a tree (?) and embraced the shade.[1] Then I stretched forth my feet in order to find out what I could put into my mouth. I found figs and vines there, and all manner of fine leeks, kau-fruit together with nekut-fruit and cucumbers . . . There were fish there and fowl, and there was nothing that was not in it.[2] Then I satisfied myself and still left over, for it was too much for my hands. When I had made me a fire-drill,[3] I kindled a fire and made a burnt-offering for the gods.

Then I heard the sound of thunder and thought it was a wave of the sea ; the trees brake, and the earth quaked. I uncovered my face [4] and found that it was a serpent that drew nigh. He was thirty cubits long, and his beard—it was longer than two cubits ; his body was overlaid with gold, his eyebrows were of real lapis lazuli,[5] and he coiled himself forward.

He opened his mouth at me, while I was on my belly in front of him, and he said unto me : " Who hath brought thee (hither), who hath brought thee (hither), little one ? Who hath brought thee (hither) ? If thou delayest in telling me who hath brought thee to this island, I will let thee know thyself to be but ashes, becoming as that which is not seen." [6] (I answered :) " Thou speakest unto me, and yet I hear it not. I am in thy presence, but my wits have gone."

Then he took me in his mouth and brought me to his lair, and set me down without touching me, and I was whole and there was nothing torn from me.[7] He opened his mouth at me, while I was on my belly in front of him. And he said unto me : " Who hath brought thee (hither), who hath brought thee (hither), little one ? Who hath brought thee to this island of

---

[1] *I.e.* probably only : I sought it.   [2] The island.

[3] An Egyptian fire-drill consists of only two pieces of wood, and so is easy to construct.

[4] In his terror he had held his hands in front of his face.

[5] The narrator conceives of the monster as the figure of an Egyptian divinity, made of gilded bronze with coloured inlay. By the beard is meant the plaited beard of a god.

[6] The serpent can spit fire like its divine companion, the snake of the sun-god.

[7] So carefully did he handle him.

the sea, which is encompassed on both sides by the waters ? "
And I made answer to him, my arms being bent [1] in his presence,
and said unto him : " I am one who went down to the mines
on an errand of the Sovereign, with a ship of an hundred and
twenty cubits in length and forty cubits in breadth, and therein
were an hundred and twenty sailors of the pick of Egypt.   They
scanned the sky, they scanned the earth, and their hearts were
more . . . than those of lions.   They foretold the storm or
ever it came, and the tempest when as yet it was not.   Each
one of them was . . . of heart and stronger of arm than his
fellow, and there was no fool among them.   A storm burs⁺
while we were yet at sea, before we had reached land.   We
flew before the wind and it made a . . ., and a wave eight
cubits high was within it.   It was a piece of wood that . . .
it to me.   Then the ship perished, and of them that were in
it not one survived save me, and behold, here I am beside thee.
And I was brought to this island by a wave of the sea."

Then he said unto me : " Fear not, fear not, little one ; let
not thy countenance . . ., now that thou art come to me.   Lo,
God hath preserved thee alive to bring thee to this Island of
the Ka [2], in which there is nothing that is not in it, and it is
full of all good things.   Lo, thou shalt spend month after month
in this island until thou completest four months.   Then a ship
will come from the Residence [3] with sailors in it whom thou
knowest, and thou shalt go with them to the Residence and
die in thine own town.

" How glad is he that relateth what he hath experienced when
the calamity hath passed !   So I will relate to thee something
like this which came to pass in this island.[4]   I was in it with
my brethren, and children were in their midst, and we numbered
in all seventy-five serpents, my children and my brethren,
without my mentioning to thee the daughter of a humble
woman that was brought to me by. . . .[5]   Then a star fell,

[1] The humble posture.

[2] With regard to the " ka," see above, p. 24, note 2.   Here " Island of
the Ka " probably only means an island in which there is food to live on.

[3] This is naturally not to be taken literally, for one cannot get by ship
to the Red Sea from any Egyptian town !

[4] For the curtailment of the following narrative, see above ; the similarity to the experience of the shipwrecked sailor lies of course in the fact
that the serpent, too, had lost all his companions.

[5] A human child cast on to the island.

and these went up (?) in fire because of it. Now it happened when I was not with the burned ones (?), and while I was not in their midst. And I (almost) died on their account when I found them as one heap of corpses.

"If thou art valiant, curb thine heart.[1] Then thou wilt embrace thy children and kiss thy wife and see thine house— that is the best thing of all. Thou wilt arrive at the Residence, and dwell there in the midst of thy brethren."

Then I extended myself on my belly and touched the ground in (his) presence. And I said unto him: "I will discourse on thy nature to the Sovereign and acquaint him with thy greatness. I will cause ibi, hekenu, iudeneb, and khesait [2] to be brought to thee, and incense of the temples, wherewith every god is made content. I will relate what befell me, and of what I have seen. . . . Thou shalt be thanked in the city in the presence of the officers of the entire land.[3] I will slay for thee oxen for burnt-offering, and geese will I sacrifice for thee. I will send thee ships laden with all the precious things of Egypt, as should be done for a god, that loveth men, in a land far off which men know not." [4]

Thereupon he laughed at me and at what I had said, as being but foolishness in his heart.[5] And he said unto me: "Thou hast not myrrh [6] in plenty, being (but) a possessor of frankincense. But I am the prince of Punt, and myrrh, that is my very own. As for that hekenu whereof thou didst say that it is to be brought (to me), why that is the chief product of this island. But it shall happen, when thou art parted from

[1] As I did then.

[2] Pure perfumes, which were accounted as most precious substances by the Egyptians.

[3] Thus a public recognition by the king of the services rendered by the serpent.

[4] To what the king is to send he himself will add something: ships full of good things, and burnt offerings, which latter indeed a far-off god is able to receive, for the wind wafts them to him.

[5] The serpent laughs at the simplicity of the man, who holds out before him valuables, on which he himself sets no store or actually possesses in better quality.

[6] "Antiu," which we are accustomed to translate "myrrh," is regarded as the chiefest of all perfumes. It was imported from Punt, the land named immediately below, Punt being probably a general designation for the incense-producing countries in the south of the Red Sea.

this place, that never shalt thou behold this island more, for it will become water." [1]

And then that ship came, even as he had foretold. And I went and climbed a tall tree, and I descried them that were in it. And I went to report it, but found that he already knew it. And he said unto me : " Safely, safely home, little one, and see thy children, and give (me) a good name in thy city. Lo, that is all I require of thee."

Then I placed me on my belly, and my arms were bent in his presence. And he gave me a freight of myrrh, hekenu, iudeneb, khesait, tishepes, shaas, eye-cosmetic, giraffes' tails, a great mass (?) of incense, elephant-tusks, greyhounds, monkeys, apes, and all goodly treasures. [2] And I stowed them on this ship.

Now when I had placed me on my belly to thank him, he said unto me : " Lo, thou shalt reach the Residence in two months, shalt hold thy children in thine embrace, grow young again at the Residence, and be buried." [3]

And I went down to the shore where this ship lay. And I hailed the contingent that was in this ship, and gave praise upon the shore to the lord of this island, and they that were on board did likewise.

Then we voyaged northwards to the Residence of the Sovereign, and we reached the Residence in two months, according to all that he had said. And I entered in before the Sovereign and presented unto him all this treasure which I had brought from this island. And he thanked me in the sight of the officers of the entire land, and I was appointed to be a henchman and was presented with people of his (?).

Look at me after I reached land, after I saw what I had experienced. [4] Hearken unto my speech. Lo, it is good for men to hearken !

And he said unto me : " Act not the superior person, [5] my

---

[1] Thou needest not therefore trouble thyself to send me anything.

[2] All these are things that the Egyptians actually imported from the incense-producing countries.

[3] *I.e.* duly buried, as is necessary, if a person desires to be happy in death.

[4] Meaning probably : See to what I have attained, in spite of my unlucky voyage.

[5] Do not try to be too sapient ?

friend ! Who giveth water at dawn to a bird that he will kill early in the morning ? " [1]

3. THE STORY OF THE HERDSMAN [2]

That this fragment has been preserved to us is due solely to the fact that a scribe of the Middle Kingdom, who wished to clean a papyrus in order to re-use it, did not complete his task, and left intact twenty-five lines from the middle of the book—unfortunately, too few for us to be able to conjecture their purport. Perhaps a goddess waylays one of the herdsmen, who live with their cattle in the swamps of the Delta.

. . . Behold ye, when I went down to the swamp which bordereth on this low ground, I saw a woman therein, and she looked not like mortal men. My hair stood on end when I saw her tresses, because her colour [3] was so bright. Never will I do what she said ; awe of her is in my body.

I say unto you : Ye bulls, let us go home (?). Let the calves cross over and the goats rest in the place of . . ., with the herdsmen behind them, and our boat for the voyage home (?), astern of which are set the bulls and cows, and the wisest of the herdsmen recite a waterspell [4] and speak thus : " My kas [5] rejoice." Ye herdsmen and ye men, there is none that shall drive me forth from this field, (even ?) in the year of a high Nile, that issueth commands to the ridges of the land, and the pool cannot be distinguished from the river. [6]

Betake thee unto thine house. [7] The cattle that had remained in their place have come. The fear of thee hath vanished, the awe of thee is passed away, until (?) the terror of the Mighty

[1] The meaning being : The king will show me no favour now, for he even has designs on my life.

[2] See GARDINER, *Hierat. Papyrus aus den königl. Museen zu Berlin,* ii. p. 15.

[3] The colour of the woman, not of her tresses.

[4] To keep the crocodiles from the herds. What is meant is known to us from the representations of the Old Kingdom. The herdsmen, who bring the cattle home and have to cross a stretch of water, go ahead in a skiff, the bulls and cows follow swimming, while the calves are kept up by the halter. At the same time, the herdsmen make a particular gesture with the fingers, which is supposed to keep off the crocodiles.

[5] See p. 24, note 2 ; divine beings possess several kas.

[6] The water now masters even the higher parts of the country, and lake and river form a single mass of water.

[7] This is probably the answer of the other herdsmen.

One, the fear of the Lady of the Two Lands,[1] hath (also) vanished.

When the earth grew bright, at early dawn, it was done even as he said. This goddess met with him as he wended his way to the pool, and she had stripped off her clothes and disarrayed her hair. . . .

4. KING KHEOPS AND THE MAGICIANS [2]

This tale, in contrast with the narratives that have so far been presented to the reader, does not belong to the higher literature. It is of a popular character, as is shown both by the simplicity of its style and of its matter, which, at times, is burlesque, and by the fact that it is written in the vernacular ; it might well be ascribed to a public story-teller.

In spite of the loss of the beginning and end of the book, the plot is easily reconstructed. King Kheops, the builder of the Great Pyramid (about 2900 B.C. at the latest), makes his sons tell him tales of the wonders which had been wrought by magicians in the past. Finally, one of his sons informs him of his acquaintanceship with a still living magician, who then works his miracles in the king's presence. But unfortunately this sage also knows the future, and so the Pharaoh is informed by him, though unwillingly, of the disaster threatening his line : at this very time three children will come into the world who will drive it from the throne. The children are then actually born and—here the papyrus breaks off — grow up notwithstanding all Kheops' machinations ; it is the pious kings of the Fifth Dynasty whose origin is here recounted.

The first of these tales deals with events in the reign of King Zoser, but only the conclusion is preserved, in which King Kheops, in recognition of their deeds, commands victuals to be presented to that king and his magician, a " chief kherheb," [3] i.e. to be placed in their tombs.

Then Prince Khephrēn [4] stood up to speak and said : " I relate to thy majesty a wonder that came to pass in the time

---

[1] In view of these designations a great goddess must be meant.

[2] The so-called *Papyrus Westcar* in Berlin. See my edition : *Mitteilungen a. d. Oriental. Sammlungen der Königl. Museen*, vols. v. and vi. The papyrus was perhaps written in the Hyksōs period.

[3] The kherheb is the learned priest who knows the sacred books, and is accordingly the magician *par excellence*.

[4] The well-known builder of the second pyramid of Gîzah.

of thy father King Nebka,[1] when he went to the temple of Ptah of Memphis.   Now when his majesty went to Memphis, he also visited (?) the chief kherheb Ubaoner – – – –.

Ubaoner had a wife who was in love with a townsman, and who kept in touch with him through the medium of a handmaid ; she had also sent him a box full of clothes *as a present, and* he came with the handmaid.

And after many days had passed [2]—now there was a pleasure-house in the lake [3] of Ubaoner—the townsman said to the wife of Ubaoner : " Why, there is a pleasure-house in the lake of Ubaoner.   Behold, we will tarry therein."   And the wife of Ubaoner sent to the house-steward that had charge of the lake, saying : " Let the pleasure-house which is in the lake be furnished." [4]   *Then went she thither* and passed the day there drinking with the townsman, *until the sun set.*   Now when it was evening, he came and went down into the lake, and the handmaid *waited on him as bath attendant.   And the house-steward observed it.*   Now when the earth became light and the next day was come,[5] the house-steward went *and reported* this matter *to his master* – – – –.   And Ubaoner said : " Fetch me my . . . of ebony and gold," *and with this gear he made* a waxen crocodile *that was seven spans long.   And he recited a spell over it and said* : " Whoso cometh to bathe in my lake, *him do thou seize."*   And he gave it to the house-steward, and said unto him : " When the townsman goeth down into the lake according to his daily wont, then do thou throw the crocodile into the water behind him."   So the house-steward went his way and took the waxen crocodile with him.

And the wife of Ubaoner sent unto the house-steward that was in charge of the lake, saying : " Let the pleasure-house which is in the lake be furnished.   Lo, I come to dwell therein."   And the pleasure-house was furnished with every good thing.   Then they [6] went and spent a mirthful day with the townsman.

[1] Nebka and the previously mentioned Zoser are kings of the Third Dynasty, who reigned not long before Kheops.

[2] A stereotyped formula in Egyptian tales, and not to be taken literally.

[3] What is meant is a large garden with a pond in it and a pavilion, in accordance with Egyptian custom (*cf.* A. M. BLACKMAN, *Luxor and its Temples*, pp. 10 f.).

[4] With provisions, etc.   [5] Also a stereotyped expression.

[6] The wife and her maid.

Now when it was evening, the townsman came according to his daily wont. And the house-steward threw the waxen crocodile behind him into the water, and it became a crocodile of seven cubits, and it laid hold on the townsman – – – –. But Ubaoner tarried for seven days with the majesty of King Nebka, *and meantime the townsman was in the water without* breathing. Now when the seven days were passed, King Nebka came . . . and the chief kherheb Ubaoner *presented himself before him.* And Ubaoner said : " . . . May thy majesty come and view the wonder that hath come to pass in the time of thy majesty." *The king went with him, and Ubaoner called the crocodile and said* : " Bring thou hither the townsman." Then the crocodile came forth *and brought him* – –. And the majesty of King Nebka said : " Your pardon, but this crocodile is frightful (?)." Thereupon Ubaoner stooped down and took it, and it became a waxen crocodile in his hand.

Then the chief kherheb Ubaoner related unto the majesty of King Nebka this thing that the townsman had done in his house with his wife. And his majesty said unto the crocodile : " Take that is thine." Then the crocodile went down into the depths (?) of the lake, and none knew the place whither he went with him.

And the majesty of King Nebka caused the wife of Ubaoner to be taken to the field to the north of the Residence, and he set fire to her, and (her ashes) were thrown into the river.

Lo, this is a wonder that came to pass in the time of thy father Nebka, one of the deeds of the chief kherheb Ubaoner.

And the majesty of King Kheops said : " Let there be offered to King Nebka a thousand loaves of bread, a hundred jars of beer, one ox, and two measures of incense, and let there be given to the chief kherheb Ubaoner one cake, one jug of beer, a large piece of flesh, and one measure of incense, for I have seen an example of his learning." And it was done, according to all that his majesty commanded.

Then Prince Baufrē stood up to speak, and said : " I relate to thy majesty a wonder that came to pass in the time of thy father Snefru,[1] one of the deeds of the chief kherheb Zazamonkh. *One day King Snefru was sad. So he assembled the officers of the palace* in order to seek for him a diversion, but he found

---

[1] The immediate predecessor of Kheops.

none. Then said he : ' Go, bring me the chief kherheb, the scribe of the book, Zazamonkh.' And he was brought unto him straight-way. And his majesty said unto him : ' *I had assembled the officers of the palace together* in order to seek for me a diversion, but I could find none.' And Zazamonkh said unto him : ' If thy majesty would but betake thee to the lake of the Great House ! [1] Man thee a boat with all fair damsels from the inner apartments of thy palace. Then will the heart of thy majesty be diverted, when thou shalt see how they row to and fro. Then, as thou viewest the pleasant nesting-places of thy lake, and viewest its fields and its pleasant banks, thine heart will be diverted there-by.' *His majesty said unto him : ' I will do this ; get thee back to thine house* (?), but I will go boating. Have brought to me twenty paddles of ebony inwrought with gold, the handles thereof being of sekeb-wood inwrought with fine gold. Have brought to me twenty women, of those with the fairest limbs, and with (beauteous) breasts and braided tresses, such as have not yet given birth, and moreover have brought to me twenty nets, and give these nets to these women instead of their clothes.' And it was done according to all that his majesty commanded. And they rowed to and fro, and the heart of his majesty was glad, when he beheld how they rowed.

" Then a leader [2] became entangled (?) with her braided tress, and a fish-pendant [3] of new malachite fell into the water. And she became silent [4] and ceased rowing, and her side became silent and ceased rowing. Then said his majesty : ' Is it that ye will not row then ? ' And they said : ' Our leader is silent and roweth not.' And his majesty said unto her : ' Wherefore rowest thou not ? " She said : ' It is the fish-pendant of new malachite that hath fallen into the water.' He had *another brought to her* (?) *and said : ' I give thee this* instead.' And she said : ' I want my pot down to its bottom.' [5]

---

[1] *I.e.* the Palace.

[2] The girls probably sit in two lines, either of which has a leader who sets the stroke.

[3] Women when boating seem sometimes to have worn a hair-orna-ment in the shape of a fish ; see BLACKMAN, *Journ. of Egypt. Archæology,* xi. pp. 212 f. She probably hit herself on the hair with her paddle.

[4] The girls sing at their rowing to keep time, as is done on Nile boats to-day.

[5] Doubtless a proverb : I want my right in full, my own thing. [Better : " I would rather mine own than its likeness " (Translator)].

" Then said his majesty : ' Go to, and bring me the chief kherheb Zazamonkh.' And he was brought straightway. And his majesty said : ' Zazamonkh, my brother, I have done as thou saidst, and the heart of my majesty was diverted when I beheld how they rowed. But a fish-pendant of new malachite belonging to a leader fell into the water, and she was silent and rowed not, and so she spoilt her side. And I said unto her : ' Wherefore rowest thou not ? ' And she said unto me : ' It is a fish-pendant of new malachite that hath fallen into the water.' And I said unto her : ' Row, and lo, I will replace it.' And she said unto me : ' I want my pot down to its bottom.' " [1]

" Then the chief kherheb Zazamonkh said his say of magic, and he placed the one side of the water of the lake upon the other,[2] and found the fish-pendant lying on a potsherd.[3] And he brought it and gave it to its mistress. — Now as for the water, it was twelve cubits deep in the middle, and it reached twenty-four cubits after it was turned back. Then he said his say of magic, and he brought the waters of the lake back to their place.

" And his majesty spent the whole day in merriment with the entire palace, and he rewarded the chief kherheb Zazamonkh with all good things.

" Lo, it is a wonder that came to pass in the time of thy father King Snefru, one of the deeds of the chief kherheb, the scribe of the book, Zazamonkh."

And the majesty of King Kheops said : " Let there be offered to the majesty of King Snefru a thousand loaves of bread, a hundred jars of beer, one ox, and two measures of incense, and let there be given to the chief kherheb, the scribe of the book, Zazamonkh, one cake, one jug of beer, and one measure of incense, for I have seen an example of his learning." And it was done according to all that his majesty commanded.

Then Prince Hardedef stood up to speak and said : " *Hitherto hast thou heard only examples* of what they knew that have gone before (us), and one knoweth not the truth from falsehood. *But even* in thine own time there is a magician." Then said his majesty : " Who is that, Har[dedef, my son ? " And Prince

[1] See above p. 39, note 5.
[2] He folds up the waters of the lake like a cloth.
[3] It had not, therefore, sunk in the mud.

Har]dedef said : [1] "There is a townsman, Dedi by name, and he dwelleth in Ded-snefru.[2] He is a townsman of 110 years, and he eateth five hundred loaves of bread, a haunch of beef in the way of meat, and drinketh one hundred jugs of beer, unto this very day.[3] He knoweth how to put on again a head that hath been cut off, and he knoweth how to make a lion follow after him, with its leash [4] trailing on the ground. He knoweth the number (?) of the locks [5] (?) of the sanctuary of Thōth." — Now the majesty of King Kheops was always seeking for himself the locks (?) of the sanctuary of Thōth, to make for himself the like thereof for his Horizon.[6]

Then said his majesty : " Thou thyself, Hardedef, my son, shalt bring him to me." And ships were made ready for Prince Hardedef, and he voyaged upstream to Ded-snefru. Now when the ships were moored to the bank, he went journeying by land, and sat in a carrying-chair of ebony, the poles of which were of sesenem-wood and overlaid with gold.

And when he was come to Dedi, the chair was set down. And he stood up to salute him, and found him lying on a mat on the threshold of his house, and a servant held his head and was stroking it for him, and another was rubbing his feet.

And Prince Hardedef said : " Thy condition is like life before growing old and before (?) old age, the place of decease, the place of enwrapping, the place of burial ; (thou art still) one that sleepeth on into the daylight, free from sickness, and without becoming old in abhorrence.[7] Greetings, revered one ! I am come hither to summon thee with a message from my father Kheops, that thou mayest eat the dainties that the king giveth, the victuals of them that are in his service, that he may

---

[1] For this reading see SETHE, *Aegyptische Lesestücke*, p. 28.

[2] A town near the modern Medûm, north of the entrance to the Fayyûm.

[3] So hale and hearty is he yet ; 110 years is the conventional number for extreme age.

[4] The rope by which he could lead the lion ; but the lion follows him even so.

[5] But see GARDINER, " The Secret Chambers in the Sanctuary of Thōth," in *Journ. of Egypt. Archæology*, xi. pp. 2 ff.

[6] The Horizon is the pyramid of the king, who is supposed to set therein like the sun. The king wished to have for it the safest locks, even those which the god of wisdom had himself invented in past time.

[7] In these greetings of the prince and the sage the narrator aims at a loftier style, and accordingly becomes hard to understand.

bring thee at a good time of life to thy fathers, who are in the realms of the dead." Said this Dedi : " In peace, in peace, Hardedef, thou king's son whom his father loveth ! May thy father Kheops reward thee ! May he advance thy station among the elders ! May thy ka contend with thine adversary ! May thy soul know the . . . way to the portal of Him-that-hideth-Weakness ! [1] Greetings, king's son ! "

And Prince Hardedef held out his hands to him and helped him up ; and then he went with him to the riverside, giving him his hand the while. And Dedi said : " Let a ship be given me, that it may bring me the children [2] together with my books." And two vessels with their crews were put at his service ; but Dedi voyaged downstream in the ship in which was Prince Hardedef.

Now when he reached the Residence, Prince Hardedef entered in to make report to the majesty of King Kheops. And Prince Hardedef said : " O king, my lord, I have brought Dedi." Said his majesty : " Go, bring him to me." Then his majesty proceeded to the pillared hall of the palace, and Dedi was brought in unto him. And his majesty said : " How is it, Dedi, that I have never seen thee before ? " And Dedi said : " It is he who is summoned that cometh. The Sovereign summoned me, and lo, I am come." [3] And his majesty said : " Is it true, what is said, that thou canst put on again a head that hath been cut off ? " And Dedi said : " Yea, that I can, O king, my lord." And his majesty said : " Have brought unto me a prisoner that is in the prison, that his punishment may be inflicted." And Dedi said : " But not on a man, [4] O king, my lord ! Lo, is not such a thing rather commanded to be done to the august [5] cattle ? "

And a goose was brought unto him, and its head was cut off ; and the goose was placed on the western side of the hall, and its head on the eastern side of the hall. And Dedi said his say of magic, and thereupon the goose stood up and waddled, and its head likewise. Now when one part had reached the other, the goose stood up and cackled. And he had a duck

---

[1] A door-keeper in the underworld.   [2] His pupils ?

[3] Sense : It is thy fault if thou hast not seen me till now ; thou hast never even inquired about me.

[4] The sage is depicted as humane.

[5] " August " because they are the property of the king.

brought unto him, and there was done unto it the like. And his majesty had an ox brought to him, and its head was made to tumble to the ground. And Dedi said his say of magic, and the ox stood up behind him, while its leash fell to the ground.[1]

And King Kheops said : " It hath been said that thou knowest the number (?) of the locks (?) [2] of the sanctuary of Thōth." And Dedi said : " So it please thee (?), I know not the number thereof, O king, my lord, but I know the place where they are." And his majesty said : " Where is that ? " And Dedi said : " There is a chest of flint in the chamber named ' The Inventory ' in Heliopolis. (Lo, they are) in the chest." [3] And Dedi said : " O king, my lord, lo, it is not I that bring it thee." And his majesty said : " Who then will bring it me ? " And Dedi said : " It is the eldest of the three children who are in the belly of Red-dedet that will bring it thee." And his majesty said : " But I desire that (?) thou say who she is, this Red-dedet." And Dedi said : " It is the wife of a priest of Rē of Sakhebu,[4] that hath conceived three children of Rē, lord of Sakhebu. He hath told her that they will exercise this excellent office [5] in this entire land, and that the eldest of them will be high priest in Heliopolis." Then his majesty's heart grew sad thereat. And Dedi said : " Pray, what is this mood, O king, my lord ? Is it because of the three children ? Then I say unto thee : thy son, his son, and then one of them." [6] And his majesty said : " When will she give birth, pray, (this) Red-dedet ? " (And Dedi said) : " She will give birth on the fifteenth day of the first winter month." And his majesty said : " She . . . the region (?) of the Canal of the Two Fishes ; I myself would set foot (?) there ; I will see the temple of Rē, lord of Sakhebu." And Dedi said : " Then will I cause the

[1] The above-mentioned wonder with the lion seems to have been omitted here in the MS. ; to it belongs the statement about the leash.

[2] See above, p. 41, note 5.

[3] An utterance of the king's has dropped out here.

[4] A little-known town in the district of Memphis and Heliopolis.

[5] The kingship. The sun-god, from whom the kings are descended, has begotten for himself a new line and rejected that of Kheops.

[6] The prophecy asserts : first thy son Khephrēn will reign, then his son Mykerinos, and then the new family is to take the helm. Actually two other kings reigned in the interval ; but of the Fourth Dynasty kings only the builders of the three great pyramids lived in the memories of the people.

water to stand four cubits deep over the region (?) of the Canal of the Two Fishes." [1]

Then his majesty betook himself to his palace. And his majesty said : " Let the . . . be instructed (to consign) Dedi to the house of Prince Hardedef, that he may dwell with him. Fix his allowance at a thousand loaves of bread, an hundred jars of beer, one ox, and an hundred bunches of leeks." And it was done according to all that his majesty commanded.

Now on one of these days it came to pass that Red-dedet suffered the pangs of childbirth. Then said the majesty of Rē of Sakhebu to Isis, Nephthys, Mesekhent, Heket, and Khnum : [2] " Up, go ye and deliver Red-dedet of the three children that are in her womb, that will exercise this excellent office in this entire land. They will build your temples, they will furnish your altars with victuals, they will replenish your libation-tables, and they will make great your offerings." [3] Then these deities went, when they had taken on the forms of dancing-girls, and Khnum was with them and bore their carrying-chair (?). [4]

And they came to the house of Rewoser [5] and found him standing with loin-cloth hanging down. [6] Then they presented to him their necklaces and rattles. [7] And he said unto them : " My mistresses, [8] behold there is a lady here who is in travail." And they said : " Let us see her ; lo, we understand mid-wifery." And he said unto them : " Come." Then they entered in before Red-dedet, and shut (the door of) the room

[1] Dedi probably wishes to make the journey easier for the king. At the season mentioned the region in question was dry, but Dedi will by magic place it under water for him, so that the king can voyage in comfort to Sakhebu.

[2] Mesekhent is the goddess of birth, Heket an ancient primordial goddess ; Khnum is the fashioner of all mankind.

[3] The kings of the Fifth Dynasty were thus pious kings, according to the popular view, in contrast with those of the Fourth. Whether they really were descended from a priest of the sun-god we do not know, but it is certainly true that they displayed special veneration for this divinity, for each one of them built at his residence a new temple for him, after the pattern of the temple of Heliopolis.

[4] They come as travelling women with a male attendant.

[5] The husband of Red-dedet.

[6] His clothing was in disorder—because of his anxiety ?

[7] *I.e.* they made music and danced before him ; *cf.* above, p. 27, note 3.

[8] He speaks to them politely, in order that they might go away.

upon them and her. And Isis placed herself in front of her, and Nephthys behind her, and Heket hastened the birth. And Isis said : " Be not lusty in her womb as truly as thou art named User-ref." [1] This child slipped forth on to her hands, a child of one cubit with strong bones ; the royal titulary of his limbs was of gold, and his head-cloth of true lapis lazuli.[2] They washed him, cut his navel-string, and laid him on a sheet upon (?) a brick. And Mesekhent drew near unto him and she said : " A king that will exercise the kingship in the entire land." And Khnum gave health to his body.

The birth of the two other children is then related, both times in the same words and in the same detail. But the adjurations are of course different : " Draw not near in her womb, as truly as thou art named Sah-rē," [3] *and* " Be not dark in her womb, as truly as thou art named Keku."

And these divinities went forth, after that they had delivered Red-dedet of the three children. And they said : " Let thy heart be glad, Rewoser ! Behold, three children are born unto thee." And he said unto them : " My mistresses, what can I do for you ? I pray you give this one measure of barley to your chairman, and take it away for yourselves as payment into (your) vessels (?)." [4] So Khnum loaded himself with the barley.

Now when they had gone their way to the place whence they had come, Isis said unto these deities : " What meaneth it, that we have come to her and yet have worked no wonder for these children, that we may make report to their father who sent us forth ? " So they fashioned three royal crowns, and they placed them in the barley. And they caused storm and rain to come in the sky, and they went back to the house.[5] And

[1] The adjurations, which Isis utters, declare the names of the children to be User-ref, Sah-rē, and Keku. The three first kings of the Fifth Dynasty are meant : Userkaf, Sahurē, and Kakai. The adjurations contain puns on the names.

[2] The children come into the world attired in the royal blue and yellow head-cloth, while the titulary, which the kings assumed on attaining the throne, is to be read on their limbs inlaid in gold. The story-teller conceives of the children as inlaid bronze figures, just as pointed out on p. 31, note 5.

[3] See BLACKMAN, *Journ. of Egypt. Archæology*, x. p. 196.

[4] He means probably the barrel-like pottery receptacles in which grain and the like are stored.

[5] They bring on the storm in order to have a pretext for bringing back the barley.

they said : " We pray you, let us lay the barley here in a locked-up chamber until we come again – – – –." And they laid the barley in a locked-up chamber.

And Red-dedet purified herself with a fourteen days' purification.[1] And she said unto her handmaid : " Hath the house been made ready ? " And she said : " It hath been made ready with every good thing, save for pots, which cannot be brought." And Red-dedet said : " Wherefore, pray, cannot pots be brought ? " And the handmaid said : " No good can be done here [2] apart from the barley for the dancing-girls, and that is in a chamber bearing their seal." And Red-dedet said : " Go down and fetch some of it, and Rewoser will recompense them therefore after he returneth."

So the handmaid went and opened the chamber. And she heard in the chamber the sound of singing, music, dancing, rejoicing (?), and all that is done in a king's honour. Then she went and told Red-dedet all that she had heard. And she (Red-dedet) went round the chamber, but could not find the place wherein it was being done. Then she laid her temple to the corn-bin, and she found that it was in this. And she put it in a chest, put this in another locker, corded it with hide, put it in a closet which contained her pots, and shut (the door) upon it.

And Rewoser came in from the field, and Red-dedet related unto him this matter. And he rejoiced greatly, and they sat them down and made merry.

Now after certain days had passed by, Red-dedet was enraged with her handmaid about a matter, and had her punished with a beating. And the handmaid said unto the people that were in the house : " Shalt thou do the . . . ? She has born three kings. I will go and tell it unto the majesty of King Kheops." So she went and found her eldest brother by her mother [3] binding yarn of flax on the threshing-floor. And he said unto her : " Whither art thou bound, little maiden ? " Then she related unto him this matter. And her brother said unto her :

---

[1] A woman, therefore, was accounted unclean for a period of time after child-birth.

[2] See GARDINER, *Recueil de Travaux*, xl. pp. 79 ff.

[3] The added designation is illustrative of the relationships of such slaves ; they belong to their mother, the father counts for nothing.

" And so thou art come even unto me (?), and I am to take part in the betrayal (?) ! " [1]   And he took a . . . of flax to her, and dealt her a grievous blow.   Then the handmaid went to fetch her a handful of water, and a crocodile seized her."

Then her brother went to tell it to Red-dedet, and he found Red-dedet sitting with her head upon her knee and her heart exceeding heavy.   And he said unto her : " Wherefore art thou so troubled ? "   And she said : " It is this girl, that hath grown up in the house.   Lo, she is even now gone forth, saying : ' I will go to reveal it ! ' "   And he hung down (?) his head and said : " My mistress, she came and said unto me – – – – beside me, and I dealt her a grievous blow.   And she went to draw her some water and a crocodile seized her."

(Here the manuscript breaks off.)

5. THE DELIVERANCE OF MANKIND

The following myth, which is a good example of a popular tale, has survived owing to the author of a charm against snakes having used it as an introduction to the same.   It thus had the honour of being included among the texts inscribed on the walls of two royal tombs of the New Kingdom, and so has been preserved for us.[2]

– – – – (Rē), the god that fashioned himself, when he was king over men and gods together.   Mankind devised an (evil) thing.   Now his majesty [3] had become old, and his bones were silver, his flesh gold, his hair real lapis lazuli.[4]

And his majesty discerned the things which were (devised) against him by mankind.   And his majesty said unto them that were in his following : " Pray, summon to me mine eye,[5] and Shu, Tefnet, Kēb, and Nut, together with the fathers and mothers that were with me when I was yet in Nun,[6] likewise

---

[1] Sense in any case : I do not want to have anything to do with your denunciation.

[2] First brought to notice by Naville in 1875 ; frequently discussed and translated, most recently by ROEDER, *Urkunden zur Religion des alten Ägyptens*, p. 142.

[3] *I.e.* Rē, the sun-god.

[4] Apparently regarded as the signs of old age.

[5] This is originally the sun himself, as eye of the sky-god.   It was then also identified with the oft-mentioned snake of the sun-god, and it is here, in addition, identical with the goddess Hathor.

[6] The ocean in which the sun originated.

also my god Nun himself. He shall bring his courtiers with
him. Thou shalt bring them stealthily (?), in order that mankind may not see, and that their hearts may not be *affrighted*.
Thou shalt come with them to the great hall, that they may
tell (us) their counsels – – – –."

So these gods were brought in, and these gods came nigh
unto him, and they touched the ground with their foreheads
in the presence of his majesty, that he might say his say in the
presence of the Father of the Eldest Ones, him that had fashioned
mankind, the king of men. They said before his majesty:
" Speak to us that we may hear it." And Rē said unto Nun :
" Thou eldest god, in whom I came into being, and ye, ye ancestor
gods, behold, mankind that came into being from mine eye [1]—
they have devised a thing against me. Tell me what ye would
do concerning it. Behold, *I still ponder*, and am slaying them
not, until I have heard what ye may say about it." And the
majesty of Nun said : " My son Rē, thou god that is mightier
than he that created him, and older than they that fashioned
him, (only) sit thee down on thy throne ; the fear of thee is
great, if thine eye is (but) turned toward them that blaspheme
thee." And the majesty of Rē said : " Behold, they are fled
unto the desert, their hearts being afraid because of what they
have said." And they said before his majesty : " Send forth
thine eye, that it may slay them for thee – – – –. Let it go
down as Hathor."

Then went this goddess and slew mankind in the desert.
The majesty of this god said : " Welcome, Hathor ! Thou hast
done *that for which I sent thee forth*. . . ." And this goddess
said : " By thy life, I have prevailed over men, and that is
pleasant in mine heart." Said the majesty of Rē : " I will
prevail over them in (Herakleopolis and ?) diminish them."
So arose the name Sekhmet [2] – – – – meal of the night, in order
to wade in their blood, beginning from Herakleopolis.[3]

And Rē said unto (his followers) : " Pray call to me swift-
running messengers, that they may run for me as the shadow
of a body." These messengers were brought straightway.

[1] According to another legend, which is based on a pun, the sun-god
wept, and from these tears mankind originated.

[2] " She that prevaileth," the name of the goddess of war, who is here
equated with Hathor.

[3] In this garbled speech Rē expresses his determination, which he
then carries out, to rescue what is left of mankind.

The majesty of this god said : " Get you to Elephantine and bring me much dedi." [1] And this dedi was brought to him, and the majesty of this great god gave it unto Him-with-the-Side-lock of Heliopolis,[2] and he ground this dedi. Now the maidservants bruised (?) barley for beer, and this dedi was added to this mash and it was as human blood. And seven thousand jars of beer were made ready.

The majesty of the king of Upper and Lower Egypt, Rē, came together with these gods to see this beer. Now it was the morning whereon the goddess purposed to slay mankind, when they should go up. Said the majesty of this god : " How goodly they are,[3] I will protect mankind thereby." And Rē said : " Carry them to the place where she said that she would slay mankind there."

The majesty of the king of Upper and Lower Egypt set to work early, under cover of the night, to have this . . . drink poured out. Then were the fields full of liquor [4] to the height of four palms through the might of the majesty of this god.

And this goddess came in the morning and found· how this was flooded. Her face looked beautiful therein. Then drank she it, and it pleased her ; she became drunken and knew not mankind.

6. THE FOUNDING OF A TEMPLE [5]

That Sesōstris I (1965–1934 B.C.) undertook building operations in the temple of Heliopolis we can see from his fine obelisk, the only noteworthy relic of the famous temple that has survived the passing of the centuries. This building of Sesōstris must have been a large one, for the king erected a special monument in order to record to posterity his resolve to undertake the work, and its inauguration. The actual stone has not come down to us, but we probably possess a copy of it, made by some one in the time of the Eighteenth Dynasty. The copy was made, no doubt, because the text was regarded as an example of good literary style. Anyhow, it was then further made use of in the schools, for, in the manuscript

---

[1] Some substance that stains red ; possibly hæmatite, which is actually to be found at Elephantine.

[2] See SETHE, *Zeitschr. für ägypt. Sprache*, lvii. pp. 18, 24 [Translator].

[3] The jars containing the beer.   [4] The beer is meant.

[5] Preserved in the so-called *Berlin Leather Roll*, a sheet of vellum dating from the time of Amenōphis II. Brought to notice in 1875 by Ludw. Stern ; see BREASTED, *Ancient Records of Egypt*, i. pp. 240 ff.

4

with which we are concerned, it is divided up into verses and sections, and the orthography has been changed into that of the New Kingdom—not without serious perversion of the text.

In the year 3, on the . . . day of the third month of Inundation, under the majesty of the king of Upper and Lower Egypt, Kheperkerē, the son of Rē, Sesōstris, who liveth for ever and ever.

The king appeared in the double crown, and it came to pass that One [1] sat down in the . . . hall, and that One asked counsel of his followers, the chamberlains of the palace and the magistrates, in the place of seclusion.[2]   One commanded, while they hearkened.   One asked counsel, and caused them to reveal their opinion : " Behold, my majesty intendeth a work, and bethinketh him of some good thing for the time to come, that I may erect a monument and set up an abiding memorial tablet [3] for Harakhti.   He hath formed me in order to do for him what should be done for him, and to execute that which he commanded to be done.   He hath made me the herdsman of this land, for he knew that I would maintain it in order for him. He hath bestowed upon me that which he protecteth, and that which the eye [4] that is in him doth illumine.   All is done in accordance with his desire – – – –.

" I am a king whom he (caused ?) to be, a sovereign – – – –. I conquered already as a babe,[5] and was great while yet in the egg – – – –.   He hath made me spacious, to be lord of the Two Halves, as a child, ere the swaddling-clothes were loosed for me.   He hath appointed me to be lord of the people, created me (. . .) in the sight of mankind, and completed me for dweller in the palace [6] when unborn, ere I came forth from between the thighs.   He hath given me (the land) in its length and breadth, and I am brought up to be an ' if he is, he conquereth.' [7]   He hath given me the land, and I am its lord.   My might hath reached the height of heaven.

[1] " One " here, and subsequently, denotes the king.

[2] The innermost part of the palace.   Probably so named because Horus had grown up in " seclusion."

[3] *I.e.* that on which the inscription was cut ?

[4] The sun ; *cf.* p. 47, note 5.   [5] Literally : young bird.

[6] " Horus, the dweller in the palace," as a designation of the king.

[7] Similar bold constructions are fancied elsewhere, *e.g.* an " if I come, it is brought to me " for something belonging to me, a " go out that he may come in," for an overcrowded place.

" It is excellent (?) to work for him that hath made me, and
to content the god with what he hath given. *I am like* his son
and protector ;[1] he hath commanded me to conquer what he
hath conquered. *I am the* guardian *of the temple* (?), Horus
– – – –. I establish the food-offerings of the gods, and do a
work for my father Atum in the great hall. (I) cause him to
have[2] it as broad as he hath caused me to conquer. I victual
his altar on earth. I build mine house in (his) vicinity.[3] Thus
my beauty will be remembered in his house ; my name will be
the benben-stone, and my memorial the lake. It is to gain
eternity, if one doeth for him that which is good, and no king
dieth that is mentioned because of his[4] possessions – – – –.
A name that standeth thereupon is . . . mentioned and
perisheth not in eternity. What I do is what will be, and what
I seek is what is excellent – – – –."

And the chamberlains of the king spake and answered before
their god :[5] " Commanding Utterance (?) is in thy mouth, and
Discernment is behind thee. O sovereign, thy designs come to
pass. O king, who hast appeared as uniter of the Two Lands,
in order to . . . in thy temple ! It is excellent to look upon
the morrow – – – –. (But) mankind together (would) complete
nothing without thee, for thy majesty is the eye of all men.
Thou art great when (thou) settest up thy monument in Heliopolis, the dwelling of the gods, before thy father, the lord of
the great hall, Atum, the Bull of the Ennead. Erect thine house
and make for it gifts for the stone of oblation, that it may serve
the statue, its favourite – – – – for all eternity."

The king himself said to the chancellor and first chamberlain,
the superintendent of the two (gold-)houses and silver-houses,
him that is over the mysteries of the two serpent-diadems :
" It will be thy counsel that causeth the work to be accomplished . . ., the coming to pass of that which my majesty
desired. Thou wilt be the director thereof, one that will do
according to that which is in my heart – – – – vigilant, that
it may come to pass without languor, and all work that apper-

---

[1] Horus—who, to be sure, actually bears this designation as the
protector of Osiris.

[2] By my work on his temple.

[3] The king thus built a second new temple beside the older one ; the
new was then also assigned the accessories of the old, a sacred benben-
stone and a lake.

[4] The god's.   [5] The king.

taineth thereto – – – –. They that work are commanded to work according to that which thou wilt ordain (concerning it)."

The king appeared in the diadem and the two feathers, and all the people accompanied him. The chief kherheb and scribe of the god's book [1] extended the line *and carried out the foundation ceremonies.*

Then his majesty caused the royal scribe of the records to go before the people, who stood united together, out of Upper and Lower Egypt. . . .

7. THE WAR OF KING KAMŌSE [2]

This beginning of a narrative is to be found on a schoolboy's writing-board.' As far as can be decided on palæographical grounds, it dates from the time in which the events recorded took place, namely, the seventeenth century B.C.

It deals with a war which Kamōse, the king of Thebes, waged against the Asiatic people known as the Hyksōs, who had conquered a large part of Egypt, and whose capital, the city of Avaris, lay in the north-eastern Delta. The late tale of King Apōphis and Sekenenrē, which I give below, is concerned with an incident of the same date. But what occurs on our writing-board is not a tale, but an historical narrative, which the teacher may well have copied from an inscription of Kamōse.

The document begins with the date of the third year of the king. It then continues :

The strong king in Thebes, Kamōse, who is granted life for ever, is an excellent king ; Rē himself hath made him king and hath granted to him victory in very sooth.

His majesty spake thus in his palace to the council of the great men that was with him : " I should like to know to what purpose serveth my strength. One prince sitteth in Avaris and another in Nubia,[3] and there sit I together with an Asiatic and a negro ! Each possesseth his slice of Egypt and divideth the land with me – – – – as far as Memphis. . . . Behold, he

---

[1] It was the duty of this adept in the sacred writings to direct the ceremonies of laying the foundations of a temple. This consisted mainly in marking out on the ground the outline of the building by means of sticks and cords.

[2] See GARDINER, *Journ. of Egypt. Archæology*, iii. pp. 95 ff. ; v. p. 45 ff. The language already displays vulgar characteristics.

[3] A Nubian state had therefore grown up at that time.

hath Shmūn,[1] and no man standeth still (?), being ruined by the imposts of the Bedouins. I will grapple with him,[2] and rip open his belly. My desire is to deliver Egypt and to smite the Asiatics."

The great men of his council spake thus : " Behold, *even if* the Asiatics *are come* as far as Cusæ, and have pulled out their tongues all together (?),[3] yet are we in quietness with our Egypt. Elephantine [4] is strong, and the middle part (of the land) belongeth to us as far as Cusæ. The finest of their fields are ploughed for us, our oxen are in the Delta,[5] wheat is sent for our swine,[6] our oxen are not taken away, – – – – he hath the land of the Asiatics and we have Egypt. (But) if any man cometh *and attacketh us* (?), we will act against him."

They were displeasing in the heart of his majesty : " Your counsel *is wrong and I will fight with* the Asiatics – – – – weepeth, the whole land – – – –. *Men shall say of me* in Thebes : Kamōse, the protector of Egypt."

Then sailed I [7] down stream to drive back the Asiatics, according to the command of Amūn, that hath the right counsels. My valiant army marched on before me like a fiery blast ; the auxiliary troop of the Matoï [8] was our . . ., in order to seek out the Bedouins and to blot out (?) their places. East and West brought fat and wine (?),[9] and the host was furnished with victuals in every place.

I sent on the strong troop of the Matoï *ahead* (?), and I remained as guard – – – – in order to *coop up* (?) Teti, the son of Pepi,[10] in the town of Nefruisi. I suffered him not to escape, and held off the Asiatics, – – – –.

I passed the night in my ship with gladsome heart. When

[1] Shmūn—Hermopolis—lies in Middle Egypt. Perhaps this passage is to be taken as stating that the Hyksōs realm actually reaches only up to Memphis, but that it has unlawfully extended itself as far as Middle Egypt, where it hinders trade with its tariffs.

[2] The enemy is not named as being obvious.

[3] Meaning that they put out their tongues derisively ?

[4] The frontier fortress against Nubia.

[5] The Upper Egyptians have thus, in spite of the Hyksōs domination, retained their property and their rights of pasturage.

[6] Wheat was the species of grain produced in the Delta.

[7] From here onwards the king recounts his deeds.

[8] A people in Northern Nubia who served as mercenaries in Egypt.

[9] The ships received presents from both banks of the Nile.

[10] He will be a vassal of the Hyksōs.

day dawned, I was on him, as it were an hawk. When it was the time of perfuming the mouth,[1] I drove him back and destroyed his wall and slew his people. I caused his wife to come down [2] to the quay, and my soldiers were like lions with their prey, with slaves, herds, fat, and honey, dividing up their possessions with joyful hearts – – – –.

All we can learn from the few following sentences is that a place, Per-shak, was in a panic when Kamōse came unto it and their horses fled inside.

B. INSTRUCTIONS IN WISDOM

The writings which compose this section bear the name " sbōyet," " instruction," and are conceived of as the addresses [3] of a sage, in which he instructs his son. In some instances we have to do with a discourse on worldly prudence and wisdom, and such books will have been intended merely for schools ; unquestionably so the *Instruction of Duauf*, which is simply a commendation of the schools. But the customary designation " sbōyet " also covers writings of different content ; what King Amenemhēt committed to his son far exceeds the bounds of school philosophy, and there is nothing whatever to do with school in a great man warning his children to be loyal to the king.

I. THE INSTRUCTION OF PTAHHOTEP [4]

This book professes to have been composed by a vizier of King Issi (about 2675 B.C. ; according to other calculation about 2870 B.C.), and, as a matter of fact, that king did have a vizier of this name, whose tomb is still known to us.[5] Though it may rightly be doubted whether the book can really claim this man as its author, it is certainly very ancient, and by the time of the Middle Kingdom had already been re-edited, obviously with a view to making it

---

[1] Perhaps breakfast, otherwise called " mouth-washing."

[2] As a captive.

[3] The " instruction in the form of a letter," which prevailed in the schools during the New Kingdom, does not appear at an earlier date.

[4] Preserved complete only in the *Papyrus Prisse* in Paris, which was written during the Middle Kingdom. The most recent edition, in which use is made of all the manuscripts, is that of DÉVAUD, *Les Maximes de Ptahhotep* (Fribourg, 1916). Translations, among others, by GRIFFITH in *The World's Best Literature*, and by LANGE (not printed).

[5] At Sakkârah (MARIETTE, *Mastabas*, D 62).

more intelligible. In this form it was still used as a school-book as late as the Eighteenth Dynasty.

It has a twofold object. It is intended to instruct the schoolboy in wise conduct and in good manners, but, at the same time, it sets out to be his model for the appropriate expression of ideas; he is to be an "artist" in speech, and is to express himself in such choice language as befits an official.

In my translation I have preferred sometimes the older, and sometimes the newer, version, according as one was more easy to understand than the other. I have only too often had to forgo translating altogether.

[TITLE.—OLDER VERSION.]

The instruction of the superintendent of the capital, the vizier, Ptahhotep, under the majesty of King Issi, who liveth for ever and ever.

[INTRODUCTION.—LATER VERSION.]

So spake he unto the majesty of King Issi: Old age hath come and dotage hath descended. The limbs are painful and the state of being old appeareth as something new. Strength hath perished for weariness. The mouth is silent and speaketh not. The eyes are shrunken and the ears deaf – – – –. The heart is forgetful and remembereth not yesterday. The bone, it suffereth in old age, and the nose is stopped up and breatheth not.[1] To stand up and to sit down are alike ill. Good is become evil. Every taste hath perished. What old age doeth to a man is that it fareth ill with him in all things.

Let therefore the servant there [2] be bidden to make him a staff of old age; let my son be set in my place, that I may instruct him in the discourse of them that hearken,[3] and in the thoughts of them that have gone before, them that have served the ancestors in times past.[4] May they do the like for thee, that strife may be banished from among the people, and the Two River-banks may serve thee.

Said his majesty: "Instruct thou him in discourse first – – – –. May he set an example to the children of the

---

[1] The nose was accounted the actual seat of life (see p. 26, note 1).

[2] Humble way of saying "me"; see also p. 22, note 5.

[3] This must have a special meaning here.

[4] The viziers of previous kings. May my pupil be as useful to you as they were to their kings.

great ; may obedience enter into him, and every right conception of him that speaketh unto him. There is no child that
(of itself) hath understanding.''

[SECOND TITLE.—EARLIER VERSION.]

The beautifully expressed utterances, spoken by the prince
and count, the father of the god and beloved of the god,[1] the
bodily son of the king, the superintendent of the capital and
vizier, Ptahhotep, while instructing the ignorant in knowledge
and in the rules of elegant discourse, the weal of him that
will hearken thereto and the woe of him that shall transgress
them.

1. [THOU CANST LEARN SOMETHING FROM EVERY ONE.—
LATER VERSION.]

Be not arrogant because of thy knowledge, and have no
confidence in that thou art a learned man. Take counsel with
the ignorant as with the wise, for the limits of art cannot be
reached, and no artist fully possesseth his skill. A good discourse is more hidden than the precious green stone, and yet
is it found with slave-girls over the mill-stones.[2]

2–4. [CONCERNING BEHAVIOUR TOWARDS AN ORATOR (?).]

If thou findest an orator (?) at his time, with sound sense
and better than thou, bend thine arm and bow thy back. *But
if he speaketh ill, then* fail not to withstand him, in order that
men may call out to him : " Thou ignorant one."
But if it is an equal of thine, show thyself by silence to be
better than he, when he speaketh ill. *Then* will he be praised
by the listeners, *but* thy name *will be accounted* good *among the
great.*[3]
If he is a humble person, who is not thine equal, be not
wrathful against him, for thou knowest that he is miserable.
– – – –. Disregard him, and so he punisheth himself. It is
bad if one injureth one that is despicable – – – –. Thou smitest
him with the punishment of the great.[4]

---

[1] Priestly title.   [2] The poorest of the poor.
[3] But see GARDINER, *Notes on the Story of Sinuhe*, p. 31.
[4] Does this mean : as great people punish, by keeping silence and
ignoring him ?

5. [THOU WILT GET ON BEST IN LIFE WITH THE AID OF RIGHT
AND TRUTH.—LATER VERSION.]

If thou art a leader and givest command to the multitude,
strive after every excellence, until there be no fault in thy
nature. Truth is good and its worth is lasting, and it hath not
been disturbed since the day of its creator,[1] whereas he that
transgresseth its ordinances is punished. It lieth as a (right)
path in front of him that knoweth nothing. Wrong-doing (?)
hath never yet brought its venture to port. Evil indeed winneth
wealth, but the strength of truth is that it endureth, and the
(upright) man saith : " It is the property of my father." [2]

6. POSSIBLY : THOU CANST OBTAIN NOTHING IN LIFE BY
BLUSTER ; what hath come to pass is the command of God.

7. [CONCERNING BEHAVIOUR AS A GUEST.—LATER VERSION.]

. If thou art one that sitteth where standeth the table [3] of one
who is greater than thou, take, when he giveth, that which is
set before thee. Look not at that which lieth before him, but
look at that which lieth before thee.[4] Shoot not many glances
at him, for it is an abhorrence to the ka [5] if one offendeth it.

Cast down thy countenance until he greeteth thee, and
speak only when he hath greeted thee. Laugh when he laugheth.
That will be well pleasing in his heart, and what thou doest
will be acceptable ; one knoweth not what is in the heart.[6]

A great man, when he sitteth behind the food, his resolves
depend upon the command of his ka. A great man giveth to

[1] Rē, who brought truth into the world.

[2] That my father brought me up in the ways of truth is the best thing
he has bequeathed me.

[3] The Egyptians at meals sat each at a low table by himself. We
are to suppose that the exalted host had his table in the middle, and the
guests theirs round about him.

[4] The host has a quantity of victuals before him ; do not look greedily
at them. [See also GUNN, Syntax, pp. 13, 74 (Translator)].

[5] Upon this vital force in a man also depended, according to the view
here held, his disposition and therewith his whole conduct. In social
intercourse, therefore, particular care must be taken to avoid what is
unpleasant to another's ka—what, as we would say to-day—gets on his
nerves.

[6] Prudence in the presence of a great man is always in place, for one
doesn't know his moods.

the man that is within reach of him, but the ka stretcheth out the hands for him (further).[1] Bread is eaten by the decree of God [2] – – – –.

8. [BE FAITHFUL IN THE DELIVERING OF MESSAGES.—LATER VERSION.]

If thou art one of the trusted ones, whom one great man sendeth to another, act rightly in the matter when he sendeth thee. Thou shalt deliver the message as he saith it. Be not secretive concerning what may be said to thee, and beware of any forgetfulness. Hold fast to the truth and overstep it not, even if thou (therewith) recountest nothing that is gratifying. Beware (also) of worsening words, such as might make one great man contemptible (?) to the other through the manner of speech of all men. " A great man, an insignificant one "—that is what the ka abhorreth.[3]

9. If thou ploughest and there is growth in the field and God giveth it thee liberally, satisfy not thy mouth beside thy kindred . . . (*all the rest unintelligible*).

10. [DO NOT SLIGHT THOSE WHO HAVE RISEN IN THE WORLD. —LATER VERSION.]

If thou art an humble person and art in the train of a man of repute, one that standeth well with the god,[4] know thou nothing of his former insignificance. Raise not up thine heart against him on account of what thou knowest about him aforetime. Reverence him in accordance with what hath happened unto him, for wealth cometh not of itself – – – –. It is God that createth repute – – – –.

11. [PERMIT THYSELF TIME FOR RECREATION.—OLDER VERSION.]

Follow thine heart [5] so long as thou livest, and do not more than is said. Diminish not the time in which thou followest

[1] Usually the great man at a meal only gives especially tasty morsels to those who sit beside him ; but if he is in good humour he will stretch out his hand even as far as you.

[2] Probably the ka ; mention is also made elsewhere of the god who is in man.

[3] Do not replace the choice language of your employer by ordinary expressions ; it sounds discordant when a great man speaks like a nobody.

[4] *I.e.* the king.

[5] Variant : thy ka.

the heart, for it is an abhorrence to the ka if its time is diminished. *In particular a warning seems to be uttered against* too much care for thine house.

12. [CONDUCT TOWARDS THY SON.—LATER VERSION.]

If thou art held in esteem, and hast an household, and begettest a son that pleaseth God—if he doeth right, and inclineth to thy nature, and hearkeneth to thine instruction, and his designs do good in thine house, and he hath regard for thy substance as it befitteth, search out for him everything that is good.

He is thy son, whom thy ka hath begotten for thee ; separate not thine heart from him.

But if he doeth wrong and trespasseth against thy designs, and acteth not after thine instructions, and his designs are worthless in thine house, and he defieth all that thou sayest – – – – then drive him away, for he is not thy son, he is not born to thee – – – –.

13. [ON BEHAVIOUR IN THE VESTIBULE OF THE GREAT.]

If thou standest or sittest *in the vestibule, wait quietly until thy turn cometh.* Give heed to the servant that announceth ; he that is called hath a broad place.[1] The vestibule hath its rule, and every arrangement therein is in accordance with the measuring-cord. It is God who assigneth the foremost place— *but one attaineth nothing (?) with* the elbow.

14. *Be discreet in thine intercourse with people.*

15. Proclaim thy business without concealment. Give out thy thoughts in the council of thy lord – – – –. *One ought to say plainly what one knoweth and what one knoweth not. The last line runs :* he is silent and saith : " I have spoken."

16. *The* leader, *i.e. the high official, ought* to have in mind the days that are yet to come, *or, as the later version more clearly puts it :* beware of the days that are yet to come, *thus probably the ever-threatening displeasure of the king.*

17. [BEHAVIOUR TOWARDS PETITIONERS.—LATER VERSION.]

If thou art one to whom petition is made, be kindly when thou hearkenest to the speech of a petitioner. Deal not roughly

---

[1] *I.e.* he need not push himself forward in unseemly fashion.

with him, until he hath swept out his body,[1] and until he hath said that on account of which he is come. A petitioner liketh it well if one noddeth to his addresses, until he hath made an end of that about which he came – – – –. A favourable audience gladdeneth the heart.

But whoso acteth the churl towards petitioners, then men say : " Why is it, pray, that he so doeth ? "

18. [WARNING AGAINST WOMEN.]

If thou wouldst prolong friendship in an house to which thou hast admittance, as master, or as brother, or as friend, into whatsoever place thou enterest, beware of approaching the women. The place where they are is not good.

On that account a thousand go to perdition : Men are made fools by their gleaming limbs, and lo ! they are (already) become herset-stones.[2] A trifle, a little, the likeness of a dream, and death cometh as the end – – – –.

19. [WARNING AGAINST COVETOUSNESS.]

If thou desirest thy conduct to be good, to set thyself free from all that is evil, then beware of covetousness, which is a malady, diseaseful, incurable. Intimacy with it is impossible ; it maketh the sweet friend bitter, it alienateth the trusted one from the master, it maketh bad both father and mother, to-together with the brothers of the mother, and it divorceth a man's wife. It is a bundle (?) of every kind of evil, and a bag of everything that is blameworthy. Long lived is the man whose rule of conduct is right, and who goeth in accordance with his (right) course ; he winneth wealth thereby, but the covetous hath no tomb.[3]

20. [THE SAME.—OLDER VERSION.]

Be not covetous regarding division, and be not exacting, except with regard to what is due to thee. Be not covetous towards thy kindred ; the request of the meek availeth more

---

[1] A similar comparison of the unburdening of the heart with the emptying of the belly is also employed in the *Complaints of the Peasant.*

[2] The shining limbs attract you, but after brief enjoyment they appear as discoloured to you as the herset-stone, which is accounted elsewhere as the sign of affliction.

[3] The sign of the extremest poverty.

than strength – – – –. Just the little of which he hath been defrauded, createth enmity (even) in one of a cool disposition.

21. [THE ADVANTAGE OF MARRIAGE.—OLDER VERSION.]

If thou art a man of note,[1] found for thyself an household, and love thy wife at home, as it beseemeth. Fill her belly, clothe her back ; unguent is the remedy for her limbs. Gladden her heart, so long as she liveth ; she is a goodly field for her lord.

To this, apparently, another warning is appended : hold her back from getting the mastery *and the like.*[2]

22. [BE LIBERAL TOWARDS THINE INTIMATES.—LATER VERSION.]

Satisfy thine intimates with that which hath accrued to thee, *as one* favoured of God. *To do this is prudent,* for there is none that knoweth his condition, if he thinketh of the morrow. *If, therefore,* a misfortune befalleth the favoured ones, it is the intimates that still say " Welcome ! " to him. . . . *Thus retain for thyself their attachment against the time of displeasure that threateneth.*

23. *Repeat not frivolous speeches, the* utterance *for instance* of one that is heated.

24. [BE CAUTIOUS IN SPEECH.]

If thou art a man of note, that sitteth in the council of his lord, fix (?) thine heart upon what is good. Be silent—this is better than teftef-flowers. Speak (only) if thou knowest that thou canst unravel (the difficulty). It is an artist that speaketh in council, and to speak is harder than any other work – – – –.

25. *Only the beginning is intelligible :* If thou art strong and inspirest respect, through knowledge or through pleasantness of speech – – – –.

26. Approach not a great one in his hour,[3] and anger not the heart of him that is laden – – – –; *this is a dangerous*

---

[1] *I.e.* hast attained eminence in thy profession.

[2] In this passage the older version employs a term for " wife " that is more than blunt, and this the later modestly replaces with " woman."

[3] *I.e.* probably, when he is at his work.

thing, which detacheth the ka from him that loveth him, *him that supplieth* food together with the god [1] – – – –.

27. Instruct a great one in that which is profitable to him ; *that will also be of advantage to thee, for thy sustenance* dependeth upon his ka, *and* thy back will be clothed thereby. – – – –

28. If thou art the son of a man of the ·bureaucracy, an envoy, that is to make the multitude content – – – –, be not partial – – – –.

29. *Do not harbour a grudge ?*

30. [TRUST NOT FORTUNE.—OLDER VERSION.]

If thou be grown great, after that thou wast of small account, and have gotten thee substance, after that thou wast aforetime needy in the city which thou knowest,[2] forget (?) not how it fared with thee in time past.   Trust (?) not in thy riches, that have accrued to thee as a gift of God.   *Thou art not better (?) than* another that is thine equal, to whom the same hath happened.[3]

31. [RESPECT FOR SUPERIORS.—OLDER VERSION.]

Bend thy back to him that is over thee, thy superior of the king's administration.   So will thine house endure with its substance, and thy pay be duly awarded.   To resist him that is set in authority is evil.   One liveth so long as he is indulgent. – – – –

32. Do not have intercourse with a woman with (?) a child (*one that is pregnant ?*).

33. [PRUDENCE IN ENGAGING IN FRIENDSHIPS.]

If thou lookest for a state of friendship, ask no question, but draw near him and be with him alone – – – –.   Prove (?) his heart by a conversation.   If he betrayeth aught that he hath seen, or doeth aught with which thou art vexed, *then take heed, even in thine answers* – – – –.

---

[1] *I.e.* the king; upon him and upon the partiality of your superior your fate depends.

[2] In thine home, not yet, as now, at court.

[3] Impoverishment ; he avoids naming the misfortune.

34. Have a cheerful countenance when thou celebratest a feast *and distributest bread thereat.*

35. *Perhaps : Riches are inconstant, but a good disposition is a lasting possession.*

36. *Quite unintelligible.*

37. [LET NOT THY CONCUBINE STARVE (?)]

If thou takest to wife one that is well-nurtured, one that is cheerful, one that the people of her city know, – – – – put her not away, but give her to eat.[1]

[*Now comes a long epilogue, in which the usefulness of this instruction is extolled : it should be handed on from generation to generation, because of its excellent contents and its beautiful form :*]

If thou hearest this that I have spoken unto thee, thy whole state will be as good as that of them who have gone before. What remaineth over of their truth is noble, and the remembrance of them perisheth not in the mouth of men, because their maxims are so goodly.   Every word (of theirs) will be used (?) always as a thing imperishable in this land, and will beautify the utterances with (?) which the princes speak.[2]

It is that which teacheth a man to speak to posterity that it may hear it, and to be an artist, one that hath heard what is good, and that now on his part speaketh to posterity that it may hear it.

If a good nature is formed in him that is the one set in authority,[3] he will be excellent for ever and all his wisdom will endure eternally ; the wise man's soul is glad when he causeth his beauty . . . to endure on earth.

Then men see how admirable he is : his heart is *evenly balanced* (?) to his tongue, *and* his lips are exact when he speaketh ; his eyes see, and his ears together hear what is profitable for his son, that doeth right and is free from lying.

[1] The other version is more explicit : make her fat by eating.

[2] Discourse is adorned with quotations from these proverbs.

[3] Or does it mean : if it is recognized by a person set in authority ? What follows possibly asserts that he will take care that the wise teaching is perpetuated on earth.

[The next section, which was certainly a masterpiece in respect of style, plays with the word " to hear." The translation is particularly difficult. He who " has heard " is he who has adopted his father's wisdom.]

To hear is excellent for a son that hath heard ; the hearer entereth [1] as one that hath heard, and he that hath heard becometh a hearer [2] that heareth well and speaketh well. Every one that hath heard is something excellent, and it is excellent for one that hath heard to hear. To hear is better than all that is, and fair favour accrueth thereby. How good is it for a son to receive it, when his father speaketh ; thereby old age becometh his portion.

He whom God loveth, heareth, but he whom God hateth, heareth not. It is the heart that maketh its owner into one that heareth or one that heareth not. His heart is a man's fortune – – – –.[3]

How good is it when a son hearkeneth to his father, and how happy is he to whom this is said.[4] A son, that is good as a lord of hearing, that hath heard, and to whom it is said . . . that is honoured of his father, the memory of him remaineth in the mouth of the living, them that are now upon earth and them that shall be.

If a son accepteth it, when his father saith it, not one of his plans miscarrieth. – – – – *He will* be esteemed among the magistrates – – – –, *whereas* evil cometh on him that heareth not. A wise man riseth early in order to establish himself,[5] but the ignorant *doeth not so.*

As for the fool that heareth not, he can do nothing at all. He regardeth knowledge as ignorance, and good as bad. He will do everything that is blameworthy, so that complaint is laid against him every day. He liveth on that wherefrom others die, and it is his food to speak ill. *This his nature* is known to the magistrates; *daily doth death threaten him (?), and men shun him* because of the multitude of misfortunes that are daily upon him.

A son that hath heard is a worshipper of Horus.[6] He prospereth after he hath heard. When he hath grown old and

[1] Into the palace ?   [2] Is this an official post ?
[3] A man's fate does not rest with him ; it depends on his talents.
[4] The father ?   [5] In his good profession ?
[6] One of the legendary primæval kings.

hath attained honour, he talketh in like manner to his children and reneweth the instruction of his father. *And every one that is so instructed should talk to his children, and they again to theirs.* . . . May the people who shall see (them) say : " He is as that one was," and also the people who shall hear (of them) shall say : " He is as that one was " — — — —.

Take no word away, and add nothing thereto, and put not one thing in the place of another.[1] — — — —

Thy lord *also shall say* : " This is the son of that one," and they that hear it (*shall say*) : " Praised be he to whom he was born " — — — —. May the magistrates that will hear it say : " How goodly are the utterances of his mouth."

So act that thy lord may say concerning thee : " How goodly was the instruction of his father. He issued from him, from his body, and he hath told (it) unto him, and it [2] is all in (his) body, and what he hath done is yet greater than what was told to him. Behold, this is a good son, one that God giveth, one that did more than what was told him by his lord. He doeth right and his heart doeth after its (right) course."

Mayest (?) thou reach me [3] being sound in body, and so that the king is satisfied with all that hath been done, and mayest thou pass many years in life. It is not little that I have wrought upon earth. I have spent an hundred and ten years [4] in life, which the king hath given me, and with rewards beyond those of them that have gone before, because I did right for the king up to the place of honour.[5]

In what esteem our book was held can be seen, moreover, from the fact that single phrases were quoted from it in inscriptions. Thus a certain Amenemhēt,[6] who lived during the Eighteenth Dynasty, says, speaking of himself and his superior : I shot not many glances at him. I cast down my countenance when he spake with me ; *this he has extracted from precept 7. And upon the monument, which glorifies King Sesōstris III's conquest of*

---

[1] Alter nothing in this book ; a warning that has certainly not protected the book from being completely recast.

[2] The instruction.   [3] Be as successful as I.

[4] The proverbial long life. The king bestows long life, inasmuch as he gives a man sustenance for a corresponding length of time.

[5] Old age.   [6] *Zeitschr. für ägypt. Sprache*, xlvii. pp. 87 ff.

5

Nubia,[1] *we read :* he is not thy son, he is not born to thee, *which is derived from our precept* 12.

2. THE INSTRUCTION FOR KAGEMNI [2]

This must have been a similar work to the *Instruction of Ptah-hotep.* In the lost beginning it was probably related that the old king Huni (dating from the end of the Third Dynasty) commanded his vizier to put his life's experiences in writing for the benefit of his children, among whom was included the future vizier Kagemni. There actually was a vizier of this name, though several hundred years later, and the author of this work will have had some dim recollection of his name.

1. [ON DISCRETION IN SPEECH.]

– – – – the humble remaineth whole, and he that dealeth uprightly is praised ; the tent is opened for the humble, and *he that is cautious in speech* (?) *hath* a broad place, *but* the knife is sharp against him that strayeth from the path – – – –.

2. [ON BEHAVIOUR AT A MEAL.]

If thou sittest with many persons, hold the food in abhorrence, even if thou desirest it ;[3] it taketh only a brief moment to master oneself, and it is disgraceful to be greedy. – – – – A cup of water quencheth the thirst, and if the mouth be full of . . ., it strengtheneth the heart. A good thing taketh the place of that which is good,[4] just a little taketh the place of much. He is a miserable man that is greedy for his body – – – –.

3. [THE SAME SUBJECT.]

If thou sittest with a greedy person, eat thou only when his meal is over, and if thou sittest with a drunkard, take thou only when his desire is satisfied. Rage not against the meat in the presence of a . . . ; take when he giveth thee, and refuse it not. Think, that softeneth him.

4. [STRIVE TO OBTAIN A GOOD PROFESSION ?]

[1] In the Berlin Museum.
[2] Preserved in the Paris papyrus of the Middle Kingdom, which also contains the *Instruction of Ptahhotep* ; translated, as is that, by Griffith and Lange.
[3] Assume this manner out of humility.
[4] A simple but good dish sufficeth thee instead of the better one.

5. [BE NOT BOASTFUL.]

Be not boastful of thy strength in the midst of those of thine own age. Be on thy guard against any withstanding thee (?). One knoweth not what may chance, what God doeth when He punisheth.

6. [CONCLUDING NARRATIVE.]

The vizier had his children called after he had completed (his treatise on) the ways of mankind and on their character as encountered by him. And he said unto them : " All that is in this book, hear it as if (?) I spake it – – – –." Then they placed themselves upon their bellies. They read it as it stood in writing, and it was better in their heart than everything that was in this entire land ; they stood and they sat in accordance therewith.[1]

The majesty of King Huni came to port,[2] and the majesty of King Snefru was raised up as beneficent king in this whole land. Then was Kagemni appointed superintendent of the capital and vizier.

3. THE INSTRUCTION OF DUAUF [3]

This *Instruction* was a favourite work in the schools of the late New Kingdom, and it is, moreover, preserved only in schoolboys' exercises of the Nineteenth Dynasty (about 1300 B.C.) — completely in two papyri, and in parts on several ostraca. The way in which the boys have mangled the text baffles description. There are not many passages in it with regard to which one does not despairingly ask what can have been written there originally ; for what the boys have written are only too often meaningless words—they simply did not understand what they had to copy out. Of many paragraphs, therefore, I can only translate a small portion.

It is not surprising that this work was such a favourite school textbook, for it is written to extol schools and a school-education, exactly as are the fictitious letters to and from schoolmasters in the New Kingdom. It can be seen from the personal names con-

---

[1] They regulated their behaviour in accordance with it.
[2] Usual euphemism for " to die."
[3] Preserved in *Pap. Sallier*, ii. and *Pap. Anastasi*, vii. in the British Museum. Brought to light by Goodwin in 1858 ; edited by MASPERO, *Genre épistolaire*, pp. 48 ff. A recent edition is wanting.

tained in this *Instruction*, that it is to be dated to the time between the Old and Middle Kingdoms.

Instruction, which a . . . man,[1] named Duauf, the son of Khety, composed for his son, named Pepi, when he voyaged up to the Residence, in order to put him in the School of Books, *among* the children of the magistrates – – – –.

He said unto him : I have seen him that is beaten, him that is beaten : thou art to set thine heart on books. I have beheld him that is set free from forced labour : behold, nothing surpasseth books.[2]

Read at the end of the Kemit ;[3] thou findest this sentence therein : " The scribe, his is every place at the Residence and he is not poor in it.[4] *But he that acteth according to* the understanding of another,[5] *he hath no success."* *The other professions also are* as this sentence purporteth.

Would that I might make thee love books more than thy mother, would that I might bring their beauty before thy face. It is greater than any calling. – – – – If he [6] hath begun to succeed, and is yet a child, men greet him.[7] He is sent to carry out behests, and he cometh not home that he may don the apron.[8]

Never have I seen a sculptor on an errand, nor a goldsmith as he was being sent forth. But I have seen the smith at his task at the mouth of his furnace. His fingers were like stuff from crocodiles,[9] he stank more than the offal (?) of fishes.

Every artisan that wieldeth the chisel (?), he is wearier than he that delveth ; his field is the wood and his hoe is the metal.[10] In the night, when he is set free, he worketh beyond what his arms can do ; in the night he burneth a light.[11]

The stone-mason seeketh for work (?) in all manner of hard stone. *When he hath finished it,* his arms *are* destroyed and

---

[1] Apparently a person of low standing.

[2] The uneducated is faced with a life of flogging, the educated need not do any rough work.

[3] Is this the name of some old book ?

[4] Meaning probably : Every office which a scribe fills is in connection with the court, and so the scribe has a share before others in all the favours which are distributed there.

[5] Thus is himself not a learned official.   [6] The schoolboy.

[7] So soon do men begin to treat him with deference.

[8] The " apron " here and further on will denote the clothing of the artisan.

[9] As crinkled and hard as their skin.   [10] *I.e.* the chisel.

[11] Even at night there is no respite for him.

he is weary. When such an one sitteth down at dusk, his thighs and his back are broken.

The barber shaveth late into the evening – – – –, he betaketh him from street to street, in order to seek (?) whom he may shave. *He straineth his arms* in order to fill his belly, even as a bee that feedeth at its work.[1]

The . . . sails down to the Delta in order to get the purchase-money,[2] and he worketh beyond that his arms can do. The gnats [3] slay him – – – –.

The small bricklayer [4] with the Nile mud (?), he spendeth his life among the cattle (?) ; *he is somehow concerned with* vines *and* swine,[5] his clothes are stiff, – – – – *he worketh* (?) with his feet, he poundeth – – – –.

Let me tell thee further of the builder of walls, *that is oft-times sick (?), his raiment is likewise vile ; what he eateth is* the bread of his fingers *and* he washeth himself once only. — *He fares so ill that the sage has to devote a second paragraph to him, of which only a little is intelligible to us :*

He is more miserable than one can rightly tell (?). *He is like a block of stone (?)* in a room, which measureth ten cubits by six cubits. – – – – The bread, he giveth it unto his house ; his children are beaten, beaten.

The gardener bringeth loads,[6] *and his arm and neck ache beneath them.* At morn he watereth the leek, and at even the vines – – – –. *It also goeth more ill with him than* any calling.

The field-worker, his reckoning endureth for ever ; [7] he hath a louder voice than the abu-bird – – – –. *He, too,* is wearier than can be told (?), *and* he fareth as well as one fareth among lions ; *he is oft-times sick (?),* – – – – *and* when he cometh unto his house at eventide, the going hath cut him to pieces (?).[8]

[1] As indefatigably as it collects honey.   [2] Thus a trader ?
[3] The pest of the Delta.
[4] This seems to be the bricklayer who makes brick out of Nile mud and builds with them.
[5] In the Egyptian there is a play on the words " vines " and " swine," and it is probably on that account that they are brought together here.
[6] The produce of the garden.
[7] Probably the settling up of accounts with the owner, so often depicted in the old tombs ; the standing jokes in the scenes being that the peasants talk a great deal and get a hiding.
[8] The long roads have worn him out ?

The weaver (?) in the workshop, he fareth more ill than any women.[1] His thighs are upon his belly,[2] and he breatheth no air. *On a day, when no weaving is done, he must* pluck (?) lotus flowers in the pond. He giveth bread to the doorkeeper,[3] that he may suffer him to come into the daylight.

The fletcher, he fareth ill exceedingly, when he goeth up into the desert.[4] Much giveth he for his ass, much giveth he for what is in the field.[5] When he setteth out on the road (?) – – – – and cometh unto his house at eventime, the going hath cut him to pieces (?).

The . . . goeth up into the desert, and (first) maketh over his goods to his children, for fear of the lions and the Asiatics – – – – and cometh unto his house at eventide, the going hath cut him to pieces (?) – – – –.

The . . ., his fingers stink, and the odour thereof is abhorrent (?) – – – –. He spendeth the day cutting reed, and clothes are his abhorrence.[6]

The cobbler, he fareth ill exceedingly ; he beggeth ever. He fareth as well as one fareth among . . . What he biteth is leather.[7]

The fuller washeth upon the river bank, a near neighbour of the crocodile – – – –. This is no peaceful calling in thine eyes, that would be more tranquil than all callings – – – –.

The fowler, he fareth ill exceedingly, when he looketh at the birds in the sky. When the passers-by [8] are joined to the heaven, he saith : " Would that I had a net here." *But God giveth him no success (?).*

Let me tell thee further, how it fareth with the fisherman ; it goeth more ill with him than any other calling. Is not his work upon the river, where he is mixed with the crocodiles ? – – – –. One saith not : " There is a crocodile there " ; fear

---

[1] Who also must always sit in the house.

[2] He squats on the ground on his haunches.   [3] He bribes him.

[4] Where he fashions the arrow-heads out of the quantities of flints that are to be found there.

[5] The donkey's fodder.   [6] Because he is standing in the water.

[7] He uses his teeth at his work in order to pull tight the sandal-straps, as he is actually shown doing in a scene on a tomb wall (ROSELLINI, *Mon. Civili.*, lxiv. 1). The jest obviously is that this is the only thing that comes between his teeth.

[8] The migratory birds, which formed a substantial item in the food-supply of the Egyptians.

hath blinded him – – – –.   Behold, there is no calling that is
without a director except (that of) the scribe, and he is the
director.[1]

If he knoweth the books, then true of him is : " They are
good for thee " – – – –.   *What I now do* on the voyage up to
the Residence, lo, I do it out of love for thee.   A day at school
is profitable to thee, *and its work endureth even like the
mountains* – – – –.

*Most of what is to be found in the following sections is unin-
telligible.   As the introduction to them shows :* Let me say to
thee further yet other words in order to instruct thee, *they deal
with a new theme ; indeed, they may be a later addition.   The
one section teaches good behaviour in the presence of the* great : If
thou enterest, while the master of the house is in his house, *and
he hath to do with another first,* while thou sittest with thine hand
to thy mouth, ask not for anything.   *Further :* Speak no hidden
words *and* speak no insolent words – – – –.   *Then :* If thou
comest from school and midday is announced to thee, and thou
goest shouting joyously in the streets, then – – – –.   If a
great man sendeth thee with a message,[2] *repeat it as he saith it ;*
take nothing therefrom and add nothing thereto – – – –.

Be content with thy diet : If three loaves satisfy thee, and
thou drinkest two pots of beer, *and the belly is not yet contented,
fight against it* (?).

Behold, it is good if thou sendest away the multitude and
hearkenest (alone) to the words of the great. – – – – Make a
friend of a man of thy generation.

Behold, Renenet [3] is upon the way of God ; Renenet, the
scribe hath her upon his arm on the day of his birth.[4]   He
arriveth at the vestibule (?) of the officials, *when he is grown up* (?).
Behold, no scribe lacketh sustenance, the things of the king's house.

Mesekhent [5] *hath vouchsafed success to the scribe ;* at the

---

[1] This thought is the culmination of all that the sage has hitherto been
saying.

[2] In the school or on the way home ?

[3] The goddess of the harvest ; the following sentences assert somehow
or other that a scribe never suffers want.

[4] This will have some connection with the custom, which we know
from statues, of having the name of one's master either branded or
tattoed on the upper part of the arm.   So the scribe is the property of the
goddess, who gives plentiful sustenance.

[5] The goddess of birth, see p. 44, note 2.

head of the officials is he set, and his father and his mother thank God *for it* – – – –. Behold, this it is *that I set before thee and thy children's children.*

4. THE INSTRUCTION OF KING AMENEMHĒT [1]

This book also seems to have been held in high esteem during the New Kingdom, for it is preserved in four different papyri, and extracts from it are found on at least nine ostraca. Unfortunately there is no older manuscript, and, with one exception, they are all writing-exercises of schoolboys of the Nineteenth Dynasty (*circa* 1300 B.C.), and teem with mistakes.

The great king Amenemhēt I (1955–1965 B.C.), in the twentieth year of his reign, as we know from other sources, made his son Sesōstris I co-regent, and withdrew from the outward activities of political life.

Our document represents the aged king as recounting to his son on this occasion, by way of admonishment, the events which induced him to take this step ; he had reaped ingratitude, and an attempt had been made on his life.

Instruction, which the majesty of King Sehetepibrē,[2] the son of Rē, Amenemhēt, made, speaking in a message of truth to his son, the Lord of All.

He saith : " Thou that hast appeared as God,[3] hearken to what I shall say to thee, that thou mayest be king over the land, and ruler over the river banks, that thou mayest do good in excess of (what is looked for). Be on thy guard against subordinates – – – – ; approach them not, and be not alone. Trust not a brother, know not a friend, and make not for thyself intimates,—that profiteth nothing.

If thou sleepest, do thou thyself guard thine heart, for in the day of adversity a man hath no adherents. I gave to the poor and nourished the orphan, I caused him that was nothing to reach the goal, even as him that was of account.

It was he who ate my food that disdained me (?) ; it was he to whom I gave my hand that aroused fear therewith.[4] They that clothed them in my fine linen looked at me as at a

---

[1] See the article by GRIFFITH in *Zeitschr. für ägypt. Sprache,* xxxiv. pp. 35 ff. ; MASPERO, *Les ensignements d'Amenemhâit Ier.* Cairo, 1914.

[2] " He who pacifies the heart of Rē," the official name of King Amenemhēt I.

[3] *I.e.* that hast become king.

[4] With the kindness which I showed him ?

shadow, and they that anointed them with my myrrh, poured water . . .

Mine images are among the living, and my shares (in the offerings) among men ; [1] (and yet ?) they contrived a conspiracy (?) against me, without it being heard, and a great contest, without it being seen.[2] Men fought on the place of combat [3] and forgat yesterday.[4]—Good fortune attendeth not one that knoweth not when he ought (?) to know.[5]

It was after supper, when night had come ; I had taken an hour of repose, and laid me down upon my bed. I was weary, and my heart began to follow after slumber. Then it was as if weapons were brandished, and as if one inquired (?) concerning me, and I became like a snake of the desert.[6]

I roused me, to fight alone (?), and I marked that it was an hand-to-hand affray of the bodyguard. When I had quickly taken weapons into mine hand, I drave back the rogues. . . . But there is no strength by night, and one cannot (?) fight alone, and success will not come without thee that protectest me.[7]

Behold, the abominable thing came to pass when I was without thee, when the Court had not yet heard that I am resigning (the sovereign power) to thee,[8] when I did not yet dwell with thee. May I act according to thy counsels,[9] for I fear them [10] no (more), . . . *and I am powerless against* the indolence of servants.

Had the women set the battle in array ? Had the conflict been fostered (?) within the house ? – – – – Were the townsmen made foolish on account of their [11] deeds. Ill fortune hath not come behind me since my birth, and nought hath happened that might equal my prowess as a doer of valiant deeds.[12]

[1] So honoured am I in the land.
[2] No one betrayed to me the plot.
[3] Literally the place where the bulls fight.   [4] My good deeds.
[5] Does he mean himself, who was unsuspicious ? The interpretation of the whole paragraph is by no means certain. (See also GUNN, *Syntax*, p. 128 [Translator]).
[6] *I.e.* I started up like a sand-viper.
[7] He fears further assaults if his son is not associated with him on the throne.
[8] That sounds as though the attempt had been made by some one who wished to see the son on the throne at once.
[9] *I.e.* your plan to take a part in governing.
[10] The courtiers.   [11] The conspirators ?
[12] For this successful administration I have had but ill thanks.

I trod Elephantine,[1] I marched into the Delta ; I stood upon the boundaries of the land and beheld its circuit. I carried forward the boundaries of my power by my might and by my prowess.

I was one that produced barley and loved the corn-god ; the Nile greeted me on every . . .[2] None hungered in my years, none thirsted in them. Men dwelt (in peace) through that which I wrought and talked of me (?) ; all that I commanded was as it should be.

I tamed (?) lions and captured crocodiles.[3] I . . . ed the Wawa,[4] and captured the Matoï ; [4] I caused the Bedouins to go as dogs.[5] I built an house adorned with gold ; its ceilings are of lapis lazuli [6] . . ., its floor is . . ., the doors are of copper and the bolts of bronze, they are made for endless time, and eternity is afraid of them.[7]

The schoolboy, on whose scribblings we are at this juncture almost entirely dependent, has so utterly garbled the conclusion, that we can only make out disconnected scraps : There is much talk in the streets. I know : " Yea " and make search because of its beauty, for he knoweth it not [8] – – – – King Sesōstris. Thy feet go. Thou art mine own heart, mine eyes gaze upon (thee). The children have an hour of happiness beside the people, when they give thee praise.

Behold, I have wrought at the beginning, and thou (?) commandest at the end – – – – the white crown of the divine seed.[9]

There is exultation in the boat of Rē.– – – –[10] Monuments are set up and thy tomb (?) is made splendid – – – –.

---

[1] The southern frontier town.

[2] The inundation reached even the most inaccessible places.

[3] Probably figurative for foreign peoples.

[4] Nubian people.

[5] *I.e.* So docile were they.

[6] *I.e.* the ceilings of the rooms are painted to represent the sky.

[7] Because it sees that it will never be able to destroy them.

[8] The whole of this meaningless sentence, as can be seen only, it is true, in the original, is derived from the verse of the *Admonitions* (p. 100), " Nay, but the children of the magistrates are thrown on to the streets. He that hath knowledge saith : ' Yea.' The fool saith : ' Nay.' He that hath no knowledge, to him seemeth it good."

[9] The king.   [10] See GUNN, *Syntax*, p. 148.

5. THE INSTRUCTION FOR KING MERIKERĒ [1]

Although this work is only known to us from an Eighteenth Dynasty copy, we need not hesitate to assign it to an earlier date. As to Merikerē, we only know that he lived in the confused period between the Old and Middle Kingdoms—in the second half of the third millenium B.C.—and was one of the kings of Herakleopolis. The kings of the Eleventh Dynasty ruled at Thebes contemporaneously with these monarchs, and, as our book asserts (an assertion now confirmed by inscriptions from Thebes), they fought with one another for the possession of the city of Thinis. The name of the father of Merikerē, who here presents his son with his life's experiences, is unknown to us.

It is worth noting that we meet with religious conceptions in this composition that are practically non-existent in the other works of the same class.

Only scanty fragments survive of the beginning of the book. It can be seen that the father who addresses Merikerē is himself a king. Further on, also, long lacunæ make interpretation difficult.

[How to act towards rebels.]

With regard to one whose dependants are many, and who is pleasant in the eyes of his serfs, *one that* talketh much, *the king's advice is :* suppress him, slay him, wipe out his name, – – – root out the memory of him and his dependants that love him.

A cause of unrest for the citizens is a quarrelsome man, one that createth two factions among the youth. If thou findest that the citizens cleave to him . . ., cite [2] him before the courtiers, suppress him ; he too is an enemy.

This was followed by two similar sections, the one about a beggar that stirs up the army, *and then came the assurance that if the son dealt justly it would be well with him :* the citizens rejoice and thou art justified before the god.[3] – – – – A good disposition is a man's heaven (?), but the cursing of a passionate (?) man is baneful.

[The value of speaking well and of wisdom.]

Be a craftsman in speech, so that thou mayest prevail, for the power of (a man) is the tongue, and speech is mightier than

[1] In a Leningrad papyrus of the time of Thutmōsis III (1478–1447 B.C.), and in fragments of a papyrus of the same period in Moscow. Discovered by Golénischeff in 1876, and published by him in 1913. See the translation by GARDINER, *Journ. of Egypt. Archæology*, i. pp. 20 ff.

[2] Thus in legal form ?

[3] Osiris, before whom the trial took place in the other world.

any fighting. – – – – *He that is clever*, him the learned attack not, if he is learned, and no (harm) happeneth where he is. Truth cometh to him fully kneaded,[1] after the manner of that which the forefathers spake.

Copy thy fathers, them that have gone before thee – – – –. Behold, their words endure in writing. Open (the book) and read, and copy the knowledge,[2] so that the craftsman too may become a wise man (?).

[BE BENEVOLENT, BUT WITH PRUDENCE.]

Be not evil, it is good to be kindly. Cause thy monument[3] to endure through the love of thee. – – – – Then men thank God *on thine account, men* praise thy goodness *and* pray for thine health.

Honour the great and prosper thy people – – – –; good is it to work for the future. *But keep thine eyes open*, one that is trusting will become one that is afflicted – – – –.

[ABOUT HIGH OFFICIALS.]

Make thy counsellors great,[4] that they may execute thy laws, for he that is rich in his house dealeth not partially, he is a possessor of substance that wanteth nought.

(But) the poor man speaketh not according to what is right for him, and he that saith " Would that I had," is not fair. He favoureth him that hath a payment for him. Great is a great one whose counsellors are great. Strong is a king that possesseth a court.[5] – – – – Speak thou the truth in thine house, that the nobles who hold sway in the land may fear thee. It goeth well with a lord that is upright of heart. It is the inside of an house that inspireth the outside with fear.[6]

---

[1] The comparison is derived from the processes of brewing; lightly baked barley loaves were kneaded in water, which then fermented and produced the beer. This task of kneading has already been done for you, for truth already worked up into shape is before you in the ancient writings.

[2] The knowledge of the forefathers, *i.e.* follow their teaching.

[3] The remembrance of thee.

[4] *I.e.* rich enough for it not to be necessary for them to suffer themselves to be bribed.

[5] That is to say, a dependable one.

[6] Your good example in the palace influences your officials all over the country.

[How the king himself should behave.]

Do right so long as thou abidest on the earth. Calm the weeper, oppress no widow, expel no man from the possessions of his father, and injure not the magistrates in respect of their posts.[1] Take heed lest thou punish wrongfully. Slaughter not, that doth not profit thee ; punish with beatings and with imprisonment (?). Therewith shall this land be well established (indeed). – – – – God knoweth the froward, God requiteth his sins in blood.[2] – – – – Slay not a man whose good qualities thou knowest, with whom thou didst once chant the writings.[3]

Read in the Sipu-book (?) : " . . . (who is with God ?) goeth boldly forward in inaccessible places. The soul cometh to the place that it knoweth ; it strayeth not from its paths of yesterday. No magic keepeth it away,[4] but it cometh to them that give it water." [5]

[Warning against the posthumous judgment.]

The judges who judge the oppressed, thou knowest that they are not lenient on that day of judging the miserable,[6] in the hour of carrying out the decision.[7] Ill fareth it when the accuser is the Wise One ![8]—Put not thy trust in length of years ; they regard a lifetime as an hour.[9] A man remaineth

[1] Do not deprive them of their positions except for most cogent reasons; it is an Egyptian king's duty to secure to the sons the positions held by their fathers.

[2] Thus you can leave vengeance to him ?

[3] *I.e.* with whom you learnt to read ? In Oriental schools this is done in a sing-song voice.

[4] Meaning probably : the soul of the slain can always haunt you, it finds its way back again to the road that it travelled yesterday. That the souls of the dead brought sickness and misery upon the living out of revenge was a widespread belief.

[5] Its relations ?

[6] Those who have been murdered by thee will accuse thee in the posthumous trial in the underworld.

[7] *I.e.* execution.

[8] Probably Thôth, the god of wisdom, who directs the posthumous trial.

[9] Think not that the judgment is still a long way off, and that by then all will have been forgotten. The judges of the dead keep all things in remembrance.

over after death and his deeds are placed beside him [1] in heaps. But it is for eternity that one is there,[2] and he is a fool that maketh light of (?) them.[3] But he that cometh unto them without wrong-doing, he shall continue yonder like a god, stepping boldly forward like the Lords of Eternity.[4]

[ON THE TREATMENT OF THE YOUNG.]

Raise up thy young troops, that the Residence may love thee, and get thee a large following. . . . Behold, thy commonalty is full of those newly grown up, of such as are twenty years old. The young generation is happy in following its heart. – – – Magnify thy great ones, advance thy . . ., and increase the young generation of thy followers, that it may be furnished with lists,[5] endowed with fields, and rewarded with cattle.

[BE JUST, ENERGETIC, AND PIOUS ?] [6]

Exalt not the son of one of high degree more than him that is of lowly birth, but take to thyself a man because of his actions. Practise every craft, – – – – protect thy boundary and command thy fortresses (?), that the troops may be of service to their master. Make . . . monuments for the god ; they cause the name of their builder to live again. A man should do that which profiteth his soul : in that he performeth the monthly service of priest,[7] putteth on white sandals, frequenteth the temple, uncovereth the mysteries, entereth the sanctuary, and eateth bread in the temple.[8]

[BE PIOUS.]

Cause the drink-table [9] to be replenished, and present many loaves. Increase the permanent offering,—that is profitable to

[1] In judgment, to be scrutinized.   [2] In the other world.
[3] The judges of the dead.   [4] Name of the blessed dead.
[5] Lists of the revenues belonging to them.
[6] In this section the beginning actually belongs to what precedes, and the end to what follows. This occurs elsewhere in this treatise and in other Egyptian compositions, and is certainly an intentional artifice. I could not always adhere to this arrangement.
[7] Or : the monthly bath ? A bath was demanded of him who entered a god's presence.
[8] *I.e.* shares in the offering. All this active participation in public worship is thus accounted as merit, that will one day be imputed to the departed soul.
[9] Upon which water and the like were offered in the temple.

him that doeth it.   Cause thy monuments to flourish, so long
as thou hast the strength : a single day giveth to eternity, and
an hour doeth good to futurity.   God knoweth him that worketh
for Him.[1]

The end : Conduct thy statues to a distant land – – – –,
*speaks also of the enemy and Egypt, and then probably leads on to
what follows.*

*The second part of the treatise, which begins here, refers to
various political affairs and to the father's deeds, and is for the
most part unintelligible to us, who are unacquainted with them.
This king's dominion, as we also know from other sources, did not
comprise the whole of Egypt, and there is a Southern Land as well.*

The young generation shall oppress the young generation,
as the forefathers have foretold concerning it.   Egypt fights in
the necropolis with violating of tombs [2] . . .   Even so did I,
and even so did it occur. – – – –

Be not on ill terms with the Southern Land, for thou knowest
what the Residence hath foretold concerning it, and that
happeneth even as this did happen.   *With regard to the city of
Thinis, which apparently formed the southern boundary of the
realm, it is then said :* I captured it like a cloud-burst.   King
Mer . . . rē did not do it.   *But now be* lenient *concerning it,
for :* it is good to work for the future.

Stand well with the Southern Land.   Then the bearers of
bags come to thee with gifts.   I did the same as the forefathers :
" Though it hath no corn that it may give it, yet let it be pleasing
to thee, seeing that they are but weak unto thee.   Satisfy
thee with thy bread and with thy beer." [3]   The red granite,
too, comes to thee without hindrance.[4]   Harm not the monument of another, but quarry thyself stone in Turah.[5]   Build

[1] God will some day reward you for all you have done during your
lifetime to promote His worship.

[2] To what extent this was carried on, tombs of all periods still show.
It was the worst injury that could be inflicted on enemies.   For the
passage *cf.* below, p. 82, note 3.

[3] Meaning probably : Forego the corn, which they should give as
tribute, rather than rouse them again to fight.

[4] The granite quarries of Hamamat and of Elephantine lay within the
Southern Land.   He who had no hold over them was driven to plundering
older buildings for his own requirements.   Hence the following reflection.

[5] The quarries south-east of Cairo, from which the fine white limestone was obtained.

not thy tomb out of what hath been pulled down – – – –.
Behold, thou king, thou lord of joy, . . . thou sleepest in thy
might.[1] Follow thine heart in that which I have done, and
so thou hast no foe within thy borders.

*What follows is concerned with conditions in the Delta, the
western side of which was perpetually harassed by the Libyans.
The only intelligible portion runs :*
There rose up one, a ruler in the city,[2] and his heart was
oppressed by reason of the Delta, – – – –. I pacified the entire
West as far as the margins (?) of the lake.[3] *Also on the east
side of the Delta matters were in evil case, it is* made into districts
and cities, and the authority of one is in the hand of ten. *But
now (?) they give a whole* list of all manner of taxes, the priest
is invested with fields, and tribute is paid thee as if they were
a single gang.   It will not come to pass that there are evil foes
thereamong.   Thou sufferest not from the Nile, that it cometh
not, and thou hast the products of the Delta.[4]

*The eastern boundary of the kingdom is now secured against
the Asiatic Bedouins :* Behold, I drave in the mooring-post,[5] . . .
in the East.   The boundary from (?) Hebenu unto the Path-of-
Horus [6] is settled with cities and filled with people of the
best of the entire land, in order to repel the arms (of the
Asiatics).

I would fain see a brave man,[7] that equalleth (me) therein,
and that doeth more than I have done. – – – –

This is said, moreover, with regard (?) to the barbarian :
The wretched Asiatic, evil is the land wherein he is, with bad
water, inaccessible by reason of the many trees, and the roads
thereof are evil by reason of the mountains.[8] Never dwelleth
he in a single place and his feet wander (?).   Since the time

[1] Unconcerned. To what the whole of this passage refers eludes us,
as the beginning of the treatise is missing.
[2] Probably the old king himself, who might have come into power
as defender of the country against the Libyans.
[3] The lagoons on the coast of the Delta ?
[4] The inundation chances to be a good one and consequently the
tax returns are large.
[5] Elsewhere an expression meaning " to land."
[6] Hebenu lies in Middle Egypt. For the Path-of-Horus, see p. 26,
note 2.
[7] He trusts in his son, who will maintain these establishments.
[8] This wooded and mountainous country with nomadic inhabitants
must be Palestine.

of Horus [1] he fighteth and conquereth not, but likewise is he not conquered, and he never announceth the day in fighting, like the . . . supporter of a confederacy.[2]

Further on, mention is made of foreigners : I caused the Delta to smite them, I made captive their people, I plundered their cattle, − − − − trouble not thyself concerning him, the Asiatic − − − − ; he plundereth a lonely settlement (?), but he captureth not a populous (?) city.

Of the cities which he has peopled, he makes special mention of Kemui, *the later Athribis* : Behold, that is the navel of the barbarians.[3]   Its walls are made ready for battle (?), its soldiers are many, subjects are in it, who know how to take the . . . *And such too is the case with the district of Ded-esut, which was probably situated near Memphis :* it counts ten thousand men as citizens, who are clean [4] and without imposts.   The great men thereof go since the time (of Horus ?) to the Residence. Established are its boundaries . . .   There are many northerners who water it − − − −, they have made a dyke as far as Herak-leopolis − − − −.

If thy boundary towards the Southern Land is in revolt, *the foreigners (of the North ?) will also begin fighting (?).*   Build (therefore) towns in the Delta.   A man's name will not be small through what he hath done, and an inhabited city is not harmed. Build towns. . . .   The enemy is glad to see that one is afflicted (?), out of evil nature (?).   King Akhthoes [5] laid it down in his instruction :   " Whoso is quiet toward one that is insolent, he injureth − − − −.   God attacketh him that is hostile towards the temple."

From this point onwards the treatise reverts to more general topics.   Of the first all that is intelligible is : − − − − reverence God, and say not :   " He hath a *weak mind* (?)."   *Let* not *thine arms* be limp.   *Further, with regard to the monuments which another king has erected :* He will not injure them, through desire

---

[1] Horus was the last of the gods to rule the world.
[2] A robber-chief.   [3] What does this mean ?
[4] Does this mean free from taxes as colonists ?
[5] Akhthoes is the founder of the royal line of Herakleopolis, to which also the kings of our treatise belonged.   Greek tradition related of him that " he was more terrible than any before him, and that he did evil to all in Egypt."   According to this passage he also composed a book of wise sayings.

6

that what he himself hath done may be maintained by another that cometh after him.   There is none that hath no enemy.

[The king ought to know everything ?]

Full of knowledge is he, the (ruler ?) of the Two River-banks, and no king is foolish while he hath courtiers.[1]   He is wise already, when he cometh forth from the womb – – – –.

[Piety towards one's predecessors.]

The kingship is a goodly calling.   Although it hath no son and no brother, who may cause the remembrance thereof to endure, yet one restoreth (the monument) of the other.   Each one doeth it for one that went before, because he desireth that what he himself hath done may be maintained by another that cometh after him.[2]

Behold, a calamity happened in my time : the regions of Thinis were violated.   It happened in sooth through that which I did, and I (only) knew it after it was done.[3]   *That was evil* – – – –.   Take heed concerning it.   A blow is rewarded with the like thereof [4] – – – –.

[God and mankind.]

A generation passeth among men, and God, who discerneth characters, hath hidden himself. – – – –

Reverence thou God upon his road,[5] even him that is fashioned of precious stones and formed of copper, even as water that is replaced by water.[6]   There is no river that suffereth itself to be concealed ; it destroyeth the dam (?) with which it was hidden.[7]

[1] He probably means to say that the knowledge of those about him is at the king's disposal.

[2] A private person without successors is soon forgotten, but kings fare better, for in their case it is the duty of successors not to allow the memory of their predecessors to perish.

[3] His soldiers destroyed the monuments of the sacred city, without his having a hand in it.   This is the " violating of tombs " which he mentions above on p. 79.

[4] The meaning being that God punishes such impiety ?   " God " is also referred to above, after the first mention of these acts of destruction.

[5] In a procession ?

[6] Meaning possibly that since God keeps Himself hidden, His image must be reverenced.   It is, of course, only a substitute, but a sufficient one.

[7] So also God is only seemingly hidden.

The soul goeth to the place which it knoweth, and strayeth not from its paths of yesterday. (Wherefore) make fair thine house of the West, and stately thy place in the necropolis, even as one that is just, as one that hath done right. That it is, whereon their heart reposeth.[1]

More acceptable (to God) is the virtue of one that is just of heart than the ox of him that doeth iniquity. Do something [2] for God, that He may do the like for thee with an offering that replenisheth the offering-table, and with an inscription, one that perpetuateth (?) thy name. God is cognizant of him that doeth something for Him.

Well tended are men, the cattle of God. He made heaven and earth according to their desire. He allayed the thirst (?) for water. He made the air that their nostrils may live. They are His images, that have proceeded from His limbs. He ariseth in heaven according to their desire. He made for them plants and cattle, fowls and fishes, in order to nourish them. *But He also punisheth :* He slew His enemies, and punished His children, because of that which they devised when they were hostile.[3]

He maketh the light according to their desire ; *but He also suffereth them to sleep* – – – – *and* when they weep, He heareth.

He made for them rulers from the womb,[4] a supporter to support the back of the weak.

He made for them magic as weapons, to ward off events (?), and dreams in the night as in the day.[5]

He hath slain the froward of heart among them, even as a man smiteth his son and his brother. God knoweth every name.[6]

At the end comes a general exhortation, of which but little is intelligible :

Mayest thou reach me without having an accuser.[7] Slay

---

[1] Souls require a good tomb, in which they may find food and lodging, when they come on earth to enjoy the light.

[2] *I.e.* make offering, then God will have a well-tended tomb allotted to thee.

[3] Allusion to the legend of the revolt of mankind against the ageing sun-god (see pp. 47 ff.).

[4] *I.e.* legitimate kings.

[5] Are dreams meant which foretell the future ?

[6] He knows every one, and therefore also knows whom He has to punish.

[7] In the other world ?

not one that standeth nigh unto thee,[1] after thou hast praised him, and God knoweth him – – – –. Cause thyself to be beloved by all the world – – – –. Behold, I have spoken unto thee the best of mine inmost thoughts ; thou wilt act according to what hath been established before thee (?).

6. THE INSTRUCTION OF SEHETEPIBRĒ

This poem to King Amenemhēt III (1844–1797 B.C.) is included in this section, because its author claims to have composed it for the instruction of his children. He was a high official in the treasury, and must also have been brought into personal contact with the king, for he speaks of himself as " one whom his lord exalted in front of millions, a real confidant of his lord, to whom hidden things were spoken." He, moreover, proclaims this close connection with his lord by placing—against all precedent—the following verses on his tomb-stone,[2] which he scholastically designates his " Instruction."

Instruction which he composed for his children.

I tell of a great matter and cause you to hear (it). I impart to you a thought for eternity, and a maxim for right living (?) [3] and for the spending of a lifetime in bliss.

Revere King Nemaatrē, who ever liveth, in your bodies, and consort with his majesty in your hearts.

He is Understanding, which is in the hearts, and his eyes search out every body. He is Rē, by whose rays men see.

He illumineth the Two Lands more than the sun. He maketh the Two Lands more verdant than doth a high Nile. He hath filled the Two Lands with strength and life.

The nostrils become cool when he inclineth to terror.[4] When he is gracious, then (?) men breathe the air.

He giveth vital force to them that serve him, he supplieth food to them that tread his path. The king is Vital Force and his mouth [5] Abundance.

[1] *I.e.* probably : Do not make away with your kinsmen on coming to the throne—as so often is done in the East.

[2] Cairo 20538. The quite obvious stanzas should be noted.

[3] A special device has been employed here by the poet. Not only do the three words " for right living " form a pun on the immediately following name of his king, but he has contrived so to arrange the signs that they look like this name.

[4] Meaning ?

[5] Which utters his commands. The passage merely states that the king sees that his faithful subjects are provided for.

He it is that nurtureth him that will be.   He is Khnum for all bodies, the Begetter that begetteth the people.[1]

He is Bastet,[2] that protecteth the Two Lands ; he that revereth him shall escape his arm.   (But) he is Sekhmet [2] against him that transgresseth his command ; he that . . . to him will have . . .

Fight for his name and defend (?) his life, that ye may be free from affliction (?).[3]

He that is a friend of the king,—he will be an honoured one.[4]   But there is no tomb for him that is a foe of his majesty, and his corpse is thrown into the water.

Do this, that your bodies may be sound, yea, it is profitable for you for ever.

C. MEDITATIONS AND COMPLAINTS

The first treatises in this section are perhaps the most interesting to be found in the whole of Egyptian literature.   They deplore the misery which the world brings upon the individual, and depict the frightful distress of a nation that has suffered from a complete collapse : it is best for mankind not to be born.   Such a mood can come upon a nation only as the result of dire misfortune, and we shall not be mistaken, therefore, in regarding the end of the Old Kingdom and the period before the Twelfth Dynasty as times of great catastrophes, times at the thought of which a generation, that had survived them, still shuddered.

Quite different in tone to these writings are the *Complaints of the Peasant*.   Here again the subject, it is true, is the wickedness of those who oppress the poor, but over the bad officials stands a good minister and a good king.   Moreover, the author is not quite in earnest about all this ; his interest lies in the ever new and eloquent words in which his hero contrives to frame his complaints.   The book is an exercise in rhetoric and a school product.

[1] As Khnum creates children, so he creates dignitaries.
[2] The kindly cat-headed, and the terrible lion-headed, goddess respectively.
[3] Possibly "disloyalty" [Translator].
[4] A dead person who has been properly buried.

1. THE DISPUTE WITH HIS SOUL OF ONE WHO IS TIRED OF LIFE [1]

This strange work is based upon the conception that the soul is an independent being apart from the man ; it can leave him at death, but it can also stand by him faithfully.

In the lost beginning of the book it must have been related how a man was impoverished, deserted, and calumniated, and how in his distress he wished to bring his life to an end, and that by burning. His soul itself had urged him to take that step, but it declined to remain by him when death was actually at hand ; for, in the case of so poor a person it feared that it would fare badly. No tomb would protect him, and no survivor would bring him victuals, and thus it was threatened with hunger, cold, and heat. So the unfortunate man endeavours to persuade his soul not to desert him in death. Where the treatise at present begins, both are arguing before certain judges, whose tongue is not biased ; the soul has turned to them, instead of answering its master.

Then opened I my mouth unto my soul, that I might answer what it had said : This is too much for me at present, that my soul speaketh not with me – – – –. My soul goeth forth ; it shall stand there for me – – – –. It fleeth on the day of misfortune.

Behold, my soul thwarteth me, and I hearken not unto it, and drag me to death ere I be come to it, [2] and cast me upon the fire in order to burn me – – – –. May it draw nigh to me on the day of misfortune and stand upon yon side, as a mourner doth [3] – – – –. My soul, it is foolish, to hold back (?) one that is sorrowful on account of life ; lead (?) me to death, ere I be come to it, and make the West [4] pleasant for me. Is that then something grievous ? – – – – Tread thou upon wrong-doing. [5] The unhappy one will endure : [6] Thoth will judge me, he that contenteth the gods ; Khons will defend me, he, the

[1] A Berlin papyrus of the Middle Kingdom, the purport of which was recognized by Maspero in 1874 ; edited by me in *Abh. der Berliner Akademie* in 1896.

[2] *I.e.* before the time appointed for me.

[3] The meaning probably is : since I have no survivor to trouble about me, let it at least remain beside my corpse. The same wish more exactly expressed below.

[4] The usual name of the abode of the dead and the necropolis.

[5] Give up thy purpose of wishing to forsake me.

[6] The following passage declares that he relies on the good and righteous gods, who will espouse his cause.

scribe of Right ; Rē will hearken unto my words, he that guideth (?) the sun's ship ; Isdes will maintain my cause – – – –. My distress is heavy upon me and he beareth it for me . . . The gods avert the secret of my body.[1]

This is what my soul said unto me in answer : Thou art not a man (of high degree) – – – – (and yet) thou carest for good things like one that possesseth treasures.[2]

I said : I go not away so long as that one [3] remaineth on the earth – – – – I will carry thee away. Thy lot (?) is to die, while thy name liveth on, and yonder [4] is the place where one alighteth – – – –. If my soul will hearken unto me – – – – and its heart agreeth (?) with me, it will be happy. I will cause it to reach the West, like the soul of one that is buried in his pyramid, and at whose burial there stood a survivor.

The expedient, whereby the luckless one proposes to attain this, is unfortunately unintelligible to us ; one can only see that he will do something which will safeguard his soul against the distresses feared. He assures it that it will despise another soul as a weary one, *and* it shall not freeze ; *it will despise* another soul that is too hot, *for he* will drink water at the place of drawing,[5] *and it will also look down on* another soul that hungereth. In this wise *it is to* lead him to death—*otherwise hast thou no possibility of* alighting in the West. Be so kind, my soul and my brother, and become mine heir (?),[6] who shall make offering and stand upon my tomb on the day of burial, that he may prepare (?) the funeral bed.

Then my soul opened its mouth to me, to answer what I had said : If thou callest burial [7] to mind, it is sadness, it is the

[1] My unspoken troubles ? The body is to the Egyptian the seat of thought.

[2] Meaning probably : the gods will not trouble themselves about a miserable person like you.

[3] The soul.   [4] The other world.

[5] *I.e.* " the part of the river where water is drawn," where it was the wish of all the dead to drink.

[6] *I.e.* the survivor, who recited the prescribed formulæ over the corpse and performed the rites necessary for the welfare of the dead. Since the luckless one has no one to render him this service, the soul is to take on the duty.

[7] To be able to appreciate all the malice of the following sentences, it must be borne in mind that to the genuine Egyptian of that day there

bringing of tears, it is making a man sorrowful, it is haling a man from his house and casting him upon the hill.[1] Never wilt thou go forth again to behold the sun.[2] They that builded in granite and fashioned a hall (?) in the pyramid, that achieved what is goodly in this goodly work—when the builders are become gods,[3] then their offering-tables are empty (and they are) even as the weary ones which die upon the dyke without a survivor ; the flood hath taken its end (of them) and likewise the heat of the sun, and the fish of the river-bank hold converse with them.[4]

Hearken thou unto me, lo, it is good for a man when he hearkeneth. Follow the glad day and forget care.[5]

Thus the advice of the soul now is that he had better give life a further trial, and then, probably in support of the theory that this is still to be endured by even the most unfortunate, he recounts to him two tales, of which we frankly understand but little :

A man of humble birth tilleth his field and loadeth his harvest on to a ship, that he may tow (it) . . ., when his festival approacheth. He seeth that the night of the flood (?) cometh on, keepeth watch in the ship until dusk, and goeth forth with his wife and his children ; they perish upon the lake, en-dangered (?) in the night amid the crocodiles. *Then he sitteth him down and when he* hath a share in the voice (*i.e. can speak again ?*), *he saith :* I am not weeping for that maid, who cannot come forth from the West to another woman upon earth [6] ; I am troubled for her children that are broken in the egg, that behold the face of the crocodile before they are yet alive.

We understand still less of the second tale [7] *of* the man of humble birth, *who begs his supper of his wife.*

---

was no higher duty than the care of the dead and of their tombs. This is represented here with bitter scorn as useless folly—arrant heresy, which, however, displays itself also in the *Song at a Banquet* (p. 133).

[1] The tombs are situated on the high ground at the desert edge.

[2] It is the constant prayer of the dead, that they might leave their tombs by day and behold the sun.

[3] *I.e.* directly the kings are dead.

[4] Meaning : they dragged themselves down to the water's edge and there they died ; they lie half on the land and half in the water, their corpses shrivel up and rot simultaneously, and the fishes nibble at them.

[5] That is the usual cry at banquets. [6] See GUNN, *Syntax*, p. 143.

[7] Perhaps it is only the conclusion of the first.

Then opened I my mouth to my soul, that I might answer what it had said : [1]

[FIRST POEM.]

Lo, my name is abhorred,
Lo, more than the odour of carrion [2]
On days in summer, when the sky is hot.

Lo, my name is abhorred,
Lo, more than catching fish
On the day of the catch, when the sky is hot.

Lo, my name is abhorred,
Lo, more than the odour of birds,
More than the hill of willows with the geese.

Lo, my name is abhorred,
Lo, more than the odour of fishermen,
More than the shores of the swamps, when they have fished.

Lo, my name is abhorred,
Lo, more than the odour of crocodiles,
More than sitting on . . ., where are the crocodiles.

Lo, my name is abhorred,
Lo, more than that of a wife
When lies are told against her to the husband.

Lo, my name is abhorred,
Lo, more than that of a stalwart child
Against whom it is said, he . . . to him that hateth him, [3]

Lo, my name is abhorred,
Lo, more than that of a . . . city,
(Than) that of a rebel, whose back is seen. [4]

---

[1] For the peculiar construction of this poem, *cf.* the remarks on pp. xxx. f.

[2] In Egyptian a name is said to " stink," meaning to " be execrated " ; the following verses express this by means of comparisons, which come readily to an Egyptian, especially those associated with fishing and fowling in the swamps.

[3] No doubt a stepchild is meant.   [4] Who has fled.

[SECOND POEM.]

To whom do I speak to-day?
Brothers are evil,
Friends of to-day, they are not lovable.

To whom do I speak to-day?
Men are covetous,
Every one seizeth his neighbour's goods.

To whom do I speak to-day?
Gentleness hath perished,
Insolence hath come to all men.[1]

To whom do I speak to-day?
He that hath a contented countenance is bad,
Good is disregarded in every place.

To whom do I speak to-day?
He that maketh wrathful a (good) man by his evil deeds,
The same moveth all men[2] to laughter, when his iniquity is
      grievous.

To whom do I speak to-day?
Men rob,
Every man seizeth his neighbour's (goods).

To whom do I speak to-day?
The sick man is the trusty friend,
The brother that is with him, hath become the enemy[3]

To whom do I speak to-day?
None remembereth the past,
None at this moment doeth good to him that hath done it.

To whom do I speak to-day?
Brothers are evil,
A man is treated as an enemy (?) in spite of (?) a right disposition.

[1] This verse occurs again in the *Admonitions*; see below, p. 99, note 1.
[2] The masses make mock of the righteous for becoming enraged against the evil-doer.
[3] The meaning may be: since his own relatives have deserted the poor man, he now has no friend save him who is in a worse plight.

To whom do I speak to-day?
Faces are invisible,
Every man hath his face downcast against his brethren.[1]

To whom do I speak to-day?
Hearts are covetous,
The man on whom men rely, hath no heart.

To whom do I speak to-day?
There are none that are righteous,
The earth is given over to the workers of iniquity.

To whom do I speak to-day?
A trusty friend is lacking,
A man is treated as one that is unknown, albeit (?) he have
  made (himself) known.[2]

To whom do I speak to-day?
There is none that is peaceable ;
That one who went (?) with him, he is not existent (?).

To whom do I speak to-day?
I am laden with misery,
And lack a trusty friend.

To whom do I speak to-day?
The sin that smiteth the land,
It hath no end.

[THIRD POEM.]

Death is before me to-day
As when a sick man becometh whole,
As when one walketh abroad after sickness.

Death is before me to-day
As the odour of myrrh,
As when one sitteth under the sail on a windy day.[3]

Death is before me to-day
As the odour of lotus flowers,
As when one sitteth on the shore of drunkenness.[4]

[1] No one now looks openly at the other.
[2] But see GUNN, *Rec. de Trav.*, xxxix. p. 105 [Translator].
[3] Meaning probably that one is released from rowing.
[4] The poet means a feast on the cool river-bank.

Death is before me to-day
As a well-trodden (?) path,
As when a man returneth from the war unto his house.

Death is before me to-day
As a clearing of the sky,
As a man . . . to that which he knew not.

Death is before me to-day
As when a man longeth to see his house again,
After he hath spent many years in captivity.

[FOURTH POEM.]

Why he that is yonder [1] will be
One that . . . as a living god,
And will inflict punishment for sin on him that doeth it.

Why he that is yonder will be
One that standeth in the sun's ship,
And will therein assign the choicest things unto the temples.

Why he that is yonder will be
A man of knowledge, and he is not hindered,[2]
And he petitioneth Rē when he speaketh.

This is what my soul said unto me : Cast aside (?) lamentation, my comrade, my brother – – – –. I will abide here, if thou rejectest the West. But when thou reachest the West, and thy body is united with the earth, then I will alight after that thou restest. Let us have an abode together.

2. THE ADMONITIONS OF A PROPHET [3]

We have only the one very inferior manuscript, in which both the beginning and end of the book are missing ; thus the narrative of events which called forth the prophet's utterances is lost to us.

---

[1] " He that is yonder " is a regular euphemism for the dead. The three concluding verses are in praise of the lot of the blessed dead, who, as the sun-god's companions, promote what is good.

[2] The man who is tired of life doubtless alludes here to his own fate.

[3] In a papyrus at Leyden, and brought to notice by H. O. Lange in 1903. See GARDINER, *The Admonitions of an Egyptian Sage*, Leipzig, 1909.

Various restorations have been proposed on the basis of indications in the text, and that here offered is also not to be regarded as certain in all respects.

Under a ruler of ancient times a terrible calamity overtakes the country ; the people rebel against the officials and those in high places ; the foreign mercenary troops are in revolt, and possibly also the Asiatics threaten the Eastern frontier. Thus ordered government breaks up completely in Egypt ; but the aged king lives on peacefully in his palace, for he is being regaled with lies. Then a sage, Ipuwer by name, appears on the scene at court [1] and tells the whole truth. He depicts the misery already prevailing, and foresees what is still to come ; he urges his hearers to fight against the enemies of the realm, and reminds them that the worship of the gods must be restored. And then he addresses the king himself, that he, too, " may taste of this misery."

The time in which this break-up of ordered government in Egypt is to be imagined as taking place, must be the end of the Old Kingdom. At the conclusion of the Sixth Dynasty (*circa* 2500 B.C.), Egypt is suddenly blotted out from our sight in obscurity, as if some great catastrophe had overwhelmed it ; furthermore, the few remains known to us from the centuries immediately following show that civilization, formerly at so high a level, has declined— exactly as one would expect from the descriptions in our book. And that the ruler, whom the sage addresses, is apparently an aged man, is also perfectly in agreement with facts, for the monarch, with whom the Old Kingdom disappears from our ken, is none other than the second Phiops, who came to the throne at the age of six, and who, according to Egyptian tradition, reigned for ninety-three years.[2]

The approximate date of the *Admonitions* can be determined from two passages therein, recurring also in other old poems. One, in the *Dispute with his Soul of One who is tired of Life*, is far more in place there than here ; with the other, the reverse is the case, for on external grounds it certainly belongs to our book, whereas, in the *Instruction of Amenemhēt*, it is interpolated in a corrupt form. The *Admonitions* is thus later than the *Dispute of One who is tired of Life*, and older than the *Instruction of Amenemhēt*.

The book consists of prose sections, and of six poems, these

---

[1] In view of the frequent references to storehouses and treasuries, it is natural to suppose that the sage was one of the treasury officials. Also from the third poem and its appendix it may be inferred that he came from the Delta to report on the lack of treasure ; possibly he had to do this himself, because his messengers refused to go. The catastrophe, however, is not confined only to the Delta, but extends, as is expressly stated on p. 95, to Upper Egypt.

[2] See, too, A. M. BLACKMAN, *Luxor and its Temples*, pp. 35 ff.

forming its actual kernel; for their formation see above, pp. xxx. and **xxxiii.** f.

Where the book now begins, the sage is already depicting the country's misfortune : The door-keepers say : " Let us go and plunder." The washerman refuseth to carry his load. The bird-catchers have made themselves ready for battle, *and others from the Delta* carry shields. *Even the most peaceful callings, such as the* confectioners *and the* brewers *are in revolt,* and a man looketh upon his son as an enemy. – – – – The virtuous man goeth in mourning because of what hath happened in the land – – – – strangers are become Egyptians [1] everywhere.

[FIRST POEM.]

It is concerned mainly with the general distress—robbery, murder, destruction, and famine. The officials are expelled, the administration destroyed, trade with abroad is at an end. Foreigners flourish in the country, and the rabble occupy the positions of the upper classes.

Every verse begins with two words, best rendered in English by " nay, but " or " forsooth," which represent the assertion as something that cannot be gainsaid.

Nay, but the face is pale – – – – ; the forefathers have foretold – – – –.[2]

Then after a lacuna of some length :

Nay, but – – – – (*and the land is*) full of confederates.   A man goeth to plough with his shield.

Nay, but the meek saith : – – – – (*destroyed*).

Nay, but the face is pale, the bowman is ready.   The wrong-doer is everywhere.   There is no man of yesterday.[3]

Nay, but plunderers are everywhere – – – –.

Nay, but Nile is in flood, yet none plougheth for him.   Every man saith : " We know not what hath happened throughout the land." [4]

---

[1] Literally " men," *i.e.* " real men " ; this designation of Egyptians is found elsewhere.   All that is meant is that the numerous foreigners who then, as now, will have lived in Egypt, venture, in the universal upheaval, to pose as Egyptians.

[2] It is apparently stated previously in a much damaged passage, that this had already been determined in the time of Horus, *i.e.* in primæval time.

[3] Who was highly esteemed yesterday.

[4] No one has enough confidence, in these times of uncertainty, to till the fields.

Nay, but women are barren, and there is no conception. Khnum fashioneth men no more because of the condition of the land.[1]

Nay, but poor men now possess fine things. He who once made for himself no sandals now possesseth riches.

Nay, but men's slaves, their hearts are sad.[2] *The great no longer take part in the rejoicings of their people (?).*

Nay, but the heart is violent. Plague stalketh through the land and blood is everywhere. – – – – The mummy-cloth speaketh (although) not drawn nigh unto.

Nay, but many dead men are buried in the river. The stream is a sepulchre, and the Pure Place [3] is become a stream.

Nay, but the high-born are full of lamentations, and the poor are full of joy. Every town saith : " Let us drive out the powerful from our midst."

Nay, but men look like gem-birds.[4] Squalor is throughout the land. There is none whose clothes are white in these times.

Nay, but the land turneth round as doth a potter's wheel. The robber possesseth riches. The . . . is (become ?) a plunderer.

(*A mutilated verse.*)

Nay, but the river is blood. Doth a man drink thereof, he rejecteth it as human, (for) one thirsteth for water.

Nay, but gates, columns, and walls are consumed with fire ; (and yet) the chamber (?) of the king's palace (still) endureth and standeth fast.

Nay, but the southern ship [5] is adrift (?). The towns are destroyed, and Upper Egypt is become an empty (waste ?).

Nay, but the crocodiles (are glutted with) what they have carried off. Men go to them of their own accord – – – –. People say : " Tread not here, *but they do tread there as though there were fish, so stupid is* the timid man through terror.

Nay, but men are few. He that layeth his brother in the ground is everywhere (to be seen) [6] – – – –.

[1] See above, p. 44, note 2. He gives up the now useless task.
[2] The slaves of the new rich ?
[3] The place of embalmment. The corpses are too numerous to be buried. They are thrown into the water like dead cattle.
[4] A kind of heron, which may have had a dirty appearance.
[5] Probably figuratively for Upper Egypt.
[6] Grave-diggers are to be seen everywhere.

Nay, but the son of the high-born man is no longer to be recognized (?). The child of his lady is become the son of his handmaid.[1]

Nay, but the Red Land [2] is spread abroad throughout the country. The homes are destroyed. The stranger people from without are come into Egypt.[3]

The next verse ends with, there are no men anywhere.[4]

Nay, but gold and lapis lazuli, silver and turquoise, carnelian and bronze, marble and . . ., are hung about the necks of slave-girls. But noble ladies (?) walk through the land, and mistresses of houses say : " Would that we had something we might eat." [5]

Nay, but – – – – ladies, their limbs are in sad plight because of their rags. Their hearts shudder (?) when (they ? are) greeted.[6]

Nay, but boxes of ebony are broken up. Precious sesnem-wood is cut in pieces for beds (?) – – – –.

Nay, but they that build . . . are become field-labourers, and they that were in the god's bark are yoked together.[7] Men do not sail to Byblos to-day.[8] What can we do to get cedars for our mummies ? Priests are buried with their produce, and princes are embalmed with their resin, as far as the land of Keftiu,[9] and now they come no more. Gold is diminished, the . . . *which is used for* all handicrafts is at an end – – – –. How great it seems to one (after all), when the people of the Oases come *bringing their products in the way of plants and birds.*[10]

[1] There is no longer any distinction between the child of the head-wife and that of the domestic slave-girl.

[2] Foreign countries in contrast to the " Black Land," *i.e.* Egypt. The expressions are taken from the yellow and black soils. The meaning is : everywhere one encounters foreigners.

[3] The expressions do not sound like a hostile invasion.

[4] See p. 94, note 1.   Only foreigners are to be seen.

[5] They are begging.

[6] No doubt meaning : they are ashamed to be recognized in their misery.

[7] Architects and commanders of the royal ships (that is what is meant by the god's ships) work as common labourers.

[8] The port for the Lebanon, whence were brought the cedar-wood and cedar-resin.

[9] Apparently Crete, which was under Egyptian influence at an early date.

[10] This trivial trading, now that all more extended commerce is at an end, is something quite gratifying.

Nay, but Elephantine and Thinis (?), and the . . . of Upper Egypt (?), they pay taxes no more by reason of the unrest. *There is a lack of fruits,* charcoal, and *all manner of joinery,* the products of the craftsmen – – – –.   To what purpose is a treasury without its revenues ?   But glad is the heart of the king when the truth cometh to him ! [1] – – – – .What can we do about it ?   All goeth to ruin !

Nay, but laughter hath perished and is no longer made. It is grief that walketh through the land, mingled with lamentations.

(*A damaged verse, treating of Egyptians and foreigners.*)

Nay, but the hair of all people is (*untended* ?).   The son of a man of rank is no more distinguished from him that hath no such (father).[2]

(*A damaged verse.*)

Nay, but great and small say : " I wish I were dead ! "   Little children say : " He ought never to have caused me to live."

Nay, but the children of princes, men dash them against walls. The children of the neck,[3] they are laid upon the high ground.[4]

Nay, but they that were in the Pure Place, they are cast forth upon the high ground.   The secret of the embalmers, *it lieth open.*[5]

Nay, but that hath perished which was still seen yesterday. The land is left over to its weariness, as when one hath pulled up the flax.[6]

Nay, but the entire Delta is no (longer) hidden.   The confidence of the North Land is (now) a trodden road.[7]   What is

---

[1] By this is probably meant the truth which the king is not told.

[2] The hair of children of high rank was probably dressed in a special way ; they wore perhaps the side-lock, which later on was ordinarily worn by princes only.

[3] Children in arms ?   Below, where the verse is repeated, this expression is replaced by " the children of the request," *i.e.* those which have been asked for in prayer.

[4] Want drives people to expose them.

[5] The mummies of persons of rank are torn from the tombs.

[6] In the flax-field no stubble is ever left.

[7] The natural protection of the Delta afforded by its swamps and lakes is no longer of any avail, the foreigners enter it in bands and practise its crafts themselves.   It is to be borne in mind that the Delta in the later periods of Antiquity and during the Middle Ages was the centre of industry and export.   Such may well have been the case also at this earlier date.

7

one to do ? – – – – Men say : " Cursed (?) be the inaccessible place ! Behold, it belongeth now (?) as much to them that know it not, as to them that know it, and strangers are versed in the crafts of the Delta.

Nay, but the citizens have been placed over the mill-stones. They that were clad in fine linen are beaten with . . . They that saw not the day are gone forth [1] . . . They that were on the beds of their husbands, let them sleep on the cushions [2] of the . . . – – – – Ladies are like slave-girls. The musicians in the chambers within the houses, their song to the goddess of music (?) is a dirge, and they that tell . . ., sit over the mill-stones.[3]

Nay, but all female slaves have power over their mouths.[4] When their mistresses speak, it is irksome to the servants.

Nay, but – – – –. People will say, when they hear it : " The . . . cakes for the children are diminished, and there is no food for . . ." How tasteth that to-day ?

Nay, but the magistrates are hungry and suffer need – – – –.

Nay, but the hot-headed man saith : " . . . If I knew where God is, then would I make offering to Him." [5]

(Two damaged verses : Truth hath become lies (?) in the land, and : The harvester (?) is robbed of all his possessions.)

Nay, but all cattle, their hearts weep. The herds lament because of the state of the land.

Nay, but the children of princes, men dash them against walls. The children that have been earnestly desired, they are laid upon the high ground. Khnum complaineth because of his weariness.[6]

(A quite unintelligible verse.)

Nay, but – – – – throughout the land, insolence hath come

[1] As in the following sentence, the writer probably means ladies of high rank, who ordinarily lived in the house ; they must now toil outside in the heat.

[2] In this and a later passage, by cushions are meant apparently some inferior kind of resting-place.

[3] The female singers (and story-tellers ?) are meant, who at other times entertained the ladies of the harim.

[4] Say what they like ; as we should say, " are free with their tongues."

[5] What is meant by this ?

[6] The trouble he takes in fashioning children seems to him to be wasted. The author has already employed the same verse similarly above.

to all men.[1] A man slayeth his brother by the same mother – – – –.

Nay, but the roads are . . . and the streets are watched.[2] Men sit in the bushes until the benighted (traveller) cometh, in order to take from him his load.   What is upon him is stolen. He getteth blows of the stick to smell and is slain wrongfully.

Nay, but that hath perished which was still seen yesterday. The land is left over to its weariness, as when one hath pulled up the flax.[3] – – – – Would that there might be an end of men, no conception, no birth ! Oh that the earth would cease from noise and strife be no more !

Nay, but men feed on herbs and drink water.   No fruit nor herbs are longer found for the birds, and *the offal* (?) is robbed from the mouth of the swine, *without it being said* (*as aforetime*) : " This is better for thee than for me," for men are so hungry.[4]

Nay, but corn hath perished everywhere. People are stripped of clothing, perfume, and oil. Every one saith : " There is no more."   The storehouse is bare, and he that kept it lieth stretched out on the ground. – – – – Would that I had lifted up my voice at that moment, that it might have saved me from the pain in which I am ! [5]

Nay, but the splendid judgment-hall, its writings are taken away ; the secret place is laid bare. . . .

Nay, but magic spells are divulged *and are now ineffectual* (?), for the people have them in mind.[6]

Nay, but the public offices are opened, and their lists are taken away.   Serfs become lords of serfs.[7]

Nay, but the (officials ?) are slain and their lists taken away. Woe is me because of the misery in such a time !

Nay, but the scribes of the sack, their writings are destroyed.

---

[1] This sentence is borrowed from the *Dispute with his Soul of One who is tired of Life* (see p. 90).

[2] *I.e.* by robbers ?   [3] The same verse already above.

[4] Men are now themselves eating that on which they used to feed the poultry and the pigs.

[5] Is the prophet reproaching himself here for not having come forward at the right moment ?

[6] Owing to their having become known, they are profaned.   It should be observed that magical spells are here reckoned as a valuable possession of the Government.

[7] Now the lists are gone, no one knows who was not free.

That whereon Egypt liveth is a " When I come, it's brought me." [1]

Nay, but the laws of the judgment-hall are placed in the vestibule. Yea, men walk upon them in the streets, and the poor tear them up in the alleys.

Nay, but the poor man hath attained to the condition (?) of the Nine Gods. That procedure of the House of the Thirty is divulged. [2]

Nay, but the great judgment-hall is a " go out, that he may come in." [3] The poor go and come in the Great Houses. [4]

Nay, but the children of the magistrates are thrown on to the streets. He that hath knowledge saith : " Yea." The fool saith : " Nay." He that hath no knowledge, to him seemeth it good. [5]

Nay, but they that were in the Pure Place, they are cast forth upon the high ground. The secret of the embalmers, it lieth open. [6]

[SECOND POEM.]

The disasters described in this poem far surpass those hitherto complained of. Even the kingship is now destroyed, and the masses are completely triumphant. It is pointed out over and over again how rich they have become, whereas the upper classes are sunk in misery.

As the first poem, with each verse introduced by " Nay, but," depicted well-known and accomplished facts ; the second, with its recurring introductory " Behold," vividly brings before us events that are just taking place or about to take place.

Behold, the fire will mount up on high. Its burning goeth forth against the enemies of the land.

Behold, a thing hath been done, that happened not afore-

---

[1] The corn-supply of the State, from which all were fed, is now at any one's mercy, for the documents regulating its distribution are lost.

[2] The thirty highest officials no longer make any impression upon the people, who have become like gods.

[3] *I.e.* is full to overflowing.

[4] The Six Great Houses are the ancient High Courts, into which the rabble now forces its way without any feeling of awe.

[5] A soliloquy of the prophet, a corrupt version of which is interpolated in the *Instruction of Amenemhēt* (see p. 74, note 8). Is the complacent, unsuspecting person the king ?

[6] This verse has already been employed above.

time ; it is come to this that the king hath been taken away by poor men.[1]

Behold, he that was buried as a hawk [2] lieth on a bier. What the pyramid hid [3] will become empty.

Behold, it is come to this, that the land is despoiled of the kingship by a few senseless people.

Behold, it is come to this, that men display enmity against the Uræus,[4] the (defender ?) of Rē, which caused the Two Lands to be in peace.

Behold, the secret of the land, whose limits were unknown,[5] is divulged. The Residence is overturned in an hour.

(*An unintelligible verse about Egypt.*)

Behold, the kerehet-snake [6] is taken from its hole. The secret of the kings of Upper and Lower Egypt is divulged.

Behold, the Residence is afraid through want. The . . . will stir up unrest, and there is no resistance.

Behold, the land . . . full of confederates. The strong man, the miserable one robbeth him of his goods.[7]

Behold, the kerehet-snake . . . the weary ones.[8] He that could make himself no sarcophagus now possesseth a tomb.[9]

Behold, the lords of the Pure Place [10] are thrown out upon the high ground. He that could not make himself a coffin is now in. . . .

Behold, this hath happened among (?) men : he that could not build himself a chamber now possesseth a walled enclosure.

Behold, the officers of the land are driven out through the land. – – – – are driven out from the houses of the kingdom.

Behold, ladies lie on cushions,[11] and magistrates in the store-house. He that could not sleep upon (?) walls now possesseth a bed.

[1] From what follows, the plundering of the royal sepulchre is meant.
[2] The king.
[3] The sarcophagus.
[4] The serpent-diadem of the king and of the sun-god.
[5] Secret affairs of which no one except the king had full knowledge.
[6] A snake which lives in consecrated places—in this case the palace—as the guardian-spirit.
[7] The hitherto powerful person is plundered by the rabble joined together in bands. The following verses develop this theme.
[8] The dead.
[9] Which he has stolen for himself.
[10] See p. 95, note 3 ; the dead are meant.
[11] See p. 98, note 2 ; the magistrates seek shelter in the storehouse.

Behold, the rich man sleepeth thirsty. He that once begged him for his dregs (?) now possesseth strong beer (?).[1]

Behold, they that possessed clothes are now in rags. He that wove not for himself now possesseth fine linen.

Behold, he that never built for himself a boat now possesseth ships. He that possessed the same looketh at them, but they are no longer his.

Behold, he that had no shade now hath shade. They that had shade are in the full blast of the storm.[2]

Behold, he that had no knowledge of harp-playing now possesseth an harp. He to whom never man sang, now praiseth the goddess of music.

Behold, they that possessed drink-tables of copper,—not one vessel is bedecked (?) [3] for one of them.

Behold, he that slept unwed through want now findeth ladies (?) – – – –.

Behold, he that had nothing now possesseth wealth. The great man [4] praiseth him.

Behold, the poor of the land have become rich ; he that possessed something is now one that hath nothing.

Behold, they that . . . now have a staff of servants. He that was a messenger now sendeth another.

Behold, he that had no bread now possesseth a barn ; (but) that wherewith his storehouse is provided is the property of another.

Behold, the bald head that used no oil now possesseth jars of pleasant myrrh.

Behold, she that had no box now possesseth a coffer. She that looked at her face in the water now possesseth a mirror.

(*A verse left incomplete.*)

Behold, a man is happy when he eateth his food : " Spend thy possessions in joy and without holding thee back ! It is good for a man to eat his food, which God assigneth to him whom he praiseth [5] ⁁ – – –."

---

[1] Literally " beer that bowls one over."

[2] They are shelterless, exposed to the sun and to the tempest.

[3] The verse is probably corrupt. Possibly there is here a reference to the custom of wreathing the wine-jars with garlands.

[4] Or, " the high official " ; he must pay court to the upstart.

[5] Apparently a quotation from some old book. But what is it doing here ?

Behold, he that knew nought of his god now maketh offering to him with the incense of another – – – –.

Behold, noble ladies, great ladies, who possessed goodly things, their children are given to the beds.[1]

Behold, *he that had* a lady to wife, her father protecteth him – – – –.

Behold, the children of officials are in rags – – – –. *Their cattle belong to* plunderers.

Behold, the butchers make onslaught upon [2] the cattle – – – –.

Behold, he that never slaughtered for himself now slaughtereth oxen – – – –.

Behold, the butchers make onslaught upon the geese, which are given to the gods instead of oxen.[3]

Behold, slave-girls . . . make offering . . ., ladies – – – –.

Behold, ladies run – – – –. Their (children ?) are laid low in fear of death.

Behold, the chiefs of the land run, without their having any employ, through want . . .

Behold, they that possessed beds now lie upon the ground. He that slept with dirt (?) upon him now stuffeth for himself a cushion.

Behold, ladies, they are becoming hungry ; but the butchers are sated with that which they have done.[4]

Behold, no office is any longer in its right place ; they are as a frightened herd without herdsmen.

Behold, the cattle rove about and there is none that careth for them. Each man fetcheth for himself therefrom and brandeth it with his name.

Behold, a man is slain beside his brother. *He leaveth him in the lurch* in order to rescue himself.

Behold, he that had no yoke of oxen now possesseth droves. He that could not procure himself oxen for ploughing now possesseth herds.

Behold, he that had no grain now possesseth barns. He that fetched for himself corn-doles now himself causeth them to be dispensed.

---

[1] Does this mean they are prostituted ?   [2] Slay them indiscriminately.

[3] The meaning probably is that the new rich give geese as offerings and prefer to eat the oxen themselves.

[4] They themselves eat the meat. (But see BLACKMAN, *Journ. of Egypt. Archæology*, xi. pp. 213 ff. [Translator]).

Behold, he that had no bondsmen now possesseth serfs. He that was a (notable ?) now himself executeth behests.

Behold, the mighty ones of the land, none reporteth to them the condition of the common people.   All goeth to ruin !

Behold, no craftsman worketh ; the enemy despoileth the land of its crafts.

(*A mutilated verse about the* harvest, *which he that gathereth* hath not tilled – – – –.)

[THIRD AND FOURTH POEM.]

Some missing and mutilated verses, each of which began with the word " Destroyed." *In the last but one can be made out :* The poor man awakeneth, when day dawneth upon him, and is without dread, *and* they are tents which they have made like the barbarians. *The last is as follows :*

Destroyed is the carrying out of that for which servants were sent on the behests of their lords ; they are without dread. Behold, they are five men.[1]   They say, they say : " Go ye upon the road which ye know, we have arrived (home ?).[2]

An isolated section follows :

The Delta weepeth, the storehouse of the king is for every one an " If I come, then it is brought unto me."   The entire palace is without its dues, and (yet) there belong to it barley and wheat, fowl and fish.   To it belong white cloth and fine linen, copper and oil.   To it belong mat and carpet, . . . and palanquin and all goodly dues – – – –.   If it is not yet proclaimed (?) in the palace, then – – – –.

In the fourth poem, of which only scraps are preserved, the six verses begin with the words : Destroy the enemies of the noble Residence ; *it thus doubtless contains the summons to resist them.   The Residence is here assigned such epithets as* with excellent officials, with many laws, and with many offices, *and in the first verse the words* the superintendent of the capital goeth forth without constables *are still legible.*

---

[1] There were labour-gangs of five persons, and perhaps that is what is meant here.   They no longer suffer themselves to be sent on errands, but expect the masters to go themselves.   Mention was made of a " messenger " in the preceding passage.

[2] For the meaning which can be assigned to this and the following passage, see above, p. 93, note 1.

[FIFTH POEM.]

Eight or more verses beginning with " Remember " ; *they deal with the worship of the gods, how this was formerly conducted, and how it is to be conducted in the future.*

All that can be said about the first verse is that it makes mention of some one in pain *and of* his god.

Remember – – – – how fumigation is made with incense, and water offered from an ewer in the early morning.

Remember how fat geese are brought, and geese and duck and the divine offering offered to the gods.

Remember how natron is chewed,[1] and white bread prepared on the day when the head is moistened.[2]

Remember how flagstaffs are erected,[3] and offering-slabs carved, how the priest purifieth the temples, and the house of God is whitened like milk, how the horizon [4] is perfumed, and the offering-bread perpetuated.

Remember how the regulations are observed, and the days of the month *adjusted.   Bad priests are to be removed* (?) – – – –.

Remember how oxen are slaughtered – – – –.

In the destroyed concluding verses we read among other things that geese are laid upon the fire, *of course as a sacrifice.*

A long section followed, in which the sage first addresses himself yet further to several persons ; of what is preserved the following is intelligible :   Behold, wherefore seeketh he – – – – ?   A timid man is not distinguished from one that is violent ;   he will bring coolness upon the heat.   It is said : he is the herdsman of all men.   No evil is in his heart.   His herd is diminished, and yet (?) he hath spent the day in order to tend them [5] – – – –. Ah, but had he perceived their nature in the first generation ; [6]

---

[1] The priest purified his mouth with natron-water.   [2] Meaning ?

[3] At the gateways of the temples.   The whole verse speaks of the restoration of ruined temples.

[4] The temple.

[5] This must primarily refer to the king, to whom the sage once more addresses himself ; he is a herdsman, from whom the herd has run away during the night.

[6] Probably an allusion to the legend which related how Rē, when he ruled over the world in primæval times, did not, in his clemency, so completely extirpate mankind as they deserved in view of their impieties (see pp. 47 ff. and the allusion on p. 83, note 3).   It might also bear the

then would he have smitten down evil ; he would have stretched forth the arm against it, and destroyed the seed thereof and their inheritance. *Then the sage laments, perhaps, over the fact that men always* desire to give birth, *and* seed issueth from the women, *while* oppression *is* on every side. *There is no* pilot in their time. Where is he to-day ? Doth he sleep then ? Behold, his might is not seen.[1] *When* we were thrown into (?) mourning I found thee not ; I was not called – – –. *After a series of long lacunæ the text again becomes intelligible :*

Command, Perception, and Truth are with thee,[2] but it is confusion that thou puttest throughout the land, together with the noise of them that contend. Behold, one thrusteth at the other – – – –. If three men journey upon a road, they are found to be two men ; it is the greater number that slayeth the lesser. Is there an herdsman that loveth death ?[3]

But thou wilt command that a reply be made – – – –. Lies are told thee ; the land is brushwood,[4] mankind is destroyed – – – – all these years are confusion. A man is slain (even) upon his roof, when he is on the watch in his boundary-house.[5] If he be strong and saveth himself, then remaineth he alive. *The text then goes on to speak of some one* that walketh upon the road. What is upon him is stolen. He getteth blows of the stick to smell and is slain wrongfully.[6]

Would that thou mightest taste some of these miseries (thyself) ! Then thou wouldest say – – – –.

[SIXTH POEM.]

A description of the happy time that the future has in store.
It is good, however, when ships sail upstream – – – –.
(*A verse destroyed.*)
It is good, however, when the net is drawn in and the birds are made fast[7] . . .

meaning : Would that Rē had realized at the time that men were incorrigible, and extirpated them.

[1] The sleeping pilot is certainly the king.

[2] You possess the qualities necessary to a king, but make no use of them.

[3] Among his herd.

[4] Literally : " It is kaka " ; kaka is elsewhere a plant that easily catches fire.

[5] What is intended by this ?

[6] This verse occurs above in the first poem (p. 99).

[7] The catching of birds with the clap-net is meant.

(A verse dealing probably with roads.)

It is good, however, when the hands of men build pyramids and dig ponds, and make for the gods plantations with trees.

It is good, however, when the folk are drunken, and when they drink . . .[1] glad of heart.

It is good, however, when rejoicing is in (men's) mouths, and the magnates of districts stand and look on at the jubilation in their houses (?), clad in fine raiment – – – –.

It is good, however, when beds are stuffed and the head-rests [2] of the great are protected (?) with amulets, and every man's wish is satisfied with a bed in the shade, behind a closed door, *(and he need not ?)* sleep in the bushes.

It is good, however, when fine linen is spread out on the day of – – – –.

After a series of lacunæ we meet with a section that must have contained a reply of the king, to which the sage makes further answer. In what is preserved of this section mention is apparently made of the " recruits," the young manhood, having revolted and of having, like foreigners, attacked Egypt. The peoples of the South, however, wish to succour Egypt, which is brother and sister to them :

– – – – .None are found to stand and protect it – – – –. If any man fight for his sister, he protecteth himself.[3]

The negroes say : " We will be your protection. Let fighting be multiplied to repel the People of the Bow. Do they consist of Temehu, then we do it again."

The Matoï, who are friendly towards Egypt, (say ?) : " How could there be a man that would slay his brother ? "

The recruits whom we enrolled (?) for us, are become a People of the Bow, that would fain destroy that from which it took its being, and showeth the Bedouins the condition of the land, But all foreign countries are afraid of them. – – – –

Then after long lacunæ : Said the recruits – – – –. *All the rest is destroyed.*

This is what Ipuwer said when he answered the majesty of the Lord of All : – – – – to be ignorant of it [4] is something

[1] Some special kind of drink.

[2] The wooden rest on which the head was laid during sleep. People liked to have them ornamented with figures of demons, who were supposed to protect sleepers.

[3] Is this Egypt's call for help to the Southern peoples ?

[4] Meaning possibly the future ?

that is pleasant in the heart. Thou hast done what is good in their hearts, thou hast kept alive the people among (?) them,[1] but (?) they (still) cover their faces for fear of the morrow.

There was once a man that was old and stood in the presence of death, and his son was still a child and without understanding − − − − and opened not yet his mouth to speak unto you. Ye took him away through a deathly doom − − − −.[2]

Isolated words still surviving show that the subject under discussion was still the plight of the land, weeping, the forcing a way into the tomb-chapels, *and the* burning of statues.

3. THE COMPLAINT OF KHEKHEPERRE-SONBU [3]

As is evident from his name, Khekheperre-sonbu (" Khekheperrē is in health "), the author lived under King Sesōstris II, *i.e.* about 1900 B.C. As the text is written on the writing-board of a school-boy of the Eighteenth Dynasty, it was evidently regarded at that time also as a classical work.

The introduction alone is preserved, and in it the author expresses a desire to discover new and unheard-of utterances, with which to adorn his complaint. The book is in the form of the colloquy of a man with his own heart as his only true friend. It is thus reminiscent of the *Dispute with his Soul of One who is tired of Life* (above, pp. 86 ff.), in whose case also his soul is the only companion left to him. We know nothing, apart from this work, about the calamity which the writer deplores, though, to be sure, in view of our inadequate knowledge of Egyptian history, we cannot exactly be surprised at this.

That the book is later than the other writings of this description, is distinctly to be concluded from the fact that the man's complaint is somewhat vague and generalizing. It might almost be supposed that to lament over the misery of the world had already become a literary convention. With this would agree the author's wish to surpass his predecessors in his phraseology.

[TITLE.]

The collection of words and gathering [4] of sayings, the quest of utterances with meditation of the heart, composed by the

---

[1] *I.e.* the Egyptians ? See p. 94, note 1.

[2] What does this story mean ? Does he tell it by way of illustration, or is it the prelude to the whole disaster ? (*cf.* above p. 93).

[3] On a writing-board of the Eighteenth Dynasty in London. See GARDINER, *The Admonitions of an Egyptian Sage,* pp. 95 ff.

[4] He thinks of himself as plucking flowers.

priest of Heliopolis, the . . ., Khekheperre-sonbu, also named Ankhu.

He saith : Would that I had words that are unknown, utterances and sayings in new language, that hath not yet passed away, and without that which hath been said repeatedly—not an utterance that hath grown stale, what the ancestors have already said.

I wring out my body [1] because of that which is therein, as one that separateth himself from (?) every one that hath spoken (aforetime), seeing that – – – –. *And now the author indulges in tricks of construction with the words " say " and " speak," of which only parts are intelligible :* What is said is said ; *a man cannot pride himself upon* the speech of men of former times ; *in this instance* there speaketh not one that hath spoken, there speaketh one that will speak. *He that doeth otherwise,* that is lies, and there is none that will make mention of his name to others. [2]

This have I said in view of that which (?) I have seen : from the first generation unto that which cometh after—they are like that which is past. [3]

Would that I knew that which others knew not yet, somewhat of that which is not (only) repetition, in order that I might say it, and that my heart might make answer to me, in order that I might make clear (?) to it (*i.e.* to the heart) my suffering, and thrust aside to it the load that is upon my back. – – – –

I am meditating upon what hath happened, on the things that have come to pass throughout the land. Changes take place ; it is not like last year, and one year is more burdensome than the other. The land is in confusion, become waste (?) – – – –. Right is cast out, and iniquity (sitteth) in the council-chamber. The plans of the gods are destroyed and their ordinances transgressed. The land is in misery, mourning is in every place, towns and villages lament. All people alike are transgressors, the back is turned upon respect – – – –.

He would fain complain of this misery, for it is painful to hide it in the body. *He cannot complain of it to another, for* another heart *would be* bowed down *therewith. Still, an* heart that is valiant in evil case, this is a comrade to its lord. Would

---

[1] The body is accounted the seat of the thoughts.

[2] See GUNN, p. 162, note 1.

[3] No one is original ; the " first generation " is of course merely a manner of speech.

that I had an heart that knoweth how to endure ! Then would I rest upon it, that I might load it with words of misery, that I might drive to it my pain.

He saith to his heart : Come, my heart, that I may speak to thee, that thou mayest answer for me my words, that thou mayest expound to me the things that are throughout the land, that are bright and lie outstretched.[1]

I meditate upon what hath happened. Affliction is come to-day – – – – and all men are silent concerning it. The whole land is in a great condition.[2] There is none free from transgression, and all men alike are doing it. Hearts are sorrowful. – – – – Every day men rise up early thereto : yesterday in that respect is like to-day. – – – –.

There is none so understanding, that he comprehendeth ; none so indignant, that he speaketh out. Men rise up early every day to suffering.

Long and heavy is my suffering ; the wretched hath no strength to (protect himself) from him that is stronger than he.

It is pain to keep silent with respect to what is heard, and it is misery to answer one that is ignorant [3] – – – –. The heart accepteth not the truth – – – –. I speak to thee, mine heart, to the intent that thou mayest answer me ; an heart that is approached doth not keep silence. Behold, the affairs of the servant [4] are like those of the master, and manifold is that which weigheth upon thee.

4. THE PROPHECY OF NEFERROHU [5]

This work is known to us from a papyrus of the time of Thutmōsis III, and from two writing-boards [6] and three ostraca of the New Kingdom. It belongs, therefore, to the literature cherished

---

[1] What is in view of all, yet is comprehended of none.

[2] " Condition " for " bad condition."

[3] The meaning of the passage probably is : It is not right, my heart, that you answer me nothing, and wherefore should I speak to you, if you wish to know nothing about it ?

[4] The servant is the heart, which also suffers, if the man, its master, suffers.

[5] Discovered and published by Golénischeff ; translated by GARDINER, *Journ. of Egypt. Archæology*, i. pp. 100 ff.

[6] One (*Brit. Mus.*, No. 5647) contains, to be sure, only a few words, for the schoolboy has wiped the surface almost clean.

in the later schools. The approximate date of its composition is revealed by its ending : the sage, who describes to the old king Snefru [1] the distress of the south-eastern Delta, foresees that a defender will rise up for it in the person of King Amenemhēt I (1995–1965 B.C.).[2] To the poet this king is not a far-away figure, one out of the long series of Pharaohs, but stands close to him ; for he mentions him familiarly by his nickname, as though he were his contemporary. One might, therefore, suppose that these prophecies were written under this king himself, whom they set out to glorify, or at least under one of his immediate successors. The horrors also, which the sage foresees at the time of Snefru, and which Amenemhēt is to bring to an end, must correspond with events of the poet's own period.

The book begins with a scene, which is employed as an intro-duction in all periods of Egyptian history, even in official inscrip-tions : the king sits with his court and deliberates upon a matter, or has some story told him.[3] That, as a result of his inquisitive searchings into the future, he also succeeds in hearing something that he had rather not know, is to be found elsewhere.[4]

Now it came to pass when the majesty of King Snefru, the blessed, was beneficent king in this whole land—on one of these days it came to pass that the officers of the Residence entered into the palace to offer greeting [5] to the king, and they came forth again that they might offer (further) greeting, as was their daily observance. Then said his majesty to the chancellor who was at his side : " Go and bring to me the officers of the Resid-ence who have gone forth hence to-day in order to offer greeting." They were led in unto him forthwith and lay on their bellies in the presence of his majesty a second time.

And his majesty said unto them : " My friends, I have caused you to be summoned, in order that ye may seek out for me a son of yours that hath understanding, or a brother of yours that excelleth, or a friend of yours that hath performed some noble act, one that will speak to me some beauteous words, choice speeches, in hearing which my majesty may find diver-sion." Then they laid themselves on their bellies in the presence of his majesty yet again.

They said before his majesty : " There is a great kherheb

---

[1] See above, p. 38, note 1. [2] See above, pp. 15 ff. and 72 ff.
[3] *Cf. e.g.*, pp. 64 ff., and 50 ff. [4] Above, p. 43.
[5] By " offer greeting " are meant the daily reports of the high officials, rendered firstly to the king, then to the vizier and other departmental chiefs.

of Bast,[1] O king our lord, named Neferrohu ; he is a commoner with valiant arm, and a scribe with cunning fingers ; he is a lordly person, who is richer than any of his equals. Oh that he might see thy majesty ! "

Said his majesty : " Go and bring him to me." And he was led in unto him forthwith,[2] and he laid himself on his belly in the presence of his majesty. Said his majesty : " Come now, Neferrohu, my friend, and speak to me some beauteous words, choice speeches, in hearing which my majesty may find diversion." And the kherheb Neferrohu said : " Shall it be of that which hath happened, or of that which will happen, O king my lord ? " Said his majesty : " Nay, of that which will happen. If ought hath happened to-day, pass it by (?)." [3]

Then he stretched out his hand to the box of writing materials, and took him a scroll and pen-and-ink case, and then he put it in writing.

What was spoken by the kherheb Neferrohu, the wise man of the East, that belongeth to Bast . . ., the child of the Heliopolitan nome,[4] while he brooded over what will come to pass in the land, and thought of the condition of the East, when the Asiatics come in their might (?), when they afflict the hearts of the harvesters, and take away their span when ploughing.

He said : " Up (?), mine heart, that thou mayest bewail this land whence thou art sprung [5] – – – –.

Rest not ! Behold, it lieth before thy face. Rise up against that which is in thy presence. – – – – That which was made is as if it were never made, and Rē might begin to found (anew).[6] The whole land hath perished, there is nought left, and the black of the nail surviveth not of what should be there !

This land is ruined ; none concerneth himself about it any more, none speaketh, and no eye weepeth.[7]

[1] *Cf.* above, p. 36, note 3. Bast is the jovial cat-headed goddess of Bubastis in the Delta.

[2] This is a regular formula in narratives of this sort and is not to be taken literally here, for Bubastis is at least ninety kilometres distant from the residence of Snefru.

[3] The meaning probably is : let the past alone.

[4] He was born in Heliopolis and has settled in Bubastis.

[5] Here, as throughout the book, what is said refers strictly to the district in which Neferrohu was born, and not, as in similar writings, to Egypt as a whole.

[6] He can begin creation over again.   [7] That is no longer worth while.

How fareth this land ?   The sun is veiled and will not shine that men may see.   None will live when the storm veileth (it) ; all men are dulled (?) through the want of it.[1]

I will speak of what is before me, and foretell nought that is not also come.

The river of Egypt is empty, men cross over the water on foot.   Men shall search for water upon which the ships may sail ; its road is become a bank and the bank is become water – – – –.[2]   The south wind will drive away the north wind,[3] and the sky hath still only the one wind.   *The birds no longer hatch their eggs* in the swamps of the Delta, *but the bird* hath *made* her a nest *nigh unto men and letteth them approach her in her necessity.*[4]   Moreover, those good things are ruined, the fish-ponds (?), where were the slittings,[5] which shone with fish and wild fowl.   All good things are passed away, and the land is laid low through misery, by reason of yon food of the Bedouins who traverse the land.[6]

Foes are in the East, Asiatics are come down into Egypt ; – – – – no helper heareth.   By night one *will suddenly be fallen upon* (?) ; men shall force their way into houses (?) ; sleep shall be banished (?) from mine eyes, and I lie there and say : " I am awake." [7]

The wild beasts of the desert [8] shall drink from the rivers of Egypt, in order that they may cool themselves upon their banks, for that there is none *to scare them away* (?).

This land is taken away and added to,[9] and none knoweth what the issue will be ; *that is* hidden *and one cannot* say, see, or hear *it* . . .

I show thee the land in lamentation and distress ; that which never happened (before) hath happened.   Men shall take

---

[1] By this obscuring of the sun, of which he also speaks below, p. 114, not a single eclipse will be intended, but dust- and sand-storms, suiting, as they do, the following descriptions of the drought.

[2] By the road is meant the course of the river ; but what does the rest signify ?

[3] Which brings coolness and humidity.

[4] The birds migrate from the dried-up swamps to inhabited regions, where water still exists.

[5] The slitting open and preparing of fish.

[6] The new misfortune, to which he now directs his attentions.   It is a food which the country has to taste to the full.

[7] He uneasily waits for the attack.

[8] The Bedouins ?   [9] An expression for disorder.

8

up weapons of war, that the land may live on uproar.[1] Men shall fashion arrows of copper, that they may beg for bread with blood. Men laugh with a laughter of disease. Men will not weep because of death, men will not sleep hungry because of death ;[2] a man's heart followeth after his own self.[3]

– – – – and one slayeth another. I show thee the son as foeman, and the brother as adversary, and a man murdereth his father.

Every mouth is full of " Love me ! "[4] All good things have departed, The land is destroyed – – – – ; that which was made is as though it had not been made. Men take the goods of a man (of high estate) from him and give them to one from without. I show thee the possessor in deprivation, and him that is (from) without contented.

Moreover, hatred *reigns among the* townsmen ; the mouth that speaketh is brought to silence, and a speech is answered, while the hand reaches out with the stick – – – –. A thing spoken is as fire for the heart, and what a mouth uttereth is not endured.

The land is minished and its governors are multiplied.[5] (The field ?) is bare, and its imposts are great ; little is the corn and great the corn-measure,[6] and it is measured to overflowing.

The sun separateth himself from men ;[7] he ariseth when it is the hour. None will know that it is midday, and his shadow will not be distinguished.[8] No face will be bright that beholdeth thee,[9] and the eyes will not be moistened with water.[10] He is in the sky like the moon, and yet he deviateth not from his accustomed time, and his rays are in (men's) faces after his former wise.

[1] In the prevailing distress all live on robbery.

[2] Did people ordinarily fast on the occasion of a death ?

[3] The passage probably means that people are so stupefied that they view the death of others with calmness. They are fully preoccupied with their own troubles.

[4] Can that have been the cry of the beggar ?

[5] In the confusion petty princes arise, who oppress the people with taxes, although the cultivated fields grow ever less.

[6] The corn-measure of the tax-collector.

[7] Here he reverts again to the calamities of the drought and the sand-storms.

[8] By which the hours were defined on the dial.

[9] In a lively turn of speech he now addresses the sun himself.

[10] One can gaze at the pallid sun without the eyes watering.

I show thee the land in lamentation and distress.[1] The man with a weak arm hath an arm – – – –. I show thee how the undermost is turned to uppermost – – – –. Men live in the necropolis. The poor man will acquire riches – – – –, paupers eat the offering-bread [2] – – – –. The nome of Heliopolis will no longer be a land (?), it, the birthplace of every god.[3]

A king shall come from the south, called Ameni,[4] the son of a woman of Nubia, and born in Upper Egypt (?). He shall receive the white crown, and wear the red crown ; he shall unite the Two Powerful Ones [5] and shall delight the Two Lords [6] with what they love – – – –.

Be glad, ye people of his time ! The son of a man (of high degree) will make himself a name for all eternity. They that would work mischief and devise hostility, they have subdued their mouthings [7] for fear of him. The Asiatics shall fall before his carnage, and the Libyans shall fall before his flame. The foes succumb to his onset, and the rebels to his might. The royal serpent that is on his forehead, it pacifieth for him the rebels.

There shall be built the "Wall of the Prince," [8] and the Asiatics shall not (again) be suffered to go down into Egypt. They beg (again) for water, after their accustomed wise, that they may be able to give their cattle to drink.

And Right shall come again into its place, and Iniquity, that is cast forth. He will rejoice who shall behold this, and who shall then serve the king.

A man of learning shall pour out [9] water for me, when he seeth that what I have spoken is fulfilled.

[1] The way in which the description ends is reminiscent of the *Admonitions* (see pp. 94 ff.).
[2] Which appertains to persons of distinction.
[3] The whole prophecy thus applies to this sacred land.
[1] The usual shortened form of the name Amenemhēt.
[5] The two diadems.
[6] Horus and Sēth, as tutelary divinities of the two divisions of Egypt.
[7] *I.e.* They do not venture to speak any more.
[8] The fortification in the east of the Delta, which was meant to bar the way against the irruptions of the Bedouins (*cf.* above, p. 17, note 2).
[9] In my tomb in honour of the dead colleague. With an offering of this sort the departed were made happy.

5. THE COMPLAINTS OF THE PEASANT [1]

The fact that we know of four manuscripts of the *Complaints of the Peasant* belonging to the Middle Kingdom, shows that they were highly esteemed at that time. None dating from the New Kingdom are so far authenticated,[2] and so we may suppose that the work had by then fallen out of favour. The reason for this is fairly obvious — these complaints are monotonous and the contents lacking in interest. Indeed, the book is primarily an example of that rhetoric which is entirely given up to elegant expression. The main point of it is that a person " who is eloquent in very sooth " delivers, on account of a matter that has occurred, nine speeches of most beautiful words. That in these speeches right is praised, and the baseness of officials condemned, is almost forgotten by us in face of the flood of far-fetched expressions. Monotonous, obscure, and far-fetched as these nine speeches may appear to us to-day, they really may not have sounded so to an Egyptian. He was sensible of much in them that was elegant and witty, which quite escapes us who only understand the book very incompletely.

The event described occurred in the reign of Nebkaurē, one of the kings of Herakleopolis, who bore the name of Akhthoes (toward the end of the third millennium B.C. ; see p. xxiv., note 2). The man whom, according to custom, I designate " the peasant " is really not one, but is a " dweller in the field," an inhabitant of the salt-field. The salt-field is the Wâdi Natrûn, the small oasis west of the Delta, the " Desert of Natron " of the Christian period. He lives in this wilderness and brings its products to Egypt, in order to exchange them for corn. That a man of such humble rank should have the gift of eloquence accords, however, with what the learned Ptahhotep teaches, namely, that fine expressions may be learnt even from slave-girls (see above, p. 56).

There was once a man whose name was Khunanūp, a peasant from the salt-field ; and he had a wife whose name was Marye.

And this peasant said unto this his wife : " Behold, I am going down into Egypt to bring food thence for my children. Go to, measure out for me the corn which we have left in the barn . . ." She measured it out for him, and there were eight bushels.

And this peasant said unto his wife : " Thou hast two bushels as food for thee and thy children ; but from the six

[1] Contained in four papyri of the Middle Kingdom (three of which are in Berlin). Brought to notice by Chabas in 1863. See F. VOGELSANG, *Kommentar zu den Klagen des Bauern*, Leipzig, 1913. For the most recent translation see GARDINER, *Journ. of Egypt. Archæology*, ix. pp. 5 ff.

[2] But see GARDINER, *Journ. of Egypt. Archæology*, ix. p. 25 [Translator].

bushels which remain over thou shalt make for me bread and beer for every day, that I may (live) thereon."

So this peasant went down into Egypt, after that he had laden his asses with iaa-plants, redemet-plants, natron, salt, sticks of the land of . . ., rods of the Land of the Cow, leopard skins, wolf furs, – – – – [1] and all kinds of other goodly products of the salt-field.

And this peasant went southwards to Herakleopolis,[2] and came to the district of Per-fiōfi, to the north of Medenit. And there he fell in with a man standing on the river-bank, named Dehutinekht, the son of a man whose name was Iseri, belonging to the vassals [3] of the high steward Rensi, the son of Meru.

And this Dehutinekht said, when he saw the asses of this peasant, which were desirable in his heart : " Would that I had some potent idol, that I might steal the belongings of this peasant withal ! " [4]

Now the house of this Dehutinekht lay on the . . . of a path,[5] that was narrow and not broad, equal only to the breadth of a loin-cloth ; and the one side of it was under water, and the other side of it under corn.

And this Dehutinekht said unto his servant : " Go, fetch me a sheet from our house." And it was brought to him straightway. Then he stretched the sheet over the . . . of the path, and its one hem rested on the water and the other on the barley.

Then came this peasant along the public road. And this Dehutinekht said : " Have a care, peasant ; wouldst tread on my clothes ? " And this peasant said : " I will do thy pleasure, my course is a good one." So he went farther up. And this Dehutinekht said : " Shalt thou have my barley for a path ? " This peasant said : " My course is a good one. The bank is high, and the only way is under barley, and still thou cumberest our path with thy clothes. Wilt thou not let us go by ? "

[1] Here follow about twenty names of plants, stones, and birds, about which we know nothing.

[2] The capital at that period.

[3] That is one who was attached to Rensi's estates. One must suppose that he was an official connected with the estates-management.

[4] Probably an oath and curse.

[5] The meaning is that a narrow path led between a somewhat higher lying field and a canal. One had only to spread out the washing upon it to dry for it to be entirely blocked.

When he had so far spoken, one of the asses filled its mouth with a wisp of barley.

And this Dehutinekht said : " Behold, I will take away thine ass, peasant, for it is eating my barley.   Behold, it shall tread (?) and thresh (?) it." [1]

And this peasant said : " My course is a good one.   Since the one side was blocked, I have brought mine ass upon the other,[2] and now thou takest it away for the filling of its mouth with a wisp of barley.   But I know the lord of this domain.   It belongeth to the high steward Rensi, the son of Meru.   He it is that restraineth every robber throughout the entire land, and shall I be robbed in his domain ? "

And this Dehutinekht said : " Is not this the proverb that men say : ' The poor man's name is (only) pronounced for his master's sake ? ' [3]   It is I that speak to thee, but it is the high steward whom thou callest to mind."   Then he took up a rod of green tamarisk against him and belaboured all his limbs therewith, took his asses, and drove (them) into his domain.

Then this peasant wept very bitterly for the pain of that which was done unto him.   But Dehutinekht said : " Cry not so loud, peasant, behold thou art bound for the city of the Lord of Silence." [4]   And this peasant said : " Thou beatest me and stealest my goods, and now thou takest away also the complaint from my mouth !   O Lord of Silence, give me back my chattels !   So may I not cry out – – – –."

And this peasant tarried ten days making petition to this Dehutinekht, but he heeded it not.

So this peasant departed to Herakleopolis to make petition to the high steward Rensi, the son of Meru, and found him as he was coming forth from the door of his house to go down into his barge belonging to the judgment-hall.   And this peasant said : " Would that it might be permitted me to apprise thee of this matter.   Perchance thy trusted servant might be sent

[1] Asses were generally employed for treading out the corn.

[2] A more exact term for this side is employed (but see GARDINER, *Journ. of Egypt. Archæology*, ix. p. 8).

[3] This is apparently a proverb, which asserts that the man of humble standing is disregarded.   What he means to say is : Mind how you treat me.   What concern has my master with you ?

[4] " Lord of Silence " is an attribute of Osiris, in whose holy places noise was forbidden.   These two are in proximity to such a place—the cemetery of Herakleopolis.

to me, so that through him I might inform thee concerning it." [1]
Then the high steward Rensi, the son of Meru, sent on his
trusted servant ahead of him, and through him this peasant
gave information concerning this matter in its every aspect.

Then the high steward Rensi, the son of Meru, brought an
accusation against this Dehutinekht before the magistrates which
were with him. And they said unto him : " This is assuredly
a peasant of his, who hath gone to some one else instead of to
him.[2] Behold thus do they unto their peasants who go to others
instead of to them. Behold, thus do they. Is it a case for one's
punishing this Dehutinekht on account of a trifle of natron and
a trifle of salt ? [3] Let him be bidden to replace it, and he will
replace it." But the high steward Rensi held his peace, and
answered not these magistrates, nor did he answer this peasant.

Then this peasant came to make petition to the high steward
Rensi, the son of Meru, and said :

" O high steward, my lord ! Greatest of the great, leader
of that which is not and of that which is.[4] If thou goest down
to the lake of truth,[5] sail over it with a fair wind ! The . . .
of thy sail shall not be stripped off, thy boat shall not lag,
misfortune shall not befall thy mast, thy pegs (?) shall not be
cut through, – – – –, the current shall not carry thee off, thou
shalt not taste the evils of the river, thou shalt not see a frightened face.[6] The timid (?) fish shall come to thee, and thou shalt
capture fat fowl ! Forasmuch as thou art the father of the
orphan, the husband of the widow, the brother of her that is
put away, the apron of him that is motherless.[7]

[1] The peasant does not venture to detain the great lord with his
complaint.

[2] The magistrates do not even inquire into the matter, but know
already that what they have to do with is an ordinary case of some one
taking the law into his own hands ; not that they intend to sanction this,
but at the same time they do not intend to inflict punishment.

[3] The asses and all the rest of the merchandise the magistrates leave
out of count. It should be noted what pleasure is taken in depicting these
magistrates as unscrupulous and biased.

[4] A favourite expression for " all."

[5] Is this an actual lake ? Or is it only a figurative designation ? In
what follows the idea is worked out of Rensi wishing to go boating in
order to catch fish and birds, the favourite pursuit of Egyptian notables.

[6] *I.e.* probably among his companions.

[7] You are the garment for the poor child, who has no mother to make
a garment for him.

" Let me make for thee a name in this land, that is worth more than every good ordinance.[1] Thou leader, in whom is no guile, thou great one in whom is no baseness ! Thou that destroyest wrong and fosterest right ! Put evil aside. I speak and do thou hear ! Do justice, thou praised one, praised by them that are praised ; dispel the wrong that hath been done me. See how burdened I am with misery. See how weak I am. Take count of me, behold, I am found lacking." [2]

Now this peasant made this speech in the time of King Nebkaurē, the blessed.

And the high steward Rensi, the son of Meru, went before his majesty and said : " My lord, I have found one of these peasants, that is eloquent in very sooth,[3] one that hath been robbed of his goods by a man who is subject to (?) me. And behold, he is come to make petition to me concerning it."

Then said his majesty : " If thou lovest to see me in health,[4] cause him to tarry here without answering aught that he may say, to the intent that he may yet go on speaking. Then let his speech be brought to us in writing that we may hear it. But provide for his wife and for his children ; behold, one of the peasants may go and relieve the penury in his house. Provide also for this peasant himself. Thou shalt cause food to be given him, without letting him know that it is thou that hast given it him." [5]

So they gave him four loaves of bread and two jugs of beer every day. These the high steward Rensi, the son of Meru, used to give—he used to give them to a companion of his, and he gave them to him. Then the high steward Rensi, the son of Meru, sent to the mayor of the salt-field and remitted to the wife of this peasant daily provision, to the amount of three bushels.[6]

[1] If you help me, men will put more trust in you than in the laws.

[2] In the bureaucratic Egyptian manner he likens his plight to a deficiency in computation.

[3] The king and his minister are both connoisseurs and lovers of elegant discourse.

[4] Probably a familiar way of introducing a request.

[5] These arrangements for the sustenance of the people are characteristic of the humane nature of the educated Egyptian.

[6] The three bushels are probably assigned as total, not as daily amount.

Then this peasant came to make petition to him a second time and said :

" O high steward, my lord ! Greatest of the great, richest of the rich. – – – –. Thou tiller of heaven, thou beam of the earth, thou plumb-line that carrieth the weight. Tiller, tumble not ; beam, tilt not ; plumb-line, swing not awry ! [1]

" The great lord helpeth himself to that which hath no possessor, and robbeth the solitary one (?). *And yet thou hast* what thou needest in thine house, the one jug of beer and the three loaves. What dost thou draw out then for the satisfying of thy poor ? [2] – – – –

" Wilt thou not be a man of eternity ? Is it not wrong, for-sooth,[3] a balance that tilteth, a plummet that deflecteth, a guardian of the laws who is become one that vacillateth (?) ?

" Behold, justice fareth ill (?) with thee and is thrust from its place. The magistrates do evil, the well-ordered speech is partial. They that give hearing, steal. – – – –. He that should give air to breathe, taketh away breath (?) – – – – ; the arbitrator is a spoiler ; – – – – ; he that should combat wrong, himself doeth evil."

Here the high steward interrupts these accusations of the peasant with the reminder that his henchman might carry him off. *But the peasant does not permit himself to be bewildered, and proceeds :* " He that measureth the corn heaps, converteth to his own use ; he that filleth up for another, apportioneth too little to his intimates ; he that should lead according to law, commandeth to rob. Who then shall redress evil, when he who should dispel wrong swingeth backwards and forwards ? – – – –"

He then calls to mind a saying : " Do to the doer so that he may do," [4] *and adds thereto :* " that is thanking him for

----

[1] That the sky, which turns with such regularity like a good ship, has a tiller, is an idea that appears elsewhere in Egypt, and that the earth is securely put together is also a natural enough conception. What would become of the world if reliance could no longer be placed on these main-stays of its order, or on the plummet of the mason ? And so you, who are like these, may not vacillate and give way.

[2] *I.e.* what do you use for that purpose out of your possessions ? From here onwards he attacks the prince as though he were a robber and a miser as well.

[3] Ironical.

[4] *I.e.* " Do the other good, that he may do it to you." All else here is quite obscure.

what he doeth, that is parrying a thing before it is shot, that is giving an order to one that hath a trade."

He wishes the prince ill: " Ah, if only a moment might destroy and (cause) upheaval in thy . . ., diminishment among thy birds, and destruction among thy water fowl! *But* he that can see is turned blind, he that can hear deaf, and he that should be the guide is become the one that leadeth astray − − − −.

" Behold, thou art strong and powerful, thou art active of arm, and thine heart is rapacious. Mercy hath passed thee by. How sorroweth the poor man that is destroyed by thee !

" Thou art like unto a messenger of the crocodile ; − − − − the Lady of Pestilence.[1] If it is not for thee, it is not for her ; if it is not against her, it is not against thee. If thou wilt not do it, the merciful man will not do it."

He further reproaches him with openly laying violent hands on the poor and committing " theft on him that hath nothing. − − − − *That is* an ill deed in one that (himself) lacketh nothing − − − −. But thou art sated with thy bread and drunken with thy beer. Thou art rich in all things.

" If the face of the steersman is turned to the front, the ship drifteth whither it will. If the king sitteth within doors and the tiller is in thy hand, evil is dealt out in thy company. Long *and* tedious *to this company seemeth the* petitioner *who is ruined :* ' Who is he that is there ? ' men say.[2]

" Be thou a place of refuge, let thy quay be sound.[3] − − − −. Let thy tongue be directed aright ; go not astray. − − − −. Speak no falsehood ! Take heed to the magistrates − − − −. They that give hearing, it is provender for them to speak lies ; that is a light matter in their hearts.

" Thou that knowest about all men, knowest thou then nought of my circumstances ? Thou that dispellest every need of the water, behold I have course without a ship.[4] Thou that

---

[1] Apparently two divinities who bring ruin are meant ; whom you resemble in what you do. The obscure sentences which follow further amplify this comparison with the goddess of pestilence. [See GUNN, *Syntax*, p. 148.]

[2] So say the magistrates, before whom the petitioner makes his claim.

[3] That ships may lie off it in safety.

[4] That in the course of travelling one should be impeded by canals, etc., is characteristic of Egypt ; to assist the traveller in such circumstances counted as a moral duty.

bringest every drowning man to land and rescuest the ship-wrecked, rescue thou me – – – –."

Then this peasant came to make petition to him for the third time and said :

" O high steward, my lord, thou art Rē,[1] the lord of heaven, in company with thy courtiers. The needs of all mankind (are supplied by thee, for) thou art like the flood.[2] Thou art the Nile, which maketh green the meadows and maketh habitable the waste places.

" Ward off the robber ! Protect the poor man ! Become not a torrent against the petitioner ! Take heed to the approach of eternity.[3] Will so to be, even as it is said : ' To do right is breath for the nose.'[4] Mete out punishment to him that should be punished.

" None shall equal thee in rectitude. Doth the hand-balance deflect ? Doth the stand-balance weigh falsely ? Doth Thōth[5] slow leniency ? (If so) then do thou work mischief. Make thyself the companion of those three, and if the three show leniency, then do thou show leniency.

" Answer not good with evil,[6] put not one thing in place of another."

What follows may mean something like : let the weeds of my speech grow, and do not water it with evil, otherwise it only grows the more. Then he warns him against wrongly handling the tiller and sail : " The exact adjustment of the land is the doing of right.

" Speak not falsehood—thou art great. Be not light—thou art heavy. Speak not falsehood—thou art the balance. Be not in error (?)—thou art rectitude."

Seven comparisons of the unjust prince follow, all of which begin with " Behold thou art," and are only partly intelligible :

" Behold, thou art on one level with the balance ; if it tilt, then do thou also tilt. Fall not, thou art to handle the tiller.

---

[1] You are like the sun-god, who, together with the gods who voyage with him in his ship, rules the world.

[2] You provide men's sustenance like the inundation.

[3] Eternity is the life after death, in which their punishment overtakes the wicked.

[4] Apparently a proverb.

[5] The god of wisdom and judge of the gods.

[6] He probably notices that he has provoked Rensi and is afraid of him.

– – – –. Rob not, thou art to act against the robber, for that great one is not great that is rapacious. Thy tongue is the plummet (of the balance), thine heart is the weight, thy two lips its arms.[1] If thou veil thy face against the impious, who will ward off crime ?

" Behold, thou art a poor man for the washerman, a rapacious one, that damageth friendship [2] – – – –.

" Behold, thou art a ferryman, who (only) conveyeth across him that hath a fare ; a straight-dealer whose straight-dealing is done away with.

" Behold, thou art an head of the granary – – – –.

" Behold, thou art a bird of prey (?) to men, living upon the meanest of the birds.

" Behold, thou art a cook, whose joy is slaughtering ; – – – –.

" Behold, thou art an herdsman – – – –.

" Thou that canst hearken, thou hearkenest not ; wherefore doest thou not hearken ? – – – –. He that concealeth the truth is found out (at the last), and the back of falsehood is laid on the ground.

" Prepare not to-morrow, ere it be come ; none knoweth the evil that will [3] come in it."

Now this peasant spake these words to the high steward Rensi, the son of Meru, at the entrance of the gate-house.[4]

Then he caused two apparitors to attend to him with whips, and they belaboured all his limbs therewith.

And this peasant said : " The son of Meru goeth on erring ; blind to what he seeth, and deaf to what he heareth, and regardless (?) of that which is related to him.

" Behold, thou art a town without its mayor, like a company without its chief, like a ship in which is no commander, a confederacy without its captain.

[1] The arms of the balance.

[2] Better : " Behold thou art a wretch of a washerman, one rapacious in damaging a comrade, one that forsaketh (?) his partner (?) for the sake of his client ; he who hath come and brought (something) for him is his brother " [Translator].

[3] Meaning probably only : Some day it may even go ill with you, all powerful though you be.

[4] The gate-house is a seat of the administration ; accordingly the prince has servants at hand there, who thrash the peasant for his impudent utterances.

" Behold, thou art a constable (?) and a thief, a mayor that taketh presents, a chief of a district that should repress plundering, and yet art become a pattern for him that doeth it (?)."

Then this peasant came to make petition to him a fourth time, and found him coming forth from the door of the temple of Harsaphes,[1] and said :

" Thou praised one, may Harsaphes, from whose temple thou art come, praise thee. Good is diminished, and there is none that can boast (?) that he hath laid out the back of falsehood upon the ground."

He then appears to speak of one's using a ferry in order to cross the river, but does not say what he means by this simile.[2]

" Why, who (still) sleepeth until daylight ? Destroyed are walking by night, and travelling by day, and suffering a man to attend to his own right cause.[3]

" Behold, one is never finished saying to thee :[4] ' Mercy hath passed thee by.' How sorroweth the poor man that is destroyed by thee !

" Behold, thou art a sportsman that followeth his desire, one bent on doing what he will, harpooning hippopotami and shooting wild bulls, striking fish and catching birds.[5] (But) none that hath a hasty mouth is free from . . . ; none that is light-minded hath weighty designs. Be patient and learn the truth – – – –. Something (?) is brought (to thee) that maketh the eyes to see, and the heart is gladdened ;[6] so be not boastful, because thou art powerful, lest mischief befall thee. – – – – It is he that eateth that tasteth, and he that is addressed answereth ;[7] it is he that sleepeth that seeth the dream – – – –.

" Fool, behold, one is come to thee. Dunce, behold thou

[1] The god of Herakleopolis.

[2] Possibly : even so justice is needed to preserve the country.

[3] That one should sleep till late, and go out unmolested by night, is spoken of elsewhere as a sign of public security. An end has been made of that ; even by day men are robbed, and they can no longer maintain their rights. *Cf.* p. 127, note 1.

[4] He has addressed the following sentence to him once already in the second complaint.

[5] Is he appealing to the cheery nature of the sportsman ?

[6] To " gladden the heart " is the regular and also official expression for " inform." Does the peasant allude to a petition which he has handed in through the medium of the trusted servant ?

[7] Accordingly, give me a final answer.

art addressed. Thou that hast baled out [1] the piss, behold thou art entered.

"Steersman, let not thy ship run aground. Thou that shouldest keep alive, suffer not to die. Destroyer,[2] suffer not to be destroyed. Shade, become not sun. Shelter, let not the crocodile seize.

"It is now the fourth time that I make petition to thee. Am I to spend (yet more) time at it?"

In the fifth *petition the peasant first produces all manner of anglers, fishers, fish-spearers, every one of whom catches a fish— one, it might be conjectured, they did not wish to catch—and then adds:* "Behold, thou art in like case," *i.e. one, probably, who does not ply his trade aright.*

"Rob not an humble man of his possessions, a feeble man whom thou knowest (to be such). The poor man's possessions are breath to him, and he that taketh them from him stoppeth up his nose.

"Thou wast appointed to hear pleas, to judge between suitors, to repress the robber. But lo, it is the upholder of the thief that thou wouldst be.[3]

"Men put their trust in thee, and thou art become a transgressor. Thou wast set for a dam unto the poor man, to prevent his being drowned—and behold, thou art his lake, thou flowing one!"

Then this peasant came to make petition to him a sixth time, and said:

"O high steward, my lord! – – – –, foster truth, foster good, and destroy (evil), even as satiety cometh, that it may end hunger, and clothing, that it may end nakedness; even as the sky becometh calm after a high storm, when it warmeth all that are cold; even as a fire that cooketh what is raw, and as water that quencheth thirst.

"Look in front of thee. The arbitrator is a spoiler.[4] The peace-maker is a maker of sorrow – – – –.

[1] *I.e.* evacuated. The same tasteful simile occurs again in greater detail in the seventh complaint! I have no idea what it means here.

[2] One expects rather some such expression as "sustainer."

[3] See GUNN, *Syntax*, p. xiv [Translator].

[4] He has already said this in the second complaint, and he has similarly employed there the following metaphor of false measurement of the corn.

" Cheating maketh justice too small, *one must* give good measure ; truth neither falleth short nor exceedeth. *The next paragraph perhaps means to assert that a petitioner ought not to be rebuffed, otherwise* one knoweth not what is in the heart ; *and then follow two utterly unintelligible metaphors, the one of urine or semen, the other of the loading of a ship.*

" Thou art instructed, thou art made perfect . . . but not for plundering. (Yet) thou dost the same as all men, – – – – a cheat for the whole land : The cultivator of evil waters his plot with wrong-doing, that he may plant his plot with lies, and pour out trouble for the estate."

Then this peasant came to make petition to him a seventh time, and said :

" O high steward, my lord ! Thou art the tiller of the entire land. The land saileth according to thy command. Thou art the peer of Thōth, who judgeth without partiality.

" My lord, permit that a man be called to what is rightfully his.[1] Be not vexed, it is nothing to thee, if (?) the man of cheerful (?) countenance becometh ill-humoured. Rail not because of that which hath not yet come, and rejoice not because of that which hath not yet happened." [2]

What follows perhaps speaks of a good judge, who re-examines a case that has been settled, and then of one " that subverteth the law and infringeth upon right reckoning. No poor man liveth whom he plundereth, and truth addresseth him not.

" But my belly is full and mine heart is laden. There issueth forth from my belly . . ., there is a breach in the dam and its water floweth ; (thus) is my mouth opened for speech – – – –. (Now) have I baled out my piss and ventilated what was in my belly.[3] I have washed my clothes ; my discourse is achieved, and my misery is concluded in thy presence. What is now thy decision (?) ? [4]

" Thy sluggishness will lead thee astray, thy rapacity will make thee a fool, thy gluttony (?) will create thee enemies.

" But wilt thou ever find another peasant like me ? A

[1] That his suit be conducted according to rule.

[2] Probably only meaning : do not come to a decision prematurely, before you have exact information about a matter.

[3] As the body rids itself of what is a burden to it—as when there is a breach in a dam—so my distress pours forth in words.

[4] The washing is ready and now it is your turn.

sluggard—will a petitioner remain standing at the door of his house ? [1] He keepeth no (longer) silence whom thou hast caused to speak ; he sleepeth no (longer) whom thou hast awakened ; – – – – ; the mouth (remaineth) not closed that thou hast opened ; he is no (longer) ignorant, whom thou hast caused to know ; he is no (longer) a fool whom thou hast instructed. They [2] are such as repel evil ; they are magistrates who possess good ; they are craftsmen who create that which is ; they are such as affix the severed head. [3]

Then this peasant came to make petition to him an eighth time, and said :

" O high steward, my lord ! Men suffer a fall because of greed, the rapacious faileth in his affair, his affair eludeth him. Thou art rapacious, that is nothing for thee ; thou robbest, that profiteth thee not, thee, that (else) wouldst suffer a man to attend to his own right cause. [4]

" What thou needest is in thine house, thy belly is full. The corn measure runneth over ; that which leapeth out (?) [5] of it perisheth, and its superfluity is on the ground. [6] They seize, plunder, and take away, do the magistrates, yet they were appointed to repel evil. A refuge for the insolent are the magistrates, yet they were appointed to repel falsehood.

" The fear of thee hath not suffered me to make petition to thee, and so thou knowest not mine heart [7] – – – –.

" Thou hast thy plot of ground in the field, thy bread in the domain, thy victuals in the storehouse. The magistrates give to thee, [8] and thou takest (yet more)—art thou not a robber ? And doth not one bring to thee, when the troops are with thee at the division of the ground-plots ? [9]

---

[1] Meaning ?   [2] Probably those who thus tell you the truth.

[3] They make even the impossible possible ; the magician in the story had also to exhibit this art (see above, p. 42).

[4] The same in the fourth appeal (p. 125). The peasant warns Rensi in this section against injustice, which only brings a man harm ; because, as he emphasizes further on, it is at variance with the will of the gods.

[5] During the measuring. In your house no one bothers about such a trifle.

[6] You are so rich, and yet you still permit robbery to go on.

[7] From fear of you I have never yet been able to tell you what I really want (?)

[8] From their plunder.

[9] When you divide the fields anew after the inundation (?)

" Do according unto truth for the Lord of Truth,[1] whose truth is the truth (indeed). Thou reed-pen, thou book, thou palette of Thōth, when thou keepest aloof from working mischief.[2] Good is it, when thou art good, yea good is it, when thou art good.

" ' But truth endureth unto everlasting, and it descendeth with him that doeth it into the nether world.[3] When he is buried and the earth is joined with him, his name is not obliterated upon earth, but he is remembered for goodness.' That is what is laid down in the word of God.[4] Is it a hand-balance ? Then it tilteth not. Is it a stand-balance ? Then it weigheth not falsely.[5]

" Whether I shall come or another shall come, greet him, but answer him not with the greeting of one that is silent, and attack not him that attacketh not.[6]

" Thou art not become a sufferer (?), thou art not become sick, thou hast not run away, and thou hast not perished, and yet hast thou given me no payment [7] for this goodly speech that cometh forth from the mouth of Rē himself : ' Speak truth, do according unto truth, for that it is great and mighty, and endureth. Its . . . will find thee and bring thee to venerable estate.' [8]

" If the balance doth tilt, or its scales which weigh the things, there is then no right result. A mean act attaineth not to the city,[9] whereas a . . . will come to land."

Then this peasant came to make petition to him a ninth time and said :

" O high steward, my lord ! The tongue of men is their

[1] Usually a name of Ptah of Memphis, but here Osiris will be meant.

[2] In accordance with your office, you are the instrument of the god of wisdom, the judge of the gods—only you must behave accordingly.

[3] It helps him in the posthumous judgment.

[4] The sacred writings which are derived from Thōth. What proceeds will therefore be a quotation from these.

[5] The word of God is probably meant ; this has been put to the proof.

[6] In the future be friendly to petitioners and do not leave them, as you have left me, without an answer, and do not fly at them.

[7] You have heard all my speeches, and yet I remain without answer.

[8] This is also probably a quotation from the sacred writings.

[9] Like a bad ship that does not reach the town ; similarly in the ninth appeal.

9

stand-balance. The hand-balance searcheth out the deficiencies,[1] and punisheth him that should be punished. Be like it in rectitude – – – –.

" If falsehood walk abroad, it strayeth ; it crosseth not over in the ferry-boat and . . . not. As for him that is rich therein, he hath no children, and hath no heir upon earth. He that voyageth with it cometh not to land, his vessel mooreth not off its city.

" Be not heavy, if (?) thou art not light. Lag not, if (?) thou art not quick. Be not partial ; hearken not unto the heart.

" Veil not thy face against one whom thou knowest. Be not blind to one whom thou seest. Rebuff not him that petitioneth thee.

" *So be* not sluggish, *and* publish thy speech and do (what is right) to him that hath done (it) to thee. Hearken not unto all men,[2] but call a man to what is rightfully his.[3] There is no yesterday [4] for the sluggard ; for him that is deaf to truth there is no friend ; for him that is rapacious there is no day of cheer. – – – –.

" Behold, I make petition to thee, and thou hast not heard it. Now will I go away and will make petition on thy behalf to Anubis." [5]

Then the high steward Rensi, the son of Meru, caused two apparitors to go and bring him back (?). And this peasant was afraid, and thought that it was being done to punish him for this speech which he had spoken.

And this peasant said : " As the thirsty man draweth near to water, as the mouth of the suckling reacheth after milk, *so I long to see how death cometh* (?)."

The high steward Rensi, the son of Meru, said : " Fear not, peasant. Behold, thou shalt dwell with me." Then this peasant swore, saying : " I will for ever eat of thy bread and drink of thy beer." And the high steward said : " Well, come this way, that thou mayest hear thy petitions." And he caused them

[1] It indicates what should be left over and yet is not there ; that is what you also should be.

[2] He means the magistrates.

[3] *Cf.* p. 127, note 1.

[4] Possibly : no pleasant recollection ?

[5] *I.e.* I will betake me to the god of the dead ; meaning, he would die and seek for justice at his hands ?

to be read out from a new [1] papyrus roll, every petition according to [its] content. And the high steward Rensi, the son of Meru, caused it to be sent in to the majesty of King Nebkaurē, the justified. And it pleased the king more than anything that was in the entire land.

And his majesty said: " Give judgment thyself,[2] O son of Meru." Then the high steward, the son of Meru, sent two apparitors to fetch him. And he was brought. An inventory was made – – – –.

From the fragments of the concluding portion of the tale one conjectures that the household of the peasant amounted to six heads, *and that he was provided with* wheat, asses . . . swine . . . *And in addition all the possessions* of Dehutinekht *were given* to this peasant.

D. SECULAR POEMS

i. SONGS OF THE WORKERS

Several of the little songs, with which the Egyptian accompanied his tasks (see above, pp. xxviii. f.), are preserved in the tombs as inscriptions appended to representations of the task in question.

Song of the shepherds [3]

When the inundation is at an end, the shepherds drive rams over the still sodden ground, in order that their sharp hoofs may " plough " the field. While thus engaged they sang in the Old Kingdom :

The shepherd is in the water among the fish,
He speaketh with the shad, and greeteth the . . . fish.
West ! Whence is the shepherd ? A shepherd of the West.

The shepherd makes fun of himself ; what the West means here is doubtful.

---

[1] Not on one that has already been used once, and that has had the writing expunged. The passage shows clearly that at that time papyrus was still an article of some value.

[2] The king replies as though he has read through the speeches of the peasant as official documents, about which he has to come to a decision.

[3] In two tombs of the Old Kingdom ; in a third was a variant version. See ERMAN, *Reden, Rufe und Lieder* (in *Abh. d. Berl. Akad.*, 1918), p. 19.

SONG OF THE FISHERS [1]

While the net is being drawn in this song is sung :
It comes and brings us a fine catch !

SONG OF THE CHAIRMEN [2]

The men carrying their master in the palanquin sing :
Better is it (for us) when full, than when it is empty !

or :
Happy are they that bear the chair !
Better is it (for us) when full, than when it is empty !

*Or again, probably in allusion to some reward which is to be
assigned to their master Ipi :*
Come down to them that are rewarded, hail !
Come down to them that are rewarded, health !
– – – –. Reward (?) of Ipi, be it as great as I desire !
Better is it (for us) when full, than when it is empty !

2. SONGS AT BANQUETS

When the deceased's survivors celebrated a festival in his
tomb, a meal was provided, at which he was conceived of as being
present, a meal which was lacking in none of the requirements
appertaining to such an occasion—wine, music, and song, flowers
and perfumes.

A tombstone of the Middle Kingdom has preserved the beginning of one of the songs with which the guests were entertained at
these banquets. A corpulent harpist is depicted on it singing :

O grave, thou art built for festivity,
Thou art founded for what is fair. [3]

But we possess complete a remarkable song, which was sung on
the same occasions, and which describes the transitoriness of all
earthly things, in order to warn the listeners to make the most of
life. The New Kingdom, which has preserved it for us, [4] knew of

---

[1] In two tombs of the Old Kingdom ; see *op. cit.* p. 34 ; *cf.* also
BLACKMAN, *Rock Tombs of Meir*, iv. Pl. VIII.

[2] See *op. cit.* p. 52.

[3] STEINDORFF, *Zeitschr. für ägypt. Sprache*, xxxii. p. 124 ; the meaning
is of course : thou art no place for woe.

[4] Preserved in *Pap. Harris*, No. 500, and partly also on a tombstone
of the Eighteenth Dynasty. See W. MAX MÜLLER, *Die Liebespoesie der
alten Ägypter* (Leipzig, 1899), pp. 31 ff.

it as coming from the *H o u s e   o f   K i n g   A n t e f*,[1] *i.e.* from his tomb, where it was also written *i n   f r o n t   o f   t h e   H a r p i s t*. An amplified version of it is to be found among the songs of the New Kingdom.

Well is it with this good prince, the goodly destiny hath suffered hurt.[2]

Bodies pass away and others remain [3] since the time of them that were before.

The gods [4] that were aforetime rest in their pyramids, and likewise the noble and the glorified, buried in their pyramids.

They that build houses, their habitations are no more. What hath been done with them ?

I have heard the discourses of Imhotep and Hardedef,[5] with whose words men speak everywhere [6]—what are their habitations (now) ?   Their walls are destroyed, their habitations are no more, as if they had never been.

None cometh from thence that he may tell us how they fare, that he may tell us what they need, that he may set our heart at rest (?), until we also go to the place whither they are gone.

Be glad, that thou mayest cause thine heart to forget that men will (one day) beatify [7] thee.   Follow thy desire, so long as thou livest.   Put myrrh on thine head, clothe thee in fine linen, and anoint thee with the genuine marvels of the things of the god.

Increase yet more the delights that thou hast, and let not thine heart grow faint.   Follow thy desire, and do good to thyself (?).   Do what thou requirest (?) upon earth, and vex not thine heart,—until that day of lamentation [8] cometh to thee.   Yet He with the Quiet Heart [9] heareth not their lamentation, and cries deliver no man from the underworld.

[1] This must be one of the Antefs from the end of the Middle Kingdom, as the language already tends to be popular.

[2] The later version has : " The goodly destiny (*i.e.* death) hath come to pass," and that is what must be meant here.

[3] According to the later version the meaning is : Come in their place.

[4] The ancient kings.

[5] The famous old sages.   Imhotep was considered to be a son of Ptah ; Hardedef is a son of King Kheops (see above, pp. 40 ff.).

[6] Whose wise sayings every one has on his lips.

[7] The beatification is a ceremony at the funeral.

[8] The lament for the dead.

[9] The god of the dead, Osiris.

*Below there is written as " refrain " (or whatever the word
may signify) :*

Spend the day happily and weary not thereof! Lo, none
can (?) take his goods with him. Lo, none that hath departed
can come again.

3. HYMNS TO KING SESŌSTRIS III [1]

The first four of these fine songs were probably composed for
the entry of the king into " his city," and they greet him in the
name of its inhabitants. From the beginning of the fourth song
we can see that the city is one in Upper Egypt, and that the king
has come there in order to be crowned ruler of the Upper Country.

The fifth and sixth songs were apparently not written for any
special purpose.

Horus, Neter-kheperu; lord of diadems, Neter-mesut,
Horus that hath overcome Sēth, Kheper, king of Upper and
Lower Egypt, Khakaurē, son of Rē, Sesōstris [2]—he carried off
the Two Lands in triumph.

[First hymn.]

Praise to thee, Khakaurē! Our Horus, Neter-kheperu!
That protecteth the land and extendeth his boundaries,
That vanquisheth the foreign countries with his crown.[3]
That encloseth the Two Lands in his arms,
And (strangleth ?) the foreign lands with his grip;
That slayeth the People of the Bow, without stroke of the club,[4]
Shooting of the arrow, or drawing of the string.
His might hath smitten the Trōglodytes [5] in their land,
And the fear of him hath slain the Nine Bows.
His slaughtering hath made thousands to die
Of the People of the Bow . . ., that attacked his borders.
He that shooteth the arrow as doth Sekhmet,[6]

---

[1] In a papyrus of the Twelfth Dynasty found in the ruins of the town of
Kahun ; see GRIFFITH, *Hieratic Papyri from Kahun and Gurob* (London,
1898), pp. 1 ff. The king reigned from 1882–1845 B.C.

[2] The titulary of the king, which stands here as a heading to the
collection of hymns.

[3] The crown with the royal serpent on it was accounted a goddess who
protected the king.

[4] They die merely from terror of him.

[5] The inhabitants of the desert between the Nile and the Red Sea, the
modern Ababdeh and Bishârîn.

[6] The lion-headed goddess of war.

When he overthroweth thousands of them that knew not his
might.
It is the tongue of his majesty that confineth [1] Nubia,
And it is his utterances that make the Bedouins to flee.
Sole youthful one that fighteth for his boundaries,
And suffereth not his people to wax faint ; [2]
That suffereth men to sleep unto daylight,
And his recruits to slumber, for his heart is their defender.
His decrees have made his boundaries,
And his word hath joined in one the Two River-banks.

[SECOND HYMN.]

How the gods rejoice : thou hast made their offerings to
flourish.
How thy . . . rejoice : thou hast made their boundaries.
How thy (fathers) which were aforetime rejoice : thou hast
increased their portions.[3]
How the Egyptians rejoice in thy might : thou hast protected . . .
How the people rejoice in thy designs : thy might hath captured
the . . .
How the Two River-banks rejoice in thy strength : thou hast
enlarged that which they need.
How thy recruits rejoice in . . . : thou hast caused them to
grow.
How thine honoured ones rejoice : thou hast renewed their
youth.
How the Two Lands rejoice in thy strength : thou hast protected their walls.
Thereafter comes the rubric : Its . . . is : " Horus, that
extendeth his boundaries, mayest thou repeat eternity," *doubtless a direction for the singer. It might be a refrain or a specifica-
tion of the tune.*

[THIRD HYMN.]

How great [4] is the lord for his city : he alone is a million,
little are other men.

---

[1] When he does not fight himself his wise orders suffice.

[2] Through fighting ? For that is his particular care.

[3] Probably the shares which the deceased kings obtained for their
tombs at the distribution of the food-offerings.

[4] *I.e.* how rich in blessing.

How great is the lord for his city : he is like a dyke, that keepeth back the river in its water-floods.

How great is the lord for his city : he is like a cool lodge that letteth a man sleep unto daylight.

(*Two unintelligible verses : the second likens the king to* a place of refuge.)

How great is the lord for his city : he is like a bulwark that delivereth the fearful from his enemy.

How great is the lord for his city : he is like the shade of the season of Overflowing for cooling in summer.[1]

How great is the lord for his city : he is like a corner warm and dry in time of winter.

How great is the lord for his city : he is like a mountain, that keepeth back the storm-blast, at the time when the sky is in riot.

How great is the lord for his city : he is like Sekhmet unto foes that overstep his boundaries.

[FOURTH HYMN.]

He hath come unto us that he may carry away Upper Egypt ; the double diadem [2] hath rested on his head.

He hath come unto us and hath united the Two Lands ; he hath mingled the reed (?) [3] with the bee.

He hath come unto us and hath brought the Black Land [4] under his sway ; he hath apportioned to himself the Red Land.[4]

He hath come unto us and hath taken the Two Lands under his protection ; he hath given peace to the Two River-banks.

He hath come unto us and hath made Egypt to live ; he hath banished its suffering.

He hath come unto us and hath made the people to live ; he hath caused the throat of the subjects to breathe.

He hath come unto us and hath trodden down the foreign

---

[1] He is as welcome as that double cooling would be in the heat.

[2] That form of the diadem, in which the crown of Upper Egypt is inserted into that of Lower Egypt.

[3] The emblem of Upper Egypt, with which also its king is written, whereas the king of Lower Egypt is denoted in the writing by the bee.

[4] Egyptian and non-Egyptian territory.

countries ; he hath smitten the Trōglodytes,[1] that knew not the dread of him.

He hath come unto us and hath (done battle for) his boundaries ; he hath delivered them that were robbed . . .

(*A destroyed verse.*)

He hath come unto us, that we may (nurture up ?) our children and bury our aged ones . . .

[FIFTH HYMN.]

It is concerned with the gods ; one can still recognize : ye love Khakaurē, that liveth for ever and ever – – – – he apportioneth your victuals – – – – our herdsman, that can give breath – – – – ye requite it him in life and happiness, numberless times.

[SIXTH HYMN.]

Praise of Khakaurē, that liveth for ever and ever – – – – when I sail in the ship – – – – adorned with gold – – – –.

E. RELIGIOUS POEMS

The Egyptians regarded the religious writings of their ancestors as sacred ; hence any such compositions of their own closely imitated these in both form and language. It is therefore very difficult for us to be certain about the age of a religious text, of which we do not possess an early version. Accordingly it is in itself possible that one or other of the hymns here given should have been assigned a place among the remains of the earliest poetry above. On the other hand, the great *Hymn to Amūn*, which I have assigned below to the New Kingdom, may actually date from as early a period as the Middle Kingdom. However, I think that on the whole I am right in my divisions.

1. TO MIN-HORUS [2]

I adore Min and praise Horus, that lifteth up his arm.[3]

Praise to thee, Min, at his appearing ![4] Thou with lofty

---

[1] A people in the desert between Upper Egypt and the Red Sea, who plundered travellers. The king had just fought against them, as is evident from the following verse.

[2] From a tombstone of the Middle Kingdom (Louvre, C 30). The ithyphallic god Min was regarded since the Middle Kingdom as Horus, son of Osiris.

[3] Min is represented with his right arm uplifted.

[4] The " Appearing of Min " is a known festival.

plumes ; [1] son of Osiris, born of divine Isis.   Great in the Senut-temple, mighty in Ipu, thou of Koptos !   Horus, that lifteth up his arm, lord of reverence, that hath reduced the might [2] to silence.   King of all gods !   Rich in perfume, when he cometh down from the Matoï-land ; revered in Nubia ! [3] – – – –.

2. TO THE SUN

In the tombs of the New Kingdom it is the custom to furnish the deceased with two songs—either in the form of an inscription, or else written out in a so-called Book of the Dead—in which he praises the morning and the evening sun ; for to be able to look upon these was the earnest wish of all dead persons.   It is probably not to be doubted that these songs, which exist in various versions,[4] are intrinsically ancient, although no example dating from the Middle Kingdom has hitherto been found.

(*a*) To the morning sun.[5]

Adoration of Rē, when he ariseth in the eastern horizon of heaven.

Praise to thee, that ariseth in Nun [6] and lighteneth the Two Lands, when he cometh forth.

Thee the whole Ennead praiseth – – – – thou goodly, beloved youth—when he ariseth, men live.

Mankind rejoiceth at him ; the Souls [7] of Heliopolis shout joyfully to him ; the Souls of Buto and Hierakonpolis [8] extol him.   The apes [9] adore him ; " Praise to thee," say all wild beasts with one consent.

Thy serpent overthroweth thy foes.[10]   Thou exultest in thy ship, thy crew is content, and the morning [11] bark receiveth thee.

---

[1] Min wears two feathers as a head-dress.

[2] That of Sēth, the foe of Horus.

[3] Min, whose sanctuary lay in the part of Egypt whence the roads lead to eastern desert territories, was accounted the patron of these. Thus it is he who brings perfumes.

[4] For translations of such songs, see SCHARFF, *Ägyptische Sonnenlieder*, Berlin, 1922.

[5] *Book of the Dead*, ch. xv. A II.   [6] The celestial ocean.

[7] The gods of the ancient cities are designated " Souls."

[8] The ancient capitals of Lower and Upper Egypt.

[9] The apes, who greet the sun at his rising.

[10] The clouds which threaten the sun, generally conceived of as the snake Apōphis.

[11] The ship which the sun uses by day ; at night, in the underworld, he has another ; both are manned by gods.

Thou rejoicest, O lord of gods, over them whom thou hast created, and they praise thee. Nut is blue alongside of thee,[1] and Nun . . . for thee with his rays.

Give me light, that I may see thy beauty.

(b) To THE EVENING SUN.[2]

Adoration of Rē-Harakhti, when he setteth in the western horizon of heaven.

Praise to thee, O Rē, when thou settest, Atum, Harakhti! Divine divinity, that came into being of himself, primæval god, that existed at the beginning.

Jubilation to thee that hast fashioned the gods ; he that hath raised up the sky to be the pathway (?) for his eyes,[3] that hath fashioned the earth to the extent (?) of his radiance, so that every man may discern the other.

The evening bark is in gladness, and the morning bark exulteth and crieth aloud for joy, when they voyage for thee in peace over Nun. They crew is happy, thy serpent hath overthrown thine enemies, and thou hast put an end to the going of Apōphis.

Thou art fair, O Rē, every day ; thy mother Nut embraceth thee.[4]

Thou settest beauteous with gladsome heart in the horizon of Manun.[5] The noble dwellers in the West exult. Thou givest light there for the great god Osiris, the ruler of eternity.

The lords of the caverns [6] in their dens, they uplift their hands and praise thee. They address to thee all their prayers, when thou shinest for them.

The lords of the underworld,[7] they are happy when thou bestowest light on the West. Their eyes open when they behold thee. How their hearts rejoice when they behold thee !

Thou hearest the petitions of them that are in the coffin. Thou dispellest their pain and drivest away their evils. Thou givest breath to their nostrils, and they take hold of the rope at the forepart of thy ship [8] in the horizon of Manun.

---

[1] The sky-goddess is here conceived of as a blue ocean over which the sun voyages.

[2] *Book of the Dead*, ch. xv. B II.   [3] The sun and moon.

[4] The sky-goddess enfolds the sun in her arms at his rising and setting ?

[5] A legendary mountain in the West, in which the sun goes down.

[6] The dead.   [7] The dead.

[8] In the underworld, where there is no wind, the boat of the sun is towed along, and this task is undertaken by the grateful dead.

Thou art fair, O Rē, every day ; thy mother Nut embraceth thee.

3. TO THŌTH

In the form of a schoolboy's exercise written on a writing-board of the Eighteenth Dynasty,[1] but probably of earlier date.

Daily adoration of Thōth.

O ye gods that are in heaven, O ye gods that are (on earth) ! (Ye southerners, northerners, westerners ?), easterners, come and behold Thōth, how he shineth forth in his crown, which the two lords [2] in Hermopolis have set in place for him, in order that he may execute the governance of mankind. Exult in the hall of Kēb over what he hath done. Adore him, extol him, give him praise. He is the lord of kindliness, the leader of the entire multitude.

Then follow a promise [3] *that for all gods and goddesses who will thus praise him* Thōth will furnish their chapels and their altars (?) in their temples, *and a prayer of the writer that Thōth may give him* an house and possessions *and sustenance ; he is to cause that he* be loved and praised . . . and pleasant and protected *with all people, and that his enemies be overthrown.*

4. HYMNS TO OSIRIS

Osiris, the most popular of all gods, was originally a god of vegetation, which dies away, it is true, but is revived again by the inundation. But he came to be generally regarded as an almost entirely human figure, and he usually appears as such in the hymns also.

He was the son of the earth-god Kēb and the sky-goddess Nut, and succeeded his father as king of Egypt. His reign was prosperous, and he was also victorious in war. But his brother, the god Sēth, murdered him and threw his corpse into the water.

Isis, his sister and spouse, sought for it for a long time, and when she had at last found it and had brought it to land, she fanned breath into it, and so restored Osiris to a sort of life. She became pregnant by him and bore a son, Horus, whom she brought up in a hidden place, that he might escape the persecutions of Sēth. When he was grown up, she led him before the tribunal of the gods,

---

[1] *Brit. Mus.*, 5656 ; *cf.* TURAJEFF, *Zeitschr. für ägypt. Sprache*, **xxxiii.** p. 120.

[2] Horus and Sēth.

[3] These practical applications may be later.

where he defended himself against Sēth, who contested the legitimacy of his birth. The gods decided in his favour and assigned to him the kingdom of his father. Since then, Osiris reigned as king of the dead in their realm, which was thought to be in the underworld or even in the sky. He has many sanctuaries on earth, the chiefest being Busiris in the Delta, and Abydos.

(a) THE LONG HYMN.[1]

Praise to thee, Osiris ! Thou lord of eternity, king of gods ! Thou with many names and lordly of being ! With mysterious ceremonies in the temples.[2]

He it is that hath the noble ka in Busiris and the abundant sustenance (?) in Letopolis ; to whom men shout for joy in the nome of Busiris, and that hath many victuals in Heliopolis.[3]

He whom men call to mind in . . ., the mysterious soul of the lord of Kerert ; that is lordly in Memphis, the soul of Rē and his own body.[4]

He that went to rest in Herakleopolis, and to whom men raised goodly shouts of joy in the Naret-tree, which came into being in order to raise up his soul.[5]

Lord of the Great Hall in Hermopolis, and very terrible in Shashotep ; lord of eternity in Abydos, that hath his seat in To-zoser.[6]

He whose name endureth in the mouth of men, that was in Primæval Time for the Two Lands together ; [7] sustenance and food at the head of the Ennead ; [8] the most excellent glorified one among the glorified.[9]

Nun [10] hath offered to him his water, and the north wind

[1] On a tombstone of the Eighteenth Dynasty in Paris. See CHABAS, *Revue archéologique*, xiv. p. 307. The hymn in its second part furnishes us with a short account of the Osiris legend, which, however, it compresses into the form of the ordinary hymns of praise.

[2] Refers probably to the mysteries, *i.e.* the dramatic performances of incidents in the Osiris myth.

[3] In every place his festivals are celebrated and offerings are made to him.

[4] Theological constructions, whose object it is to connect Osiris with other divinities.

[5] This verse and the following deal with events in the myth of which we know nothing.

[6] The necropolis of Abydos.   [7] Who ruled over them ?

[8] The gods are indebted to him for their sustenance ?

[9] He is the ruler of the dead.

[10] The celestial ocean, to which Osiris is indebted for the water which he gives the earth in the inundation.

journeys southward to him ; the sky createth air for his nose, for the contentment of his heart. The plants grow according to his desire, and the field createth for him its [1] food.

The firmament and its stars hearken unto him, and the great portals open to him ; to whom men shout for joy in the southern sky, whom men adore in the northern sky.[2] The imperishable stars [3] are under his authority, and the neverwearying ones are his place of abode.

Offering is made to him by the command of Kēb,[4] and the Nine Gods adore him ; they that are in the underworld kiss the ground, and they that are in the necropolis make an obeisance. The . . . shout for joy when they behold him, they that are there [5] are in fear of him. The Two Lands together give him praise at the approach of his majesty.

The lordly noble at the head of the nobles, with enduring office and established rule. The goodly Mighty One for the Nine Gods, he with the kindly face, on whom men love to look.

He that put the fear of him in all lands, to the intent that they might make mention of his name [6] *in respect of all that they offered* (?) *unto him* ; he that is remembered in heaven and on earth. *To whom many shouts of joy are raised* at the Wag-festival,[7] over whom the Two Lands rejoice together. The most chiefest of his brethren, the eldest of the Nine Gods.[8]

He that established right throughout the Two River-banks, and placed the son upon his father's seat ; [9] praised of his father Kēb, beloved of his mother Nut.

Great of strength when he overthrew the adversary, powerful of arm when he slew his foe. He that put the fear of him in the enemies, and reached (?) the boundaries of them that plotted mischief. Firm of heart when he trod down (?) the foemen.

The heir of Kēb in the kingship of the Two Lands. He [10]

---

[1] The field's.

[2] An allusion to the resurrection and ascension of Osiris.

[3] The circumpolar stars, which are accounted the most eminent, because they never set.

[4] Kēb, as earth-god, furnishes the victuals.

[5] Usual designation of the dead.

[6] Probably refers to the deeds which the myth ascribes to him. Similarly all that follows.

[7] Apparently a harvest-festival.

[8] That he certainly was not; it is only poetical exaggeration.

[9] As a good king does.   [10] Kēb.

saw how excellent he was, and he entrusted it to him to lead the Two Lands to good fortune.

He placed this land in his hand, its water and its air, its herbs and all its cattle. All that flieth and all that fluttereth, its worms and its wild beasts, were made over to the son of Nut, and the Two Lands were contented therewith.

He that appeared upon the throne of his father, like Rē when he ariseth in the horizon, that he might give light to him that was in darkness. He illumined – – – – and flooded [1] the Two Lands, like the sun at dawn of day.

His crown cleft the sky and consorted with the stars ; [2] he, the leader of every god, admirable in command, whom the Great Ennead of gods praised, and the Lesser Ennead [3] loved.

His sister protected him,[4] she that held the foes aloof and warded off the deeds of the *miscreant* by the beneficent things of her mouth,[5] she with the excellent tongue, whose words come not to nought, and admirable in command.

Beneficent Isis, that protected her brother, that sought for him without wearying, that traversed this land mourning, and took no rest until she found him.

She that afforded him shade with her feathers, and with her wings created air. She that cried aloud for joy and brought her brother to land.

She that revived the faintness of the Weary One, that took in his seed and provided an heir, that suckled the child in solitude, the place where he was being unknown, that brought him, when his arm was strong, into the hall of Kēb.

The Ennead cried out full of joy :

> " Welcome, Horus, son of Osiris !
> Stalwart hearted, justified ! [6]
> Son of Isis, heir of Osiris ! "

[1] With light.

[2] It was so tall. The height of the crown is a thing that earthly kings boast about ; this will go back to the earliest times, when the ruler actually wore his crown in order to be visible above all people. In historic times also the crowns were still as much as fifty centimetres high.

[3] The ordinary Ennead comprised the gods up to the generation of Osiris ; for the remaining gods a second " Lesser " Ennead was invented.

[4] Isis protected Osiris ; the murder of the god is passed over as something too terrible to be spoken of.

[5] Her magical spells.

[6] Horus is actually not yet justified, for the trial has not yet taken place.

The Tribunal of Truth assembled for him, the Ennead and the Lord of All himself, the lords of truth that were united therein, that turned their backs on iniquity.

They sat them down in the hall of Kēb with the intent to assign the office to its lord, the kingdom to whom it should be given.

It was found that the word of Horus was true, and the office of his father was given unto him. He came forth crowned by the command of Kēb, he received the lordship of the Two River-banks, and the crown rested securely on his head.

The earth was accounted unto him for his possession (?), and heaven and earth were under his authority. Men, folk, people, mankind [1] were made over to him, Egypt and the Northerners, [2] and what the sun encircleth, were under his governance, the north wind, the river, the flood, the fruit-tree, and all plants.

The corn-god gave all his herbage and (?) sustenance to the glorified one ; [3] he brought (?) satiety and placed it in all lands.

All people were happy, cheerful of mind, and with glad hearts ; all men cried out for joy, and all people adored his goodness : " How deeply we love him ! His goodness traverseth the hearts, and great in all is the love of him.[4]

"They have given his enemies to the son of Isis – – – –. Evil hath been inflicted on the miscreant (?) – – – –.

" The son of Isis hath protected his father, and his name hath been made noble and excellent. Might hath taken its seat, and Prosperity endureth by its ordinances. The roads lie out-spread, and the ways are open.[5]

"How contented are the Two Lands ! Wickedness hath vanished, and evil hath fled. The land is happy under its lord. Right is established for its lord, and the back is turned on iniquity.

" Be glad of heart, Wennōfre ! [6] The son of Isis hath assumed

---

[1] In the original are ancient stereotyped expressions for men, the exact meanings of which are unknown to us.

[2] The " Hautiu-nebt," properly the designation for the peoples of the Mediterranean.

[3] Probably Osiris is meant.

[4] All that follows is still to be regarded as the utterance of men who are rejoicing over the accession of Horus.

[5] Security reigns throughout the land. All these are expressions employed in connection with earthly kings.

[6] Name for Osiris.

the diadem. The office of his father hath been assigned unto him in the hall of Kēb. Rē, he speaketh, Thōth, he writeth,[1] and the tribunal assenteth thereto. Thy father Kēb hath given command [2] for thee (?) and it is done according to that which he spake."

(b) Shorter hymns [3]

Praise to thee, Osiris, son of Nut ! Lord of the horns ; with tall atef-crown ! [4] To whom the crown was given (in) joy in the presence of the Ennead of gods.

He, the reverence for whom Atum hath fashioned in the hearts of men and of gods, of the glorified and of the dead.

He to whom the lordship was given in Heliopolis ; of great estate in Busiris ; fearful in the Two Places, terrible in Rosetau, revered in Ehnas, mighty in Tenent.

The greatly loved upon earth, of goodly memory in the god's palace, that appeared in greatness at Abydos.

He to whom justification was ascribed before the entire Ennead, for whom a slaughtering was made in the great hall at Herwer.

He of whom the great mighty ones were in terror, and before whom the great ones rose up from their mats.

Shu hath inspired fear of him, and Tefnet hath created reverence for him.

The two sanctuaries of Upper and Lower Egypt came making obeisance to him, because the fear of him is so great and the reverence for him so immense.

This one,[5] Osiris, king of gods, the great Mighty One of heaven, and the king of them that are there.[6] Thousands praise him in Babylon,[7] and men are in jubilation over him in Heliopolis. Lord of the portions of meat in the Upper Houses, to whom sacrifice is made in Memphis.

[1] As scribe of the gods.

[2] Meaning ?

[3] Often found on tombstones of the Middle Kingdom, e.g. Louvre, C 30, Leiden, v. 65.

[4] The god wears a crown ornamented with horns.

[5] Upon the tombstone, Louvre, C 30, but as a separate hymn.

[6] In the realm of the dead.

[7] An Egyptian city, the modern Old Cairo.

5. TO THE NILE [1]

The Nile was, it is true, regarded as a god, but unlike the other great divinities he had no regular organized cult.　Thus, this hymn, which is designated *A d o r a t i o n o f t h e N i l e*, is different in character from the old hymns to divinities; it thanks the god for all the blessings which he bestows on men.　It must have been composed for an inundation festival.　This, according to the hymn, took place in Thebes, at a time when it was the city of " a sovereign," thus possibly in the later Hyksōs period.

Praise to thee, O Nile, that issueth from the earth, and cometh to nourish Egypt.　Of hidden nature, a darkness in the daytime – – – –.

That watereth the meadows, he that Rē hath created to nourish all cattle.　That giveth drink to the desert places, which are far from water ; it is his dew that falleth from heaven.[2]

Beloved of Kēb,[3] director of the corn-god ; that maketh to flourish every workshop of Ptah.[4]

Lord of fish, that maketh the water-fowl to go upstream,[5] – – – –.

That maketh barley and createth wheat, so that he may cause the temples to keep festivals.

If he be sluggish,[6] the nostrils are stopped up,[7] and all men are impoverished ; the victuals of the gods are diminished, and millions of men perish.

If he be niggardly (?) the whole land is in terror *and* great and small *lament*. – – – – Khnum hath fashioned him.　When he riseth, the land is in exultation and every body is in joy. All jaws begin to laugh and every tooth is revealed.[8]

---

[1] Preserved in two school manuscripts of the Nineteenth Dynasty, and fragmentarily in a papyrus at Turin and on ostraca.　One of these last-named has made the first verses intelligible, for the rest of the hymn has been completely corrupted by the schoolboys.　See MASPERO, *Hymne au Nil*, Cairo, 1912.

[2] The rain which waters the desert is thus accounted a product of the Nile.

[3] The earth-god.

[4] Ptah, the craftsman, who fashions everything, could effect nothing without the Nile.

[5] To Upper Egypt.

[6] On the occasion of a deficient inundation.

[7] Men no longer breathe and live.　　　　[8] With laughing.

He that bringeth victuals and is rich in food, that createth all that is good. The revered, sweet-smelling – – – –. That createth herbage for the cattle, and giveth sacrifice to every god,[1] be he in the underworld, in heaven, or upon earth – – – –. That filleth the storehouses, and maketh wide the granaries, that giveth things to the poor.

He that maketh trees to grow according to every wish, and men have no lack thereof ; the ship is built by his power, for there is no joinery with stones.[2] *What follows possibly compares him to an invisible king, who imposes no taxes ; where he is, no one knows.*

All that is intelligible is : thy young folk and thy children shout for joy over thee, and men hail thee as king. Unchanging of laws,[3] *when he* cometh forth in the presence of Upper and Lower Egypt. Men drink the water – – – –.

He that was in sorrow is become glad, and every heart is joyful. Sobk, the child of Neith,[4] laugheth, and the divine Ennead, that is in thee,[5] is glorious.

Thou that vomitest forth, giving the fields to drink and making strong the people. He that maketh the one rich and loveth the other. *He maketh no distinctions, and boundaries are not made for him.*

Thou light, that cometh from the darkness ! Thou fat for his cattle ! He is a strong one, that createth . . . (*all the rest unintelligible*).

The beginning is entirely obscure ; then, perhaps, the poem goes on to speak of all going to work in the field : One beholdeth the wealthy as him that is full of care (?), one beholdeth each one with his implements ; – – – – None, that (otherwise) goeth clad, is clad,[6] and the children of notables are unadorned – – – –.

---

[1] By the fact that the cattle flourish.

[2] Timber is a rarity in Egypt, stone a common thing.

[3] Always at the same time.

[4] Sobk has the form of a crocodile and will originally have been a water-god, who rejoices in the inundation.

[5] Meaning ?   [6] For hard work, clothes are taken off.

He that establisheth right, whom men love. – – – –. *It would be but lies to compare* (?) *thee with* the sea, that bringeth no corn. – – – – no bird descendeth in the desert.

Farther on, mention is made of gold *and of* ingots of silver, *which avail nothing* ; men eat not real lapis lazuli ; barley *is better*.

Men begin to play to thee on the harp, and men sing to thee with the hand.[1] Thy young folk and thy children shout for joy over thee, and deputations [2] to thee are appointed.

He that cometh with splendid things and adorneth the earth ! That causeth the ship to prosper before (?) men ; that quickeneth the hearts in them that are with child ; that would fain have there be a multitude of all kinds of cattle.

When thou art risen in the city of the sovereign,[3] then men are satisfied with a goodly list.[4] " I would like lotus flowers," saith the little one, " and all manner of things," saith the . . . commander, " and all manner of herbs," say the children. Eating bringeth forgetfulness of him.[5] Good things are scattered over the dwelling – – – –.

When the Nile floodeth, offering is made to thee, cattle are slaughtered for thee, a great oblation is made for thee. Birds are fattened for thee, antelopes are hunted for thee in the desert. Good is recompensed unto thee.

Offering is also made to every other god, even as is done for the Nile, with incense, oxen, cattle, and birds (upon ?) the flame. The Nile hath made him his cave in Thebes, and his name shall be known no more in the underworld [6] – – – –.

All ye men, extol the Nine Gods, and stand in awe of the might which his son, the Lord of All,[7] *hath displayed*, even he

[1] It is an old custom to beat time with the hand while singing.

[2] To greet thee.

[3] When the inundation has reached the royal residence.

[4] *I.e.* a multitude of good things.

[5] The Nile.

[6] He will henceforth abide in Thebes, where he is so well fêted. His original home knows him no more.

[7] Whose son ? Is the king the subject of discussion, or the Nile ?

that maketh green the Two River-banks. Thou art verdant,
O Nile, thou art verdant.[1] He that maketh man to live on
his cattle, and his cattle on the meadow ! Thou art verdant,
thou art verdant ; O Nile, thou art verdant.

[1] *I.e.* thou dost flourish ; however, the formula should perhaps be
understood quite differently.

III. FROM THE NEW KINGDOM

(So far as not stated to the contrary, in New Egyptian throughout)

A. NARRATIVES

1. THE TALE OF THE TWO BROTHERS [1]

IN form and contents this is more naïve and more racy of the soil than any Egyptian tale that we possess, and we may congratulate ourselves that the young scribe Ennana,[2] who was a pupil of the scribe of the treasury Kagabu, copied out so entirely an unliterary piece of writing.

This delightful story is certainly based on a myth, as is shown by the names of the two brothers. The one is called Anubis, like the ancient jackal-god of the dead ; and if the other, Bata, does not possess so distinguished a namesake, he is also, however, a divine being, for in the Upper Egyptian town of Saka, in the period of the New Kingdom, a god called Bata [3] was worshipped side by side with the chief local divinity Anubis.

It will accordingly be a myth belonging to this town that the story-teller has here transferred to the sphere of human activities, a transference, thanks to which it has acquired a charm that it could scarcely have possessed as a mere legend about the gods.

The world, however, in which the events related take place is, naturally, not the actual world, but the supernatural world of faerie, in which the cedar has large blossoms, oxen speak, and all kinds of marvellous and impossible things occur. Two incidents in the story, which are puzzling at first, have been unexpectedly explained by comparison with other folk-tales.

It is related that there were once two brothers by one mother and one father ; and the name of the elder was Anubis,

---

[1] Preserved in the so-called *Papyrus d'Orbiney* in the British Museum. Already brought to notice by de Rougé in 1852, and since then frequently translated. See, *e.g.*, GRIFFITH in *The World's Best Literature*, p. 5253 ; MASPERO, *Contes populaires*[4], pp. 1 ff.

[2] He lived under Merneptah and Sēthos II, towards the end of the Nineteenth Dynasty (*circa* 1200 B.C.).

[3] In view of the writing of the name, it must be of quite late origin. See my note below in the poem on the king's war-chariot, p. 281.

and the name of the younger Bata. Now Anubis, he had an house and he had a wife, while his younger brother dwelt with him as a son. It was he who made clothes for him, tended his cattle in the field, ploughed and reaped for him, and did for him all the tasks that are in the field. Yea, his younger brother was a good husbandman, who had not his equal in the whole land, and the strength (?) of a god was in him.

Now many days after this [1] his younger brother tended his cattle, as he did every day, and he came home to his house every evening laden with all manner of herbs of the field, and with milk, and with . . . wood [2] of the field, and set it down before his elder brother, while he sat with his wife ; and then he drank and ate, and (laid him down to sleep) in his stall, and (kept watch over) his kine.

Now when it was dawn and another day had come, [3] he (made ready) cooked (victuals) and set them before his elder brother, and he gave him bread for the field, and he drave out his cattle in order to pasture them in the field. He walked behind his cattle, and they said unto him : " The herbage is good in such and such a place," and he heard all that they said and took them to the place where was the good herbage which they desired. Thus the cattle which he tended flourished exceedingly and calved very, very often.

Now at the season of ploughing his elder brother said unto him : " Make ready an yoke (of oxen) for ploughing, for the land hath come forth and it is now good for ploughing. [4] Also come to the field with seed, for we will plough with a will in the early morn." So spake he unto him, and his younger brother did all the things that his elder brother said unto him, " Do them."

Now when day dawned and another day had come, they went afield with their . . . and ploughed with a will, and were exceeding glad of heart because of their work at their beginning of work. [5]

And many days after this they were in the field and were

---

[1] One of those formulæ of unsophisticated narrative that have quite lost their real meaning.

[2] Is dry wood for fuel meant ?

[3] Formula, as note 1 above.

[4] The inundation has so far subsided.

[5] The commencement of the year's agriculture.

short of seed. And he sent his younger brother, saying : "Go and fetch us seed from the village." And his younger brother found the wife of his elder brother as she sat having her hair done. And he said unto her : "Up, and give me seed, that I may go to the field, for mine elder brother waiteth for me. Tarry not."

And she said unto him : "Go, open the bin (thyself), and take away for thee what thou willest ; make me not to leave unfinished the dressing of my hair."

And the lad went into his stall and took a great vessel, with the intent to take away much seed. And he loaded himself with barley and wheat and went out with it. And she said unto him : "How much is it that thou hast upon thy shoulder ? " And he said unto her : "Three sacks of wheat and two sacks of barley, five in all, have I upon my shoulder." So spake he unto her. And she . . . and said : "Then thou hast great strength. Yea, I see daily how strong thou art." And her desire was to know him as one knoweth a youth.

And she arose and took hold of him and said : " Come, we will take our pleasure and sleep. It will also be for thine advantage, for I will make thee goodly garments."

And the lad became enraged like a leopard . . . at this wicked thing which she said unto him, and she was sore afraid. And he spake unto her, saying : " Lo, thou art unto me as a mother, and thine husband is unto me as a father, for as the elder hath he brought me up. What is this great abomination that thou hast spoken ? Say it not again unto me. But I will tell it to no man, and will not suffer it to come forth from my mouth to any man." And he took up his burden and went into the field. And he came to his elder brother, and they worked at their work with a will.

Then at eventide his elder brother went home to his house, but his younger brother tended his cattle, and loaded himself with all manner of things of the field, and he drave his cattle before him, in order to let them sleep in their stall in the village.

Now the wife of his elder brother was afraid because of that which she had said. So she took fat and . . .,[1] and made as though she had been cruelly beaten, desiring to say to her

---

[1] Apparently another word for " fat," but how the woman could attain her end by that means is not clear. Does she thus cause the subsequently mentioned vomiting ?

husband : " It was thy younger brother that did beat me." And
her husband came home at even, as was his daily wont. He came
to his house and found his wife lying down and made cruelly
sick. She poured no water upon his hands according to his
wont ; she had kindled no light against his return, and his
house was in darkness ; and there she lay and vomited. And
her husband said unto her : " Who hath spoken with thee ? "
And she said unto him : " No one hath spoken with me save
thy younger brother. When he came to fetch the seed and
found me sitting all alone, he said unto me : ' Come, we will
take our pleasure and sleep. Put on thy ringlets.' [1] So spake
he unto me, but I heeded him not. ' Lo, am I not thy mother,
and thine elder brother is unto thee as a father,' so spake I unto
him. Then he was afraid, and he beat me so that I might not
report it unto thee. If, therefore, thou sufferest him to live,
I will take mine own life ; for behold, when he cometh home at
even and I tell this evil tale, he will have made it (look) white."

Then his elder brother became (enraged) as a leopard, and
made his lance sharp and took it in his hand.

And his elder brother took up his stand behind the door of
his stall, in order to slay his younger brother, when he came
home at even to drive his cattle into the stall.

And when the sun set, he loaded himself with all herbs of
the field, according to his daily wont. He came, and the first
cow entered the stall. And she said unto her herdsman : " Have
a care ! Thine elder brother standeth before thee with his lance,
in order to slay thee. Flee from before him." And he understood what his first cow said. The next entered, and she said
likewise. And he looked under the door of his stall and saw
the feet of his elder brother, as he stood behind the door with
his lance in his hand. So he laid his load down on the ground
and started to run away quickly, and his elder brother pursued
after him with his lance.

And his younger brother called to Rē-Harakhti, saying :
" My good lord, thou art he that judgest between the wrong-
doer and the righteous ! " And Rē heard all his petitions, and
Rē caused a great stretch of water, that was full of crocodiles,
to spring up between him and his elder brother, and one of them

---

[1] Literally, " Clothe thee with thy ringlets," probably meaning that
she is to put on the great wig which Egyptian women wore over their
own hair for show.

came to be upon the one side and the other upon the other. And his elder brother smote twice upon his hand,[1] because he had not slain him.

And his younger brother called to him from the (other) side, saying : " Abide here until day-break.   When the sun ariseth, I will be judged with thee in his presence, and he will give the wrong-doer to the righteous.[2]   For I will never more be with thee, nor be in a place where thou art.   I will go to the Valley of the Cedar."[3]   Now, when it was dawn and another day had come, Rē-Harakhti arose, and the one beheld the other.   And the lad communed with his elder brother, saying : " What meaneth thy pursuing after me in order to slay me by guile, without first hearing what I had to say ?   For I am indeed thy younger brother, and thou art unto me as a father and thy wife is unto me as a mother.   Is it not so ?   Now when I was sent to fetch us seed, thy wife said unto me : ' Come, let us take our pleasure and sleep.'   But behold, that hath been perverted for thee into some different thing."   And he acquainted him with all that had befallen him with his wife.

And he swore by Rē-Harakhti, saying :   " Alas, that thou desiredst to slay me by guile, and didst (take) thy lance on the word of a dirty (?) strumpet ! "[4]   And he took a reed knife [5] and cut off his privy member and cast it unto the water, and the shad swallowed it.[6]   And he was faint and became wretched.   And his elder brother was exceeding sorrowful, and stood and wept loudly (?) over him, yet could he not cross over to where his younger brother was because of the crocodiles.

Then his younger brother cried unto him, saying : " If thou hast thought of an evil thing, wilt thou not think of a good thing, or of something that I (also) might do for thee ?[7]   Go now to thine house, and (thyself) tend thy cattle, for I will no more abide in the place where thou art.   I shall go away to the

---

[1] In vexation.   [2] Meaning : let the righteous triumph.

[3] This name may well have been derived from accounts of the Lebanon, whence the Egyptians from early times obtained their timber.

[4] The expression is still coarser.

[5] Probably not a knife for cutting reeds, but a sharp reed-stalk growing by the water.

[6] Why he mutilated himself is obscure ; the swallowing of the member by the fish is an incident in the Osiris legend.

[7] He means the immediately following request—to betake himself to him in time of need.

Valley of the Cedar. Now as for what thou shalt do for me, it is that thou art to come to tend me, if thou learnest that ought hath befallen me. *Now it will come to pass* that I shall take mine heart and place it on the top of the flower of the cedar.[1] If the cedar be hewn down and fall to the ground, and thou comest to seek it—if thou spendest seven years seeking for it, grow not weary thereof. And when thou findest it and placest it in a pot of cold water, I shall live again [2] and make answer to the trespass committed against me. Hereby thou wilt learn that mischief hath befallen me, in that one handeth thee a bowl of beer and it fermenteth. Then tarry not, for this concerneth thee (?)."

And he went away to the Valley of the Cedar, and his elder brother went unto his house, his hand laid on his head,[3] and he was smeared with mud.[3] And he came unto his house, and he slew his wife, cast her to the dogs, and sat mourning for his younger brother.

And many days after this his younger brother was in the Valley of the Cedar, and there was none with him. And he spent the day hunting the game of the desert, and at even he came to sleep under the cedar, on the top of the flower whereof lay his heart.

And many days after this he built him a castle in the Valley of the Cedar, and it was full of all good things, because he wished to set up house for himself.

And (one day) he went forth from his castle, and he met the Nine Gods, as they went and surveyed their whole land. And the Nine Gods spake with one (mouth ?) and said unto him : " Ho, Bata, thou bull of the Nine Gods ! [4] Art thou here alone, and hast left thy city before the wife of Anubis thine elder brother ? Behold, his wife is slain, for thou hast made clear to him all the trespass committed against thee." And they had great compassion on him. And Rē-Harakhti said unto Khnum : [5]

[1] The heart is thus made safe against enemies and thereby secured to the person to whom it belongs. The same feature also appears in the stories of other peoples, particularly clearly in a Norwegian tale (see MAX BURCHARDT, *Zeitschr. für ägypt. Sprache*, l. p. 18.)

[2] In a Hottentot story the heart of a dead girl is placed in milk and sucks it up, and the girl then comes to life again (see *loc. cit.*).

[3] Token of grief.

[4] This is elsewhere a designation for gods, particularly for the moon.

[5] Who creates men severally ; see p. 44, note 2 ; p. 95, note 1.

" Do thou fashion a wife for Bata, that he may not dwell alone."
And Khnum made him a companion that had fairer limbs than
any woman in the whole land, and every god was in her.[1]

And the seven Hathors [2] came to see her and said with one
mouth : " She will die a violent death."

And he was greatly enamoured of her, and she dwelt
in his house. And he spent the day hunting the game of the
desert, and brought it and laid it before her. And he said unto
her : " Go not out, lest the sea carry thee away ; for I cannot
rescue thee from it, because I am a woman even as thou. Mine
heart lieth on the top of the flower of the cedar, and if another
find it, I am in his power (?)." And he opened to her his heart
in its fullness.

And many days after this Bata went to hunt, according to
his daily wont. Then went the maiden forth to walk about
under the cedar which was beside her house. And the sea saw
her and swept up behind her, and she started to run from before
it, and went into the house. But the sea called to the cedar,
saying : " Catch hold of her for me." And the cedar took away
a lock of her hair ; and the sea brought it to Egypt, and laid it
in the place in which were the fullers of Pharaoh.[3]

And the smell of the lock of hair got into the garments of
Pharaoh, and One [4] contended with the fullers of Pharaoh,
saying : " The smell of unguent is in the garments of Pharaoh." [5]
And One contended with them daily, and they wist not what
they should do. And the chief fuller of Pharaoh went to the
river-bank and was sore vexed because of these daily conten-
tions. And he stood still upon the sand,[6] and took his stand
over against the lock of hair that was in the water. And he
caused some one to go down (into the water), and it was brought

---

[1] *I.e.* something of the divine essence.

[2] The ancient sky-goddess Hathor, who at an early date had become
the goddess of women and love, has assumed in these stories the rôle of
fairies. Similarly in the following tale.

[3] Of course on the Nile near the Residence ; that the lock has floated
up the river from the sea is no matter for wonder in this world of marvels !

[4] The writing shows that " one," as often, denotes the king.

[5] The Egyptian method of anointing resulted in the unguent trickling
down from the head on to the clothes. It was therefore a sign of bad
washing if the clean linen still smelt of unguent.

[6] Literally, "the desert" ; what is meant is the sand-bank deposited
by the current on the river's edge.

unto him; and there was found an exceeding sweet smell. And he took it to Pharaoh.

Then were fetched the scribes and wise men of Pharaoh,[1] and they said unto Pharaoh: " This lock of hair belongeth to a daughter of Rē-Harakhti, and the essence of every god is in her. Yea, it is a present for thee from another land. Send messengers unto every land to seek for her. But as for the messenger that is bound for the Valley of the Cedar, with him send thou many men in order to fetch her hither."[2] And his majesty said: " What ye have said is very good." And (the men) were sent.

And many days after this, the men that had gone abroad came back to render report to his majesty, albeit they that had gone to the Valley of the Cedar came not back, for Bata had slain them, leaving only one of them to render report to his majesty.

And his majesty sent again many soldiers, and chariotry likewise, to fetch her back, and with them was a woman, into whose hand was given all manner of goodly adornment for a woman. And the woman came with her to Egypt, and there was rejoicing over her in the whole land.

And his majesty loved her exceedingly, and appointed her Great Princess.[3] And One held converse with her, that she might tell how the matter stood with her husband. And she said unto his majesty: " Have the cedar cut down and destroyed." So soldiers were sent with their weapons to cut down the cedar; and they came to the cedar and cut off the flower upon which was the heart of Bata, and on the instant he fell down dead.

Now when it was dawn and another day had come, and the cedar was cut down, Anubis, the elder brother of Bata, went into his house and sat down and washed his hands.[4] And there was given unto him a bowl of beer, and it had fermented, and there was given him another of wine, and it had gone bad.

[1] These are naturally not actual official terms, but popular expressions for the " wise men."

[2] That she should be sought for in all lands, when it is already known where she is to be found, is altogether too naïve even for a fairy-tale.

[3] Literally: " the august, the great lady "; here a rank in the royal *harim*. Later on she is actually spoken of as the consort of the king. " One " is again Pharaoh.

[4] Before partaking of a meal.

Then took he his staff and his sandals, his garments likewise and his weapons, and he started off to go unto the Valley of the Cedar. He entered the castle of his younger brother, and he found his younger brother lying on his bed, and he was dead. And he wept when he beheld his younger brother lying thus dead, and he went to seek for the heart of his younger brother under the cedar, whereunder his younger brother was wont to sleep at even. He spent three years seeking it, and found it not. But when he had begun the fourth year, his heart longed to come back to Egypt, and he said : " I will depart on the morrow." So said he in his heart.

Now when it was dawn and another day had come, he began to walk under the cedar, and he spent the whole day seeking it. And he ceased at even, and looked once more (only) to seek it, and he found a fruit. And he went home with it, and lo, this was the heart of his younger brother. And he brought a cup of cold water and dropped it into it, and sat down as was his daily wont.

And when it was night and his heart had sucked up the water, Bata shuddered in all his limbs and began to look at his elder brother, while his heart was still in the cup. Then Anubis, his elder brother, took the cup of cold water, in which was the heart of his younger brother, and gave it him to drink. And when his heart stood in its place, he became as he had been. And they embraced one another, and the one communed with the other.

And Bata said unto his elder brother : " Behold, I shall become a great bull, that is of every goodly colour,[1] whose nature none knoweth, and thou shalt set thee on my back. When the sun ariseth we shall be in the place where my wife is, that I may return answer to her. And thou shalt take me to where the king is, for there shalt be done for thee all manner of good things. Thou shalt be rewarded with silver and gold for taking me to Pharaoh, because I shall become a great wonder, and men will rejoice over me in the whole land. And thou shalt then depart to thine own village."

Now when it was dawn and another day had come, Bata took upon him the form whereof he had spoken to his elder brother. And Anubis, his elder brother, sat him upon his back.

[1] The markings are meant, by which sacred oxen, like the Apis, were recognized ; this will be one of a kind unheard of.

At dawn he came to where the king was. And his majesty was informed about him, and he examined him himself, and rejoiced over him exceedingly. And he presented unto him two great offerings, saying : " A great marvel is this that hath come to pass." And they rejoiced over him in the whole land.

And they made up his weight in silver and gold for his elder brother, and he settled down in his village. And One [1] gave him much people and much gear, and Pharaoh loved him exceedingly, more than all people that were in the whole land.

And many days after this, he [2] entered the kitchen,[3] and stood in the place where the princess was. And he began to commune with her, saying : " Behold, I am yet alive." She said unto him : " Who art thou, pray ? " He said unto her : " I am Bata. (Surely) thou knowest when thou didst cause Pharaoh to destroy the cedar at thy (?) bidding, that I might no longer live ? But behold, I am now alive and am a bull." Then was the princess sore afraid because of the tale which her husband had told her.

And he went forth from the kitchen. And his majesty sat and made merry with her ; and she poured out for his majesty, and One [4] was very gracious towards her. Then said she unto his majesty : " Swear to me by God, saying : ' Whatsoever thou shalt say, I will hearken unto it for thee.' " And he hearkened unto all that she said. " Let me eat of the liver of this bull, for he will not do anything," [5] she said unto him. And One [4] was distressed exceedingly, because of what she had said, and Pharaoh's heart was very sore for him.

Now when it was dawn and another day had come, a great sacrificial festival was proclaimed, as a sacrifice of the bull.[6] And the chief butcher of his majesty was sent to slaughter the bull. And thereafter he was slaughtered. And when he now lay upon the shoulders of the men, he shook (?) his neck and caused two drops of blood to fall beside the two door-posts (?) of his majesty, and the one fell upon the one side of the great portal of Pharaoh, and the other upon the other. And they grew into two great persea trees, each of which was excellent. And one went to say unto his majesty : " Two great persea

[1] The king.   [2] The bull.
[3] A general expression for the domestic offices.
[4] The king.   [5] He is good for nothing.
[6] The sacred animal is anyhow to meet his end at a festival.

trees are grown up as a great wonder for his majesty in the night, beside the great portal of his majesty." And they rejoiced over them in the whole land, and One [1] made offering unto them.

And many days after this his majesty appeared in the window of lapis lazuli,[2] and he had a garland of all manner of flowers about his neck, and he was upon a chariot of gold and drove forth from the palace to see the persea trees. And the princess rode forth on horseback [3] behind Pharaoh.

And his majesty sat down under one of the persea trees. Then (Bata) spake with his wife : " Ah, thou false one ! I am Bata. I yet live in spite (?) of thee. (Surely) thou knowest how thou didst cause Pharaoh to cut down (the cedar) at thy (?) bidding ! And I became a bull, and thou hadst me slaughtered."

And many days after this the princess arose and poured out for his majesty, and One [4] was very gracious towards her. And she said unto his majesty : " Swear to me by God, saying : ' Whatsoever the princess saith to me, I will hearken unto it.' Thus shalt thou speak." And he hearkened unto all that she said. And she said : " Have the two persea trees cut down, and make them into goodly furniture." And One hearkened unto all that she said.

And many days after this his majesty sent cunning craftsmen, and the persea trees (of Pharaoh) were cut down. And Pharaoh stood to behold (together with) the consort of the king, the princess. And a splinter flew off and entered the mouth of the princess, and she swallowed it, and in the same moment she conceived. And there was made of them all / that she desired.[5]

And many days after this she bore a son. And one went and told his majesty : " A son is born to thee." And he was brought in, and there were given unto him a nurse and attendants. And there was rejoicing in the whole land, and One sat down and made merry. And he was brought up (?), and straightway his majesty loved him exceedingly, and he was appointed King's Son of Ethiopia.[6]

[1] The king.
[2] The state window of the palace, in which the king showed himself on ceremonial occasions. After this a sentence is probably missing.
[3] This probably only means that she rode in a chariot.
[4] The king.
[5] Namely, the articles of furniture from the trees.
[6] The title of the viceroy of Nubia in the New Kingdom

And many days after this his majesty made him crown prince for the whole land.

And many days after this, when he had passed many years as crown prince in the whole land, his majesty flew into heaven.[1] And One [2] said : " Let my great royal counsellors be brought unto me, that I may acquaint them of all things that have befallen me." And his wife was brought unto him, and he entered into judgment with her before them, and they were in agreement with him concerning it.[3] And his elder brother was brought unto him, and he appointed him crown prince in his whole land. And he was thirty years king of Egypt ; and he departed this life, and his elder brother stood in his place on the day of his death.

2. THE ENCHANTED PRINCE [4]

I have not changed the title under which this tale was first introduced into Germany by Georg Ebers. It is, of course, quite unsuitable, for mention is never made of any enchantment. The tale would more rightly be entitled *The Foredoomed Prince*, as, although the end is missing, it is obvious that, in spite of all precautions, the prince was overtaken by his fate.

The story has something of what might be called a romantic air about it, and if the crocodile were eliminated and the names changed, it might quite as well belong to our world of fairy tales as to that of Ancient Egypt.

There was once a king to whom no son was born. So he prayed the gods whom he served for a son, and they decreed that one should be born to him. That night he slept with his wife, and she conceived. And when she had fulfilled the months of childbirth, a son was born.

Then the Hathors [5] came to decree him his destiny, and they

---

[1] Died. [2] The new king.

[3] The sentence and punishment are not recounted, being taken for granted and also regarded as an unpleasant topic.

[4] *Pap. Harris*, 500, verso, 4–8 (see BUDGE, *Facsimiles of Egyptian Hieratic Papyri in the British Museum*, second series, Pls. xlviii.–lii.), written in the reign of Ramesses II. Brought to notice by Goodwin ; often translated, *e.g.* by GRIFFITH in *The World's Best Literature*, pp. 5250 ff. ; MASPERO, *Contes populaires*, pp. 196 ff. ; PEET, *Journ. of Egypt. Archæology*, xi. pp. 227 ff.

[5] See above, p. 156, note 2.

said : " He shall die either by the crocodile, or by the snake, or by the dog."

The people who were about the child heard [1] that, and repeated it to his majesty. And his majesty became very, very sad of heart.

And his majesty had built for him an house of stone in the desert, that was equipped with people and all good things of the palace, and the child went not out of it.

Now when the child grew up, he went up on to his roof, and descried a greyhound that was following a man who was walking upon the road. And he said unto his servant that was beside him : " What is this that goeth behind the man that cometh along the road ? " And he said unto him : " It is a greyhound." And the lad said unto him : " Let one like it be brought to me also." Then went the servant and told it to his majesty. And his majesty said : " Let a little one that jumpeth about [2] be taken to him, that his heart be not grieved." [3] So the greyhound was taken to him.

Now when the days had gone by after this, the child was full grown in all his body. And he sent unto his father, saying : " To what purpose is it that I sit here ? Lo, I am doomed to the three destinies. It should therefore be granted me to do according to my desire ; God will do that which is in his heart." Then there was given unto him a chariot fully equipped with all manner of weapons, and (there was given unto him) his (servant) as henchman. And he was conveyed over to the eastern side, and it was said unto him : " Go as thou willest," and his greyhound was with him.

And he journeyed northwards, according to his pleasure, through the wilderness, and lived on the choicest of all the wild beasts of the desert. And so came he to the prince of Naharina.

Now the prince of Naharina had no child save a daughter. And he had built an house for her, the window whereof was seventy cubits distant from the ground. And he caused all the children of all the princes of the land of Kharu [4] to be brought, and he said unto them : " Whosoever shall reach the window of my daughter, he shall have her to wife."

[1] The goddesses were thus invisible.
[2] The king thinks a " little " dog could do no harm.
[3] Or possibly, " for his heart is sore."
[4] Palestine, whereas Naharina lies on the upper Euphrates.

Now when many days had gone by after this, and they were occupied as they were daily wont, the lad passed by them. Then took they the lad to their house, and they bathed him, gave his span provender, did every (good) thing for the lad, anointed him, wrapped up his feet,[1] and gave bread unto his henchman. And they said unto him, by way of discourse : [2] " Whence comest thou, fair youth ? " He said unto them : " I am a son of an officer of the land of Egypt.[3] My mother died, and my father took to him another wife, a stepmother (?). She began to hate me, and so I came fleeing from before her." And they embraced him and kissed him very many times.[4]

Now when many days had gone by after this, he said unto the youths : " What is it (that ye) do ? " *They answered him :* " Whosoever shall reach the window of the daughter of the prince of Naharina, to him will he give her to wife." And he said unto them : " Would that I could also. If I might enchant (?) my feet, I would also go to climb up with you." So they went to climb, as was their daily wont, and the lad stood afar off and watched, and the glance of the daughter of the prince of Naharina (lighted) upon him.

Now when (many days) had gone by after this, the lad came also to climb with the lads of the princes. He climbed, and he reached the window of the daughter of the prince of Naharina. And she kissed him and embraced him very many times.

Then went they to rejoice the heart of her father with these tidings, and said unto him : " A man hath reached the window of thy daughter." And the prince asked him, saying : " Whose son among the princes is it ? " And they said unto him : " It is the son of an officer, that hath come fleeing from the land of Egypt from before his stepmother (?)." Then the prince of Naharina waxed exceeding wroth, and said : " Shall I give my daughter to the Egyptian runaway ? Let him take himself off again."

And they came and said unto him : " Get thee back to the place whence thou art come." But the daughter took hold of him and swore by God : " By Rē-Harakhti ! If he is taken

---

[1] What does this mean ?

[2] The chivalrous children of the princes are well brought up and do not pump him !

[3] Why he makes this false assertion is not revealed by what follows.

[4] Literally : on all his body.

from me, I will not eat, I will not drink, I will die straightway."
And the messenger went and related to her father all that she
had said.

Then the prince sent men to slay him there and then.
And the daughter said unto them : " By Rē ! If he is slain—
when the sun sets, I too am dead. I live not an hour longer
than he." So they went and told it to her father.

The prince had the lad and his daughter summoned – – – –.
He embraced him and kissed him very many times. And he said
unto him : " Tell me of thy condition, for behold, thou art as
a son unto me." And he said unto him : " I am the son of an
officer of the land of Egypt. My mother died, and my father
took to him another wife. And she began to hate me, and I
came fleeing from before her."

Then he gave him his daughter to wife, and he gave him
an house and lands, and cattle likewise, and every good thing.

And when (many days) had gone by after this, the youth
said unto his wife : " I am doomed to three destinies—the
crocodile, the snake, and the dog." And she said unto him :
" Have the greyhound that followeth thee slain." He said
unto her : " (By Rē !) I will not have my greyhound slain, which
I brought up when it was yet little." So she began to guard
her husband carefully, and suffered him not to go out alone.

But the youth . . . the land of Egypt to wander about.[1]
And the crocodile of the lake – – – – it came against him in the
town in which the youth was – – – –. Now there was a
mighty man [2] in it, and the mighty man suffered not the crocodile to come forth – – – –. *When the crocodile slept* (?), the
mighty man came forth to stroll about. And when the sun
arose, they stood . . ., the two of them, every day for the space
of two months.

Now when (many) days had gone by after this, the youth
sat him down and made merry in his house. And when the
night came, the youth slept upon his bed, and sleep prevailed
over all his limbs. Then his wife filled a bowl (with) . . . and
another bowl with beer. And a (snake came out of its) hole
to bite the youth, but his wife sat beside him and slept not.
The maidservants (?) *gave* the snake the beer, and it drank and

---

[1] This probably implies that he journeys to Egypt.

[2] Or rather " water-spirit " ; see PEET, *op. cit.* p. 228, note 2 [Trans-
lator].

became drunken, and went to sleep *and lay on its back* (?).   *And his wife hewed it* in pieces with her axe.   And they awoke her husband – – – – and she said unto him : " Behold, thy god hath given one of thy destinies into thine hand.   He will *also give thee the others."*   Then she made an oblation to Rē, and worshipped him, and daily extolled his power.

Now when (many days had gone by after this), the youth went forth to stroll about upon the . . . in his domain (?) ; – – – – and his dog followed him.   Then his dog seized upon – – – – ran in front of him.   And he came to the lake and went down – – – – *after his* dog.[1]   Then the crocodile carried (? him off and took him to the place wherein was the mighty man – – – –.   And the crocodile said unto the youth : " I am thy destiny, that (?) followeth thee. – – – – But behold, I will let thee go . . ."   *The crocodile then speaks of the* slaying of the mighty man, *etc., and finally gives him a sign :* " but when thou seest . . .," *all unfortunately destroyed.*

Now when it was dawn and another day had come, there came—*we cannot guess who.   But the end of the story certainly was that the good dog unwittingly brought his master's life to an end.*

3. KING APŌPHIS AND SEKENENRĒ [2]

Sekenenrē was a prince of Thebes under the suzerainty of the Hyksōs, whose yoke he finally succeeded in throwing off.   The tale is probably a narrative of the events leading up to this struggle with his overlord, the Hyksōs king Apōphis.   Unfortunately, only the beginning of the tale is preserved, and even that is full of long lacunæ ; it has, moreover, been sadly corrupted by the ignorant schoolboy who had to copy it out.

The papyrus was written under King Merneptah (*circa* 1230 B.C.), and the composition itself is not necessarily much older.

Now it came to pass that the land of Egypt was in distress (?), and there was no sovereign (as) king – – – –.

And King Sekenenrē, he was (at that time only) ruler of the Southern City [3] – – – – Apōphis was in Avaris,[4] and the

---

[1] The dog probably seized something in play, the youth wanted to take it from him and so ca me to the lake.

[2] *Pap. Sallier*, i. 1–3, in the British Museum.   Its purport recognized by de Rougé as long ago as 1854, and since then frequently dealt with. See GARDINER, *Journ. of Egypt. Archæology*, v. pp. 36 ff.

[3] Thebes.

[4] The capital of the Hyksōs, on the north-east frontier of Egypt.

whole land paid him tribute with its dues. (The South paid tribute to him ?), and likewise the North, with all the goodly products of the Delta.

And King Apōphis took to him Sutekh[1] for lord, and served not any god that was in the whole land save only Sutekh. He built (him) a temple in good everlasting work. *He had* offerings made daily *to Sutekh, and the* councillors *of the king stood there* with flowers, even as is done for the temple of Rē-Harakhti.

From all that follows it is to be conjectured that King Apōphis felt himself somehow or other aggrieved by his vassal, and sought for an accusation against him. He called the scribes and wise men,[2] *and they advised him to complain of the " hippopotamus canal " which robbed him of sleep. At the same time the wise men remark that Sekenenrē undoubtedly has Amūn* with him as protector, he relieth not on any god that is in the whole land, save Amunrē, king of gods.

Now many days after this King Apōphis sent unto the prince of the Southern City concerning the . . . accusation which his scribes and wise men had said unto him. And the messenger, whom King Apōphis had sent, reached the prince of the Southern City ; and he was taken into the presence of the prince of the Southern City. And One[3] said to the messenger of King Apōphis : " Wherefore art thou sent to the Southern City ; and wherefore didst *thou venture upon* the joyrney ? " And the messenger said unto him : " It is King Apōphis that sendeth me to thee, saying : ' Cause to be abandoned (?) the hippopotamus canal, that lieth in the Well-spring of the City,[4] for it suffereth not sleep to come to me either by day or by night ; its noise is in mine (?) ear.' "[5]

And the prince of the Southern City lamented and wept a long time, and it befell-him that he could not answer the messenger of King Apōphis. *Finally he promised :* " All that thou

[1] This is not a foreign god, but a form of Sēth worshipped in the Delta.

[2] See p. 157, note 1.   [3] The king.

[4] The name of a district ?

[5] This need only mean that Apōphis believes he has a right to this canal : he hears how the canal cries out for its rightful owner. On the other hand, this statement may possibly be just some element from a folk-tale, and it may be questioned whether the hippopotami in the canal are not supposed to bellow so loudly that the king hears, or alleges he hears, the noise in far-off Avaris.

sayest to me (?) I will do." *Then the messenger of King* Apōphis betook him to journey to the place where his lord was.

And the prince of the Southern City had his great councillors summoned, and likewise the officers and leaders of the host that he had, and repeated to them every accusation concerning which King Apōphis had sent unto him. And they were silent with one accord for a long time, and knew not what to answer him, whether good or bad.

And King Apōphis sent unto – – – –.

4. THE CAPTURE OF JOPPA [1]

The tale is concerned with an otherwise unknown incident in the wars of Thutmōsis III (1478–1447 B.C.). On the other hand, we are probably acquainted with the hero of the tale, General Thutii. Among the contemporaries of Thutmōsis III, whose tombs are preserved to us at Thebes, there is also a Thuti, who must have been one of this sovereign's most important generals and diplomatists. He speaks of himself as " Confidant of the King in all Foreign Countries and in the Isles in the midst of the Sea " ; he was " Superintendent of the Northern Countries " ; he was also " General " and " accompanied the King in all Foreign Lands." His dagger is in the possession of the Museum at Darmstadt, and a gold dish, which the king presented to him, is in the Louvre. He was apparently a great personality, whose name was familiar even to subsequent generations.

Joppa is the well-known port in southern Palestine, on the road to the north.

Only the end of the tale is preserved, but the situation is quite clear. The king himself is still in Egypt, the general is besieging Joppa, and, since he cannot take the town by assault, he has recourse to a stratagem. He entices its prince out of the city to a conference, entertains him, and tells him in confidence that he will come over to his side ; he will also hand over to him his wife and children.

– – – – the troops of Pharaoh – – – –.

Now after an hour, when they were drunken, Thutii said unto (the prince of Joppa) : " *I will come to thee* with my wife and child (into) thine own city. *Let the grooms (?) bring hither the horses and give* them provender. Or an Aper [2] may also

---

[1] *Pap. Harris*, 500, verso, 1–3 (see above, p. 161, note 4). Brought to notice by Goodwin in 1874. See MASPERO, *Contes populaires*[4], pp. 115 ff. ; PEET, *Journ. of Egypt. Archæology*, xi. pp. 226 f.

[2] Aper is apparently the name for a body of foreign troops in Egyptian service.

– – – –." Then they laid hold on the horses and gave them provender.[1]

Then the prince of Joppa desired also to see the club of King Thutmōsis,[2] and one came and told it to Thutii. *And the prince of Joppa came* and said to Thutii : " My desire is to see the great club of King Thutmōsis, which is called ' The Beauteous . . .' By King Thutmōsis, thou hast it with thee to-day ! *Be so good (?)*, and bring it me ! " And he did so, and brought the club of King Thutmōsis – – – –. And he stood before him and said : " Look at me, O Prince of Joppa, *this is the club* of King Thutmōsis, the fierce-eyed lion, the son of Sekhmet.[3] His father Amūn hath *given* him his *strength in order to slay the enemy.*" And he smote the prince of Joppa on the temple, and he fell down *senseless* before him. *Then he bound him with leather thongs (?) and put* copper *chains with four rings (?)* on his feet.

And he caused to be brought five hundred sacks (?), which he had had made, and caused two hundred soldiers [4] to enter into them, and their arms were filled with fetters and handcuffs (?), and they were sealed up. And they were assigned their . . . and their carrying-poles . . . And brave soldiers all were made to carry them—five hundred in number—and it was said unto them : " When ye be come into the city, let out your comrades, and lay hold on all the people that are in the city and put the fetters on them."

And one went out [5] and said unto the charioteer of the prince of Joppa : " Thy lord *bids tell thee (?)* : Go and say to thy mistress : [6] Be glad of heart, for that Sutekh hath given unto us Thutii together with his wife and children. Lo, *here is* their tribute "—*meaning thereby (?)* the two hundred [7] sacks full of people with handcuffs (?) and fetters. And *he* went in front of

---

[1] Have his horses no fodder, and does he thus allow them to be fed by the enemy ? Or is it just a stratagem to bring his people in this wise into the city along with the horses ?

[2] There must be some peculiarity about this club. Perhaps it is the distinguishing mark of the leader of the army, which Thutii may carry as representative of the king.

[3] The war-goddess.

[4] Why there are in the one case five hundred and in the other two hundred is not clear.

[5] From the camp of the Egyptians, before which waited the chariot of the prince.

[6] The wife of the prince.   [7] See note 4 above.

them in order to gladden the heart of his mistress, saying : " We have Thutii " ; and they opened the closed gates of the city before the soldiers. So they entered into the city, and they let out their comrades.

And they laid hold on the (people of) the city, both small and great, and put on them the fetters and handcuffs (?). The strong arm of Pharaoh captured the city.

And in the night Thutii sent to Egypt unto King Thutmōsis his lord, saying : " Be glad ! Amūn, thy good father, hath given unto thee the prince of Joppa and all his people and his city likewise. Now send men to take them away as captives, that thou mayest fill the house of thy father Amūn, king of gods, with male and female slaves, that are fallen down for ever and ever under thy feet."

5. CONCERNING ASTARTE [1]

The Phœnician goddess Astarte was a familiar figure to the Egyptians of the Nineteenth Dynasty ; under Ramesses II she possessed a special temple in his residence, and such will have been the case in other cities also. This intrusion of a foreign goddess may have given rise to a tale, of which, unhappily, only small fragments are preserved. It seems to have related how Astarte was brought to Egypt from abroad.[2]

From the first fragment it is seen that a god claims tribute as sovereign, *and there appear to have been proceedings with respect to this in* a court of law. Renenutet [3] *addresses Astarte (?) :* " Behold, if thou bringest him tribute, *he will be gracious unto thee (?),* but *if thou doest it not,* he will carry us away captive. *Therefore give him (?)* his tribute in silver, gold, lapis lazuli, and . . . wood." And she said unto the Ennead of gods : " . . . the tribute of the sea ; may he hearken unto us – – – –."

In another fragment, where the subject is still the tribute of the sea, *one can make out :* Then Renenutet took a – – – – *and said :* [4] " Hear what I say. Go not forth *to another*. Up, go to

[1] First remarked upon by BIRCH, *Zeitschr. für ägypt. Sprache,* 1871, p. 119. Published by NEWBERRY, *The Amherst Papyri,* Pls. xix.–xxi.

[2] If this explanation is correct, the story will have been modelled upon the legend of the lion-goddess who fled to Nubia and was brought back by Thōth.

[3] The harvest-goddess.   [4] Perhaps to a bird.

Astarte *in* her house, and thou shalt speak under (her ?) bed (-chamber ?), and thou shalt say unto her : ' If thou awakest (?) – – – –; but if thou slumberest, I will make – – – –. Mayest thou come to them – – – –.' "

– – – – Behold, Astarte dwelleth in a region of the sea – – – – the daughter of Ptah, the raging, terrible goddess. Are the sandals, which thou hast on thy feet, . . . ? Are thy (?) clothes, which thou wearest, torn with the going and coming which (thou) hast made in heaven and on earth ? He said – – – –.

– – – – What shall I do against them ? Astarte heard the . . . of the sea, she set out and entered into the presence of the Ennead of gods, where they were. . . . The great ones beheld her, and they stood up before her. The lesser ones saw her, and they laid them on their bellies. And there was given unto her her throne, and she sat her down. And there was brought unto her – – – –.

– – – – the messenger of Ptah went, saying : " Pay homage to Ptah and to Nut." And Nut . . . the . . . which was about her neck, and placed (it) on the balance – – – –.

We must all agree with the discoverer of these fragments in saying that only enough is preserved to make us deplore the loss of the whole.

6. A GHOST STORY

Three fragments of a story are preserved to us in very faulty copies on four ostraca [1]—not enough for us to be quite certain that we fully understand the purport of it.

The matter treated of is the appearance of a person, who had died long since, to a high priest of Amūn, and his commanding him with threats to restore his ruined and forgotten tomb. After persistent search, the tomb is found.

King Rehotep, under whom the dead man lived, belongs to the obscure period at the end of the Middle Kingdom ; we must place the high priest, however, in view of his name, in the Nineteenth or Twentieth Dynasty.

The high priest, who certainly seems to be spoken of as a youth, probably speaks first, and complains as follows : I see not the

---

[1] *Rec. de Trav.*, iii. p. 3 ; *ibid.* xvi. p. 31 ; BERGMANN, *Hierat. dem. Texte*, Vienna, 1886, Pl. IV.—A translation with arbitrary restorations in MASPERO, *Contes populaires*[4], iv. p. 295.

light of the sun, and breathe not the . . . of the air ; darkness is upon me daily and they come not – – – –.[1]

The ghost said unto him : " When I lived on earth, I was Chief Treasurer of King Rehotep, and I was Representative of the Army,[2] I was at the head of men and nigh unto (?) the gods.[3]

" In the year 14, in the second (?) month of Summer, I went to my rest under King Mentuhotep (?). He presented unto me four funerary vases[4] and my sarcophagus of alabaster, and had a pyramid built for me, as appertaineth to a man of my station. He caused me to go to my rest – – – –. Behold, the ground below (?) hath become old (?) and falleth out (?)[5] – – – –.

" But as for what thou hast said (?) unto me : ' I will have the burial place made anew,' *I have already heard (?) that* four times, but what are they doing *to it (?)* – – – – *This is not* achieved with all the words – – – –."[6]

The high priest of Amunrē, king of gods, Khonsemheb, said unto him : " Mayest thou pronounce to me a good command, that appointeth : ' He is to make (this) for me or is to have it made for me (?). Five male and five female slaves, in all ten are to be given me, in order to pour out water for me, and a sack of wheat is to be assigned me daily in order to offer it unto me, and the overseer of . . . is to pour out water for me.' "[7]

The ghost was *wroth (?)* and said unto him : " To what purpose is that which thou doest ?[8] Is not the wood exposed (?) to the sun – – – – the stone that hath become old *holdeth no longer (?)* ; it tumbleth – – – –."

After mention of the sending *of people to the* tomb, *we read* : Then *said the ghost to him* : " He is also to perpetuate *the name* of the father of my father, and the name of my mother." And *the high priest said* : " I will have him do (it) for thee. I will

---

[1] This is probably the disease which the ghost has sent him.
[2] A well-known title for one of the highest officers.
[3] So distinguished ?
[4] The so-called canopic jars, in which the intestines were placed.
[5] The tomb is sinking ?
[6] If the passage is so to be understood, the ghost will have already appeared three times to the high priest and been put off with fair promises.
[7] He must have a perfectly plain contract with which he can easily comply.
[8] The ghost insists upon the restoration of his ruined tomb.

have him make a burying for thee – – – – and I will have him do it for thee as is done for a man *of thy station.*"

He probably further promises him that he shall not freeze in winter, and then after an unintelligible passage : The (high priest) Khonsemheb sat him down and wept – – – – and ate not and drank not – – – – *perhaps, because he did not know where to find the tomb he had to restore.*

Since the deceased would have been an official of Rehotep, it is assumed that he would have been buried near him.
And there were despatched the . . . of Amunrē, king of gods, three men – – – –. He crossed over (the Nile), and he climbed up *to a tomb* beside the noble house of King Rehotep – – – –.
This was the grave that was being looked for. They went down to the river-bank and crossed over to the high priest of Amunrē, king of gods, Khonsemheb, and they found him as he was officiating in the temple.
He receives them with a speech that perhaps expresses some doubt as to whether the good place *has already been found.*
Then said the three men with one mouth : " We have found the good place." And they sat down before him and made merry, and his heart also rejoiced when they said unto him : " – – – – the sun hath risen out of the horizon."
And he called the Representative of the House of Amūn, Mentuka, (and entrusted him) with his work.
In the evening he came back to sleep in the city, and he – – – –.

7. CONCERNING A KING AND A GODDESS

Miserable fragments of a papyrus in Berlin and in Vienna tell of a king, a goddess, and an official named Harmin. I give here, as a mere curiosity, the bits that permit of translation ; the imagination of the reader must fill in the rest.[1]
I might add that the official in Memphis, bearing the rare name of Harmin, with whom the king spends ten days, and in whose house the beautiful girl appears, involuntarily recalls an actual person, the eminent " Superintendent of the Royal Women's Apartment of the *Harîm* of Memphis," Harmin. This personage was rewarded with the gold by his king, Sēthos I, when he had attained " a long life and a goodly old age, without becoming childish and without

---

[1] The sequence of the fragments is not certain.

having committed a fault in the royal house." [1] All museums
have been enriched from his tomb at Sakkârah.[2] A folk-tale may
have attached itself to this man no less than to the officer Thutii
(see p. 167).

All kinds of gifts were brought to the king. And at eventide
she came (?) at the head of the people, who were laden *with the
gifts.* – – – – her house, and she said unto his majesty – – – –.

– – – – brought him the cup. He – – – – on the roof, he
called – – – – captain of the auxiliary troops of the army.

– – – – with an officer that had been beaten – – – –
bringeth me baskets with silver and gold. He did – – – –.
Now many days after this, – – – –. She (?) saw it. And
she took to him – – – – these three years in it ; they lie before
(the king ?) – – – –.

– – – – (I will do what ?) mine heart saith – – – – fifty
jars of honey, – – – – wheat – – – –. And his majesty
caused – – – – (he caused) the load to be brought before him
– – – – come (?) to Memphis, then there shall be (?) made for
thee – – – –. And many days after this, his majesty (came)
to Memphis unto the Superintendent of the (Women's ?)
Apartment, Harmin. And they spent ten days and – – – –.
And many days after this, – – – – and she changed herself
into a fair damsel – – – –.

And many days after this, – – – – be not afraid ! Come up,
thou – – – –. And many days after this, his majesty mounted
(his chariot ?) and they came to the North country – – – –
the people said to the Pharaoh : " What (wouldst thou ?) do ? "
– – – – (none returneth ?) again, the goddess (slayeth ?) the
people – – – –. And many days after this – – – –.

8. THE QUARREL OF THE BODY AND THE HEAD [3]

On a writing-board, which may date from the Twenty-Second
Dynasty, a schoolboy has written, with many mistakes, the beginning of a tale, in which the parts of the body squabble about their

---

[1] *Louvre*, C 213.

[2] His tombstones are in Berlin.

[3] Brought to notice by Maspero ; see his *Études égyptiennes*, i. pp. 260 ff.
A satisfactory publication is wanting, and the translation is on that
account very difficult.

precedence.   That this poem recalls the fable of the quarrel of the belly and the limbs, has been observed by its first editor, though it is impossible to ascertain how far this similarity went.

The belly disputed with the head, in order to solve . . . (*with ?*) loud talking (?) before the Thirty.   *These were to* bring to light the outrage, *over which* the eye *of the head* wept, *and the truth was to be established before* (?) the god, who abhorreth iniquity.

When the belly had uttered his accusation, the head cried out exceedingly with his mouth : " I, I am this beam (?) of the whole house, that supporteth (?) the beams (?), and yoketh the beams (?) together, and every member that (is supported ?) on me is happy.   My heart is happy, my limbs flourish (?), my neck sitteth firm under the head, mine eyes look into the distance, my nose breatheth and draweth in air, mine ear standeth open and heareth, my mouth is opened and knoweth how to make answer, his arms [1] flourish (?) and work.

The topic then seems to be a man who is proud and regardeth notables as being of low estate ; *who is meant by this is uncertain.   Then it proceeds :* " I am your mistress, I am the head, whom her brethren would accuse (?)."

This is what the mouth said unto him : " Is not this wrong ? Let the head speak unto me.   I am he that keepeth alive — — — —."

9. THE VOYAGE OF UNAMŪN [2]

The directness of this narrative testifies to its being the account of a traveller's actual experiences, although he will certainly have devoted more space to them here, and given them a more telling form, than in the original report, in which he must have offered excuses for his misadventures to those who had sent him on this errand.

The famous old state-barge Userhēt, which Amūn of Thebes made use of at his festivals, had in course of time constantly to be restored, or else replaced by an entirely new construction.   For such a purpose, cedar-wood, which had to be obtained from Lebanon, was required.   This presented no difficulty so long as Egypt was a great power, for the prince of Byblos was only too ready to render

---

[1] Which are subject to the mouth ?

[2] A papyrus in Moscow.   Discovered by Golénischeff and published and translated by him in 1899.   See also my revised translation in *Zeitschr. für ägypt. Sprache,* **xxxviii.** pp. 1 ff.

such service to the god, though, of course, for payment. But about
1100 B.C. the days of Egypt's greatness were over. At Thebes the
last of the many Ramessids still nominally reigned, though actually
Egypt was subject to various petty rulers.

At Thebes, Hrihor, the high priest of Amūn, held sway, and
Tanis, the important city of the north-eastern Delta, belonged to a
certain Smendes and a woman Tentamūn.[1] When the sacred barge
of Amūn once more needed completely renovating, Thebes was in
dire straits. There was insufficient money and insufficient influence to procure the wood needed for the rebuilding. However,
the money was raised by subscriptions from the different rulers of
Egypt, though a state embassy was not feasible as in better days.

In this necessity the idea was adopted of sending Amūn himself to Byblos, and there was chosen for that purpose an image of
the god, which, as it was called " Amūn of the Road," had probably
been sent away from Thebes on other occasions also. With this
image was dispatched a temple official, " the Eldest of the Hall,
Unamūn," but even he was left to depend upon charity for his
journey. He was sent with letters of introduction to Smendes and
Tentamūn, who were then to further him on his way to Byblos.

This document presents us with a vivid picture of the voyage,
and of trading operations in the eastern Mediterranean ; it enables
us to see, as it actually was, that world, the reflection of which still
delights us in the *Odyssey*. Its author writes the simplest prose,
without any learned and archaistic embellishments ; but so much
the more does he appeal to us, and not least by his delicate humour,
which often unaffectedly breaks out in the course of the narrative.

Year 5, day 16 of the third month of Summer. On this day
Unamūn, Eldest of the Hall of the Administration of Amūn
of Karnak, departed in order to fetch the timber for the great
august ship of Amunrē, king of gods, which is on (the river) and
is called Userhēt-Amūn.

On the day whereon I came to Tanis, the abode of Smendes
and Tentamūn, I gave unto them the writings of Amunrē, king
of gods. They had them read in their presence and said : " Yea,
I will do even as Amunrē, king of gods, our lord, saith."

I remained until the fourth month of Summer in Tanis.
Smendes and Tentamūn then sent me with the ship-captain,
Mengebet,[2] and on the first day of the fourth month of Summer
I went down to the great Syrian sea.

---

[1] Both Hrihor and Smendes proclaimed themselves kings later, but
neither yet held that position at the time this document was composed.

[2] As is shown later on, this is a Syrian, *i.e.* Phœnician, captain.

And I came to Dor, a city of the Zakar,[1] and its prince Beder caused to brought to me fifty (?) loaves, one measure of wine, and a leg of beef.[2]

A man of my ship ran away and stole in

Gold : . . . (vessels), . amounting to 5 deben.
Silver : 4 vessels,   . amounting to 20 deben.
Silver : in a bag,   . amounting to 11 deben.
(Total of what he stole :) Gold, 5 deben ; silver, 31 deben.[3]

On the same (?) morning I arose and went to where the prince was, and said unto him : " I have been robbed in thine harbour. Now thou art the prince of this land, and thou art its judge,[4] so look for my money. Of a truth the money belongeth to Amunrē, king of gods, the lord of the countries ; it belongeth to Smendes ; it belongeth to Hrihor, my lord, and the other great men of Egypt.[5] To thee it belongeth, and it belongeth to Weret, and belongeth to Mekemer, and belongeth to Zakarbaal, the prince of Byblos." [6]

And he said unto me : " Art thou aggrieved (?), or art thou friendly ? " [7] For behold, I understand nought of this matter that thou hast told me. Had it been a thief belonging to mine own country that went aboard thy ship and stole thy money, then would I have repaid it thee out of my treasury, until thy thief aforesaid had been apprehended. But the thief that hath robbed thee, he is thine, he belongeth to thy ship. So tarry a few days here with me, that I may seek for him."

So I spent nine days moored in his harbour. Then I went unto him and said : " Behold, thou hast not found my money, (so I will now depart) with the captain and with them that go away . . ."

[1] The Zakar are a people that eight years earlier had, together with the Philistines, conquered the coast of Palestine.

[2] As a present for a guest.

[3] A deben = 91 grammes ; we are thus concerned with about 455 grammes of gold and almost 3 kilograms of silver—a considerable sum, which was mainly to serve to pay for the timber. In the bag were pieces of silver, which were used as money, in addition to the vessels.

[4] Literally : its " inquisitor," *i.e.* its police.

[5] Who have collected it.

[6] These are the Phœnician princes, whose harbours he has to visit, and who would also come in for some of the money when he recovered it.

[7] Meaning probably : you may take offence at my answer, but this affair is no concern of mine at all, for the thief is not my subject.

In the long lacuna, which the papyrus here shows, something like the following must have been narrated. Unamūn had a heated argument with the prince of Dor : He said unto me : " Be silent ! " *and some one gives him bad advice, namely, to do as others would do, and get back his money again himself :* they go to look for their thief.—*Thence he comes to Tyre :* I came at dawn of day from Tyre, *and proceeded further on his voyage to* Zakarbaal, the prince of Byblos. *As ill luck would have it, somewhere on this journey he encountered certain Zakar-people, and thought himself justified in compensating himself out of their property for the theft of which he had been the victim in their city. He took from them a bag (?) :* I found thirty deben of silver therein and took it. *They complain, but he replies :* " (*Certainly it is*) your money, but it remaineth with me, until my money shall have been found. *He had thus made enemies of the Zakar-people.* They departed *and he* came to the harbour of Byblos. *There he sought for himself some place of safety :* (I hid therein) Amūn of the Road and placed his possessions in it.[1] *But the prince of Byblos was apparently not pleased at this visit of a man who was on bad terms with the Zakar :* The prince of Byblos sent unto me and said : " Get thee out of my harbour."

Of Unamūn's answer to this demand only the last words are preserved : " If men sail, let them take me away to Egypt." *Apparently Unamūn was himself ready enough to give up the unsuccessful journey, but had no chance of a safe voyage home, if the prince of Byblos would not secure him a passage on a ship sailing to Egypt. The text continues :* I passed nineteen days in his harbour, and every day he continued sending to me, saying : " Get thee out of my harbour."

Now when he was making offering to his gods, the god seized one of his noble youths [2] and made him frenzied, and he said : " Bring the god hither ! Bring the messenger, that hath him. It is Amūn that sent him, it is he that caused him to come." [3]

Thus the frenzied one continued in frenzy throughout this night, when I had just found a ship bound for Egypt, and I

---

[1] That will be the money of the Zakar and Unamūn's own baggage.

[2] *I.e.* a page or the like.

[3] The news that a god's image had arrived was thus talked about in the king's entourage, and works upon the boy, already excited by the sacrificial festivities. His ecstatic ejaculations might be divine manifestations, and so the prince does not in any case wish to expel Unamūn, without having spoken to him.

was stowing all that I had aboard her, and was watching for the darkness, thinking that when it descends I will also embark the god, so that no other eye may see him.[1]

And the harbour-master came to me, saying : " Remain until morning at the disposition of the prince." I said unto him : " Art thou not he that continued coming to me every day, saying : ' Get thee out of my harbour,' and never didst thou say : ' Remain ' ? And now the prince will let the ship, which I have found, depart, and thou wilt come again saying : ' Get thee gone ! ' "

So he went and told it to the prince, and the prince sent unto the ship's captain, saying : " Remain until morning at the disposition of the prince."

And when the morning was come he sent and had me brought up, while the god rested in the . . . in which he was,[2] on the shore of the sea. I found him sitting in his upper chamber, with his back leaning against a window, while the waves of the great Syrian sea beat upon his neck.[3]

I said unto him : " The kindness (?) of Amūn ! " He said unto me : " How long is it until to-day since thou camest from the abode of Amūn ? "[4] I said unto him : " Five full months until now." He said unto me : " Dost thou indeed speak the truth ? Where then is the writing of Amūn, which thou (shouldest) have ? Where is the letter of the High Priest of Amūn, which thou (shouldest) have ? " And I said unto him : " I gave them to Smendes and Tentamūn." And he was very wroth, and said unto me : " Behold, writing and letter hast thou none. Where is then (at least) the ship of cedar-wood that Smendes hath given thee ? And where is her Syrian crew ? He surely did not hand thee over to this ship's captain, to be slain and to be cast into the sea ![5] From whom had

---

[1] The god's image is something that profane eyes might not ordinarily look upon.

[2] He again emphasizes the fact that, according to custom, he has made the god secure.

[3] This is, of course, not to be taken literally. He means that through the window he saw the surf fly in spray behind the king.

[4] All the following questions clearly show that the prince is inclined to regard Unamūn as an impostor.

[5] Still to-day the favourite method in the East of getting rid of un-desirable persons. The prince's suspicions are aroused, because Smendes has let Unamūn sail with a foreign captain. He thinks that might well

they sought the god then ? And thee, pray, from whom had they sought thee, pray ? " So spake he unto me. And I said unto him : " But it is an Egyptian ship, and it is also an Egyptian crew, that saileth for Smendes. He hath no Syrian crew." [1] And he said unto me : " But there are twenty ships here in my harbour that are in kheber [2] with Smendes, and as for this Sidon, past which thou didst also (?) sail, there are other fifty (?) ships there, which are in kheber [2] with Birkat-el,[3] and they sail (?) to his house."

I was silent in this great moment. And he answered and said unto me : " Upon what kind of behest art thou come hither ? " I said unto him : " I am come after the timber for the great august vessel of Amunrē, king of gods. Thy father used to do it, thy grandfather used to do it, and thou wilt do it also." So spake I unto him. And he said unto me : " They did it in sooth, and if thou wilt give me something for doing it, I will do it. Of a truth my people did execute this behest, but the Pharaoh had six ships sent hither, laden with the wares of Egypt, and they unloaded them into their storehouses. So do thou bring somewhat for me also." And he had fetched the daily registers of his fathers, and he had them read aloud in my presence, and it was found that it was a thousand deben of every kind of silver [4] that was entered in his book.

And he said unto me : " If the ruler of Egypt were the lord of my possessions, and I were also his servant, he would not have sent silver and gold, when he said : ' Execute the behest of Amun.' Nor was it a king's gift [5] that they assigned to my father. And I too, I am not thy servant, nor yet am I the

happen, since nobody could have called him to account if he had made away with Unamūn.

[1] This, and what follows, seems to be an empty argument : the sailors are Phœnicians, but since the ship has an Egyptian owner, they can be regarded as Egyptians.

[2] The Phœnician word for " association," " partnership." Phœnician was just at that time the commercial language of this part of the world.

[3] The name must so be read, i.e. " Blessing of God." According to the context he will have been a Phœnician merchant resident in Tanis. Similarly, Smendes himself will actually have been an Egyptian merchant.

[4] He means vessels, ingots, pieces of silver, etc.

[5] No gift, such as is usual among friendly rulers. He wishes to stress the fact that the money was simply the purchase price of the timber.

servant of him that sent thee.[1] If I cry out to the Lebanon, the heaven openeth, and the trees are here lying on the shore of the sea.[2] Give me the sails that thou hast brought [3] with thee, to take thy ships that carry thy timber back to (Egypt). Give me also the ropes, *that thou hast brought with thee*, in order *to bind fast* (?) [4] the . . . trees which I (am to) fell, in order to make them . . . for thee . . . *For without all this thou canst not sail away* (?) *with the timber, and* if I make them for thee (into ?) the sails of thy ships, the ends (?) [5] will be too heavy and (the ship) will break in pieces, and thou wilt perish in the middle of the sea. (For) behold, Amūn thundereth in the sky and causeth Sutekh [6] to (rave ?) in his season. For Amūn [7] hath equipped all lands ; he hath equipped them, and the land of Egypt, whence thou comest, he did first equip. For cunning work [8] came forth from it to reach mine abode, and teaching [9] came forth from it to reach mine abode—what are these childish journeyings that they have caused thee to make ! "

And I said unto him : " Fie ! They be no childish journeyings in any wise that I make. There is not a ship upon the water that belongeth not to Amūn. His is the sea and his is Lebanon, whereof thou sayest : ' It belongeth unto me.' (Nay rather) is it a plantation for the bark Userhēt-Amūn, the lord of all ships. Of a truth thus spake Amunrē, king of gods, saying unto Hrihor, my lord : ' Send me forth,' [10] and made me travel with this great god. But behold, thou hast caused this

---

[1] He thus contemptuously designates the high priest.

[2] The trees fall as though from heaven, for the mountain range, on which they grow, soars up into it.

[3] Ironical ; he points out to him that he has not taken even the most necessary precautions for so difficult an undertaking.

[4] A cargo of logs on the deck of a ship is always dangerous, if it is not made thoroughly fast. For what purpose he was supposed to bring special sails remains doubtful.

[5] Later on he gives the name of " ends " to the stem- and stern-post of a ship ; he may thus mean the great beams which were to furnish these parts of the boat of Amūn. The details of this passage are obscure.

[6] Sēth-Sutekh was thus regarded as god of the tempest.

[7] He here speaks to the Egyptian of his Amūn as supreme god, and that leads him on in the following sentence to the fact that his own people also had respect for this god and for Egypt.

[8] The arts and crafts.　　　　　[9] Wisdom and learning.

[10] Amūn had thus himself ordained the journey of his image by means of an oracle.

great god to spend twenty-nine days, after that he had landed in thy harbour, and thou knewest well that he was here ! He is still the same as ever he was, and thou standest and wouldest bargain about Lebanon with Amūn its lord.

" As for thy saying : ' The former kings sent silver and gold '—if they had offered life and health, they would not have sent these things. Rather they sent thy fathers these things instead of life and health.[1]

" Now as for Amunrē, king of gods, he is the lord of life and health, and he was the lord of your fathers, who passed their term of life making offering to Amūn. And thou too, thou art a servant of Amūn. If now thou sayest : ' Yea, I will do it,' and fulfillest his behest, thou wilt live and prosper and be in health, and thou wilt be a benefactor to thy whole land and to thy people. But covet not for thyself anything that belongeth to Amunrē, king of gods ; verily a lion loveth his own !

" Let my [2] scribe be brought unto me, that I may send him to Smendes and Tentamūn, the officers of the land, whom Amūn hath given to the northern portion of his land, and they will send all that is needed. I will write to them, saying : ' Send it, until I be come to the south and send thee all that I owe thee.' " [3] So spake I unto him.

And he gave my letter into the hand of his messenger, and loaded the keel (?) and the bow- and stern-post, together with four other hewn logs—seven in all—and had them brought to Egypt.

And his messenger went to Egypt and came back to me to Syria in the first month of Winter. And Smendes and Tentamūn sent me :

> Gold : 4 ewers and 1 kakment-vessel.
> Silver : 5 ewers.
> Garments of royal linen : 10 pieces.
> Good Upper Egyptian linen : 10 khered.

[1] " Life and health " is the blessing which the gods bestow, which I bring you through the medium of the god's image. That is surely more than the money which you received in times past.

[2] Emend " thy " ?

[3] Smendes is to advance the money, which Unamūn will cause to be refunded to him after his return home. In view of this projected loan the prince shows himself complaisant, and sends a portion of the timber.

Fine papyrus : 500.
Ox-hides : 500.
Ropes : 500.
Lentils : 20 sacks.
Fish : 30 baskets.

They also had brought to me : [1]

Garments of good Upper Egyptian linen : 5 (?) pieces.
Good Upper Egyptian linen : 5 khered.
Lentils : 1 sack.
Fish : 5 baskets.

And the prince rejoiced, and appointed three hundred men and three hundred oxen, and set overseers at their head, in order that they might fell the trees. And they felled them, and they remained lying over the winter. But in the third month of summer they were dragged to the shore of the sea.

And the prince came forth and took up his stand upon them, and sent for me, saying : " Come." Now when I was brought nigh unto him, the shadow of his fan (?) fell upon me. And Penamūn,[2] a butler belonging unto him, placed himself between me (and him), saying : " The shadow of Pharaoh, thy lord, hath fallen on thee." And he was wroth with him, saying : " Let him alone." And I was brought nigh unto him, and he answered and said unto me : " Behold, the behest that my fathers fulfilled in times past, I have also fulfilled it, albeit thou on thy part hast not done for me what thy fathers did for me. Behold, the last of thy timber hath now arrived and there it is stacked. Now do according to my wish and come to stow it, for in truth it is given unto thee. But come not to regard the terror of the sea.[3] If thou regardest the terror of the sea, regard that of me also. Verily, I have not done to thee what they did to the messengers of Khamwese,[4] when they passed seventeen years in this land. They died where

---

[1] Tentamūn sends him this personally.

[2] An Egyptian : we are unable to determine where lay the malice of his jest. (But see BAUER, *Orientalistische Literaturzeitung*, 1925, 571. [Translator]).

[3] Meaning : now make haste to get away, and do not make the bad season of the year a pretext for remaining on here.

[4] Possibly Ramesses IX ? We are not in a position to guess what actually had occurred, but in any case a threat lurks in the allusion to this event,

they were." And he said unto his butler : " Take him and show him their grave wherein they rest."

And I said unto him : " Show it me not ! As for Khamwese, they were men whom he sent unto thee as messengers, and he himself was a man. I have none of his messengers, and yet thou sayest : " Go and look on thy comrades." [1] Dost thou not rather rejoice and have a tablet made for thee and say upon it : ' Amunrē, king of gods, sent unto me his messenger, Amūn of the Road, together with Unamūn, his human messenger, after the timber for the great august bark of Amunrē, king of gods. I felled it, I stowed it, and I despatched it with my ships and my crews. I sent them to Egypt in order to beseech for me ten thousand years of life from Amūn over and above that ordained for me (by destiny), and so shall (?) it come to pass.' When, therefore, in the time to come another messenger shall come from the land of Egypt, one that knoweth writing, and readeth thy name on the tablet, thou wilt receive water in the West like the gods that are here." [2]

And he said unto me : " It is a great testimony that thou hast recounted unto me."

I said unto him : " As for the many things that thou hast said unto me, if I reach the abode of the High Priest of Amūn, and he seeth thy behest,[3] then shall thy behest bring thee in somewhat." [4]

And I went to the shore of the sea to where the timber was stacked, and I descried eleven ships drawing nigh on the sea. They belongeth to the Zakar (*and came with the order*) : " Take him prisoner, suffer not a ship of his to get to the land of Egypt." Thereupon I sat down and wept.

And the letter-writer of the prince came out to me and said unto me : " What aileth thee ? " And I said unto him : " Surely thou seest the birds that for the second time [5] go down into Egypt. Look at them ! They go to the cool pool, but how

[1] Meaning : my mission, however, is of a divine character.
[2] The dead kings. For the offering of water, see p. 115, note 9.
[3] The timber which you are delivering.
[4] Meaning : then we shall pay also for the second consignment of timber.

[5] Since his departure from Thebes a full year has now gone by, and so with some exaggeration he can well say that he sees the birds of passage for the second time.

long am I to be left here ? Surely thou seest them that come back to take me prisoner."

And he went and told it to the prince, and the prince began to weep because of the tidings told him, that were so grievous. And he sent out his letter-writer unto me, and he brought me two measures of wine and a ram. Moreover, he had brought unto me Tentnut, an Egyptian singer that was with him, saying unto her : " Sing unto him ; let not his heart harbour cares ! " And he sent unto me, saying : " Eat and drink ! Let not thine heart harbour cares ! Thou wilt hear all that I shall say to-morrow." And when the morrow came he had his . . . called, and he stood in their midst and said unto the Zakar : " What meaneth this coming of yours ? " And they said unto him : " We are come after the shivered [1] ships which thou sendest unto Egypt with our . . . comrades." And he said unto them : " I cannot take the messenger of Amūn prisoner in my land. Let me send him away, and then do ye pursue him in order to take him prisoner." [2]

He put me on board and sent me away . . . to the harbour of the sea. And the wind drave me to the land of Arsa.[3] And they of the city came forth against me to slay me, and between them I was hustled to the place of abode of Heteb, the queen of the city. And I found her as she was coming from her one house and was entering into her other.[4]

And I saluted her, and said unto the people that stood beside her : " Surely there is one among you that understandeth Egyptian." And one of them said : " I understand it." And I said unto him : " Say unto my mistress : ' As far as Thebes, even unto the abode of Amūn, I have heard it said that wrong is done in every city, but right is done in the land of Arsa.[5] And now here also wrong is done every day.' " And she said unto me : " But what meaneth it, that thou sayest this ? " And I said unto her : " If the sea raged and the wind drave me to the land wherein thou dwellest, thou wilt not suffer them to arrest me in order to slay me, seeing that I am a messenger of Amūn. Look well to it. I am one

[1] Meaning : which should be shivered.
[2] The expedient is truly Oriental.
[3] Here begins a new series of adventures ; the story of how he got safely away from the Zakar is left untold—Arsa is probably Cyprus.
[4] Thus in the street.
[5] This sounds like a quotation from a poem or like a proverb.

for whom search will be made unceasingly.[1] And as for this crew of the prince of Byblos that they seek to slay, if their lord findeth ten crews of thine he too will slay them."

So she had the people summoned and they were brought forward. And she said unto me : " Lie down and sleep——"

Here the papyrus breaks off, and so we do not know how Unamūn escaped from these new dangers. Did he succeed in bringing the timber to Egypt ? Was it paid for ? And did Amūn of the Road, who had been so utterly useless on the journey, march safely back again into Karnak ?

B. THE SCHOOLS AND THEIR WRITINGS

We have frequently throughout this book pointed out that we in great measure owe our knowledge of the old and later literature to the papyri, writing-boards, and ostraca, upon which the schoolboys of the New Kingdom copied out extracts from standard or didactic compositions. Our sincere thanks are therefore due to the compulsory energy of these lads. But the body of writings, which the schools of the New Kingdom produced themselves, and which I have gathered together in this section, supplies us with much that is interesting, and the reader might well like to know something about the system of education which has bequeathed us all this.

It consisted apparently of two stages. In the lower, which corresponds more or less to what we call " school," the boys learnt writing and the ancient literature. For their writing exercises they used potsherds and limestone flakes, which cost nothing, rather than expensive rolls of papyrus.

About one such school at least we possess a certain amount of information. It was attached to the temple which Ramesses II built for Amūn on the west bank of Thebes, the so-called Ramesseum, and it was included in the great groups of offices surrounding the temple on three sides. A strikingly large number of such ostraca have been found there, particularly on a small rubbish mound ; apparently the temple-school stood there, and what the lads had finished writing out, they threw away on the spot. If we examine the material which the boys in this school had placed before them, we find that, besides

[1] I am held in such esteem that you cannot make me disappear unnoticed.

certain later compositions,[1] it consists of three books, which turn up repeatedly : the *Instruction of King Amenemhēt* (p. 72), the *Instruction of Duauf* (p. 67), and the *Hymn to the Nile* (p. 46), and it is interesting that the same three compositions occur all together in two school-papyri,[2] whose provenance is apparently Memphis—they thus formed the usual main subject of the school-curriculum. In these papyri they are complete, on the ostraca we invariably find only short selections from them and from other writings, and for the most part always the same selections ; perhaps they were the " choice " passages, which every educated person had to know.

When the schoolboy had finished with this elementary course of instruction, and was entered as " scribe " in some administration, he received there also yet further instruction, and that at the hands of an older official, possibly his immediate superior. While undergoing this higher education, the pupil had still to write out model compositions, though not, as heretofore, a few lines a day only, but larger portions, in one case three pages a day. What the pupil thus wrote out his teacher corrected in the margin of the papyrus, unfortunately but seldom paying attention to the nonsense which the pupil had written, but so much the more to the shape of his characters ; we might really think that we are merely concerned with an exercise in calligraphy ! Of course it was not that alone, and the contents of most [3] of these " school manuscripts " clearly show what objects were actually had in view : education on the one side, and training in commercial style and in orthography on the other. The orthography was no light matter, for scarcely any system of writing provides so many possibilities for mistakes as the hieroglyphic. How the writing of the individual word was imparted to the schoolboys, can still be seen in a book,[4] which must have been much used in the schools,

---

[1] The warning against becoming a soldier, given below on p. 195, is also included in these.

[2] *Pap. Sallier*, ii., and *Pap. Anastasi*, vii.

[3] Not all, for several teachers had wider interests and let their pupils write out things that cannot have been of much use educationally, though for us they are certainly all the more interesting.

[4] Preserved in *Pap. Hood* (MASPERO, *Études égyptiennes*, ii. 1 ff.), and more completely in a papyrus in Moscow. It must have been also used in the above-mentioned school attached to the Ramesseum, and its title at least occurs on the *verso* of a papyrus in Cairo. See also GLANVILLE, *Journ. of Egypt. Archæology*, xii. pp. 171 ff.

and which "the scribe of the God's Book in the House of Life,[1] Amenemōpe, son of Amenemōpe, devised." It bears the long-winded title : " The teaching that maketh clever and instructeth the ignorant, the knowledge of all that existeth, what Ptah hath created and Thōth hath written (?), the heaven with its stars, the earth and what therein is, what the mountains disgorge, and what floweth forth from the ocean, concerning all things that the sun enlighteneth and all that groweth on the earth." This sounds grandiose enough, yet the work is nothing more than a large collection of substantives and names of frequent and rare occurrence, placed in tolerably systematic order. First comes the heaven and what is in it : " Heaven, sun, moon, star, Orion, Great Bear, Ape, Giant, Sow,[2] clouds, tempest, dawn, darkness, sun, shadow, . . ., sun's rays." Then follow expressions for water and fields, and then in six groups the words which denote individuals. First, " God, goddess, blessed dead (male and female), king, queen," etc. ; next come the highest officials, the high priests and learned men, then the great mass of lower officials and artisans, and lastly the expressions for mankind and for troops, and the names of foreign peoples and localities. The pupil then gets to know ninety-six Egyptian cities, forty-two expressions for buildings and their parts, designations for lands and fields, and then all that one may eat and drink, including forty-eight different baked meats, twenty-four drinks, and thirty-three sorts of flesh. In the concluding portion which is destroyed, the different birds and the numerous words for cattle were listed, and of course much else besides. All this Amenemōpe carefully compiled, in order to show the world all that exists, thanks to Ptah and Thōth, though, to be sure, only with the very simple object of imparting to his pupils the correct writing of the individual words.

A serious obstacle, even for advanced students, must have been presented by the many foreign words and barbarous names, in which New Egyptian abounded, and therefore particular attention was paid to the learning of them. A schoolboy of the Eighteenth Dynasty had to busy himself on his writing-board [3] with the " drawing up of Keftiu-names " ; and the model letters on pp. 205 ff., were set before the schoolboy so that,

---

[1] Ancient designation of the schools.
[2] Constellations.
[3] See W. Max Müller, *Mitt. der Vorderasiat. Ges.*, v. pp. 7 ff.

through the foreign words which they contained, he might acquire this difficult art.

Special importance was also attached to the learning of the correct style for letter-writing. Accordingly the schoolboy had to copy out model letters of all kinds, actual and fictitious, and even the admonitions and warnings, which appertained to this instruction, he wrote out in the form of letters. What the schoolboy thus compiled on his papyrus, obtained the title of "epistolary teaching," and he often inserts in the individual letters his own name and that of his teacher, as if they were actually corresponding with one another. The schoolboy accordingly writes to himself that he is lazy and dissolute and deserves a hundred blows.

We find that officials of the most varied kind were thus occupied with the education of schoolboys,—a "scribe of the treasury of Pharaoh," a "chief registrar of the treasury," a "scribe of the workshop of Pharaoh," and the like ; and he who reads the *Literary Controversy* below, will see that even an official in the royal stable can be a famous teacher. So when the tomb of Ramesses IX was being hewn out of the rock in the desert valley of Bibân el-Mulûk, an official, who was employed on this work, could not give up teaching even in this solitude. On the large limestone flakes, which the work provided, his assistant had to write out all kinds of things for practice : a model letter, an old poem to Ramesses II, and the beautiful *Prayers of one unjustly persecuted*[1] (see pp. 302 ff.). And the teacher himself has made a certain number of corrections.

1. EXHORTATIONS AND WARNINGS TO SCHOOLBOYS [2]

These short compositions have rightly aroused great interest, as describing contemporary, social conditions. The reader must not lose sight of their object ; the pictures which they paint of the happy lot of the scribe and the misery of the other professions, are of course thoroughly biased and exaggerated.

The epistolary formulæ, which in many manuscripts precede the various compositions, have been omitted. The reader can gain

---

[1] *Zeitschr. für ägypt. Sprache*, xxxviii. p. 19 ff.

[2] Preserved separately in the different schoolboy manuscripts of the Nineteenth Dynasty. See MASPERO, *Du genre épistolaire*, Paris, 1872 (out of date) ; also ERMAN, *Die ägypt. Schülerhandsschriften* (in *Abh. d, Berl. Akad.*, 1925).

a sufficient knowledge of them from the genuine letters in the next section.

[LIFE AT SCHOOL.] [1]

I place thee at school along with the children of notables, to educate thee and to have thee trained for this aggrandizing calling.

Behold, I relate to thee how it fareth with the scribe when he . . . " Wake up, at thy place, the books lie (already) before thy comrades. Place thine hand on thy clothes and look to thy sandals (?)." When thou gettest thy daily (task ?) . . ., be not idle – – – –.[2]

– – – – and read diligently from the book. When thou reckonest in silence,[3] let no word be heard – – – –.

Write with thine hand and read with thy mouth. Ask counsel of (them that are clever ?). Be not slack, and spend not a day in idleness, or woe betide thy limbs ! Enter into the methods of thy teacher and hear his instructions . . . Behold, I am with thee every (day ?). Beware of saying . . . !

[BE DILIGENT.] [4]

O scribe, be not idle, be not idle, or thou wilt be soundly chastised. Set not thine heart on pleasures, or thou wilt be ruined. Write with thine hand, read with thy mouth, and ask counsel of them that have more knowledge than thou.

Procure for thyself this calling of a magistrate, that thou mayest attain it when thou art become old. Fortunate is a scribe that is skilled in his calling, a master of education. Persevere every day ; thus shalt thou obtain the mastery over it (writing or the knowledge of writing). Spend no day in idleness or thou wilt be beaten. The ear of the boy is on his back, and he hearkeneth when he is beaten.

Set thine heart upon hearing my words ; they will be profitable unto thee.

The Kaeri [5] is taught to dance, horses are broken in, a kite (?) is put in a nest (?), a hawk's wings are bound.[6]

[1] *Pap. Anastasi*, v. 22. 6 ff.

[2] Possibly arithmetical exercises are the subject of the omitted passage.

[3] *I.e.* in your head.

[4] *Pap. Anastasi*, iii. 3. 9 ff. ; *ibid.* v. 8. 1 ff. Translated by Griffith.

[5] An Ethiopian animal, which is spoken of elsewhere as an example of what can be done in the way of training.

[6] Meaning : if one can tame all these, one will probably be able to do the same with you.

Persevere in asking counsel, neglect it not ; and in writing, sicken not of it.

Set thine heart upon hearing my words, thou wilt find them profitable.

[BE DILIGENT.] [1]

Be not a foolish man, that hath no instruction.

By night one teacheth thee, and by day one instructeth thee, but thou hearkenest not unto instruction, and thou doest after thine own devices.

The Kaeri [2] listeneth to words, when it is brought from Ethiopia. Lions are taught, horses are broken in—but thou, the like of thee is not known in the whole land. Prithee, know that.

BE DILIGENT.] [3]

Mine heart is sick of giving (thee further) teaching – – – –.

I may give thee an hundred blows, and yet thou castest them all off. Thou art as a beaten ass unto me, that is stubborn (?) . . . Thou art as a jabbering negro unto me, that is brought with the tribute.[4]

The kite (?) is put in a nest (?), the wings of the kite are bound [5]—I will also make thee play the man, thou bad boy. Prithee, know that.

[BEER AND THE MAIDEN.] [6]

I am told, thou forsakest writing, thou givest thyself up (?) to pleasures ; thou goest from street to street, where (?) it smelleth of beer, to destruction (?). Beer, it scareth men (from thee), it sendeth thy soul to perdition (?).

Thou art [7] like a broken steering-oar in a ship, that is obedient on neither side. Thou art like a shrine without its god, and like a house without bread.

Thou art encountered climbing a wall and breaking the

---

[1] *Pap. Bologna*, 1094, 3. 5 ff.   [2] See p. 189, note 5.

[3] *Pap. Sallier*, i. 7. 9ff.

[4] The newly imported slave, who has no knowledge of Egyptian.

[5] The same passage above, p. 189.

[6] *Pap. Anastasi*, iv. 11. 8 ff. ; *Pap. Sallier*, i. 9. 9 ff. ; was contained also in *Pap. Anastasi*, v.

[7] In your drunkenness.

. . . ; men run away from before thee, for thou inflictest wounds on them.

Would that thou knewest that wine is an abomination, that thou wouldst take an oath in respect to shedeh,[1] that thou wouldst set not thine heart on the bottle (?), and wouldst forget telek.[2]

Thou art taught to sing to the flute and to . . . to the pipe (?), to speak to the kinnor in anen, and to sing to the nezekh.[3]

Thou sittest in the house and the girls encircle thee ; thou standest and makest . . ., thou – – – –.

Thou sittest in front of the wench and art besprinkled with oil ; thy garland of ishet-penu[4] hangeth about thy neck, and thou drummest on thy paunch.

Thou dost reel, and (then) fallest upon thy belly and art besmirched with dirt – – – –.

[THE SCHOOLBOY IS PUT IN FETTERS.][5]

I have heard that thou followest pleasures. Turn not thy back on my words. Dost thou give thy mind to all manner of deaf (?) things ? – – – –

I will cause thy foot to stumble (?), when it goeth in the streets,[6] and thou shalt be beaten with the hippopotamus whip.

Howbeit, I have seen many like thee, that did sit in the writing academy and that said not " by God," without swearing : " Books are nothing at all." (Yet) they became scribes, and One remembered[7] their names, to despatch them on errands.

If thou lookest at me myself, when I was as young as thou, I passed my time with the handcuff on me, and this it was that bound my limbs, when it stayed on me for three months and I was imprisoned in the temple, while my father and my mother were on the land and my brethren also. When it left me and mine hand was free, then surpassed I what had been aforetime,

---

[1] A sweet intoxicating beverage.
[2] A foreign word for some kind of beverage.
[3] Nothing but foreign words. " Kinnor " is the foreign lyre, " nezekh " probably something similar ; " anen " perhaps means warbling.
[4] A plant.   [5] *Pap. Anastasi*, v. 17. 3 ff.
[6] When you go gadding about.
[7] The king or the highest officials.

and was the first of all my (comrades), and surpassed them in books.

Do as I say, and thy body will be healthy, and thou wilt be found in the morning [1] to have no superior.

[BE DILIGENT.] [2]

I am told thou forsakest writing, thou departest and dost flee. Thou forsakest writing as fast as thy feet can manage it, thou art like a pair of horses of the . . . [3]

Thine heart fluttereth, and thou art like an akhy-bird ; thine ear . . ., and thou art like an ass when it getteth a beating. Thou art like an antelope in flight. [4]

But thou art not an hunter of the desert nor a Matoï of the west.

But thou art not one that is deaf, that cannot hear, and one speaketh unto him with the hand.

Thou art like a skipper's mate that is skilful in the boat, [5] when he is skipper in the boat and standeth at the prow (?). He looketh not out for the adverse winds, he searcheth not for the wave. [6] If the outer rope is let go, the . . . rope hangeth about his neck. [7] When he pulleth the rope – – – –.

All that follows is obscure. We are informed that he pluckÉth *flowers* on the banks, *and a probably comic description is given of his dress :* his wig with its curled locks, that reach to his feet, is of Ethiopian work, *etc. etc.*

The ending is : he hath a full [8] ear on the day of the ass, and is a steering-oar on the day of the boat. [9]

[1] The schoolboy wrote " morning " incorrectly and the teacher wrongly corrected it to " month."

[2] *Pap. Koller*, 2. 3 ff. = *Pap. Anastasi*, iv. 2. 4 ff. ; was also in *Pap. Anastasi*, v. Translated by GARDINER in *Hieratic Texts*, p. 38.

[3] One naturally thinks of a race-course or the like, though no such thing is known of in Egypt.

[4] The purpose of this and the following paragraphs probably is : you are wayward and have an aversion to my teaching.

[5] Perhaps a sailor is meant who would act the captain and who fails in his attempt. But the whole is obscure. (Gardiner's rendering differs somewhat [Translator]).

[6] He pays no heed to the current ?

[7] He becomes entangled in the sail ropes ?

[8] The pupil does not hear ?

[9] This probably applies to the ass and the skipper, with which he previously compared him.

I will do all this to him,[1] if he turneth his back on his calling.

[Do not be a husbandman.] [2]

I am told, thou dost forsake writing, thou givest thyself up (?) to pleasures ; thou settest thy mind on work in the field, and turnest thy back on the God's Words.[3] Dost thou not bethink thee how it fareth with the husbandman, when the harvest is registered ? [4] The worm hath taken half of the corn, the hippopotamus hath devoured the rest. The mice abound in the field, and the locust hath descended. The cattle devour, and the sparrows steal. Woe to the husbandman !

The remainder, that lieth upon the threshing floor, the thieves make an end of that. The . . . of copper is destroyed ; the pair of horses dieth at the threshing and ploughing.

And now the scribe landeth on the embankment and will register the harvest. The porters [5] carry sticks, and the negroes palm-ribs. They say : " Give corn." " There is none there." He is stretched out and beaten ; he is bound and thrown into the canal – – – –. His wife is bound in his presence, his children are put in fetters (?). His neighbours leave them, they take to flight, and look after their corn.[6]

But the scribe, he directeth the work of all people. For him there are no taxes, for he payeth tribute in writing, and there are no dues for him. Prithee, know that.

[Do not be a soldier.] [7]

Put writing [8] in thine heart, that thou mayest protect thyself from hard labour of any kind and be a magistrate of high repute.

[1] But he has not threatened him with anything !
[2] *Pap. Sallier*, i. 5. 11 ff. = *Pap. Anastasi*, v. 15. 6 ff. Translated by Griffith.
[3] Hieroglyphic writing and the ancient texts.
[4] *I.e.* the taxes deducted from it.
[5] These appear here as minor officials, the negroes as police.
[6] Bring it into safety.
[7] Ostracon in Florence (see ERMAN, *Zeitschr. für ägypt. Sprache*, xviii. p. 96) ; *Pap. Lansing*, recto, 9. 3 ff. ; see ERMAN - LANGE, *Pap. Lansing*, Copenhagen, 1925, pp. 82 ff. ; BLACKMAN - PEET, *Journ. of Egypt. Archæology*, xi. pp. 291 f.
[8] Ostracon reads " the scribe " here.

Dost thou not recall the indolent one whose name is unknown ? He will be loaded like an ass, while he carrieth in
front of the scribe that knoweth what he is worth (?).

Come, let me tell thee how woefully fareth the soldier,
according as his superiors are many—the general, the commander
of the auxiliary troops, the saket who is at their head, the
standard-bearer, the lieutenant, the scribe, the captain of fifty,
and the commander of the Iwai-troops.[1] They go in and out
of their courts in the royal palace, they say : " Let them (?)
know (?) work."

He is awakened, when an hour hath gone by, and he is
driven like an ass. He worketh until the sun goeth down
under (?) its darkness (?) of night. He is hungry, and his body
is . . ., he is dead while yet alive.

[Do not be a soldier.] [2]

Ah, what meanest thou by saying : " It is thought that the
soldier is better off than the scribe " ?

Come, let me tell thee how the soldier fareth, the oft-
belaboured, when he is brought, while yet a . . . child, to be
shut up in the barracks (?). He receiveth a burning (?) blow
on his body, a ruinous blow on his eye, a blow that layeth him
out on his eyebrow, and his pate is cleft with a wound. He
is laid down and beaten, like a document.[3] He is battered
and bruised with flogging.

Come, let me tell thee how he goeth to Syria, and how he
marcheth over the mountains. His bread and his water are
borne upon his shoulder like the load of an ass ; they make his
neck as . . . as that of an ass, and the joints of his back are
bowed. His drink is stinking water. He falleth out only to
keep watch. When he reacheth the enemy, he is like a
trapped (?) bird, and he hath no strength in his limbs.

If he cometh back home to Egypt, he is like wood that the
worm eateth. He is sick and becometh bedridden. He is
brought back upon the ass ; his clothes are stolen, and his
servant hath run away.

[1] Employed in particular abroad.
[2] *Pap. Anastasi*, iv. 9. 4 ff. = *Ibid.* iii. 5. 6 .
[3] It is uncertain what is meant by this comparison—probably not
the preparing of a sheet of papyrus.

O scribe Ennana,[1] turn thee away from the thought that the soldier is better off than the scribe.

[Do not be a soldier.] [2]

Turn thy face by day to writing, and read by night, for thou knowest that which the Sovereign doeth as touching all his measures in their entirety. All the subjects are mustered, and the best are taken. The man is made into a soldier, and the stripling into a recruit. The boy, he is only bred to be torn from the arms of his mother ; if he attaineth manhood, his bones are battered.

Art thou an ass that is led, (for) it hath no understanding in its body ?

Acquire for thyself this great calling of a scribe ; pleasant and abounding in possessions are thy palette and thy papyrus roll, and blithesome art thou every day.

Prithee, know that.

[Do not be a charioteer.] [3]

Set thine heart on being a scribe, that thou mayest direct the whole earth.

Come, let me tell thee of a miserable calling, that of the officer of chariotry. He is placed in the stable [4] because of the father of his mother,[5] with five slaves ; two men of them are given him as helpers (?).

He hasteneth to get steeds from the stall in his majesty's presence. When he hath obtained goodly horses, he is glad and exulteth. He cometh with them (?) to his town, and he trampleth it underfoot [6] with zest. Happy is he when he thus trampleth underfoot . . ., (but) he knoweth not (yet) how it is with him.[7]

He expendeth his wealth which he hath from the father of

---

[1] The schoolboy who copied out the letter in *Pap. Anastasi*, iv., has introduced his own name here.

[2] *Pap. Sallier*, i. 3. 6 ff. = *Pap. Anastasi*, v. 10. 3 ff.

[3] *Pap. Anastasi*, iii. 6. 2 ff.

[4] Of the charioteers of the king, their barracks.

[5] Out of regard for his good family.

[6] The town, in his attempt to drive.

[7] He has no thought for his coming fate.

his mother, that he may acquire a chariot. Its pole costeth three deben and the chariot costeth five deben.[1]

He hasteneth to trample underfoot from upon it.[2] He maketh himself into one that is shod . . ., he taketh himself and thrusteth himself into the sandals (?). He casteth it (?) (*i.e.* the chariot) away in the thicket, and his feet are cut by the sandals (?), and his shirt is pierced with thorns.

When one cometh to muster the troops (?), he is grievously tormented (?) ; he is beaten upon the ground, beaten with an hundred stripes.

⌜Do not be a soldier, a priest, or a baker.⌝ [3]

Be a scribe, who is freed from forced labour, and protected from all work. He is released from hoeing with the hoe, and thou needest not carry a basket.[4]

It [5] separateth thee from plying the oar, and it is free from vexation. Thou hast not many masters, nor an host of superiors.

No sooner hath a man [6] come forth from his mother's womb, than he is stretched out before his superior. The boy becometh a soldier's henchman, the stripling a recruit, the grown man is made into an husbandman, and the townsman into a groom. The halt (?) is made into a doorkeeper, and the (short-sighted ?) into one that feedeth cattle ; the fowler goeth upon the . . ., and the fisherman standeth in the wet.

The superintendent of the stable standeth at the work, while his span is left in the field.[7] Corn is thrown down to his wife, and his daughter is on the embankment (?). If his span leaveth him and runneth away, he is carried off to the Iwai-troops.[8]

---

[1] That would be 273 and 455 grammes, a considerable amount, if silver is meant.

[2] *I.e.* to ride in it. The meaning of the paragraph probably is : he goes forth eagerly to war, but he cannot always ride in mountainous Palestine, and has finally to abandon the chariot.

[3] *Pap. Sallier*, i. 6. 9 ff., and, with variations, *Pap. Anastasi*, ii. 6. 7 ff.

[4] A peasant's tasks.　　　　　　　　[5] The scribe's profession.

[6] Who has not become a scribe.

[7] He has to inspect the work in the fields. What follows must mean that while thus engaged he cannot concern himself with his family. The other manuscript also introduces his own servant and maidservant.

[8] See p. 194, note 1. Meaning probably : if during these non-military activities his horses get lost, he is put into the infantry.

The soldier, when he goeth up to Syria, hath no staff and no sandals. He knoweth not whether he be dead or alive, by reason of the (fierce ?) lions. The foe lieth hidden in the scrub, and the enemy standeth ready for battle. The soldier marcheth and crieth out to his god : " Come to me and deliver me ! "

The priest standeth there as an husbandman, and the wḗ'eb-priest worketh in the canal [1] – – – – he is drenched in the river ; it maketh no difference to him whether it be winter or summer, whether the sky be windy or rainy.

When the baker standeth and baketh and layeth bread on the fire, his head is inside the oven, and his son holdeth fast his feet. Cometh it to pass that he slippeth from his son's hand, he falleth into the blaze.

But the scribe, he directeth every work that is in this land.

[BE AN OFFICIAL.] [2]

Let not thine heart go afluttering like leaves before the wind – – – –. Set not thine heart on pleasures. Alas, they profit not, they render a man no service – – – –. When he worketh [3] and *it is his lot* to serve the Thirty,[4] he worketh *and* extendeth not his strength,[5] *for* evil toil lieth (yet) in front of him. No servant bringeth him water, and no women will make bread for him, whereas his companions [6] *live* according to their desire, and their servants act in their stead.[7] (But) the man of no sense standeth there and toileth, and his eye looketh enviously at them.[8]

Therefore give heed, thou naughty one ; thou obstinate one, that will not hear when thou art spoken to. Hasten to it, the calling with the gay. . . .[9] It is the one that directeth all the Councils of Thirty [10] and the courtiers of the (Royal) Circle. Prithee, know that.

---

[1] Even the priesthood is not immune from forced labour.
[2] *Pap. Sallier*, i. 5. 4 ff.
[3] Performs manual labour.
[4] The college of high officials.
[5] He dares not sleep.
[6] His erstwhile schoolfellows who have become scribes.
[7] Relieve them of domestic tasks, or compulsory labour on the embankments, etc.
[8] The schoolfellows.
[9] The scribe's profession.
[10] There were thus several such councils.

[A FRAGMENT.] [1]

I am told that thou dost forsake writing and givest thyself up to pleasures ; thou turnest thy back on the God's Words, and runnest away from this calling of Thōth. Thine heart knoweth not that thou art . . . in order to lead others – – – –.

The subject of the fragments following is perhaps again the woes of the soldier.

2. ACTUAL LETTERS AS MODELS FOR SCHOOLBOYS

Among the letters, which the teacher set his pupils to copy, are several apparently real business, or private, letters, similar to a number of fairly well-preserved originals still in our possession. If they have gained the distinction of being employed as models, the teacher at any rate must have considered their style to be good, and besides, his pupil could learn from them the various forms of epistolary composition.

That the teacher selected them from his own family or official correspondence is quite clear from the fact that these letters occur in only one of the schoolboy manuscripts, whereas the fictitious letters, dealt with later, recur in various manuscripts.

Here, only certain specimens are given. The differences in the formulæ employed in the letters are to be noted ; these being determined by whether, as in the first example, persons of the same standing are writing to one another, or, as in the second, a superior to an underling, or, as in the third, an underling to "his master."

[PURSUIT OF A RUNAWAY SLAVE.] [2]

The Commandant of the Auxiliaries of Zeku,[3] Kakemur, (writeth) to the Commandant of the Auxiliaries, Anii, and to the Commandant of the Auxiliaries, Bekenptah.

In life, prosperity, and health, and in the favour of Amunrē, king of gods, and of the Ka of King Sēthos II, our good lord.[4]

I say to Rē-Harakhti : " Keep Pharaoh, our good lord, in health ! Let him celebrate millions of jubilees, while we are daily in his favour."

Furthermore : I was sent forth from the halls of the royal palace after these two slaves on the ninth day of the third month of Summer at the time of evening. And when I came

[1] *Pap. Anastasi*, v. 6. 1 ff.
[2] *Ibid.* v. 19. 2 ff.
[3] Frontier station not far from the Bitter Lakes.
[4] Meaning : May you receive this letter in life, prosperity, etc.

on the tenth day of the third month of Summer to the castle (?) of Zeku, I was told that the news from the south was that they had gone past on the . . . th day of the third month of Summer. And when I came to the fortress, I was told that the groom (?) had come from the desert (and had reported) that they had crossed the boundary north of the Migdol [1] of Sēthos, who is . . . like Sēth.

When my letter reacheth you, write unto me about all that hath come to pass with you. Where were their tracks found? Which watch (?) found their tracks? What men pursued after them? Write unto me of all that was done about them, and how many men followed them.

Live ye happily!

[ORDER TO CARRY OUT A PIECE OF WORK.] [2]

The king's scribe and general, Ramōse, saith to the mason, Auroi: This letter is brought unto thee.

Further: When my letter reacheth thee, thou art to go to the town of . . . rē in Bubastis, and thou art to execute every behest, and art then to come to make report unto me. Look thou to it, have a care, take heed to thyself! Hold not back in any respect!

My letter cometh unto thee by the hand of the priest Ramōse. (He was?) present, when thou camest unto me near by the canal, and I beat thee, saying: "How comes it that thou neglectest my business? I will set thee to work on the canal."

Prithee, know that!

[BUSINESS OF VARIOUS SORTS.] [3]

The scribe Pe-uhem gladdeneth [4] his lord Anhorrekh.

In life, prosperity, and health! This is written to let my lord know.

A further matter to gladden my lord. I have heard the order that my lord sent me, that I am to give fodder to the horses of the great stable of Ramesses-Beloved-of-Amūn, likewise to the horses of the great . . . stable of Binerē-Beloved-of-Amūn, [5] of the Residence.

[1] Canaanite word for "fort."   [2] *Pap. Anastasi*, v. 21. 8 ff.
[3] *Pap. Bologna*, 1094, 2: 7 ff.
[4] Probably only means: makes him a communication, which (as just below) need by no means be gladdening.
[5] Merneptah, the reigning king (*circa* 1230 B.C.).

A further matter to gladden my lord. The peasants of the domain of Pharaoh, which is in the charge of my lord, three men of these ran away from the superintendent of the stable, Neferhotep, when he beat them. Now behold, the fields of the domain of Pharaoh, which are in the charge of my lord, are neglected and there is none to till them.

This is written to let my lord know.

[REQUEST FOR ASSISTANCE IN A MATTER OF TAXATION.][1]

The priest Pramheb of the temple of Sutekh enquireth after the steward Sēthos. In life, prosperity, and health, and in the favour of Amunrē, king of gods !

I say unto Rē-Harakhti, to Seth, to Nephthys, and to all the gods and goddesses of Pe-u-nozem : " Mayest thou prosper, mayest thou live, may I see thee again in safety, and fold thee in my embrace."

Furthermore : I have heard of the many good things which thou hast done for my ship, in that thou didst dispatch it. May Month reward thee ! May the sun, thy good lord,[2] reward thee !

When my letter reacheth thee, thou shalt go with the standard-bearer,[3] Ptahemmenu, and shalt make a declaration to the vizier with respect to the much silver, concerning which the henchman Eai saith : " Hand it over," though it is not my tax at all. And take the copy of the silver [4] and of the dues (?) in writing to the south,[5] and place them before the vizier, and tell him, he is not to tax (me on account of the) people, for I (personally) have no people. For I am responsible for the galley, and I am responsible likewise for the House-of-Nephthys,[6] and behold, the multitude [7] of temples, that are in the district, it is not conformable to me.[8] I am very miserable, in extremest misery, because of what hath been done unto me.

---

[1] *Pap. Bologna*, 1094, 5. 8 ff.   [2] The king.
[3] An officer of sorts.   [4] *I.e.* the tax assessment.
[5] The vizier will be in Thebes.
[6] Sense of the passage : I cannot be assessed in accordance with the large number of people that I employ, for they are necessary for all the state property which I unfortunately must administer.
[7] Literally " heap " ; *cf.* the familiar use of the word " heap " in English.
[8] It is out of keeping with my personal circumstances, that I should have to look after all of them.

Now behold, – – – – and speak also with some one else with regard to the excessive administrative work, that is imposed upon me as dues attaching to the temple of Sutekh, and to the domain of Pharaoh, that are in my charge.

Behold, that is (for thee) a small matter, and omit nothing (thereof), together with the standard-bearer Ptahemmenu.

Fare thee well !

[ENQUIRIES.] [1]

The scribe Pe-uhem gladdeneth his lord, the scribe Mehu of the workshop of Pharaoh.

In life, prosperity, and health ! This is written to let my lord know.

Something further to gladden my lord. The vizier sent three boys, saying : " Make them priests in the temple of Merneptah in the House-of-Ptah." (But) one laid hold on them and took them away . . . and said : " They shall be soldiers." Pray, hasten and pass by them, and write to me as to how they fare.

Likewise look up the merchant and see whether he hath come back from Syria.

Likewise thou shalt pass (by me) here in Memphis ; my heart is in ill humour and I cannot write (it) to thee.

Pray send the servant Taennana, and write to me as to how thou farest, by the hand of any one who may be coming here from thee.

Fare thee well !

[FAMILY LETTER.] [2]

The scribe Amenmōse inquireth after his father, the Commandant of the Auxiliaries, Bekenptah.

In life, prosperity, and health, and in the favour of Amunrē, king of gods.

I say to Rē-Harakhti, and to Atum and his Ennead : " Mayest thou be in health daily."

Furthermore : Pray write to me as to the state of thy health by the hand of any persons who are coming hither from thee, for I desire daily to hear as to how thou farest. Thou writest to me neither good nor ill, and no person of them that thou sendest passeth by me, that he may tell me how thou

---

[1] *Pap. Bologna*, 1094, 4. 10 ff.   [2] *Pap. Anastasi*, v. 20. 6 ff.

farest. Pray write to me as to how thou farest, and how thy servants fare in regard to all their concerns, for I have an exceeding longing for them.

Furthermore : I had brought to thee (only) fifty good kyllestis-loaves, for the carrier threw away thirty of them saying : " I am too heavily laden." And he would not wait for me to have vegetables brought to him from the store-house (?), although he had not informed me as to what evening he would be coming to me. I send thee by him two plates of fat for unguent.

Fare thee well !

[Congratulations.] [1]

The Commandant of Auxiliaries and Overseer of the Foreign Country, Penamūn, to the Commandant of Auxiliaries, Pehri-pide.

In life, prosperity, health, and in the favour of Amunrē, king of gods, and of the Ka of King Sēthos II ! [2]

I say to Rē-Harakhti : " Keep Pharaoh, our good lord, in health. May he celebrate millions of jubilees, whilst thou [3] art daily in his favour ! "

Furthermore, I have heard what thou hast written, saying : " Pharaoh, my good lord, hath carried out for me his good designs. Pharaoh hath appointed me (chief captain) of the auxiliaries of the well." [4] So hast thou written unto me.

It is a goodly disposition of Rē that thou art now in the place of thy father. Bravo ! The same, (and again) the same ! [5]

When thy letter reached me I rejoiced exceedingly. May Rē-Harakhti grant thee a long life filling thy father's place ! May Pharaoh regard thee yet again ! Mayest thou grow stronger, and write to me again as to how thou farest, and how thy father fareth, by the hand of the letter-carriers who come hither from thee.

Furthermore : All goeth well with me, and all goeth well with the domain [6] of Pharaoh. Have no anxiety about me.

Fare thee well !

[1] *Pap. Anastasi*, v. 11. 7 ff.
[2] Merneptah's successor.   [3] The person addressed.
[4] One of the fortified well-stations on the road to Palestine.
[5] May just the same good fortune attend you yet further !
[6] Which the writer has to administer.

[REPROOF OF A HIGH OFFICIAL.] [1]

This royal decree is brought to thee.

What concern hast thou with the Tekten of the Oasis country, that thou hast sent forth this scribe of thine to remove them from their Niau ? [2]

If now . . . Rē and Ptah suffer (us) not to hear aught respecting (?) these rumours (?) that one heareth, and this prince [3] then writeth saying : " Thou art to bring hither the Tekten that can spy "—whither wilt thou (turn) ? To whose house wilt thou (go) ? He cometh down on thine head like a sand dune. Thou art taken away and art placed there – – – –.

Even so is it with thine other very grave offence, which thou now committest : thou lettest Pharaoh come, in order to betake himself unto Heliopolis, without causing tools for the workshop to be brought as equipment behind thy lord – – – –.

Art thou not put in the place of other superintendents of the treasury, who abstained from removing a Tekten from his Niau, and only thou (doest this) ?

When the decree of Pharaoh reacheth thee, thou art to write a letter to this scribe of thine, whom thou didst despatch to the Oasis country, saying : " Beware ! Abstain from taking away even one of the Tekten, or it will be accounted unto thee as a crime worthy of death." And thou shalt hand over thy letter to an henchman of thine, and thou shalt despatch him with the runner [4] with all speed.

[ENNUI IN A LONELY PLACE.] [5]

It is concerned with an officer who, instead of marching to Palestine, has to erect buildings on the frontier. But he can do no work, and can only give information about dogs and gnats. The whole is of course ironical.

[1] *Pap. Anastasi*, iv. 10. 8 ; was also in *Pap. Anastasi*, v. The letter might be purely fictitious.

[2] The Tekten and Niau are barbarians of sorts, who were kept in the western desert as light troops. They are mentioned also in Merneptah's hymn of victory.

[3] The title indicates one of the highest officials in the administration.

[4] A courier who maintained communications with the Oases.

[5] *Pap. Anastasi*, iv. 12. 5 ; was also in *Pap. Anastasi*, v. It may well be a purely fictitious letter. It appears to be composed in verses of four lines.

I reside in Kenkentaui,[1] and I am without equipment. There are no people to make bricks, and there is no straw [2] in the district.

Where are they that bring me? – – – – Are there no asses? —They are stolen.

I spend the day gazing at what is in the sky, as though (?) I were catching birds. Mine eye glanceth furtively at the road, in order to go up to Palestine.

I pass the night under trees that bear no fruit (?) to eat. Where are their dates? They have none (?), they bear not.

The gnat is there in the twilight, and the zewet-gnat at noon, – – – – and it sucketh at every vein.

I go like one that is firm upon the bones, I traverse the lands on my feet.[3]

If ever one openeth a bottle, it is full of beer of Kedi, and people came forth to . . . the cup outside.[4]

There are two hundred large dogs here, and three hundred wolf-hounds, in all five hundred,[5] which stand ready every day at the door of the house whenever I go out, because they smelt the seber [6] when the jar was opened. However (?), have I not got the little wolf-hound of Teherhu, a royal scribe, here in the house? And he delivereth (?) me from them. At every hour, whensoever I sally forth, he is with me as guide upon the road. As soon as he barketh I run to undo (?) the bolt.[7]

" Isheb " is the name of a wolf-hound, red, with a long tail. He goeth by night into the stalls of the cattle. He beginneth with the largest [8] first, for he maketh no distinction whatsoever, when he is fierce.

God will deliver whom He will (from ?) this fire, which is here and which hath no compassion.[9]

Furthermore: A . . . scribe is here with me, every vein

[1] An unknown place. The name, " Flogging of Egypt," is perhaps only a joke.

[2] Which was necessary for the manufacture of crude brick.

[3] He complains again that he has no donkey.

[4] Is the meaning: one is glad even if one can only admire such a drink from outside?

[5] The street-dogs of the Orient are meant.

[6] From the writing, a drink or the like.

[7] Or " to fasten " ? Meaning probably: this tame dog keeps me from going out.

[8] Of the cattle.

[9] Meaning: God (the King ?) may let me go from here.

of whose face . . . ; the . . . disease hath developed in his eye, and the worm gnaweth at his tooth. I cannot leave him destitute, when my company goeth forward. So let his ration be given unto him here, that he may have rest in the region of Kenkentaui.

[LONGING FOR MEMPHIS.] [1]

Behold, mine heart hath gone forth secretly. It hasteneth to a place that it knoweth ; it voyageth downstream, that it may see Memphis – – – –. But I sit and wait for (a messenger), that he may tell me how Memphis fareth. I have no message, and mine heart leapeth in its place.

Come to me, Ptah,[2] to take (me) to Memphis, and let me view thee unhindered.

I spend the day with mine heart dreaming (?). Mine heart is not in my body, all my limbs – – – –, mine eye is weary with looking,[3] mine ear is not . . ., my voice is . . ., so that it speaketh all manner of things pervertedly. Be gracious to me, and suffer (me ?) to mount up (?) to them.

3. FICTITIOUS MODEL LETTERS

Besides actual letters, which schoolboys were given to copy out, literary productions in the form of letters were placed before them. Firstly, all the exhortations and warnings given above on pp. 189 ff. ; these have in every case been given an epistolary form, having prefixed to them " The official A. saith to the scribe B." Secondly, compositions, which from their contents might really be letters, but in which the business element almost escapes notice, as it is cloaked in such flowery language, and is so spun out and expanded.

Many of these texts recur in different manuscripts—one at a considerably later date [4]—and were thus certainly prized as examples of elegant style. In the case of several, the suspicion is unavoidable that the whole purport of the mass of unusual names and words, which they contain, was to familiarize the schoolboy with the writing of them.

---

[1] *Pap. Anastasi*, iv. 4. 11 ff. The letter might be fictitious.
[2] The god of Memphis.   [3] For a messenger ?
[4] A *Pap. Rainer* in Vienna, belonging to the Twenty-First Dynasty. The letter, which is known to us from a MS. of the time of Merneptah, must have been written under Ramesses II. It thus continued to be used in the schools for at least two hundred years.

[In praise of the new city called House-of-Ramesses.] [1]

House-of-Ramesses is the famous newly founded residence of Ramesses II, which lay on the site of the later Pelusium. It was regarded as the centre of an empire that was supposed to embrace Palestine and Egypt. The letter is probably based on a poem similar to that given below (pp. 270 ff.), celebrating the entry of the king into this city.

The scribe Paibes greeteth his lord, the scribe Amenemōpe.[2]

In life, prosperity, and health! This is written in order to give information to my lord.

Another greeting to my lord: I have arrived at House-of-Ramesses-Beloved-of-Amūn and have found it flourishing exceedingly, a fair throne (?), whereof the like existeth not; after the pattern of Thebes. It was Rē who founded it himself, the residence where life is pleasant.

Its field is full of all good things, and it hath provisions and sustenance every day. Its ponds (?) are full of fishes, and its lakes of birds. Its plots are verdant with herbage, and its banks bear dates. – – – – Its granaries are full of barley and wheat, and they reach unto the sky. Garlic and leeks for victuals (are there), and lettuce (?) of the . . . -garden; pomegranates, apples, and olives; figs from the orchard, sweet wine of Kankēme,[3] *surpassing* honey; red uz-fish from the canal of . . . ; betin(?)-fish *from Lake* Neher; – – – –.[4]

Shihor [5] yieldeth salt, and Lake Her natron. Its ships fare forth and come to port.

Provisions and sustenance are in it daily. One rejoiceth when one dwelleth in it, and none saith unto it, "Would that!" The small in it are like unto the great.[6]

---

[1] *Pap. Anastasi*, iii. 1. 11 ff.; *Pap. Rainer*, and an ostracon. See Gardiner, *Journ. of Egypt. Archæology*, v. p. 185. *Cf.* also Blackman and Peet, "Papyrus Lansing: A Translation with Notes," in *Journ. of Egypt. Archæology*, xi. pp. 293 ff.

[2] In *Pap. Anastasi*, iii., Amenemōpe is the teacher, Paibes the pupil.

[3] The frequently mentioned vineyard, which was probably situated in the neighbourhood of House-of-Ramesses.

[4] There then follow five other kinds of fish from different pools—all unknown to us.

[5] The stretch of water, also mentioned in the Old Testament, which forms the boundary of Egypt, *i.e.* the Pelusiac arm of the Nile, or rather, since here it yields salt, the lagoons created by it.

[6] The humble person here lives like a great person in other cities.

Come, let us celebrate for it its festivals of the sky,[1] and its beginnings of seasons.

The Zouf-swamp cometh to it with papyrus, and Shihor with rushes. Vine-trailers hath it from the orchards, and garlands from the vineyards. Birds (are brought to it ?) from the cool water – – – –. The sea hath beg-fish and ad-fish, and the lagoons present unto it their . . .

The youths of Great-of-Victories [2] are in festive attire every day, and sweet oil is upon their heads in the newly dressed hair. They stand beside their doors, their hands weighed down with foliage (?), with greenery from the House of Hathor, and with flax (?) from Lake Her, on the day whereon Ramesses entereth, even Month [3]-in-the-Two-Lands, on the morning of the feast of Khoiakh. Every man and his fellow likewise utter their petitions.

The draughts of Great-of-Victories are sweet ; its tebi [4] are as shaau ; [5] its khiwawa [4] taste like inu,[5] surpassing (?) honey ; beer of Kedi [6] from the port, and wine from the vineyards.

Sweet unguents (are there) from the waters of Segbain, and garlands from the . . . -garden, sweet singers of Great-of-Victories, who have been instructed in Memphis.

Dwell (there) happily, and stride freely forth, not moving thence, O Usimarē-Chosen-of-Amūn, Month-in-the-Two-Lands, Ramesses-Beloved-of-Amūn, thou god !

[LETTER OF A GOVERNOR TO A VASSAL.] [7]

The Fan-bearer at the right hand of the King, Captain of Auxiliaries and Superintendent of the foreign lands of Ethiopia, Paser,[8] saith unto the Protector of his People.[9] This letter is brought unto thee.

[1] Determined by events in the sky (new moon, rising of Sōthis, etc.), in contrast to the conventional ones (New Year, first day of the month, etc.).

[2] A name for House-of-Ramesses.   [3] The war-god.

[4] Drinks of sorts.   [5] Fruit.

[6] Kedi is an oft-mentioned country, possibly Cilicia. The "port" is the harbour belonging to House-of-Ramesses.

[7] *Pap. Koller*, 3. 3 ff. ; also on an ostracon. See GARDINER, *Hieratic Texts*, p. 40.

[8] A viceroy of Ethiopia of this name lived under Ramesses II, another under King Ai ; the ostracon also gives the writer of the letter this name.

[9] *I.e.* probably some petty Nubian dynast.

Furthermore : When my letter reacheth thee, thou shalt cause the tribute [1] to be furnished with all that appertaineth thereto. With cattle and young oxen and short-horned bulls, with gazelles, oryxes, ibexes, and ostriches. Their cargo boats, their cattle-transports, and their boats *are ready to hand* (?), their sailors and their crews are prepared for starting. With much gold wrought into dishes, and fine gold in bushels, and good gold-dust (?) from the desert in a bag of red linen. With ivory and ebony, with ostrich feathers, with nebes-fruit as . . ., and bread of the nebes, shakarkaba, meyenyekhis, behkek, and shesa,[2] which look like panther-skins, with gummi-resin and hæmatite, with red jasper, amethyst, and crystal, with cats from Miu, monkeys and apes – – – –. Numerous men of Irmi [3] walk in front of the tribute, their eberez-staves (?) overlaid with gold – – – – ;[4] tall men of Tirek in . . . -garments, their fans of gold, wearing high feathers, and their bracelets are of woven work (?) ; many negroes of all sorts.

Increase thy contributions every year ! Have a care for thine head, and cease from thine indolence. – – – – See thou to it, give heed, be on thy guard ! Be mindful of the day when the tribute is brought, when thou passest before the king beneath the window,[5] and the counsellors are ranged on either side in front of his majesty, and the chiefs and envoys of all lands stand there marvelling and viewing the tribute. Thou art afraid . . ., thine hand sinketh, and thou knowest not whether death or life lieth before thee. Thou hast (only) the strength to petition thy gods : " Deliver me ! Prosper me but this once ! "

[EQUIPMENT FOR A ROYAL JOURNEY.] [6]

The scribe Amenemōpe saith unto the scribe Paibes : This letter is brought unto thee.

Furthermore : Take heed to have (full) preparations made

---

[1] Which he is delivering to the king.

[2] Probably all are fruits. The writer throughout the letter piles one rare foreign word on the top of another.

[3] A Nubian tribe.

[4] A series of barbarous words, which probably refer to the adornment of the people.

[5] The great window of the palace in which the king shows himself on ceremonial occasions.

[6] *Pap. Anastasi*, iv. 13. 8 ff. ; commencement in *Pap. Koller*, 5. 5 ff.

in front of Pharaoh, thy good lord, in fair and excellent order, and let not thyself be blamed. Look thou to it, give heed, and beware. Be not remiss.

List of all that thou must have provided.

Cause to be procured what the basket-makers need in the way of reeds and rushes. Likewise have made ten flat baskets for heaps, one hundred round (?) baskets for making presentation, and five hundred baskets for food-stuffs (?).

List of the things which thou shalt have made for them.[1]

(*A long list of victuals. First* 29,000 *loaves of bread in ten different varieties, including at the end,* 1200 assorted Asiatic loaves. *Then cakes in* baskets *and* cups, *next* 100 baskets of dried meat, 250 handfuls of entrails, 60 measures of milk, 90 measures of cream. *Furthermore* 100 heaps of vegetables, *50 geese, 70 rams, bunches of grapes, pomegranates, figs, flowers, garlands, etc. etc. Lastly, wood-fuel and charcoal.*)

Behold, I write to thee, to instruct thee in the regulations for equipping the ports,[2] which thou wilt execute before Pharaoh, thy good lord. Thou art thus not lacking in any counsels, whereof thou wilt stand in need. Suffer not thyself to be wanting in understanding in the . . ., and suffer not thyself to be wanting in vigour in the equipping. (*Then comes an additional note concerning honey, leeks, etc.*)

[EQUIPMENT FOR THE KING.] [3]

Take heed to have full preparation made in front of Pharaoh, thy good lord, in fair and excellent order, with bread, beer, meat, cakes . . ., and likewise with incense and with a pleasant oil (*here follow seven varieties of oil bearing foreign names, from the countries of Arsa, Khatti, Singar, Emor, Tekhis, and Naharina*), and with many oils of the harbour, for the anointing of his soldiery and chariotry; with oxen and short-horned oxen, goodly, castrated, from the west, with fat calves from the south, and many fat birds from the reed-swamp.

Next come twelve sorts of fish, with notification of their places of origin, then fat quails (?) *and* pigeons of the season of harvest,[4]

---

[1] The baskets.

[2] This " equipping of the ports " is known to us under Thutmōsis III as an annual undertaking.

[3] *Pap. Anastasi,* iv. 15. 1 ff.; *ibid.* iii. 8. 1 ff.

[4] *I.e.* which have been fattened up in the field.

14

furthermore honey, oil for eating, fat of geese, cream, *milk, lentils, etc. etc.*, jars of pewer-drink for the servants,[1] beer from Kedi, wine from Syria, and beans in heaps.

Bottles (?) and cups of silver and gold,[2] which are set out in array (?) beneath the (palace) window.

Slaves from the land of Kerke, youths in relays in the capacity of butlers of his majesty; they are washed, anointed, and clothed (?) in . . ., when they pass under the window. The man who is among them is bound for the kitchen, and will provide beer of Kedi for the palace – – – –.

Canaanite slaves from Syria, goodly youths, and goodly negroes from Ethiopia, destined to carry the fan; they are shod with white sandals and clad (?) in . . ., their armlets (?) are on their hands.

Then follow all kinds of effects needed by the king: firstly, goodly . . . from the land of Emor, whose staves are of meri-wood and inlaid in the work of the land of Kedi. *Next the* beauteous chariots of berri-wood, that glitter more than lapis lazuli; *eleven parts of them are enumerated, and in every case what they are made of is notified, or from what country they originate. Furthermore:* Bows and many quivers . . ., sword, lance, and knife, goodly weapons for his majesty. Goodly whips of zaga-wood, their lashes being of red linen – – – –. Long staves for his majesty, whose handles are wrought with gold, *etc. etc., all consisting of as many foreign words and names as possible.*

Flour in many heaps, and heaps of flour of wheat, beans, figs of Syria, pomegranates and apples, *and lastly charcoal* – – – –.

Large and well-baked loaves, appointed for the sustenance of the notables, and assorted Asiatic wheaten loaves, which are for the sustenance of the soldiery, and which lie in heaps under the window of the right side. Copper ore in many ingots, and jugs of . . ., which the children of Arsa bring upon the neck as gifts for his majesty; the horns which they hold in their hands are filled with oil of . . .

Beauteous steeds reared in Singar, steers of the first quality from the land of Khatti, and cows from Arsa, which are brought by their princes, who stand bowing beneath the (window) – – – –.

---

[1] Thus a beverage of an inferior kind; see also p. 217 with note 5.

[2] It might be supposed that another document actually begins here, describing the presentation of tribute.

[EQUIPMENT OF A WAR-CHARIOT.] [1]

Furthermore : Take good heed to have made ready the pair of horses bound for Syria, together with their stable-men and their grooms. Their coats are . . . ; (they [2] are) full of provender and straw, and rubbed down twice over.

Their bags are full of kyllestis-bread, *and each single ass carries them* between two men. [3]

Their chariots are of berri-wood and full of weapons. Eighty arrows are in the quiver ; (there is) the . . ., the lance, the sword, the knife, – – – – the whip of zaga-wood fully supplied with lashes (?), the chariot-club, the staff of the watch, the spear of the land of Khatti, the . . . Their [4] points are of bronze of six-fold alloy, graven, – – – –. Their cuirasses lie beside them. The bows – – – –.

4. GREETINGS TO TEACHERS AND SUPERIORS

[TO THE TEACHER.] [5]

(Thou didst) bring (me) up as a child, when I was with thee ; thou didst beat my back and thy teaching went into mine ear.

I am like a frisky horse ; sleep cometh not to me by day into mine heart, and it is not upon me by night, for I would be one that is profitable unto his lord, like a servant profitable unto his lord.

I would build for thee a new mansion, which is upon the ground of thy city and is planted with trees upon every side of it.

Thy stalls within (it are full of cattle), and its granaries are full of barley and wheat ; there is corn therein and – – – –, beans and lentils – – – –, flax and vegetables – – – – and love-apples, [6] which are to be measured with baskets.

---

[1] *Pap. Koller*, i. 1 ff. See GARDINER, *Hieratic Texts*, p. 36.

[2] The horses ?

[3] The horses are thus accompanied by a train bearing provisions for those in charge of them.

[4] The weapons.

[5] *Pap. Anastasi*, iv. 8. 7 ff. ; see also BLACKMAN-PEET, *Journ. of Egypt. Archæology*, xi. p. 293.

[6] A fruit often mentioned in poems of the time ; the translation " love-apples " only rests upon the comparison with the fruit dudaïm mentioned in Genesis and the Song of Songs.

Thy herd doubleth the backs,[1] and thy breeding-cows are pregnant.

I will plant for thee five acres as a vegetable garden to the south of thy city, with cucumbers and – – – – as the sand for multitude.

Let ships come in order to stow them aboard, whereby thou mayest know what thou offerest to Ptah Nefer-hor, that he may fulfil for thee thy desire.

[To the teacher.] [2]

May Amūn afford thee joy in thine heart, may he grant thee a good old age, that thou mayest pass a happy life, until thou attainest honour. Thy lip is in health, thy limbs flourish, and thine eye seeth afar.

Thou puttest on fine linen; thou ridest the horses,[3] with a golden whip in thine hand; thou hast a new . . ., *and the yoke is of Syrian workmanship.* The negroes run in front of thee and execute what thou wouldest (have done).

Thou embarkest on thy ship of cedar-wood, that is manned from bow to stern, and thou arrivest at this thy fair mansion, which thou hast builded for thyself.

Thy mouth is full of wine and beer, of bread, and meat, and cakes. Oxen are slain and wine(-jars) opened, and pleasant singing is before thee.

The chief anointer anointeth with kemi-unguent, thy water-bailiff beareth garlands, thine overseer of the country folk presenteth fowl, and thy fisherman presenteth fish.

Thy galley cometh from Syria laden with all good things. Thy stall is full of calves, and thine herd (?) flourisheth.

Thou endurest, and thine enemy hath fallen; he that spake against thee, he is no more. Thou enterest in before the Nine Gods and comest forth justified.[4]

[To an official.] [5]

Thou livest, art prosperous, and art in health. Thou art not wretched and sufferest no distress. – – – – Thou endurest like the hours,[6] and thy counsel endureth; long is thy life-

---

[1] *I.e.* its numbers.

[2] *Pap. Anastasi*, iv. 3. 2 ff., and two ostraca.

[3] *I.e.* drivest thy chariot.   [4] At the posthumous trial.

[5] *Pap. Anastasi*, v. 14. 6 ff.; see also the *verso* of *Pap. Anastasi*, ii.

[6] Which recur without intermission.

time, and thine utterances are excellent.   Thine eye seeth what is beautiful, and thou hearest what is pleasant. − − − −

Thou art the herdsman whom God hath given, and thou carest for many.   Thou givest thine hand to him that is miserable, and raiseth up him that hath fallen.

Thou endurest, and thine enemy hath fallen ; he that spake against thee, he is no more.

Thou enterest in before the Nine Gods and comest forth justified.

[To THE TEACHER ?] [1]

Good sir, thou wilt endure and wilt every day have victuals by thee, cheerful and flourishing daily, and praised numberless times.

Joy and gladness join themselves unto thee, and thy limbs proclaim health.   Every day growest thou younger, and nought harmful (?) hath the mastery over thee.

There cometh a year wherein (?) one calleth to mind thy beauty, and thy like is found not.   Thine eye is bright every day, and thine ear is sharpened (?)

Thou hast many beauteous years.   Thy months (thou spendest) in prosperity, thy days in life, and thine hours in health.   Thy gods are satisfied with thee and are gladdened by thy words.

Thou sendest away (?) the beauteous West,[2] thou becomest not old and art not sick. Thou completest one hundred and ten years upon earth, and thy limbs are strong, as happeneth to one that is praised like thee, when his god rewardeth him.

Then the lord of the gods entrusteth thee to the lords of the Western Mountain,[3] and bouquets are assigned thee in Busiris,[4] and cool water in the necropolis. Thy soul cometh forth that it may walk about wherever it willeth.[5]

[1] *Pap. Anastasi*, iii. 4. 4.

[2] Since the West is the realm of the dead, this will mean : thou puttest off the day of death.

[3] *I.e.* when God at last sendeth death to thee.

[4] The holy city of Osiris, in the Delta.

[5] The desire of the dead was to be able to leave their tombs.

5. A LITERARY CONTROVERSY [1]

I put this remarkable composition immediately after the school-letters, because, like them, it was actually used in the schools as a standard work, and the spirit which it breathes is the same as that which prevails in them.   On the other hand, it is not to a young scholar that the official of the royal stable, Hori, recommends, in the capacity of instructor, good style and clear ideas, but to the scribe in command of the army, Amenemōpe.   Nor does Hori cherish the hope of converting Amenemōpe, but makes fun of him.   The work is a satirical letter, and indeed originated in an actual correspondence, which gradually developed into a literary controversy.

Hori, it would seem, had last written to his adversary bidding him furnish corn for the soldiers, and the latter had not properly carried out the instructions, but had sent back a reply which aimed at being malicious, but which was, in Hori's opinion, a mere jumble of praise and blame.   To this Hori again makes answer in his long dispatch, telling his opponent what he on his part thinks of him as regards both his knowledge and the deeds about which he brags. At the same time he defends himself against the attack which his adversary has directed against him.

This ink-slinging on the part of two officials can in itself have possessed no interest ; it must therefore have been the style and the humour which gave the work its value.   Though we naturally cannot fully appreciate either, yet even a modern reader will enjoy the polite and ironical way in which Hori deals with his luckless victim.   He is an educated Egyptian, to whom crudity was a thing to be avoided.   If the work strikes us as monotonous in parts, it yet atones for this by presenting us with a series of remarkable pictures of the civilized world of the day, particularly in the account of the journey through Palestine.   When reading this work, it must never be forgotten that the author is presenting us with an over-coloured and exaggerated description.

The work belongs to the time of Ramesses II ; that the author was actually called Hori, and his opponent Amenemōpe, cannot be doubted, for the different manuscripts all agree in giving them the same names.

[1. THE WRITER OF THE LETTER.]

The scribe of choice perception, patient in discussion (?), at whose utterances men rejoice when they are heard, a craftsman

---

[1] Preserved completely in *Pap. Anastasi*, i., in London ; a fragment in a Turin papyrus.   In addition, single excerpts on eight ostraca.—Dealt with seriously for the first time in 1866 by CHABAS in his *Voyage d'un Égyptien en Syrie*, but only in 1885 recognized by Erman to be a satire.   See GARDINER, *Hieratic Texts*, i., Leipzig, 1911.

in the God's Words ;[1] there is nothing that he knoweth not.
He is a champion in valour and in the work of Seshat,[2] and a
servant of the lord of Hermopolis in his academy of writing ; a
teacher of subordinates [3] in the office of books. The most
eminent of his companions, and the commencement of his family ;
the prince of his contemporaries, without his peer. He is to be
detected [4] in all lads ; of active (?) hand, and his fingers make
the child become great. Exquisite – – – – wise of understanding – – – – his laughter (?). Beloved in (men's) hearts
without being resisted (?) ; men desire to be friends with him
and tire not of him. He is swift to inscribe empty pages.
Youthful, eminent of charm, pleasant of grace ; who expoundeth
the difficult passages like him that composed them.[5] All that
issueth from his mouth is steeped in honey, and hearts are made
healthy therewith, as it were with medicine. Groom of his
majesty,[6] who accompanieth the sovereign and traineth the
king's foals, a keen cultivator of the stable,[7] – – – – Hori, son
of Wennofre, of Abydos, region of the righteous ;[8] born of
Tewosre in the district of Barset,[9] singer of Bast in the Field of
God.[10]

[2. Salutation to the recipient.]

He inquireth after his friend, his excellent brother, the royal
scribe who issueth commands to the victorious army, of exquisite taste, goodly of character, wise of understanding, who
hath not his equal in any scribe. The darling of all men, as
beautiful to him that beholdeth his charm as is a papyrus-plant
in the heart of strangers.[11] In every aspect a scribe, and
there is nothing that he knoweth not. Men enquire of him in
respect to his answer, in quest of what is choice. Clever and
of friendly heart ; one that loveth men, that rejoiceth at a

---

[1] Writing and sacred books.   [2] The goddess of writing.
[3] Or " assistant teacher."   [4] *I.e.* his instruction is to be detected.
[5] Obscure passages in ancient books. To be able to understand them
is a wish elsewhere expressed by scribes and addressed to their god
Thōth.
[6] This is his actual occupation ; he only gives instruction as a hobby.
As horses at this time were the most precious treasure of the king, Hori
had no mean position, although he was certainly not of high family, for
he would not have concealed that fact from us.
[7] *I.e.* a diligent worker.   [8] The city of Osiris, the god of the dead.
[9] In the Delta, the modern Belbeis.   [10] The region of Bubastis.
[11] To whom this common Egyptian plant is something exotic.

righteous act, and that turneth his back on iniquity. The scribe of the young (?) . . . , Amenemōpe, son of the steward Mōse, the revered.[1]

[3. Introductory part of the letter.] [2]

Mayest thou live, prosper, and be in health, my excellent brother, being wealthy, strongly established, and without " Ah that I had ! ",[3] while thou hast what thou needest for life in the way of sustenance and victuals ; joy and gladness being united in thy path. – – – – Mayest thou see the rays of the sun and sate thyself therewith ; mayest thou pass thy term of life – – – –, thy gods being pleased with thee, not being wroth. *Mayest thou receive rewards* after old age – – – – ;[4] mayest thou enter into thy tomb in the necropolis, and mix with the noble souls ; mayest thou be judged among them and be acquitted in Busiris before Wennofre,[5] being established in Abydos in the presence of Shu-Onuris.[6] Mayest thou cross to U-peker [7] in the train of the god. Mayest thou traverse the Region of the Goddess (?) in the train of Sokaris.[8] Mayest thou join the crew of the Neshmet barque without being held back. Mayest thou see the sun in the sky, when he divideth the year.[9]

May Anubis attach for thee thine head to thy bones.[10] Mayest thou come forth from the hidden place and not be destroyed. Mayest thou behold the light (of the sun) in the nether world, as it passeth by thee.[11] May ocean overflow in thine house,[12] to inundate thy path ; may it stand seven cubits high beside thy tomb. Mayest thou sit upon the river bank – – – –. Mayest thou lave thy face and thine hand. Mayest thou receive offerings, and may thy nose inhale the breeze – – – –. May the corn-god give thee bread, and Hathor beer ;

---

[1] His father is therefore dead.

[2] This paragraph is purposely couched in extravagant phraseology, for Hori wishes to show his opponent how he ought to have written.

[3] Without a wish.

[4] All the ensuing wishes refer to the life after death.

[5] Name of Osiris.

[6] Onuris is an appellation of Shu, under which he was also worshipped at Abydos.

[7] A locality at Abydos, which played a part in the Osirian celebrations.

[8] The funerary god of Memphis.

[9] *I.e.* on New Year's Day.   [10] As he did for Osiris.

[11] The dead rejoice when the sun passes by night through their realm.

[12] Probably meaning : mayest thou have no lack of water in thy grave.

mayest thou suck at the udder of the Sekhait-cow. – – – –
May thy Ushebti-figures [1] *help thee and bear* sand from the
eastern to the western hill. *May* thy sycamore [2] moisten thy
throat – – – – without thy being destroyed. Mayest thou
change thyself into whatsoever thou listest, like the Phœnix,
every form of thine being that of a god – – – –.

[4. HOW HE RECEIVED THE LETTER.]

Furthermore : Thy letter came to me in an hour of leisure (?).
I found [3] thy message as I sat beside the horse, which is in my
charge, and was happy and cheerful, and ready to reply. When
I entered into thy [4] stall to look at thy letter, I found that it
consisted neither of praises nor of insults. Thine utterances
confuse this with that, all thy words are perverted, they are not
linked together. All thine imaginings are – – – –, *thou mixest*
evil things with choice, and best with . . . Thy words are
(not ?) sweet and are not bitter. – – – – shedeh-wine mingled
with pewer. [5]

[5. THOU HAST NOT WRITTEN THY LETTER ALONE.] [6]

I write to thee and testify to thee (?) – – – – I stood not
in awe of thee, for I know thy nature. I imagined that thou
wouldest answer it all by thyself, whereas thy defenders [7] stand
behind thee ; thou procurest for thyself many . . . as helpers,
as if thou wert summoning magistrates to a session (?).

Thy looks are troubled, as thou standest there coaxing the
assistants (?) and saying : " Come with me and lend me a
hand." Thou presentest them with gifts, each man severally,
and they say to thee : " Take heart, we will overcome him." [8]
Thou standest there and – – – – and they sit and deliberate,
they, the six scribes. Thou goest with them – – – – and

[1] The little figurines which were supposed to relieve the dead of
agricultural labour in the other world. In this connection mention is
always made, as here, of the transport of sand, though we have no idea
of what is meant by it.

[2] The tree out of which a goddess gives the dead food and drink.

[3] I received it ? [4] Read " my " ?

[5] Shedeh is a frequently mentioned good, and pewer inferior, beverage ;
cf. p. 210, note 1.

[6] In accordance with the sense, a new paragraph ought to begin here,
though the manuscript does not indicate it.

[7] Figuratively for " thy helpers."

[8] The controversy had thus already lasted some time.

chargest each one with two sections (?),[1] that thou mayest complete thy letter again. (One ?) praiseth, two insult ; [2] the other standeth and instructeth them in the rules. The fifth saith : " Hurry (?) not, have patience (?), *and make it perfect."* The sixth hasteneth to the (corn) to measure − − − − to have it withdrawn. The seventh standeth hard by and . . . taketh in charge the rations [3] for the soldiers.

Thine orders are confused and are not rightly expressed (?). Kheriuf[4] playeth the deaf man and heareth not ; he taketh an oath by Ptah saying : " I suffer not the seal to be set on the granary." [5] He goeth forth in a rage. By how many bushels art thou *short, and how many hin are wanting to every measure ?*

Behold thou art a scribe that issueth commands to the army ; men hearken to what thou sayest, and thou art not disregarded. Thou art skilled as a scribe, and there is nothing thou dost not know. *And yet* thy letter is *too badly put together* to permit of it being listened to − − − −.

The close of the paragraph is unintelligible ; Amenemōpe said of something or other : it sitteth on my fingers like a papyrus roll on the neck of a sick man [6] − − − − *it groweth* not weary and is tied with the string of my seal.[7]

[6. MY REPLY WILL BE BETTER THAN THY LETTER.]

I reply to thee in like manner in a letter, which, (however,) is new from beginning (?) to end (?). It is filled with expressions of my lips, which I have fashioned by myself alone, none other being with me. By the ka of (my god ?) Thōth, I com-

---

[1] Of the reply.

[2] They compose the friendly and aggressive sections. What follows is obscure in detail.

[3] Which he is to have delivered for Hori.

[4] Probably the superintendent of the granary ; he will not deliver in view of such doubtful instructions. We actually know of a superintendent of the granary of this name, who, however, could at the most be only the grandfather of this person.

[5] Possibly the superintendent of the granary had to seal it up again after every delivery of grain ; if he declined to do this, it was a sign that things were not in order.

[6] An amulet.

[7] The ancient seals, in the form of a small cylinder, were hung round the neck on a string.

posed it by myself, without summoning any scribe [1] that he might assist.

I will give thee more [2] in twenty sections, and repeat unto thee what thou hast said, (every) section in its place, (all) the fourteen divisions (?) of thy letter.[3]

Take hold of the papyrus, that I may tell thee many things, that I may pour out for thee choice words, that a Nile [4] may be in full flood, with waters shimmering in the season of inundation, when it hath taken possession of the fields (?).

All my words are sweet and pleasant . . . and I act not as thou hast *acted* ; for thou beginnest with insults against me in the first section, and in the beginning of thy letter thou dost not enquire after my health. (But) what thou sayest [5] is far from me and affecteth me not. My god Thōth is a shield about me. By the ka of Ptah, lord of truth, – – – – Behold, what thou hast said may not come to pass ! And all that hath come forth from thy mouth may be turned against some (other) foe ! Yet shall I be buried in Abydos in the dwelling-place of my father, (for) I am the son of a righteous one in the city of the lord (of right ?), and I shall be buried among mine own people in the hill of To-Zozer.

Wherein am I become evilly disposed towards thee in my heart, *that thou so attackest me* ? To whom have I made mention of thee in evil wise ? I only wrote for thee a work like unto a pleasant jest, which turned out a diversion for all men.[6]

[7. Answer to the abuse of Amenemōpe.]

Thou hast said concerning me, that I am broken of arm [7] and devoid of strength ; thou hast undervalued me as scribe

---

[1] As thou hast done. [2] Write a still longer letter.

[3] What is meant is that Hori intends to write in all twenty sections, of which fourteen will concern themselves with the corresponding portions in the letter of Amenemōpe. In point of fact the five or six introductory sections are followed by fourteen others, and these contain the actual controversy.

[4] A flood of eloquence.

[5] Amenemōpe has therefore cursed him in his letter, and in particular, as appears from what follows, has expressed the wish that he should remain unburied.

[6] Why have you taken my harmless jests about your letter so seriously ?

[7] Usual expression for feeble, indolent.

and said : " He knoweth nothing ! " Am I to pass my time at thy side coaxing thee and saying : " Be my protector, if another persecuteth me " ? [1] By (?) the decree of the mighty lord, whose name is mighty and whose statutes abide firmly established, like those of Thōth, I am myself a helper of all my kindred.[2] – – – –

(But) I know many men who are devoid of strength,[3] broken of arm, cut to pieces, lacking in power, and yet are made rich in their houses in food and sustenance and say not *of aught* : " Ah, if I but had ! " Come, let me tell thee how it is with the scribe Roi, who is called the firebrand (?) of the granary. He moveth not and never ran since his birth. The work of an active man he abhorreth, and he knoweth it not. He hath (already) gone down into the West,[4] although his limbs are still healthy, and fear of the Good God [5] bringeth him not forth.

Thou art more foolish (?) than (?) Kasa, the reckoner of cattle [6] . . ., if I tell thee how it fareth with him, that thou mayest not . . .

Thou hast surely heard the name of Amun-wah-su, one of the old men of the Treasury. He passeth his life as controller in the workshop beside the smithy.[7]

Come, that I may tell thee of Nakht, him of the wine-store ; [8] he is ten times better for thee than these.

I will tell thee of the captain of auxiliaries, who was in Heliopolis, and is (now) an elder of the Palace. He is smaller than a tom-cat and larger than a monkey.[9] He prospereth in his house – – – –.

[1] Meaning : if I were to ask you for your protection, would you pass any other judgment upon me ?

[2] I do not need your protection ; the oath by the king is to show on what assistance he would prefer to rely.

[3] The sloth which you cast in my teeth I know to exist in others. The slothful officials whom he now brings forward as examples will certainly be well-known persons and good friends of Amenemōpe.

[4] He is as good as dead.   [5] The king.

[6] We know of an " Overseer of the Cattle," by name Kasa, a vessel for whose intestines (canopic jar) is in the Berlin Museum ; this may be the person in question, for the name is rare.

[7] The meaning probably is that, instead of discharging his own duties, he is always sitting and chattering in a workshop, as if he were the high official set in authority there.

[8] *I.e.* probably the drunkard.

[9] *I.e.* probably from age, but the point of the jest is not clear.

If thou art here in the stable – – – –, thou hearest the name of Kisep . . . He moveth over the ground unnoticed, in disorderly (?) raiment and tightly swathed (?). If thou seest him at eventide in the darkness, thou sayest : " It is a bird that passeth by." Place him in the scale that thou mayest see how heavy he is ; he will come out at twenty deben [1] – – – –. If thou blowest beside him as he passeth, he will drop down afar off like as if he were a leaf of foliage.

If I were to tell thee of Wah, him of the cattle-stalls, thou wouldst give me my weight in thrice refined gold.[2] I swear by the lord of Hermopolis and by Nehem-await : [3] thou art strong of arm and wilt overthrow them.[4] Let them be examined, those and these, that I may smite them with mine arms and mine hands (not) let go (of them).

Good sir, my friend, who knoweth not what he saith, behold, I solve thy grievous difficulties and make them pleasant for thee.[5]

[8. Thou playest at being the sage.]

Thou art come furnished with great secrets and tellest to me a proverb of Hardedef,[6] and (yet) thou knowest not whether it be good or bad. What chapter precedeth it ? – – – –

Thou art a man of learning at the head of his fellows,[7] and the lore of books (?) is graven on thine heart ; felicitous (?) is thy tongue, wide are thy words, and a proverb cometh forth from thy mouth that weigheth more than three deben – – – –. Mine eyes are dazzled at what thou doest, and I am agape (?) when thou sayest : " As scribe I am immersed in heaven, in earth, and in the underworld, and I know the mountains in deben and hin.[8] The house of books is hidden and is not seen ; its company of gods is concealed and far from – – – –." [9]

---

[1] 1820 grammes.

[2] Meaning, probably : so amusing would it be—of course ironical.

[3] Thōth and a consort of his, who also was venerated in Hermopolis.

[4] Ironical : on the grounds of my description you will certainly now proceed against them.

[5] Leads on to the next section.

[6] Son of Kheops ; see pp. 40, 133. He had therefore left behind him a book of wise sayings. Amenemōpe quoted a proverb in his letter, although he had certainly never read the book.

[7] Ironical : you come forward as such.

[8] I know how much they weigh and what their capacity is.

[9] Meaning, probably : however secret it may be, I know it.

Thus I answer thee : " Take care that thy fingers approach not the God's Words [1] – – – –. *Of what follows all that is intelligible is :* as . . . sitteth, to play draughts.

[9. IT IS NOT TRUE, IF THOU ART CASTING DOUBTS ON MY ATTAINMENTS.]

Thou hast said unto me : " Thou art no scribe, thou art no soldier ! Thou hast made thyself out to be a superior . . ., and thou art not on the list." Now thou art a scribe of the king, who enrolleth the soldiers, and before whom all . . . of heaven [2] are opened. Run then to the place of the books, that they may let thee see the chest with the registers. If thou takest with thee a bouquet for Heresh,[3] he will speedily open for thee – – – – and thou wilt find my name upon the roll as officer in the great stable of Ramesses-Beloved-of-Amūn. *Thou hast further evidence* in the command of the stable,[4] (for) a food-allowance is entered in my name. So I am a soldier, and I am a scribe.

There is no stripling of my generation that may compare (?) himself with me. " Ask about a man of his mother " [5]—so hie thee to my superiors, that they may inform thee about me.

[10. AS TO WHAT THOU REQUIREST OF ME, FIRST SHOW ME HOW TO DO IT THYSELF.]

Again thou hast said unto me : " A high mountain range [6] standeth in front of thee. Enter thou into the dreadful range, (even if ?) thou knowest it not." [7] Enter thou in ahead of me, and I will come after thee. However (?), thou hast not drawn nigh unto it, and hast not approached it. If thou art discovered in it, then I (also) will come hither (?) behind thee. Beware of stretching forth the hand to pull me out (?).

---

[1] *Cf.* p. 215, note 1 ; perhaps the meaning is : beware even of the elements of learning, of which thou understandest nothing.

[2] This will be some jocose expression for the scribes' bureaux.

[3] Name of the keeper of the archives ; the bouquet will be *bakshish*.

[4] Perhaps the enactment regulating his salary.

[5] Probably a proverb.

[6] Apparently the Canaanite word *har*, "mountain," but, in view of the writing, conceived of as wooded.

[7] Amenemōpe of course said this figuratively, in the sense of : Carry out the task that has been set you.

[11. Once more a doubt as to the attainments of Hori.] [1]

Thou hast said unto me : "Thou art in no respect a scribe, an empty and cold (?) name ; [2] thou bearest the palette *wrongfully* – – – –." – – – – and so thou dost harness thyself against me yet again, but thy sayings do me injustice, and they will not be hearkened to. Let thy letters rather be taken before Onuris, that he may decide for us who is right, that thou mayest not be wroth. [3]

[12. Amenemōpe cannot calculate, as is revealed in the digging of a lake and the building of a ramp.]

Another topic. Behold, thou comest and fillest me with thine office. [4] I will cause thee to know how matters stand with thee, when thou sayest : " I am the scribe that issueth commands to the army."

There is given thee a lake to dig. Thou comest to me to inquire concerning the rations for the soldiers, and sayest : " Reckon it out." Thou desertest thine office, and the task of teaching thee to perform it falleth on my shoulders.

Come, that I may tell thee more than thou hast said : [5] I cause thee to be abashed (?) when I disclose to thee a command of thy lord, thee, who art his royal scribe, when thou art led beneath the window [6] in respect of any goodly (?) work, when the mountains are disgorging great monuments for Horus, the lord of the Two Lands. [7] For see, thou art the clever scribe who is at the head of the troops. [8] A ramp [9] is to be con-

---

[1] Amenemōpe in his letter will have returned once more to this doubt, and, since Hori goes through his letter with him section by section, he must yet again tackle the question.

[2] Is the meaning : thou hast only a name without title ?

[3] He now proposes a decision by means of an oracle, a frequent practice at this period. On these occasions two writings were laid before the god, one affirmative and the other negative, and the god decided between them by nodding.

[4] Probably meaning : you talk to me a great deal about it.

[5] *I.e.* something of which no mention was made in your letter.

[6] The palace window, from which the king issued commands and the like. See, *e.g.*, p. 208, note 5.

[7] *I.e.* when the king has had stones quarried, which are now to be used for building purposes.

[8] Ironical : you must indeed understand everything.

[9] In order to hoist into position the great blocks used in building, a huge ramp of bricks was erected, upon which they were dragged up.

structed, 730 cubits [1] long, 55 cubits wide, containing 120 compartments,[2] and filled with reeds and beams ; [3] 60 cubits high at its summit, 30 cubits in the middle, with a . . . of 15 cubits,[4] and its . . . 5 cubits.   The quantity of bricks needed for it is asked of the generals, and the scribes are all collected together, without one of them knowing anything.   They all put their trust in· thee and say : " Thou art a clever scribe, my friend ! Decide for us quickly !   Behold, thy name is famous ; let one be found in this place to magnify the other thirty ! [5]   Do not let it be said of thee that there is aught thou dost not know. Answer us, how many bricks are needed for it ? "   See, its measurements (?) are before thee.   Each one of its compartments is of 30 cubits and is 7 cubits broad.[6]

[13. AMENEMŌPE ALSO DOES NOT UNDERSTAND HOW TO ESTIMATE THE WEIGHT OF AN OBELISK.]

Ah, good sir, thou vigilant scribe, who is at the head of the army, who distinguisheth himself when he standeth at the Two Great Gates,[7] and who boweth down in comely fashion below the window !   A despatch hath come from the crown-prince at Raka in order to rejoice the heart of the victorious Horus, and to appease (?) [8] the raging lion, and it telleth how an obelisk hath been newly made, graven with the name of his majesty ; it is 110 cubits in length of shaft, its pedestal measureth 10 cubits, and the block (?) at its end measureth 7 cubits on every side.   The tapering (?) amounteth to 1 cubit and 1 finger ;

[1] The cubit = 51 cm.

[2] In order to save bricks, large chambers were left free in the ramp and these were filled with sand.

[3] Great brick walls had reed mats and beams interspersed between the courses.

[4] Apparently what is meant is that the base of the sloping side walls projects 15 cubits behind.

[5] The questioners.   Do they all belong, therefore, to the frequently mentioned College of the Thirty ?   (See pp. 100, 197.)

[6] Observe the light and airy way in which Hori writes ; he forgot to insert these specifications above, and now calmly inserts them here at t'.e end, just as one would do in actual conversation.
   Of the palace ; for the window, see p. 223, note 6.

[7] This is only an exaggerated development of the epistolary formula " in order to rejoice the heart," *i.e.* to make a communication.   The meaning is that the crown-prince has written to the king to say that the obelisk is ready for transport.

its pyramidion [1] is 1 cubit in height, and its . . . measureth 2 fingers. *Reckon up now* (?), that thou mayest supply every man that *is needed* for the dragging, and send them to the Red Mountain. [2] Behold, they are waiting for them. *Be of assistance* to the crown-prince, the child of the sun. Decide for us how many men are needed to drag it. Let them not have to send again, for the monument lieth (ready) in the quarry ! Answer quickly and hesitate not !

Behold, thou art seeking it for thyself. [3] Get thee on ! Lo, if thou wilt bestir thyself, I will make thee happy. I used formerly to *labour* even as thou. So let us join the fray [4] together. My heart is shrewd (?) and my fingei.. are docile, *and are* skilled where thou goest astray. Get thee onwards and weep not ; thy helper standeth behind thee. I will cause thee to say : " There is a royal scribe with Horus, the Strong Bull," [5] and thou orderest men to make a box into which to put the letters. (*The rest is unintelligible.*)

[14. At the erecting of a colossus also Amenemōpe's calculations are false.]

It is said untó thee : " Empty the magazine [6] that hath been loaded with sand under the monument of thy lord, [7] which hath been brought from the Red Mountain. It measureth 30 cubits, when lying extended on the ground, and 20 cubits in breadth. *From further statements we only learn that the " magazine " consists of several divisions*, filled with sand from the river-bank, *and that* they are all 50 cubits in height.

Thou art commissioned to find out, *and the matter that is*

---

[1] The pointed apex of the obelisk ; its height is probably reckoned at too low a figure.

[2] The sandstone quarry near Cairo ; see above, p. 17, note 1.

[3] You are trying at first to do it alone, but are not succeeding.

[4] The battle with the problem, of which I have had experience for a long time past.

[5] Meaning, perhaps : in accordance with your character you will not, of course, mention my name, but you will see to it that what is written is well packed up.

[6] Literally : " corn-bin."

[7] The colossal statue of a king. The passage deals with a method employed in Egypt for the erecting of heavy loads. They were dragged up above a chamber (the " magazine ") filled with sand, and the sand was gradually emptied so that the block settled down in the required place.

15

now engaging the king's attention (?) is : [1] " How many men will demolish it in six hours ? " Their hearts are apt,[2] (but) their desire to demolish it is small, for the time does not come (in which ?) thou givest a rest to the soldiers, that they may take their meal.[3] Let the monument be set in its place, for One's [4] desire is to see it beautiful !

[15. AMENEMŌPE CANNOT EVEN CALCULATE THE PROVISION REQUIRED FOR A MILITARY EXPEDITION.]

Thou clever scribe with understanding heart—there is nothing whatever that he knoweth not ; thou torch in the darkness before the host, and it giveth light unto them ! Thou are despatched on a mission to Phœnicia (?), at the head of the victorious army, to crush those rebels who are called Neârîn.[5] The auxiliary troops which thou commandest number 1900, 520 Shardana,[6] 1600 Kehek, (100) Mashawasha, 880 negroes— in all 5000, not reckoning their officers. A present hath been brought before thee of bread, cattle, and wine.[7] The number of men is too great for thee (?) [8] and the provision is too small for them : 300 wheaten loaves, 1800 . . . loaves, 120 goats of different kinds, 30 measures of wine—the soldiers are so many and the provision is underestimated (?) – – – –. Thou receivest the provision, and it is placed in the camp. The army is ready and equipped ; so divide it up quickly and give to each man his portion. The Bedouins look on furtively (and say ?) : " Sopher yode." [9] Midday hath come, the camp is hot. *They say :* " It is time to start." " Be not wroth, O commandant of the auxiliaries. We have yet far to march," we say. " *Why is*

[1] It is thus all the more annoying that you do not know.

[2] They understand their work.

[3] The meaning probably is : the number of people employed in accordance with your advice is not sufficient, for you have assumed that they would work six hours without a break.

[4] The king (*cf.* note 3) wishes to inspect the statue ; hence the set term of six hours in which the work is to be finished.

[5] Canaanitish : young warriors.

[6] The Shardana are a seafaring people, who were at this time in the habit of visiting Egypt, and who also entered Egyptian employment. Such was the case also with the Libyan tribes of Mashawasha and Kehek.

[7] Sent by the inhabitants of the country.

[8] Too great for you to feed from this present.

[9] " O sapient scribe " ; shortly afterwards, Hori himself so designates him in Egyptian.

there then no bread ? Our night-quarters are far off! What meaneth it, good sir, that thou beatest us, for thou art a clever scribe ? [1] Approach to give the food. *An hour cometh, in which one is* without a scribe from the Ruler. *That thou shouldest take it upon thee* (?) to beat us, that is not good, comrade ; he will hear of it and he will send to undo thee." [2]

[16. THOU KNOWEST BUT LITTLE OF SYRIA.]

In the five concluding sections, which begin here, Hori concerns himself with the " end of the letter " of his antagonist, which seems particularly to have amused him with its " great words." In it Amenemōpe had drawn attention to his deeds and experiences in Syria, and proudly assigned himself a foreign designation, that of Mahir,[3] i.e. a hero. Hori " tests " this narrative and follows the whole journey of his antagonist from Northern Syria to the confines of Egypt. But he represents the journey as full of small and great misadventures, as, according to his view, it might actually have been, and he intimates, moreover, by means of artful questions, that his antagonist possesses very little knowledge indeed of the country he had visited, and has seen but little of it. Rightly to appreciate this raillery, we ought also to be acquainted with Amenemōpe's own narrative which is here parodied. But even without that, we can enjoy the vivid description of Palestine, a country which Hori himself apparently knew well, or at any rate better than his bragging antagonist.

Thy letter aboundeth in thrusts (?), and is loaded with great words. Behold, they shall reward thee, even as them that look for a load, and shall lay more on thee (?) than thou wouldest.[4]

" I am a scribe, a Mahir," thou sayest again. There is truth in thy words, say we. Come forth, that thou mayest be tested.

---

[1] The soldiers should receive their rations in the morning when about to set out on the march ; they have not yet received them, and so have not started by midday ; they now become restless (" hot "), they complain, and he beats them.

[2] They will complain to the king, who will depose him.

[3] The Canaanite word for " nimble," " adept," which here, however, and subsequently, is the designation of the Egyptian officer who travels about in Syria.

[4] If it is to be so translated, it will be a proverb : the porter cannot complain if he is given loads to carry. Meaning : you have provoked me, and you are being paid back.

A horse is harnessed for thee, swift as a jackal with . . ., and it is like unto a storm of wind, when it goeth forth. *Thou loosenest the reins* (?) and seizest the bow. We shall see what thine hand will do. I will expound to thee the nature of a Mahir, and show thee what he doth.

Hast thou not gone to the land of Khatti, and hast thou not seen the land of Upe ? [1] Khedem—dost thou not know the nature of it, and Igedii, too, what it is like ? Sumur of Sesse [2]— on which side of it lieth the town of Kher . . . ? What is its stream like ? Hast thou not marched to Kadesh [3] and Tubikhi ? Hast thou not gone unto the region of the Bedouins with the auxiliary troops of the army ?

Hast thou not trodden the road to Meger,[4] where the sky is dark by day, and it is overgrown with cypresses (?) and oaks, and with cedars that reach heaven ? There are more lions there than panthers and hyenas (?), and it is girt about with Bedouins on (every) side.

Hast thou not climbed Mount Shewe ? Hast thou not trodden (it), while thy hands are laid upon . . ., and thy chariot is battered by the ropes as thy horse is dragged (?) ? [5]

Prithee let *me tell thee of* . . . beret. Thou shrinkest from climbing it and crossest (rather) its stream . . . Thou beholdest how it tastes to be a Mahir, when thou bearest thy chariot on thy shoulder – – – –.

When thou comest to a halt in the evening, thy whole body is crushed – – – – and thy limbs are broken. – – – – Thou awakenest, when it is the hour for starting, in the . . . night. Thou art alone to do the harnessing, brother cometh not to

---

[1] Locality near Damascus. Of the Canaanite place-names, which appear in the following passages, some are known to us from the Old Testament, from cuneiform texts, and from Greek sources ; to these I can give an approximately correct form. The others I must, of course, make pronounceable, and accordingly employ the method described in the preface ; any one who wishes for information about their consonants, which alone are known, must have recourse to GARDINER, *Hieratic Texts*, i.

[2] Sesse is the pet-name for Ramesses. Sumur is the later Simyra in Phœnicia ; the addition " of Ramesses " indicates that the king had erected a building there of some size.

[3] The city on the Orontes.

[4] Probably a part of the Lebanon.

[5] Meaning, approximately : chariot and horses must be toilfully dragged up.

brother ; [1] the fugitives (?) have come into the camp, the horse hath been let loose, the . . . hath been ransacked (?) in the night, thy clothes have been stolen.   Thy groom hath awakened in the night and hath marked *what they* (?) *have done;* he hath taken what was left, and hath joined (the ranks of) the wicked. He hath mingled with the tribes of the Bedouins and changed himself into an Asiatic.   The foe came to pillage (?) in secret, and they found thee inert, and when thou didst awake thou didst find no trace of them, and they have made away with thy things.   Thou art become a fully equipped Mahir, and takest hold of thine ear.[2]

[17. ABOUT PHŒNICIA.]

I will tell thee of another mysterious city, Byblos by name. What is it like ?   Their goddess—of her another time.[3]   Hast thou not trodden it ?

Come teach me about Berytus, and about Sidon and Sarepta. Where is the stream of Nezen,[4] and what is Us like ?

They say that another city lieth in the sea, whose name is Tyre of the Port (?).   Water is taken [5] unto it in boats, and it is richer in fish than in sand.

[18. VARIOUS CITIES.]

I will tell thee of another misery—the crossing of Seram. Thou wilt say : " It burneth more than a sting." [6]   Very ill fareth the Mahir.

Come, set me on the road southward to the region of Akka. Where is the road to Aksaph ?   Beside what city ?

Pray instruct me as to mountain of User.   What is its peak like ?   Where is the mountain of Sichem ?   Who will take its . . . ?   The Mahir—where doth he make the journey to Hazor ?   What is its stream like ?

---

[1] *I.e.* without any assistance, as the next sentences show.

[2] Probably as a gesture expressive of affliction ; " fully equipped " is, of course, ironical.

[3] For Byblos, see p. 17, note 5, pp. 177 ff. ; the goddess of this city was identified by the Egyptians with their goddess Hathor, and was greatly revered by them.

[4] The Litani, which runs into the sea north of Tyre.

[5] That such was the case with the dweller in Tyre we know from other sources ; the city lay on a small rocky island.

[6] It has been suggested that there is here a pun on the Canaanite word for " hornets."

Put me on the way to Hamath, to Deger, and to Deger-el.
the playground of all Mahirs.   Pray teach me about his road ;
show me Yan.   If one be travelling to Edemem, whither turneth
he the face ?

Turn not back from teaching (us ?), and lead us (?) to know
them !

[19. OTHER CITIES.]

Come, that I may tell thee of other towns, which lie above
them (?).

Hast thou not gone to the land of Takhsi,[1] Kafr-Mereren,
Tement, Kadesh, Deper, Azai, Har-nemi ?   Hast thou not seen
Kirjath-enab and Beth-sopher ?   Knowest thou not Ederen
and Zedepet likewise ?   Knowest thou not the name of Khelez,
which is in the land of Upe, as a bull upon its boundary, the
scene of the battles of all warriors ? [2]

Pray teach me concerning the appearance (?) of Keyen ;
acquaint me with Rehob ;   explain Beth-sha-el and Kirjath-
el (?).   The stream of Jordan, how is it crossed ?   Show me
how to pass by Megiddo which lieth above it.[3]   Thou art a
Mahir, who is skilled in the deeds of valour !   A Mahir, such
as thou art, is qualified (?) to march (?) at the head of the host !
Forward, O Maryen,[4] to shoot !   Behold, there is (?) the . . .
in a ravine (?) two thousand cubits deep, filled with boulders
and shingle.   Thou makest a detour (?).   Thou graspest the
bow ;   thou . . . on thy left, thou lettest the chieftains [5] see
what is pleasing to their eyes until thine hand groweth weary :
" Abata kemo ari, mahir naem." [6]   Thou gainest the name of
a . . . Mahir (among the ?) officers of Egypt.   Thy name
becometh like that of Kazardi, the chief of Eser,[7] when the
hyena found him in the terebinth-tree.

---

[1] A frequently mentioned country that was situated in the North.

[2] Thus a much-contested locality on the frontier.

[3] So literally.   A name may well have been left out.   Megiddo lies
north of Karmel, the crossing of which is described in the ensuing
paragraphs.

[4] A similar expression to Mahir ;   it often occurs elsewhere.

[5] The friendly barbarians.

[6] The reading of these Canaanite words is, as regards the vowels, of
course, quite uncertain.   One may suppose some such meaning as " Thou
slayest like a lion, O pleasant Mahir."

[7] Asher ?   Apparently an allusion to a legend with which the Egyptian
reader was also familiar.

Behold, there is (?) the narrow defile, made perilous by Bedouins, who are hidden beneath the bushes ; some of them are of four cubits and five cubits from the nose (?) unto the sole of the foot, fierce of face, their heart not mild, and they hearken not to coaxing.

Thou art alone, no helper is with thee, and no army is behind thee. Thou findest no guide (?) to show (?) thee a way of crossing. Thou determinest (?) to go forwards, albeit thou knowest not the way. Shuddering (?) seizeth thee, the (hair of) thy head standeth on end, thy soul lieth in thine hand.[1] Thy path is full of boulders and shingle, and there is no *passable track, for* it is overgrown with . . ., thorns, neh-plants, and wolfs-pad.[2] The ravine is on one side of thee, the mountain riseth on the other. On thou goest and guidest (?) thy chariot beside thee, and fearest to . . . thy horse. *If the horse falleth down* (?), thine hand [3] falleth and is left bare (?), and thy . . . leather falleth. Thou unharnessest the horse, in order to repair the hand in the middle (?) of the defile ; thou art not expert in the way of binding it, and thou knowest not how to fasten it together (?). The . . . falleth from its place, and the horse is (already) too heavily (laden) to load him (with it). Thou art sick at heart, and thou startest to go on foot. The sky is open,[4] and thou fanciest that the enemy is behind thee. Then trembling taketh hold of thee. Ah, would that thou hadst an hedge of . . ., that thou mightest put it upon the other side ! Thy horse is galled [5] up to the time that thou findest quarters for the night. Thou perceivest how pain tasteth.

When thou enterest Joppa, thou findest the meadow growing green in its time.[6] Thou forcest a way into [7] . . . and findest the fair maiden that keepeth watch over the vineyards. She taketh thee to herself as a companion, and giveth thee the colour of her bosom.[8] Thou art recognized and bearest witness ; [9] the Mahir is put on trial, and thy tunic of good

---

[1] That is to say, you are half-dead.   [2] Names of plants.

[3] A part of the chariot, as are also the unknown words in the next sentences.

[4] Unclouded, hot.   [5] Literally : " shaved."

[6] *I.e.* in the season when it is at its loveliest.

[7] Through the wall of the vineyard.

[8] She surrenders to you her charms.

[9] You confess ?

Upper Egyptian linen, thou sellest it [1] . . . thou sleepest every evening, with a piece of woollen cloth (?) about thee, thou slumberest, and art inert. Thy . . ., thy bow, thy . . . knife, and thy quiver are stolen, and thy reins are cut in the darkness.

Thine horse is gone and . . . over the slippery ground. The road stretcheth out before it. It smasheth thy chariot – – – – thy weapons fall to the ground and are buried (?) in the sand – – – –

Thou beggest : " Give food (?) and water, for I have arrived safely." They turn a deaf ear, they do not listen, they pay no heed to thy tales.

Thou makest thy way into the smithy, and the workshop surroundeth thee. Smiths and cobblers [2] are all about thee. They do all that thou wishest. They attend to thy chariot, and it ceaseth to be slack.[3] Thy . . . are cut aright (?) ; its . . . are adjusted. They place leather . . . on thine hand.[4] They put thy yoke to rights. They adjust thy . . ., which is engraved. . . . They give a . . . to thy whip, and attach to it lashes (?). Forth thou goest quickly to fight on the field of battle, to accomplish deeds of valour.[5]

[20. THE FRONTIER STATIONS AND THE END OF THE COMPOSITION.]

Good sir, thou choice scribe, thou Mahir that knoweth his hand,[6] leader of the Neârîn, chief of the Zaba,[7] I have described to thee the foreign countries (as far as ?) the extremity of the land of Canaan. Thou answerest me neither good nor ill, and returnest me no report. Come, that I may tell thee of *yet more as far as* (?) the fortress of Paths-of-Horus.[8]

---

[1] The meaning of the passage will be that the people of Joppa allow payment to be made for the escapade.

[2] These were for the repairing of leather articles, etc.

[3] They repair it. The subsequently enumerated parts of the chariot are unfortunately all unknown.

[4] See p. 231, note 3.

[5] Ironical, of course. Amenemōpe is already at the end of his journey, and is having his chariot prepared in order to cut a good appearance in Egypt.

[6] Who aims well.

[7] Canaanite word for " army " ; for the Neârîn, see above, p. 226. note 5. The use of these words here is also a spiteful thrust.

[8] The frontier fortress of Zaru. See p. 26, note 2. The subsequently mentioned places are in part stations on the desert road near the frontier.

I begin for thee with the House of Sesse.[1] Hast thou never trodden it ? Hast thou not eaten the fish of the water of . . . ? Hast thou not bathed in it ? Come, let me recall to thee Hezin. Where is its fortress ? Come, let me tell thee of the region of Buto of Ramesses and of House-of-Victories of Usimarē,[1] of Seb-el and Ebsekeb. I tell thee how it is with Ainen ; knowest thou not its ordinance (?) ? [2] Nekhes and Khebret, hast thou not seen them since thy birth ? [2]. O Mahir, where are they ?

Repeh [3]—what is its wall like ? How many leagues march is it to Gaza ? Answer quickly ! Render me a report, that I may name thee " Mahir," and may make boast of thy name to others ; " Maryen " will I say to them (in respect of thee).

Thou art angry at what I (now) say to thee. I . . . thine heart in all callings. My father taught me what he knew, and instructed me times out of number. I know how to hold the reins far better than thou knowest. There is no gallant that can set himself up over me, *and I am versed in the service* of Month.[4]

Very hurtful is all that which hath come over thy tongue, and very . . . are thine utterances [5] ; thou comest to me wrapt up in confusion, and loaded with their wrongfulness. Thou dividest the words as one that goeth recklessly ahead, and thou dost not tire of . . .

Be strong ! Forward ! Haste thee ! Comest thou not down ? What is it like, not to know what one hath reached ? – – – – I retreat (?). Behold, I have arrived (?). Bow thee ; [5] is thine heart heavy, so is thine heart composed. Be not vexed ! – – – – [6]

I have shorn for thee the end of thy letter, and have answered for thee what thou hast said ; thy narratives were collected upon my tongue, and remained upon my lips. They are confused when heard, and no uninstructed person (?) can under-

---

[1] Ramesses II ; see p. 228, note 2.

[2] Meaning ?   [3] Raphia, south of Gaza.

[4] The war-god. Amenemōpe will therefore have belittled the military exploits of Hori.

[5] He probably means : slanderous and moreover badly expressed.

[6] Be friendly.

[7] The meaning of this difficult passage may perhaps be : If you wish to continue the contest, go ahead. I have gained all I want and so bring the controversy to a close. But do not be vexed.

stand them. They are like the talk of a man of the Delta with a man of Elephantine.[1]

Nay, but thou art a scribe of the Two Great Gates,[2] one that reporteth the needs of the lands (to the king), goodly and fair to him that seeth it.[3]

Say not : " Thou hast made my name to stink before others and before all." Behold, I have only told thee what it is to be a Mahir ; I have traversed for thee the land of Retenu.[4] I have led before thee the foreign countries all together, and the towns in their order (?). Incline thyself to us [5] and look at it calmly, that thou mayest be found able to describe them (in the future) [6] and that thou mayest be accounted by (us ?) a . . . counsellor.

6. THE WISDOM OF ANII [7]

This book is a late imitation of the old books of wisdom, and resembles them in this respect also, that in it, as in them, a father is propounding his teaching to his son. But the scope of this work seems to be wider and its tone livelier—I say " seems," for, unfortunately, unless a new manuscript turns up, we shall never be able to understand more than isolated fragments of this wisdom. The schoolboy, who copied out the papyrus, has made mistakes in the writing of most of the words, and for the length of whole passages one has absolutely no idea of what is the subject under discussion. Possibly he did not understand much of what this book contained, for although it is written in New Egyptian, this language already belonged to a period separated some three to four hundred years from a schoolboy of the Twenty-First or Twenty-Second Dynasty, and thus much of it might have been obscure to him. We have evidence, moreover, that this was actually the case. The Berlin Museum possesses the writing-equipment of a schoolboy, who likewise lived in the Twenty-Second Dynasty, comprising a writing-board,[8] upon which are written what were origin-

---

[1] Who speak entirely different dialects. Meaning : your style is so unintelligible.

[2] Of the Palace.

[3] Meaning, probably : In your high position you need not write clearly, for it is all good in the eyes of those who read it.

[4] Palestine.   [5] Be friendly.

[6] Be not wroth, but be glad to learn from me.

[7] Papyrus of the Twenty-Second Dynasty in Cairo ; published by Chabas in 1874 in the periodical, *L'Égyptologie*, under the title of *Les maximes du scribe Ani*.

[8] *Zeitschr. für ägypt. Sprache*, xxxii. p. 127.

ally the opening words of our book. And yet he already had to add to these words a rendering in the language that was familiar to him. "Beginning of the exhortatory instruction (the commencement of the exhortatory instructions) composed by the scribe Anii (which the scribe Anii composed) of the house of Nefer(ke)rē-teri." With this last name we might possibly associate a similarly named king at the end of the Old Kingdom, and suppose that the author of the work wished to place his sage in that period, although he gave him and his son names belonging to the New Kingdom.

[FOLLOW MY WORDS.]

(I tell thee) that which is excellent, that which thou shalt observe (?) in thine heart. Do it, *and so thou wilt be good,* and all evil is far from thee. – – – – *It will be said of thee :* a good character, *and not* : he is ruined, he is idle. *Accept my words,* and so will all evil be far from thee.

[BE PRUDENT IN SPEECH ?]
Unintelligible.

[BE RETICENT.]

Guard thyself against ought that injureth (?) great people, by talking of secret affairs. If (anyone) speaketh (of them) in thine house, make (thyself ?) deaf – – – –.

[BOAST NOT OF THY STRENGTH ?]
Unintelligible.

[FOUND A FAMILY.]

Take to thyself a wife when thou art a youth, that she may give thee a son. Thou shouldest beget him for thee whilst thou art yet young, *and shouldest live to see* him become a man (?). Happy is the man who hath much people, and he is respected because of his children (?).

[BE PIOUS.]

Celebrate the feast of thy god – – – –. God is wroth with him that disregardeth it. Let witnesses stand by thine offering ; it is best (?) for him that hath done it (?) – – – – Singing, dancing, and frankincense appertain to his maintenance (?), and the receiving of reverence appertaineth to his possessions.[1] Bestow them on the god in order to magnify his name – – – –.

---

[1] God has a right to be reverenced.

[BE DISCREET ON VISITS.]

Enter not the (house ?) of another, – – – –. Gaze not on that which is not right in (his ?) house ; thine eye may see it, but thou keepest silent. Speak not of it to another outside, that it may not become for thee a great crime worthy of death, when it is heard (?).

[BEWARE OF THE HARLOT.]

Beware of a strange woman, one that is not known in her city. Wink (?) not at her – – – – have no carnal knowledge of her (?). (She is) a deep water whose twisting men know not.[1] A woman that is far from her husband, " I am fair," she saith to thee every day, when she hath no witnesses – – – –. It is a great crime worthy of death, when one heareth of it, and although it is not related outside – – – –.

[BE RESERVED IN THY CONDUCT.]

Go not in and out in the court of justice, that thy name may not stink – – – –. Speak not much, be silent, that thou mayest be happy. Be not a gossip.

[THE TRUE PIETY.]

The dwelling of God, it abhorreth clamour. Pray with a loving heart, all the words whereof are hidden. Then he will do what thou needest ; he will hear what thou sayest and accept thine offering.

[PIETY TOWARDS PARENTS.]

Offer water to thy father and thy mother, who rest in the desert-valley – – – –. Omit not to do it, that thy son may do the like for thee.

[BE NOT A DRUNKARD.]

Take not upon thyself (?) [2] to drink a jug of beer. Thou speakest, and an unintelligible utterance issueth from thy mouth. If thou fallest down and thy limbs break, there is none to hold out a hand to thee. Thy companions in drink stand up and say : " *Away with this sot !* " If there (then) cometh one to

---

[1] The changing current ? eddy ?

[2] Possible meaning : Boast not that you can drink, etc.

seek thee in order to question thee, thou art found lying on the ground, and thou art like a little child.

[LEAD AN HONEST LIFE ?]

Go not forth from thine house to one that thou knowest not (?) – – – – let every place that thou favourest be known.

[BE MINDFUL OF DEATH.]

Make for thyself a fair abode in the desert-valley, the deep which will hide thy corpse. Have it before thine eyes in thine occupations – – – – even as (?) the great elders, who rest in their sepulchre (?). He who maketh it (for himself) meeteth with no reproof ; good is it if thou too art furnished in like manner. Thy messenger [1] cometh to thee – – – – *he placeth himself in front of thee (?)*. Say not : " I am too young for thee to carry off," for thou knowest not thy death. Death cometh and leadeth away the babe that is still in the bosom of its mother, even as the man when he hath become old.

Here begins a fresh section of some length, in which, firstly, caution in social intercourse is enjoined—most of it frankly unintelligible.

Behold, I tell thee yet other excellent things, which thou shalt heed (?) in thine heart. Do them, and thou wilt be happy, and all evil will be far from thee – – – –.

[CAUTION IN SOCIAL INTERCOURSE.]

Keep thyself far from an hostile man, and take him not to thee for a companion. Make to thyself a friend (rather) of one that is upright and righteous, when thou seest what he hath done (?) – – – –.

Make not a friend of the slave of another, whose name stinketh – – – –. If one pursueth him in order to seize him, and to take away him that is in his house, thou art wretched and sayest : " What am I to do ? " – – – –

[POSSESSIONS DO NOT MAKE FOR HAPPINESS ?]

A man constructeth a house for himself. A piece of ground (?) is laid out for thee, thou hast fenced in (?) a garden of herbs in front of thine arable land ; thou hast planted sycamores inside – – – – and thou fillest thine hand with all

---

[1] Probably meaning Death, who comes to summon you.

flowers that thine eye perceiveth. (But) with them all one is wretched – – – –.

Put not thy trust in the possessions of another; guard thyself *from doing that* (?). Rely not on the things of another – – – – say not : " The father of my mother hath an house – – – –. For *when it cometh to the* division with thy brethren, thy share (is only) a storehouse. If thy god grants that a child be born to thee – – – –.

[BE RESPECTFUL.]

Sit not when another standeth, one that is older than thou, or that hath occupied himself in his calling longer than thou – – – –.

The subject with which the passages immediately following are concerned, cannot even be conjectured.

[USEFULNESS OF KNOWLEDGE.]

Men do all that thou sayest, if thou art skilled in the writings. Devote thyself to the writings, and put them in thine heart, and then all that thou sayest is excellent. To whatsoever office the scribe is appointed, he consulteth the writings.[1] There is no son for the superintendent of the treasury, no heir for the superintendent of the fortress – – – – the offices, which have no children – – – –.[2]

[BE CAUTIOUS IN SPEECH.]

Speak not out thine heart to the . . . man – – – –. A wrong word that hath come forth from thy mouth, if (he ?) repeateth it, thou makest enemies (for thyself). A man falleth in ruin because of his tongue – – – –. A man's belly is broader than a granary, and is full of all manner of answers. Choose thou out the good and speak them, while the bad remain imprisoned in thy belly. – – – –

Of a truth thou will ever be with me and answer him that injureth me with falsehood, in spite of God who judgeth the righteous. His fate cometh to carry him off.[3]

---

[1] Through them he is always successful and is therefore fit to succeed to any office, as is amplified in what follows.

[2] The most worthy obtains them, *i.e.* he who has learnt most.

[3] If the sentence is to be thus translated, the sage is here referring to some wrong which had been done him by an enemy, and of which an account may have been given in the lost beginning of the book.

[RELATIONS WITH GOD.]

Make offering to thy god and keep thyself from trespassing against him. Inquire not concerning his form ; *walk not with swaggering gait*, when he goeth forth in procession ; press not forward to carry him.[1] – – – – Let thine eye mark how he is wroth, *and have respect for* his – name. It is he that giveth power (?) to millions of forms, and (only) he is made great whom he maketh great. The god of this land is the sun which is in the horizon, (but) his images are on earth ; *to them let incense be offered daily*.

[BE GRATEFUL TO THY MOTHER.]

Double the bread that thou givest to thy mother, and carry her as she carried (thee). She had a heavy load in thee, and never left it to me.[2] When thou wast born after thy months, she carried thee yet again about her neck, and for three years her breast was in thy mouth. *She was not* disgusted at thy dung, she was not disgusted and said not : " What do I ? " She put thee to school, when thou hadst been taught to write, and daily she stood there . . .[3] with bread and beer from her house.

When thou art a young man and takest to thee a wife and art settled in thine house, keep before thee how thy mother gave birth to thee, and how she brought thee up further in all manner of ways. May she not do thee harm nor lift up her hands to God, and may he not hear her cry.

[ON WEALTH AND ITS INSTABILITY.]

Eat not bread, if another is suffering want, and thou dost not stretch out the hand to him with bread. – – – –. One is rich and another is poor – – – –. He that was rich in past years, is this year a groom. Be not greedy about filling thy belly – – – –. The course of the water of last year, it is this year in another place. Great seas have become dry places, and banks have become abysses. – – – –

[ON PAYING VISITS ?]

Go not freely to a man in (his) house, but enter in (only) when thou art bidden. When he hath said to thee " Praise to

---

[1] In the procession.

[2] I (thy father) could not help her.   [3] *I.e.* outside the school.

thee" with his mouth, – – – –. *Then after an unintelligible passage:* give him to God and give him daily again to God. The morrow is as to-day. Thou wilt see what God will do, if he besmircheth (?) him that hath besmirched (?) thee.[1]

[KEEP THYSELF FAR FROM TUMULTS.]

Enter not into a crowd, if thou findest *that it standeth ready for* beating – – – – that thou mayest not be blamed in the Court before the magistrates after the tendering of evidence, Keep thee far from hostile people – – – –.

[TREAT THY WIFE WELL.]

Act not the official over thy wife in her house, if thou knowest that she is excellent. Say not unto her: "Where is it? Bring it us," if (?) she hath put (it) in the right place. Let thine eye observe and be silent, that so (?) thou mayest know her good deeds. (She is) happy when thine hand is with her – – – –. Thereby the man ceaseth to stir up strife in his house – – – –.

[BE CAREFUL OF WOMEN.]

Go not after a woman, in order that she may not steal thine heart away.[2]

[BEHAVIOUR TOWARDS SUPERIORS.]

Answer not a superior who is enraged, *get out of his way.* Say what is sweet, when he saith what is bitter to any one, and make calm his heart. Contentious answers carry rods,[3] and thy strength collapseth. *Rage directeth itself* (?) *against thy business, therefore vex* (?) *not thine own self.* He turneth about and praiseth thee quickly, after his terrible hour. If thy words are soothing for the heart, the heart inclineth to receive them. Seek out silence for thyself, and submit to what he doeth.

[STAND WELL WITH THE POLICE.]

Make a friend of the herald[4] of thy quarter, and let him not become enraged with thee. Give him dainties when there

---

[1] Might apply to some one who had committed a wrong, the punishment of whom let God see to?

[2] Probably only the beginning of a section.

[3] Lead to thy being beaten.

[4] Here and elsewhere merely the title of an official.

are any in thine house,[1] and pass him not by at his prayers.
Say to him : " Praise to thee " – – – –.

*An unintelligible passage is followed by a dialogue, with which
the book concludes.*

The scribe Khenshotep answered his father, the scribe Anii :
" Ah, would that I were *as thou* (?) – – – – so would (?) I act
in accordance with thy teaching, that (?) the son should be pro-
moted to his father's place – – – –. *Thou art a man* with lofty
desires, all of whose words are choice. *A son that* imagineth (?)
evil within himself, he saith – – – – in books. Thy words are
soothing for mine heart, and mine heart inclineth to receive them.
Mine heart rejoiceth. (But) let not thine excellence be too
abundant, – – – – a boy *doth not yet do* according to the
teaching that instructs, albeit (?) the books are on his tongue." [2]

The scribe Anii answered his son, the scribe Khenshotep :
" Trust not in these hazardous things (?). *Avoid further com-
plaining, mine heart heedeth it not.* Even the fighting bull, that
hath slain the stall,[3] cannot leave the ring, *and receiveth* his
instructions *from the* drover. The fierce lion abateth his rage and
doefully passeth by the ass. The horse submitteth to his yoke
– – – – –. The dog, he hearkeneth to words and followeth
his master. The kaeri-animal [4] carrieth the . . . vessel, which
his mother carried not. The goose alighteth on the cool pool,
when it is chased, and then fretteth itself in the net. Negroes
are taught to speak Egyptian, and Syrians, and all strangers
likewise. *I too have discoursed on* all the callings that thou
mayest hear, and know what is to be done."

*What the son replies to this is unintelligible ; he probably
alludes to the fact that most men are worthless.* There is a multitude of all that is evil (?), and none knoweth his teaching. If
there be one that is prudent, the bulk is *foolish. He then
probably would vow obedience to his father :* All thy words are
excellent – – – – I give thee oaths, place them upon thy way.

The scribe Anii answered his son, the scribe Khenshotep :
" Turn thy back on these many words, which are far from
being heard. The bent (?) stick that lieth in the field, *exposed*

––––––––––

[1] On festival days.

[2] The meaning of the whole passage may be : Go not too far in thy
demands, or else, though I may carry thy wisdom in my mouth, I shall
not conduct myself in accordance with it.

[3] The other oxen of the stall.   [4] See above, p. 189, note 5.

to (?) sun and shade, the craftsman fetcheth it and maketh it straight, and maketh it into the whip of a notable. But the straight piece of wood, that maketh he into a board (?).[1] O heart that cannot deliberate, is it thy will to give oaths, or dost thou miscarry ? "

Anii then probably expresses the hope that his son, who already knoweth the strength in his hand,[2] *may be as sensible as* the child in its mother's arms. *When it cometh to years of discretion and no longer wishes to suck,* it findeth its mouth in order to say : " Give me bread."

C. LOVE SONGS

Though the love songs of the earlier period are still unknown to us, as many as five small collections survive from the New Kingdom. However much chance may have had a hand in the game, there can be but little doubt as to that period having been the golden age of this kind of lyric poetry ; if for no other reason than that all these songs strike one as being productions of a similar tendency.

They are mostly short songs without any rigid structure, simple discourses, in which now the beloved speaks, and now the lover. Every song was followed, so one is led to suppose from indications in the manuscripts, by the playing of some musical instrument, and that probably accounts for the fact that the song which follows hardly ever bears any relation to that which precedes.

Associated with love in this poetry is a joy in nature, in the trees and flowers in the garden and on the water. But other often very pretty and naïve pictures and ideas occur, and on the whole a great deal of pleasure can be derived from these songs.

Their tone, allowing for the southern point of view, is markedly decent ; though one cannot avoid the suspicion that behind many a striking expression some double meaning was concealed for the enjoyment of the audience !

The resemblance of these songs to the Song of Songs will strike every reader, and a connection is favoured by another feature also, namely, that the lovers call themselves there as

---

[1] Meaning probably : one can train every one, but the result is of varying value. It remains doubtful, however, whether the sage gives the preference to the beautiful whip or the level board.

[2] *I.e.* feels himself strong.

here "brother" and "sister." When we read in the *Voyage of Unamūn* (p. 174 ff.) that the prince of Byblos (*circa* 1100 B.C.) had acquired for himself an Egyptian female singer, we can well imagine along what road the lyric poetry of Egypt found its way into Canaan.

Let me find place here for a couplet, too pretty to be left out. On the *verso* of a papyrus, containing all manner of high-flown stuff out of the schools (*Pap. Anastasi*, ii.), is cursorily jotted down in a running hand :

> When the wind cometh, he desireth the sycamore :
> When thou comest, – – – –

" thou desirest me," so the line might be completed.

1. DISCOURSES OF THE LOVERS. FIRST COLLECTION [1]

Some little songs, which have no connection with one another. Sometimes it is the one, sometimes the other, of the amorous pair who laments his or her pain and expresses his or her desire.

[THE MAIDEN SPEAKS.]

– – – – my god. My brother, it is pleasant to go to the (pond) in order to bathe me in thy presence, that I may let thee see my beauty in my tunic of finest royal linen, when it is wet [2] . . . I go down with thee into the water, and come forth again to thee with a red fish, which lieth (?) beautiful on my fingers – – – – Come and look at me.

[THE YOUTH SPEAKS.]

The love of my sister is upon yonder side, a stretch of water is between (us both), and a crocodile waiteth on the sand-bank. But when I go down into the water, I tread upon the flood ; mine heart is courageous upon the waters . . . and the water is like land to my feet. Her love, it is, that maketh me so strong ; yea, it maketh the water-spell [3] for me.

I see my sister coming and mine heart rejoiceth. Mine arms are opened wide to embrace her, and mine heart rejoiceth upon

---

[1] On an ostracon in Cairo. First brought to notice by Spiegelberg. See W. MAX MÜLLER, *Liebespoesie der alten Ägypter*, Leipzig, 1899.

[2] And so clings to the body.

[3] Against the crocodiles, see p. 35, note 4.

its place [1] like . . . eternally, when the mistress cometh unto me.

If I embrace her and her arms are opened, it is for me as if I were one that is from Punt [2] – – – – unguent.

If I kiss her and her lips are open, I am happy (even) without beer. – – – –. *What follows is probably spoken by the youth to a maid-servant.* I say to thee : Put the finest linen between her limbs, make not her bed with royal linen [3] and beware of white linen.[3] Adorn (her couch with . . .) and sprinkle it with tishepes-oil.[4]

Ah, would I were her negress that is her handmaid, then would I behold the colour of all her limbs.

Ah, would I were the washerman . . . in a single month, . . . I would wash out the unguents which are in her clothing – – – –.

Ah, would I were her signet-ring which is on (her finger ?) – – – –.

2. DISCOURSES OF THE LOVERS. SECOND COLLECTION [5]

[THE MAIDEN SPEAKS.]

– – – – diversion. If thou desirest to caress my thigh, my breast will . . . thee. Wilt thou go away because thou hast bethought thee of eating ? Art thou a glutton ? [6] Wilt thou go away and clothe thyself ? But I have a sheet. Wilt thou go away, because (thou art thirsty ?) ? Take to thee my breast ; what it hath overfloweth for thee. Fair is the day whereon – – – –

The love of thee penetrateth my body like . . . mixed with

---

[1] According to the Egyptian conception, the heart rests on a support, and is only happy as long as it remains thereon.

[2] The land of perfumes. So sweetly smells the beloved by reason of her unguents.

[3] These must be inferior sorts of linen, anyhow at this period.

[4] A famous perfume ; see p. 34.

[5] On the *recto* of *Pap. Harris*, 500, in London, which was written under Sēthos I. Brought to notice by Goodwin. See W. MAX MÜLLER, *Liebespoesie.*

[6] Literally : " a man of his belly."

water, like the love-apple,[1] when . . . is mingled therewith, and like as dough is mixed with . . .

Hasten to see thy sister, as an horse – – – –

[THE YOUTH SPEAKS.]

– – – – the . . . of the sister is a field (?) with lotus buds, and her breast one with love-apples. Her arms are – – – – Her brow is the bird-trap of meru-wood, and I am the goose *which is snared by the* worm.

[THE MAIDEN SPEAKS.]

Hath not mine heart compassion on thy love for me ? My young wolf is . . . thy drunkenness. *I will not let go of thy love, even if I (?) am* beaten – – – – as far as the land of Palestine with shebet [2] and clubs, and unto the land of Ethiopia with palm-ribs, as far as the hill with sticks, and unto the field with cudgels. I will not heed their [3] designs, so as to forsake love.

[THE YOUTH SPEAKS.]

I voyage downstream in the ferry-boat – – – – with my bundle of reeds on my shoulder.[4] I will go to Memphis and will say unto Ptah, Lord of Truth : " Give me my sister to-night." The stream is wine,[5] Ptah [6] is its reeds ; Sekhmet its lotus, Earit its bud, and Nefertem its flower (?) – – – – The dawn breaks through her beauty. Memphis is a dish of love-apples set before the Fair of Face.[7]

I will lay me down in mine house and be sick for the wrong (done me). My neighbours will enter to see me. If my sister cometh with them, she will put to shame the physicians, for she knoweth my malady.

The castle of the sister, her doorway (?) is in the midst of her house, and her doors, they stand open . . . the sister

[1] See p. 211, note 6.   [2] The Hebrew word for " stick."

[3] Those who threaten her.

[4] Has he gathered them, and does he then bring them to Memphis ?

[5] In his joy at coming to the beloved, the world seems transfigured ; everywhere he sees the gods of her city.

[6] Ptah is the god of Memphis ; the war-goddess Sekhmet is the consort of Ptah, and Nefertem, who himself has the form of a flower, is the child of that pair.

[7] Name of Ptah.

cometh forth wroth.[1] Ah, that I were made the porter, so
that she might chide me. Then would I hear her voice, when
she is wroth, like a child in dread of her.

[THE MAIDEN SPEAKS.]

I voyage down stream (on) the Water of the Ruler (?) [2]
and enter into that of Rē.[2] My desire is to go where the tents
are set up at the opening of the mouth of the Mertiu.[2] I will
start to run ; I hold not my peace, when mine heart thinketh
of Rē. Then will I see how my brother entereth, when he goeth
to the . . .[3]

When I stand with thee at the mouth of the Mertiu, thou
(leadest ?) mine heart unto Heliopolis (to) Rē. I journey back
with thee to the trees of the . . . -houses.[4] I will take the
trees of the . . . -houses (for the ?) handle on my fan. I will
see what he doeth, when my face looketh on the . . . Mine arms
are full of branches of the persea, and my hair is weighed down
with unguent. I am like a (princess ?) of the lord of the Two
Lands, when I am *in thine arms*.

3. THE MAIDEN IN THE MEADOW [5]

This time the maiden alone speaks, and her several songs have,
it may be conceded, some sort of connection with one another.
The bird-catching spoken of in these poems is not carried out on a
large scale, as, for example, when geese and duck were captured in
the swamps for utilitarian purposes ; it was just a pastime, requiring
only the employment of a small trap.

The beautiful cheerful songs of thy sister, whom thine heart
loveth, who cometh from the meadow.

My beloved brother, my heart aspireth to thy love – – – –.
I say to thee : " See what I do. I have come and catch with
my trap in mine hand, and my . . . and my . . ." All birds

[1] Wroth with the little doorkeeper, who does not keep the door closed.

[2] Probably all canals at Heliopolis. What is treated of here is probably the ceremonial opening of the main canal at the beginning of the
inundation—a popular festival—such as was celebrated until quite
recently in Cairo ; on that occasion tents actually were erected for the
officials.

[3] She runs to meet him, rejoicing, when he sails into the canal.

[4] This will be a place or garden at Heliopolis. What follows depicts
apparently her proud happiness, but the details are obscure.

[5] As above, p. 244, note 5.

of Punt,[1] they settle upon Egypt, anointed with myrrh. The one that first cometh, it taketh my worm ; [2] its savour is brought from Punt, and its talons are full of unguent.

My wish concerning thee is that we loose them [3] together, I alone with thee, that thou hear the crying of my myrrh-anointed one.

How good it would be, if thou wert there with me, when I set the trap. Most good is it to go to the meadow unto him who is beloved.

The voice of the goose, caught on its worm, crieth out, but love for thee holdeth me back and I cannot loose it. I will *take away* my nets. What shall I say to my mother, to whom I go every evening laden with birds ? " Hast thou set no trap to-day ? " [4] Thy love hath carried me off.

The goose flieth and settleth – – –, the many birds wander around, *yet I trouble not myself concerning them, for I have only* my love, that of me alone. Mine heart is in full accord (?) with thine, and I go not far from thy beauty.

– – – – I see sweet cake, *and it tasteth like* salt, and shedeh,[5] which erst was sweet in my mouth, it is like birds' gall. The breath of thy nostrils alone [6] is that which maketh mine heart to live. I have found that Amūn is given me [7] for ever and ever.

Fairest one, my desire shall be *that I love thee* as thy house-wife, that thine arm be laid upon mine arm – – – – *If mine* elder brother *is not with me* to-night, then am I like him who is in the grave, for art thou not health and life ? – – – –

The voice of the swallow speaketh, saying : " The land is bright, what is thy road ? " [8] Ah no, O bird ! Thou makest me to sicken (?). I have found my brother in his bed, and mine heart is glad . . . He saith unto me : I will not betake me afar off ; my hand is in thy hand. I walk to and fro and I

---

[1] See p. 244, note 2.
[2] The bait of the trap.
[3] The birds from the trap.
[4] The mother's question.
[5] See p. 191, note 1.
[6] The Egyptians kissed, at least in the earliest times, by rubbing noses ; perhaps here is a reference to that practice.
[7] Meaning ?
[8] Thou must go away ?

am with thee in every pleasant place." He maketh me the chief of the maidens and causeth not mine heart to be sick.

I fix my gaze on the outer door. Behold, my brother cometh to me. Mine eyes are turned upon the road, and mine ear heareth – – – – I make the love of my brother to be my sole (?) concern, for that for him mine heart is not silent.

He sendeth me a swift-footed messenger, who cometh and goeth, to say unto me: Wrong *is done unto me* (?) [1] – – – –. What meaneth it, that thou wrongest another's heart and . . . me?

Mine heart recalleth thy love. The half of my temple (only) is braided, when I come running to seek thee. *I trouble myself no (longer) over my* hair-dressing, *yet, if thou still lovest me* (?), I will put on my curls, that I may be ready at any time.[2]

4. THE FLOWERS IN THE GARDEN [3]

The girl looks at the flowers of the garden—is she weaving a garland ?—and with each one thinks of her love. Every song begins with the name of a flower, to which the first verse is attached by a pun.

The " Cheerful Songs." [4]

Mekhmekh-flowers ! Thou makest the heart equable.[5] I do unto thee that which it desireth, when I am in thine arms.

My chief (?) request is paint for mine eye,[6] and my seeing of thee is light for mine eyes. I nestle close to thee, because I see thy love, thou man, for whom most (?) I crave.

How pleasant is mine hour ! Might an hour only become for me eternity, when I sleep with thee. Thou didst (?) lift up mine heart – – – – when it was in night (?).

Seamu-flowers are in it ! One is made great in their presence.[7] I am thy first sister. I am unto thee like a garden,

[1] The meaning of what follows is that he excuses himself and she does not believe it.

[2] *Cf.* p. 153, note 1.   [3] As above, p. 244, note 5.

[4] The same title is borne by the songs on p. 246, which are in the same papyrus.

[5] Paronomasia.

[6] Meaning, perhaps : when thou carryest out my request, it is to me as if I cool my eyes with cosmetic. The painting of the eyelids with antimony still plays a great rôle in Egypt at the present day.

[7] Paronomasia. Does it mean, one feels great in the presence of the little flowers ?

which I have planted with flowers and with all manner of sweet smelling herbs.

Pleasant is the channel in it, which thine hand hath digged, at the cooling of the north wind. The beautiful place where I walk about, when thine hand resteth on mine, and mine heart is satisfied with joy, because we walk together. Shedeh [1] is it, my hearing of thy voice, and I live because I hear it. Whenever I see thee, it is better for me than food and drink.

Zait-flowers are in it ! I take [2] thy chaplets, when thou comest drunken and thou liest on thy bed. I will stroke thy feet – – – –.

5. THE TREES IN THE GARDEN [3]

The trees in the maiden's garden speak to her and to the beloved, and invite them to the feast in their shade. Possibly the maiden had spoken to the trees in the lost beginning, for one of them complains that it was not regarded as " first."

The manuscript, as is shown by a note at the end, belonged to an official whose duty it was to issue copper to the metal-workers.

 – – – – The . . . -tree speaketh : My stones are like unto her teeth, and my shape unto [4] her breasts. (I am the best) of the orchard, I abide at every season, that the sister may recline (beneath me ?) with her brother, when they are drunken with wine and shedeh, and besprinkled with kemi-oil. – – – – All (trees) in the garden save me fade away ; I endure twelve months – – – – I stand . . ., and if the blossom falleth off, that of the year before is still upon me.[5]

I am the first *of all trees and will not that I* should be regarded as second. If this is done again, I will no longer keep silence *and will betray them, that* the wrong-doing may be seen and the beloved be chastised, that she may not – – – –. *The poet then speaks of the feast* with *its* lotus flowers, blossoms and buds, *its* unguent *and* beer of all kinds, that she may cause thee [6] to pass

[1] *I.e.* as sweet as that.

[2] A pun. Probably the chaplets with which he was adorned at the banquet.

[3] Papyrus in Turin. First brought to notice by Maspero in 1886. See W. MAX MÜLLER, *Liebespoesie.*

[4] Probably the shape of the fruit, not that of the tree.

[5] Thus a tree which flowers the whole year through.

[6] The lover who is just coming.

the day in merriment. The booth of rushes is a sheltered spot – – – – I see him, he is really coming. Let us go and flatter him. May he pass the whole day – – – –.

The fig-tree moveth its mouth, and its foliage (?) cometh and saith : – – – – to the mistress. Was there ever a lady like me ? (Yet) if thou [1] hast no slave, I will be thy servant.

I was brought from the land of . . . as a spoil for the beloved. She hath had me set in her orchard, she putteth not for me – – – –. I (busy?) myself with drinking, and my belly hath not become full of well-water.[2]

I am found for pleasure, – – – – to one that drinketh not. By my ka ! O beloved, – – – – bringeth me into thy presence.

The little sycamore, which she hath planted with her hand, it moveth its mouth to speak. The whispering (?) of its leaves is as sweet as refined honey. How charming are its pretty branches, verdant as . . . It is laden with neku-fruits, that are redder than jasper. Its leaves are like unto malachite, and are . . . as glass. Its wood is in colour like unto neshmet-stone,[3] and is . . . as the besbes-tree. It draweth them that be not (already) under it,[4] its shadow is (so) cool.

It slippeth a letter into the hand of a little maid, the daughter of its chief gardener, and maketh her run to the beloved : " Come, and pass the time in the midst of thy maiden (?). The garden is in its day.[5] There are bowers and shelters (?) there for thee. My gardeners are glad and rejoice when they see thee. Send thy slaves ahead of thee, supplied with their utensils. (Of a truth) one is (already) drunken when one hasteneth to thee, ere one hath yet drunken. (But) the servants come from thee with their vessels, and bring beer of every sort and all manner of mixed loaves, and many flowers of yesterday and to-day, and all manner of refreshing fruit.

[1] The beloved. The tree will act as her attendant. It can all the more be accounted a slave, as it was brought like such an one from abroad for the service of the maiden. It is, therefore, not an ordinary Egyptian fig-tree that is here spoken of.

[2] It can go on drinking perpetually, it is so well watered.

[3] Whitish-blue felspar.

[4] It entices people into its shade.

[5] In full bloom.

"Come, and spend the day in merriment, and to-morrow, and the day after, three whole days, and sit in my shadow."

Her lover sitteth on her right hand. She maketh him drunken, and heedeth all that he saith. The feast is disordered with drunkenness, and she stayeth on with her brother.

Her . . . is spread out under me, when the sister walketh about.[1] But I am discreet, and speak not of what I see. I will say no word.

D. VARIOUS SONGS

1. SONGS OF THE THRESHERS

As the thresher drives his oxen round and round the threshing-floor, that they may tread out the grain, he suggests to them that something will accrue to them out of this labour, and sings : [2]

Thresh for yourselves, thresh for yourselves, oxen !
Thresh for yourselves, thresh for yourselves ;
Straw to eat,[3] barley for your masters ;
Give yourselves no rest, it is cool (to-day).

or thus : [4]

Work for yourselves, work for yourselves, ye oxen !
Work for yourselves, the offal for yourselves, the barley
    for your masters.[5]

2. SONGS AT BANQUETS

This charming song, which bids one enjoy this fleeting life, and comes down to us from an earlier period (see p. 133), is to be found in an amplified version in the tomb of a Theban priest : [6]

How quiet is this righteous prince ! The goodly destiny hath come to pass.

Bodies pass away since the time of the god, and a generation cometh in their place.

---

[1] When the guests are drunken, the lovers walk about in the garden and recline under the tree.

[2] In the tomb of Paheri at El-Kâb ; already brought to notice by Champollion. See Lepsius, *Denkmaeler aus Aegypten und Aethiopien*, iii. 10c ; Tylor and Griffith, *The Tomb of Paheri*, p. 15.

[3] They get this for payment.   [4] Lepsius, *op. cit.* 10d.

[5] *Ie.* for the masters of your poor driver.

[6] See W. Max Müller, *Liebespoesie.* It is written in the old language.

Rē showeth himself in the morning, and Atum goeth down in Manun.[1] Men beget, women conceive, and every nose breatheth air—day dawneth, and their children go one and all to their places.[2]

Spend the day merrily, O priest ! Put unguent and fine oil together to thy nostrils, and garlands and lotus flowers . . . on the body of thy sister [3] whom thou favourest, as she sitteth beside thee. Set singing and music before thy face. Cast all evil behind thee, and bethink thee of joy, until that day cometh when one reacheth port in the land that loveth silence – – – –.

Spend the day merrily, Neferhotep, thou excellent priest with clean hands.

I have heard what came to pass – – – –,[4] their walls are destroyed, their places are no more, they are as if they had never been since the time of the god – – – –.

So much for the first of the three divisions of the poem. What is still preserved of the remaining portions shows that the singer spoke of the burial rites, of life as led in the nether world, and of those acts of kindness for which the memory of the dead is cherished ; but in between is to be recognized : be mindful of the day when thou shalt be drawn *to the land of the dead,* there is none that hath returned. *And the refrain occurs repeatedly :* Spend the day merrily.

Fragments of songs with which the musicians are entertaining the guests, are occasionally to be found appended to ... ner pictures representing a banquet held in the tomb. There is, for example, the well-known painting in the British Museum,[5] *showing three girls singing, while a fourth accompanies them on the flute, and two others dance. The words of their song come, apparently, from one which celebrates the blessings of the recent inundation :*

Kēb [6] hath planted his beauty in every body. Ptah [7] hath made this with his hands to be unguent (?) for his heart.

---

[1] Mythical country in the West.

[2] Meaning : the next day sees them already in the tomb.

[3] *I.e.* thy beloved, as in the love songs.

[4] Here, as in the original version of the song, mention must have been made of the ancient sages, or other famous men of old time.

[5] W. WRESZINSKI, *Atlas zur altaegyptischen Kulturgeschichte*, Pl. 91.

[6] The earth-god.   [7] The creator and fashioner of all things.

The canals are full of water anew,[1] and the earth is flooded over with his love.

3. THE GOOD FORTUNE OF THE DEAD

The old drinking song, with its advice to make the most of life, seeing that no one knows how it fares with the dead, must have painfully affected a pious Egyptian. So a song was composed which protested against the drinking song. If the harp-player at the banquet did sing these old profanities, he also sang after them by way of apology, as it were, the following song,[2] which begins with an address to the dead and to the gods of the Theban necropolis—for they hear what is sung at the banquet in the tomb.

All ye excellent nobles, and ye gods of the Mistress of Life,[3] hear ye how praises are rendered to this priest, and homage done to this excellent noble's lordly soul, now that he is a god that liveth for ever, magnified in the West. So may they become [4] a remembrance in after days, and for every one that cometh to (this tomb).[5]

I have heard [6] these songs that are in the tombs of ancient time. What they say, when they extol the (life) on earth, and belittle the region of the dead—to what purpose is it that they act thus towards the Land of Eternity, the just and the right, where no terrors are ? Wrangling is its abhorrence, and there is none that girdeth himself against his fellow.

This land that hath no foe,[7] all our kindred rest in it, since the earliest day of time, and they that shall be in millions of millions of years, they come thither every one. There is none that may tarry in the Land of Egypt, there is not one that doth not pass yonder.

The duration of that which is done upon earth is as a dream. (Anon) " Welcome, safe and sound " is said to him that hath reached the West.

[1] With fourfold alliteration.

[2] So in the just-mentioned (p. 251) tomb of the priest Neferhotep ; see GARDINER, *Proceedings of the Society of Biblical Archæology*, xxxv. pp. 165 ff. The song is preserved to us in the old language.

[3] The necropolis, in which there is supposed to be no death, but only new life.

[4] The praises, *i.e.* the usual mortuary prayers and invocations.

[5] Visitors to the tomb are to pray for the dead.

[6] This is the real beginning of the song.

[7] Or : where no foe existeth ?

It is remarkable to see how the poet of a modern time defends his hereafter. He no longer speaks in praise of its choice victuals and its water, and he does not even mention Osiris, the kindly king of the dead. All he has to say in praise of it is that it brings man rest at the last, after the confused dream of life. This is fundamentally the same pessimism as is found in the old drinking song, except that reverence for the hereafter is outwardly preserved.

E. POEMS TO THE KING

The poems of this nature that I lay before my readers are only single examples. They might be greatly increased, for whatever its purport in other respects, every inscription of a New Kingdom Pharaoh contains a hymn in praise of him.

I. THE VICTORIES OF THUTMŌSIS III [1]

This hymn, composed about 1470 B.C., in the old language and on the old lines, must have been a famous composition, for two later kings, Sēthos I and Ramesses II, have reproduced it on monuments of their own and applied it to themselves.

It consists of an introduction and a conclusion written in poetic language, with ten intervening strophes composed in the strictly regular form discussed on p. xxxi.

Saith Amunrē, lord of Karnak : Thou comest to me [2] and exultest, when thou seest my beauty, my son, my protector, Menkheperrē,[3] living for ever. I shine forth [4] for love of thee. Mine heart is gladdened by thy beauteous coming to my temple, and mine hands impart protection and life to thy limbs.

How pleasing is the kindliness which thou displayest towards my body ; so will I establish thee in my dwelling, and work a wonder for thee.[5]

I give thee might and victory over all the hill countries ; I

---

[1] Upon a splendid memorial stela (see SETHE, *Urkunden*, iv. 611 ff.) which stood in the temple of Karnak ; now in the Cairo Museum. Often translated ; see BREASTED, *Records*, ii. §§ 656 ff.

[2] The king comes victorious to Thebes, and the image of the god goes in procession to meet him and to greet him. The whole poem will actually have been composed for such a festival and recited at it.

[3] The king's official name.

[4] *I.e.* come forth in procession from the temple.

[5] You have so beautified my image, which is now displayed to you, and I will show my gratitude by erecting one of you in the temple.

set thy glory and the fear of thee in all the low countries, the terror of thee as far as the four pillars of the sky.[1] I make great the reverence for thee in all bodies, and cause the war-cry of thy majesty to resound among the Nine Peoples of the Bow.

The great ones of all foreign lands are held together in thy fist. I myself stretch out mine hands and tie them for thee.[2] I bind [3] together the Trōglodytes [4] by tens of thousands and thousands, the Northerners by hundreds of thousands, as captives.

I cause thy foes to fall beneath thy sandals, so that thou treadest down the . . . of the rebels ; even as I consign to thee the earth in its length and its breadth, and the Westerners and Easterners are under thine authority.

Thou traversest all foreign lands with joyful heart, and wheresoe'er thy majesty is, there is none that attacketh. I am thy guide, so that thou attainest unto them. Thou hast crossed the water of the Great Bend [5] of Naharina in victory and strength, which I have bestowed on thee. They hear thy battle-cry and enter into dens. I have bereft their nostrils of the breath of life. I send the terror of thy majesty coursing through their hearts.

The serpent which is upon thy brow, she consumeth them. She maketh an easy spoil of the malignant ones.[6] She burneth up them that are in their . . . [6] with her flame. She cutteth off the heads of the Asiatics, and none of them are lost (to her), fallen and abased (?) by reason of her might.

I cause thy victories to spread abroad into all lands. That which she who is on my brow illumineth [7] is subject to thee. There is none that rebelleth against thee as far as that which the sky encircleth. They come with gifts upon their backs and make obeisance to thy majesty, even as I ordain.

I have made to faint them that make inroads,[8] that come nigh thee ; their hearts are burnt up, and their limbs tremble.

---

[1] The sky, according to one conception, was supported on props.
[2] The simile is probably derived from fowling.
[3] The word is used of binding sheaves ; the enemy are his harvest.
[4] See p. 137, note 1.
[5] The Euphrates.
[6] Designation of a people.
[7] The royal serpent shines like the sun, to whom she actually belongs.
[8] Bedouins, sea-rovers, etc.

I have come [1] that I may cause thee to tread down the princes
of Palestine ;
I spread them out under thy feet throughout their countries.
I cause them to behold thy majesty as The Lord of Radiance, [2]
Thou shinest in their faces as my similitude.

I have come that I may cause thee to tread down them that
are in Asia ;
Thou smitest the heads of the Asiatics of Retenu. [3]
I cause them to behold thy majesty equipped with thy
panoply,
When thou layest hold on the weapons of war in the chariot.

I have come that I may cause thee to tread down the Eastern
land ;
Thou tramplest on them that are in the regions of God's Land, [4]
I cause them to behold thy majesty as the star Seshed,
Which scattereth its flame in fire, when it giveth forth its dew. [5]

I have come that I may cause thee to tread down the Western
land ;
Keftiu and Isi [6] are in awe of thee.
I cause them to behold thy majesty as a young bull,
Firm of heart, with horns ready, that is not felled (?).

I have come that I may cause thee to tread down them that
are in their . . . ;
The lands of Meten [7] tremble for fear of thee,
I cause them to behold thy majesty as a crocodile,
Lord of terror in the water, unapproachable.

I have come that I may cause thee to tread down them that
are in the islands ;
They that are in the midst of the great green sea are aware
of thy battle-cry.
I cause them to behold thy majesty as the Champion, [8]
Who appeared gloriously upon the back of his victim.

[1] *I.e.* to meet you.   [2] The sun.
[3] Palestine ; see above, pp. 17 and 234.
[4] The land of sunrise, *i.e.* Arabia and the like.
[5] Possibly rather " blight " or " pestilence " [Translator].
[6] Crete and Cyprus ?
[7] Unidentified : probably in the Mediterranean Sea.
[8] Horus, the " Champion " of Osiris. He sits as a hawk upon the
defeated Sêth.

I have come that I may cause thee to tread down the Tehenu ; [1]
The Utentiu are subject to the might of thy fame.
I cause them to behold thy majesty as a fierce-eyed lion,
While thou makest them to be corpses throughout their valley.

I have come that I may cause thee to tread down the utter-
  most ends of the lands ;
What the ocean encircleth is held in thy grasp.
I cause them to behold thy majesty as a lord of the wing, [2]
Which seizeth on what he seeth according as he desireth.

I have come that I may cause thee to tread down them that
  are in the country nigh at hand ;
Thou bindest the sand-dwellers as captives.
I cause them to behold thy majesty as a jackal of Upper Egypt,
A master of speed, a runner, traversing the two lands.

I have come that I may cause thee to tread down the Trõglo-
  dytes of Nubia ;
As far as . . . , all is in thy grasp ;
I cause them to behold thy majesty as thy twain brethren, [3]
Whose hands I have joined for thee in victory, [4]

and thy two sisters [5] have I put behind thee as a protection,
while the arms of my majesty are uplifted and dispel what is
evil. [6]

  I afford thee protection, my beloved son, Horus, Strong
Bull, who shone forth in Thebes, whom I have begotten from
my divine limbs, Thutmõsis, who liveth ever, who hath done for
me all that my ka desireth. Thou hast erected my dwelling in
everlasting work, made longer and broader than it was aforetime, and the great doorway . . . whose beauty makes festive
the House of Amūn (?). Greater are thy monuments than those
of any king that hath been. I gave thee command to make
them, and am now contented therewith ; I establish thee upon

---

[1] The Libyans ; the Utentiu are unknown.
  [2] The hawk.　　　　　　　　　[3] Horus and Sēth.
  [4] They both give it thee. It will be noticed how the strophic part is
linked to what follows. This will also have been brought out in the
chanting of the poem.
  [5] Isis and Nephthys.
  [6] The last sentence is garnished with alliterations, five words beginning
with *h* following one another. See above, p. xxxiv.

  17

the throne of Horus for millions of years, that thou mayest lead the living for ever.

2. HYMN TO RAMESSES II [1]

This fine poem is to be found on various stelae near to, and inside, the rock temple of Abu Simbel, in Nubia. Since it has no special connection with the temple or the district, we must suppose that this poem, like that on the battle with the Khatti, was one which particularly took the king's fancy and accordingly was immortalized.

The beginning contains actually only the king's names, which, however, by the addition of epithets, are expanded into a hymn. Then follow five strophes of varying length, each of which ends with " King Ramesses."

[EXPANDED TITULARY OF THE KING.]

Horus, Strong Bull, who is loved by Truth, Month [2] of kings, bull of rulers, of great strength like his father Sēth of Ombos.

Lord of the two diadems, who protecteth Egypt and subdueth foreign countries, the fearful, (greatly ?) reverenced in all lands ; who suffereth not the land of Ethiopia to exist, and putteth an end to the boasting of the land of Khatti.

The subjugator of the adversary, rich in years, great in victories, who reacheth the ends of the earth when seeking for battle, who maketh narrow the wide mouth of foreign princes.[3]

King of Upper and Lower Egypt, lord of the Two Lands, Usimarē-Chosen-of-Rē.

Son of Rē, who treadeth down the land of the Khatti, Ramesses-Beloved-of-Amūn, given life. Beloved by Rē-Harakhti-Atum,[4] lord of the Two Lands of Heliopolis ; by Amunrē,[4] king of gods, and by Ptah, the great, who dwelleth south of his Wall,[4] lord of Ankh-taui [5] ; who appeared upon the Horus-throne of the living.

[THE ACTUAL POEM.]

The good god, the strong one, whom men praise, the lord, in whom men make their boast ; who protecteth his soldiers,[6] who maketh his boundaries on earth as he will, like Rē when

---

[1] LEPSIUS, *Denkmaeler*, iii. 195*a*.   Still composed in the old language.
[2] The god of war.   [3] Their boasting.
[4] The three great gods to whom the temple of Abu Simbel is dedicated.
[5] Part of Memphis, where Ptah dwells.   [6] Cf. below, p. 267.

he shineth over the circle of the world,—he, the king of Upper
and Lower Egypt, Usimarē-Chosen-of-Rē, son of Rē, lord of
diadems, Ramesses-Beloved-of-Amūn, who is given life.[1]

He who bringeth the rebellious one as captive to Timūris,
and the princes with their gifts to his palace. The fear of him
courseth through their bodies, their limbs tremble in the time
of his terribleness, lord of the Two Lands,—he, King Ramesses.

He who treadeth down the land of the Khatti, and maketh
it a heap of corpses like Sekhmet,[2] when she rageth after the
pestilence. He who sendeth forth his arrows against them,
and hath the mastery over their limbs. The princes of every
foreign country come forth from their land, wakeful and un-
sleeping,[3] and their bodies faint. Their gifts are an assortment
of the products of their land ; their soldiers and their children
are in the forepart thereof, in order to sue for peace from his
majesty—from him, King Ramesses.

Their princes tremble, when they behold him, how that in
his might and strength he is like unto Month. He who – – – –
like the son of Nut. He is as it were a bull with sharpened
horns, great in . . ., (only) letting go (again) when he hath
made an end of his enemies—he, King Ramesses.

The strong lion with . . . claws, loud roaring, sending forth
his voice in the valley of the wild game,—he, King Ramesses.

The jackal that runneth swiftly, when seeking his assailant,
traversing the circle of the earth in a moment of time. Divine
and lordly hawk, furnished with wings, swooping down among
the small and the great, that he may cause them no more to
know themselves—he, King Ramesses.

He who causeth the Asiatics (?) to retreat, who fighteth upon
the field of battle ; they break their bows and are given over
to the fire ; his might hath the mastery over them, like unto
a flame, when it hath seized upon the scrub,[4] and the storm-
wind is behind it, like unto a fierce fire when it hath tasted of
the blaze ; every one that encountereth (?) it becometh ashes—
he, King Ramesses.

The ruler, strong when he slayeth them that know not his
name, like unto a tempest that shrieketh terribly on the sea,
its waves are like mountains, and none can come nigh unto it ;

---

[1] I abbreviate these names in the other verses.
[2] The goddess of war. [3] In such haste are they to reach Egypt.
[4] Actually a light, inflammable plant. See p. 106, note 4.

every one that is in it is drowned in the nether world—he, King Ramesses.

The king, shining forth in the White Crown, the strength of Egypt, skilled in warfare upon the battle-field, valiant in the mêlée ; fierce fighter with stout heart ; who setteth his arms as a wall about (?) his soldiers—he, King Ramesses, who is given life like Rē.

3. THE BATTLE OF KADESH [1]

The long and bitter war, which Ramesses II (*circa* 1300–1234 B.C.) waged with the Asiatic kingdom of the Khatti and their allies, culminated in a battle fought at Kadesh in the valley of the Orontes. Inscriptions and representations in Egyptian temples supply us with ample information as to the course of events in this battle. The king had pressed on ahead with the first of his four armies, without any suspicion that the whole of the enemy forces lay in wait for him behind the fortress of Kadesh. He was surrounded and was in terrible danger, but succeeded in holding out until an unexpected body of troops came to his help. Finally, when a second army was brought up, the defeat was turned into a victory for the Egyptians.[2]

This victory of the young king was celebrated in a long poem written in the ninth year of his reign by an unknown poet. The poet has dealt freely with the actual happenings, in order to give more prominence to the king's achievement. The poem must have met with the king's approval, for he has had it introduced into his great temples.

The title : The Victory which Ramesses II won *over the Khatti and all their confederates, is immediately followed by a glorification of the king* : a champion without his peer, with strong arms and stout heart – – – –, beautiful of form like Atum – – – –, victorious in all lands. None can take up arms against him ; he is a wall *for his soldiers, and* their shield in the day of battle. A bowman whom none equalleth, stronger than hundreds of thousands together ; who goeth forward – – – –. With (stout) heart in the hour of the encounter – – – – ; a thousand men cannot stand before him, and an hundred

---

[1] Already brought to notice by Champollion in 1828. Treated of for the first time by de Rougé, and frequently since. Almost completely preserved in manuscript (*Pap. Sallier*, iii., in the British Museum), and imperfectly in the temples of Luxor, Karnak, and Abydos.

[2] For full details, see BREASTED, *Ancient Records of Egypt*, iii. pp. 123 ff.

thousand are faint, when they see him. The terrible one, loudly shouting ; who (causeth) the hearts of the foreign peoples (to quail), as doth a fierce lion in the desert valley. – – – – Excellent in plans, good at (giving) directions, and his utterance is found to be admirable. Who rescueth his army, (protecteth ?) his body-guard, and delivereth his troops [1] – – – – ; his heart is like a mountain of ore,—he, King Ramesses.

[INTRODUCTION.]

Now his majesty had made ready his infantry and his chariotry, besides the Shardana, whom his majesty had taken captive by the victories of his arm,[2] *and he had* given them the directions [3] for the battle. His majesty proceeded northwards with his infantry and his chariotry, and he began the goodly march. In the fifth year, on the ninth day of the second month of Summer, his majesty passed the fortress of Zaru.[4]

He was like Month at his appearing, and all foreign countries trembled before him. – – – – All (rebels ?) came bowing down for fear of the might of his majesty. His army marched along the narrow defiles,[5] and they were there as though upon the roadways of Egypt.

And many days after this [6] his majesty was in Ramesses-Beloved-of-Amūn, the city *which lieth in the land of the* cedars.[7] His majesty proceeded northward, and came to the mountain range of Kadesh. And his majesty went forward like his father Month, lord of Thebes, and crossed the ford of the Orontes [8] with the first army of Amūn.[9] – – – – His majesty came to the city of Kadesh.

And the wretched, vanquished chief of Khatti had come, after he had gathered to himself all lands as far as the ends of the sea ; the whole land of Khatti had come, and likewise

[1] These attributes refer to the rôle which the king played in the battle, according to the conception of the poet.

[2] See p. 226, note 6.   [3] The plan of campaign.

[4] Fortress on the east frontier of the Delta ; see p. 232, note 8.

[5] Or : narrow paths.

[6] The usual, almost meaningless, formula of narrative; see above, p. 151, note 1.

[7] Some city in the Lebanon, which the king has thus renamed.

[8] The river between Lebanon and Anti-Lebanon on which Kadesh was situated.

[9] The four subsequently mentioned armies of the king are named after his chief gods.

Naharina, Aradus, Pedes, Irun, Kerkesh, Reke, Kizwadna, Carchemish, Ekeret, Kedi, the whole land of Nushashi, Meshenet, and Kadesh.[1] He had left no land which he had not brought with him ; all their princes were with him, and every one had his foot-soldiers with him and chariotry, a very great multitude without limit. They covered mountains and valleys, and were like grasshoppers in their multitude. He had left no silver in his land, and had stripped it of all its possessions ; he had given them to all countries, in order to lead them with him to the battle.[2]

Now the wretched chief of Khatti, with the many nations which were with him, stood hidden and ready for battle on the north-west of Kadesh. His majesty was all alone (with) his body-guard.[3] The army of Amūn marched behind him, the army of Rē crossed over the ford in the region south of the city of Shebten – – – –, the army of Ptah was south of the city of Erenem, and the army of Sutekh [4] was (yet) marching upon the road. His majesty had made a vanguard of all the captains of his army ; these were on the coast in the land of Emor.[5]

The wretched chief of Khatti stood in the midst of the army, which he had with him, and for fear of his majesty he came not forth to the battle. He had caused very many people and horses to come, multitudinous as the sand ; they stood three men to a span, and had joined themselves with warriors of every sort – – – – furnished with all the weapons of war, without number. They stood in battle array, concealed on the north-west of the city of Kadesh, and they came forth from the south side of Kadesh. They attacked the army of Rē in its centre, as it marched unheeding and unready for battle. The infantry and chariotry of his majesty fainted before them.

Now his majesty had halted north of Kadesh, on the west side of the Orontes ; and one came and told it to his majesty.

[1] The reading and interpretation of these names is still very questionable. The capital of Khatti lay in Northern Asia Minor (ruins of Boghazköi) ; Naharina was situated on the upper Euphrates, Aradus in Phœnicia, Carchemish on the Euphrates. In any case, it was an enormous region.

[2] *I.e.* he had exhausted it in order to give his confederates their pay.

[3] The papyrus indeed allows " no one to be with him."

[4] Another form of the name of Sēth, who at this time held the position of war-god.

[5] They were marching along the Phœnician coast, no one having any idea as to where the enemy was to be located.

[THE KING'S FIGHT.]

His majesty issued forth [1] like his father Month, after he had seized his panoply of war, and had put on his corselet ; he was like Baal in his hour.[2] The great span, which bore his majesty, was called Victory-in-Thebes and was from the great stable of Ramesses. His majesty (rode) at a gallop, and charged the hostile army of Khatti, being all alone and having none with him.

When his majesty looked behind him he marked that two thousand five hundred chariots encircled him on his way out, with all the warriors of the wretched land of Khatti and of the many countries which were with him, from Aradus, Mese, Pedes, Keshkesh, Irun, Kizwadna, Khereb, Ekeret, Kadesh, and Reke. They stood three men to a span, and had banded themselves together.

No chief [3] is with me, no charioteer, no officer of foot-soldiery nor of chariotry. My foot-soldiery and my chariotry left me for a prey before them, and not one of them stood fast in order to fight with them.

And his majesty said : " What is it then, my father Amūn ? Hath a father indeed forgotten his son ? Have I done ought without thee ? Have I not gone or stood still because of thine utterance ? And I never swerved from the counsels of thy mouth. How great is the great lord of Thebes, too great to suffer the foreign peoples to come nigh him ! What are these Asiatics to thee, Amūn ? Wretches that know not God ! Have I not fashioned for thee very many monuments, and filled thy temple with my captives ? I have built for thee my temple of millions of years,[4] and have given thee my goods for a possession.[5] I present unto thee all countries together, in order to furnish thine offering with victuals. I cause to be offered unto thee tens of thousands of oxen, together with all sweet-smelling plants.

[1] From his tent.

[2] *I.e.* when this god, whom the Egyptians equated with their Sutekh, was most terrifying.

[3] Here begins the actual poem, which largely consists of speeches by the king.

[4] *I.e.* Amūn's temple of endless duration ; he means especially Karnak.

[5] Or " made over to thee my possessions by deed " [Translator].

"No good thing leave I undone in thy sanctuary. I build for thee great pylons, and I myself set up their flag-staffs. I bring thee obelisks from Elephantine, and I it is who conveyeth stone. I cause galleys to voyage for thee upon the sea, in order to fetch for thee the tribute of the countries. Mischief shall befall him who thwarteth thy counsels, but well fareth he that understandeth (?) thee. One should work (?) for thee with loving heart.

"I call to thee, my father Amūn. I am in the midst of foes whom I know not. All lands have joined themselves together against me, and I am all alone and none other is with me. My soldiers have forsaken me, and not one among my chariotry hath looked round for me. If I cry to them, not one of them hearkeneth. But I call, and I find that Amūn is worth more to me than millions of foot-soldiers, and hundreds of thousands of chariots, than ten thousand men in brethren and children, who with one mind hold together. The work of many men is nothing ; Amūn is worth more than they. I have come hither by reason of the counsels of thy mouth, O Amūn, and from thy counsels have I not swerved."

I pray at the limits of the lands, and yet my voice reacheth unto Hermonthis ; [1] Amūn hearkeneth unto me and cometh, when I cry to him. He stretcheth out his hand to me, and I rejoice ; he calleth out behind me : "Forward, forward ! I am with thee, I thy father. Mine hand is with thee, and I am of more avail than an hundred thousand men, I, the lord of victory, that loveth strength ! "

I have found my courage again, mine heart swelleth for joy, all that I was fain to do cometh to pass. I am like Month, I shoot on the right hand and fight on the left. I am as Baal in his time before them. I find that the two thousand five hundred chariots, in whose midst I was, lie hewn in pieces before my steeds. Not one of them hath found his hand to fight. Their hearts are become faint in their bodies for fear, their arms are all become powerless. They are unable to shoot, and have not the heart to take their lances. I cause them to plunge into the water, as plunge the crocodiles.[2] They stumble one over the other, and I slay of them whom I will. Not one of

[1] A city south of Thebes, but probably used for Thebes here.
[2] A number of the enemy was actually drowned in the Orontes during the battle, as the reliefs show.

them looketh back, and there is none that turneth him about. Whosoever of them falleth lifteth not up himself again.

Now the wretched Prince of Khatti stood in the midst of his army and watched the fight, which his majesty fought all alone without foot-soldiery or chariotry. He stood with face averted and irresolute.

He caused many chieftains to come ; all of them had horse-chariots, and they were equipped with all their weapons of war : namely, the prince of Aradus, of Mese, of Irun, of Reke, and of Derdeni ; the prince of Carchemish, of Kerkesh, and of Khereb, and the brethren of the princes of Khatti—all these together were two thousand horse-chariots, who came straight ahead on to the fire.[1]

I made for them, I was like Month, I caused them to taste my hand in a single moment. I slaughtered them, slaying them where they stood, and one cried out to the other, saying : " This is no man that is among us, he is Sutekh, great of strength ; Baal is in his limbs. They are not the deeds of a man that he doeth. (Never yet) hath one man alone, without foot-soldiers and chariotry, overcome hundreds of thousands. Come quickly, that we may flee from before him, that we may seek for ourselves life and yet draw breath. Lo, as for anyone that ventureth to approach him, his hand is paralysed and every limb. None can grasp bow or lance, when it is seen how he cometh, having run the course."

His majesty was behind them as it were a gryphon ; I slew among them and none escaped me.   I shouted out to my army : " Steady, steady your hearts, my soldiers. Ye behold my victory, I being alone.   But Amūn is my protector, and his hand is with me.   How faint-hearted ye are, my chariotry, and it is useless to trust in you.   There is not one among you to whom I had not done good in my land.   Stood I not as lord there, while ye were in poverty ?   Yet I caused you to become notables, and daily ye partook of my sustenance.   I set the son over the possessions of his father. All that was evil in this land is abolished.   I remitted to you your dues, and gave to you other things that had been taken away from you.[2]   Whosoever came

---

[1] *I.e.* to the king, whose snake-diadem spat out fire.
[2] The king had thus favoured the soldiers above all other classes ; indeed, his dynasty found in them its support. The somewhat later

with a petition, to him I said at all times : ' Yea, I will do it.'
Never has a lord done for his soldiers what I have done according
to your desire, (for) I made you dwell in your houses and your
cities, albeit ye did no soldier's service. My chariotry likewise,
to them gave I the road to many cities,[1] and thought to experience to-day a like thing [2] in you in this hour of entering into
battle. But behold, ye all with one consent do a coward's
deed ; not one of you standeth firm in order to reach me his
hand, while I am fighting.

" As the ka of my father, Amūn, endureth, would that I were
in Egypt like my fathers, who saw not the Syrians – – – – and
not one of you had come in order to tell his news in the land of
Egypt. What a goodly existence he hath, who conveyeth
many monuments to Thebes, the city of Amūn [3] ! "

The crime which my foot-soldiery and chariotry have
committed is greater than can be told. But, behold, Amūn
gave me his victory, although no foot-soldiery and no chariotry
were with me. I let every far-off land see my victory and
my might, while I was all alone, without a great one to follow
me, and without a charioteer, without an officer of the foot-
soldiery or of the chariotry. The foreign countries who see
me shall speak of my name as far as the farthest lands which
are unknown. Whosoever of them escapeth from mine hand,[4]
he standeth turned about and seeth what I do. When I attack
millions of them, their feet stand not firm, but they flee away.
All who shoot at me, their arrows are dispersed when they
reach me.

But when Menna, my charioteer, saw that a great multitude
of chariots compassed me round about, he became faint, and
his heart failed him, and very great fear entered into his limbs.
Then said he unto his majesty : " My good lord, valiant prince,
great protector of Egypt in the day of battle, we stand alone

letters, on pp. 193 ff. above, present the other side of the picture ; they
view the life of the soldier from the standpoint of the scribe.

[1] He has formed soldiers' settlements both of the infantry and of the
chariotry.

[2] He means : a like friendly deed.

[3] Meaning, perhaps : would that ye had spared me news of Syria so
that I might still be building in peace at Thebes.

[4] The papyrus reads here : All warriors whom mine hand spareth.

in the midst of the foe. Behold, the foot-soldiery and chariotry have abandoned us. Wherefore wilt thou stay until they bereave (us of breath)? Let us remain unscathed, save us, Ramesses." Then said his majesty unto his charioteer: "Steady, steady thine heart, my charioteer. I shall enter in among them even as a hawk striketh; I slay, hew in pieces, and cast to the ground. What mean these cowards to thee? My face groweth not pale for a million of them." His majesty hastened forwards; he charged the foe and charged them until the sixth time. I am behind them as Baal in the hour of his might. I make slaughter of them and am not slothful.

Now when my foot-soldiers and chariotry saw that I was like Month in might and strength, and that Amūn, my father, was joined with me and made every land straw before me, they approached one by one in order to (creep?) at eventide into the camp, and they found that all peoples, among whom I had forced my way, were lying slaughtered in heaps in their blood, even all the best warriors of Khatti, and the children and brethren of their prince. I had caused the field of Kadesh to become white,[1] and one knew not where to tread because of their multitude.

And my soldiers came to reverence my name, when they saw what I had done; my notables came to extol my might, and my chariotry likewise, who glorified my name: "Ah, thou goodly warrior, who maketh steady the heart, thou rescuest thy foot-soldiery and thy chariotry. O son of Amūn, deft of hands, thou destroyest the land of Khatti with thy mighty arms. Thou art a goodly warrier without thy like, a king that fighteth for his soldiers on the day of battle. Thou art stout of heart, and art foremost when the fight is joined. All lands, united in one, have not withstood (?) thee; thou wast victorious in the presence of the host, in the sight of the whole earth—that is no boast. Thou art the protector of Egypt, the subduer of the foreign countries,[2] thou hast broken the back of Khatti for ever."

And his majesty said unto his foot-soldiers, his chief captains, and his chariotry: "*What a crime ye have committed* (?) my

---

[1] With the corpses and their white clothes.

[2] Protector of Egypt, etc., is the second name in the titulary of Ramesses II.

chief captains, my foot-soldiery and my chariotry, ye who have not fought ! Hath not one boasted in his city – – – –, he will do a deed of valour *for* his good lord – – – –? Have I not done good to one of you ? Your leaving me alone in the midst of the enemy, how excellent that is in you ! – – – – your breathing the air while I am alone. Could ye then not say in your hearts that I am your wall of iron – – – –. It will be heard say that ye left me alone, without another, and no chief captain, no officer either of chariotry or of foot-soldiery came to hold out his hand to me. I fought and overcame millions of lands, all alone. I was with Victory-in-Thebes and Mut-is-Content,[1] my great steeds ; in them (alone) found I succour, when I was all alone in the midst of many countries. Furthermore, I myself will cause them eat their provender in my presence every day, when I shall be once more in my palace, for it was in them that I found succour, and also in Menna, my charioteer, and in the butlers of the palace, who were beside me. These were present at the battle. Lo, I found that they came to my majesty in valour and victory, after that I had overthrown with my mighty arm hundreds of thousands united together." [2]

[THE SECOND DAY OF BATTLE AND THE OVERTHROW OF THE ENEMY.]

When the day dawned, I began (?) the fighting in the battle.[3] I was ready for the fray like a bull on the alert ; I shone forth against them like Month, furnished with fighters and with mighty men. I forced my way into the mêlée and fought even as a hawk striketh. The royal snake upon my brow, it overthrew mine enemies ; it spat forth fire into the face of the foe. I was like Rē when he ascendeth in the morning, and my rays burnt the limbs of the enemy.

One cried out to the other : " Look to yourselves ! Protect yourselves ! Lo, the mighty Sekhmet is with him ; she is by him on his horses, and her hand is with him. If any draweth nigh unto him, the blast of fire cometh and burneth his limbs."

[2] Names of the horses ; Mut is the consort of Amūn, and she is also identified with the war-goddess, Sekhmet.

[2] If this remark refers to the butlers, it will explain why they were not hitherto mentioned in the poem.

[3] Or " I marshalled the squadrons in battle " [Translator].

Then they began to kiss the ground before me. My majesty was mighty behind them, I made slaughter among them, and was not slack (?). They were cut to pieces before my steeds, they lay together stretched out in their blood.

Then the wretched fallen prince of Khatti sent and revered the great name of his majesty : " Thou are Rē-Harakhti, thou art Sutekh, great in strength, son of Nut ; Baal is in thy limbs, and terror of thee is in the land of Khatti. Thou hast broken for ever the back of the prince of Khatti." He sent his envoy with a letter, which was addressed to the great name of my majesty, and apprised the Majesty of the Palace of Horus, Strong Bull, Beloved of Truth,[1] as followeth : " O King, who protecteth his soldiers, valiant in his might, a wall for his troops in the day of battle, king of Upper and Lower Egypt, Usimarē-Chosen-of-Rē, son of Rē, Ramesses-Beloved-of-Amūn ! The servant there saith,[2] and would have thee know that thou art the son of Rē, who issued from his limbs, and he hath given thee all lands united in one. The land of Egypt and the land of Khatti, they are thy servants and they lie at thy feet. Thine august father, Rē, hath given them unto thee. Be not violent with us ! Behold, thy prowess is great, and thy might is heavy upon the land of Khatti. Is it good that thou shouldest slay thy servants ? – – – – Yesterday thou didst slay hundreds of thousands, and to-day thou comest and leavest (us) no heirs surviving. Be not severe in thine utterance, O mighty king ; peaceableness is better than strife of battle. Give us breath ! "

My majesty allowed myself repose, full of life and good fortune, and I was as Month in his time, when his victory hath been achieved.[3] My majesty caused to be brought all the generals of the foot-soldiers, of the chariotry, *and all other troops*, altogether, in order to inform them of what the great prince of Khatti had written unto Pharaoh. They answered and said unto his majesty : " Mercy is good exceedingly, our lord O king ; in peaceableness is there nought to harm (?) – – – –. Who will revere thee on the day wherein thou art wroth ?[4]

[1] Name of Ramesses II.

[2] The old epistolary formula ; see p. 22, note 5.

[3] *I.e.* when this war-god rests after victory.

[4] Meaning possibly : You can only enjoy men's respect in time of peace, at other times men are only afraid of you.

Then his majesty commanded his [1] words to be heard, and extended his hand in peace upon the march southwards. [2]

And when his majesty drew near in peace to Egypt with his chief captains, his foot-soldiers, and his chariotry—life, stability, and happiness were with him, and gods and goddesses – – – – and all lands praised his fair countenance— he arrived safely at House-of-Ramesses-Great-of-Victories, [3] and rested in his palace, full of life like Rē upon his throne, *and the gods* greeted his ka, saying unto him: "Welcome, our beloved son, Ramesses-Beloved-of-Amūn!" They gave him millions of jubilees, and eternity upon the throne of his father (?) Atum, while all lands and all foreign countries lie under his feet.

4. POEMS ON THE CITY OF RAMESSES

Ramesses II built himself a new residence in the extreme northeastern corner of the Delta, on the site of what was probably the later Pelusium (thus east of the Suez Canal). This is the often-mentioned "House-of-Ramesses-Great-of-Victories," which, in accordance with Jewish tradition, we call the city of "Ramesses." Its geographical position permitted it to be regarded as the capital of a dominion which embraced Palestine and Egypt. Both hymns are preserved as school writing-exercises, and, as they were written under Merneptah, the successor of Ramesses II, the boys have inserted his name Binerē, instead of Usimarē, that of his father.—See also the letter on p. 206.

[LONGER POEM.] [4]

The recital of the victories of the Lord of Egypt.

His majesty hath builded him a castle called Great-of-Victories. It lieth betwixt Palestine and Egypt, and is full of provision and victuals. It is like unto Hermonthis, [5] and its duration is that of Memphis. The sun ariseth in its horizon, and setteth

---

[1] The prince of Khatti's.

[2] *I.e.* he turned homewards after the battle, and on this return journey concluded a peace. The actual peace-treaty, however, was only concluded sixteen years later.

[3] See above, p. 206, and the two immediately following poems.

[4] *Pap. Anastasi*, ii. 1. 1 ff.; the first two sections also occur in *Pap. Anastasi*, iv. 6. 1 ff., and are translated by GARDINER, *Journ. of Egypt. Archæology*, v. pp. 187 f.

[5] An ancient city not far from Thebes.

within it.[1] All men forsake their towns and settle down in its territory. Its western part is a temple of Amūn, its southern part a temple of Sutekh. Astarte is in its Orient, and Buto in its northern part. The castle which is within it is like unto the horizon of heaven. Ramesses-Beloved-of-Amūn is in it as god ; Month-in-the-Two-Lands [2] as herald ; Sun-of-Princes [2] as Vizier ; Joy-of-Egypt, Beloved-of-Atum,[2] as mayor, to whose dwelling the world goeth down.

The great chief of the land of Khatti writeth to the chief of Kedi : [3] " Make thee ready, that we may hasten to Egypt, that we may say : ' The will of God prevaileth,' and that we may speak smooth words to Ramesses. He giveth breath to whom he will. Every land existeth according to his pleasure, and the land of Khatti according to his will alone. If the god receive not his offering, it beholdeth not the rain of heaven.[4] It is in the power of Usimarē, the Bull that loveth valour."

Good god, strong as Month, victorious king, the . . . who issued from Rē, child and likeness of the Bull of Heliopolis.[5] Who standeth upon the field of battle, and in his valour fighteth like the Strong One in the ship " Ruler of Eternity." [6] He who was a king in the egg, like the majesty of Horus. He hath captured the lands by his victory, he hath subdued the Two Lands by his designs. The Nine Peoples lie trodden down under his feet. All foreign peoples are dragged to him with their gifts, and all countries are set for him upon the one road.[7] He hath no adversary, the princes of the rebellious countries are impotent, become as wild goats for terror of him ; he entereth in among them like the son of Nut,[8] and they fall down by reason of his fiery breath in the space of a moment. The Libyan falleth to his slaughtering, men fall to his blade.

[1] *I.e.* the king abides in it day and night.

[2] Official attributes of the king. They function beside him as his highest officials, for the whole administration devolves on him personally.

[3] Kedi lies in the north and is perhaps Cilicia.

[4] The Egyptian looked with but scant respect upon the countries which were dependent upon him. The god, *i.e.* Ramesses, had it in his power even to withhold rain from the Khatti.

[5] The sun-god Rē.

[6] Sēth in the ship of the sun, whom he protects from his enemies.

[7] The road to his palace.   [8] Sēth or Osiris.

His strength is given unto him eternally, and his will enfold-
eth the mountains.   O Ramesses-Beloved-of-Amūn, lord of
strength, who protecteth his soldiers.[1]   Thou . . . son of
Amūn ;   thou dauntless one, who protecteth his soldiers.
Strong Bull, who curbeth the confederacies (?), who standeth
fast on his war-chariot like the Lord of Thebes [2] – – – –.   His
strength invadeth all foreign countries ;   he traverseth the
(lands) seeking him that attacketh him.   His battle-cry is in
their hearts, which are afraid of his countenance.   The good
ruler, the watchful one, excellent in counsel, he putteth his
name, as that of one who is valiant, in all lands.   O king and
lord of the Two Lands like the majesty of Horus, the princes
of the lands are put in awe of thee, Binerē-Beloved-of-Amūn,
son of Rē, Merneptah-Contented-with-Truth."

Good god, king that liveth on truth !   King beloved of the
gods !   Excellent egg, son of Kheprē ! [3]   Child, similitude of
the Bull of Heliopolis !   Hawk that did enter the royal ring,[4]
born of Isis, Horus !   " Binerē " who appeared gloriously in
Egypt, unto whose throne the world cometh.

How strong is " Binerē " !   How enduring his counsels !
His words are excellent like those of Thōth, and all that he saith
cometh to pass.   He is like one that sheweth the way at the
head of his army, and his words are a wall for them.

How loved is he that bendeth to him his back, to the
Beloved-of-Amūn.

Victorious soldiers come to his triumph (?) in strength and
might ;   they cast fire in Isdirekti (?) and burn up . . .
ryena (?).[5]   The Shardana,[6] whom thou carriedst away in thy
strength, they take captive the tribes of the deserts.

How pleasant it is, when thou goest to Thebes, and thy
chariot is weighed down with hands.[7]   The chieftains go bound

[1] Instead of his army protecting him, he protects it.   See p. 261,
note 1.

[2] He looks as noble in battle as Amūn.

[3] Name of the sun-god.   The youthful Horus, to whom the king is
here likened, is his descendant.

[4] The ring (cartouche) in which the royal names are written.

[5] Unreadable names of countries.

[6] See p. 226, note 6 ; p. 261, note 2.

[7] The hands of the slain were cut off.   The king here carries them with
him as tokens of victory.

in front of thee, and thou wilt present[1] them to thine august father Amūn, Bull of his Mother.

Castle of Sese,[2] that repeateth jubilees ! Throne of Tenen ![3] Thou shinest forth as . . . like Atum, like the lamp of thy father Rē.

[SHORTER POEM.][4]

O Binerē-Beloved-of-Amūn, thou chief galley ! Club that shattereth, sword that slayeth the stranger peoples, lance of the hand !

He came down from heaven, and was born in Heliopolis, and victory was decreed to him in every land.

How fair was the day of thy presence (?), and how fair was thy voice as thou spakest, when thou didst build House-of-Ramesses-Beloved-of-Amūn, the beginning of every foreign land and the end of Egypt,[5] (the city), with beauteous balconies and dazzling halls of lapis lazuli and turquoise, the place where thy chariotry is marshalled, the place where thine infantry is mustered, the place where thy ship's troops come to port, when they bring thee tribute.

Praise be to thee, when thou comest among thy slaves (chosen) from the Asiatics,[6] men of fierce countenances and burning fingers, (whom thou didst ?) carry away when they beheld the Prince[7] standing and fighting. Mountains cannot stand before him, and they are afraid of thine awfulness.

O Binerē-Beloved-of-Amūn, thou shalt exist so long as eternity existeth,[8] and ˆeternity shall exist so long as thou existeth. Thou shalt abide upon the throne of thy father Rē-Harakhti.

[1] The temple obtained them as slaves.

[2] " Sese " is the pet name for Ramesses.

[3] Name of Ptah of Memphis.

[4] *Pap. Anastasi*, iii. 7. 2 ff. Translated by GARDINER, *Journ. of Egypt. Archæology*, v. pp. 186 f.

[5] It lies on the frontier.

[6] Or: amid thy regiments of archers [Translator].

[7] Or: who advance (?) when they behold the Prince [Translator].

[8] This ending is made up of antiquated phrases, the tone of which contrasts strongly with that of the rest of this poem.

5. POEM ON THE VICTORY OF MERNEPTAH [1]

This poem is engraved on a memorial tablet, the so-called Israel Stela, set up in the funerary temple of the king, and also as is shown by a fragment, on one erected in the temple of Karnak. It was, therefore, without doubt a poem to which the king attached a great value.

It is mainly a glorification of the great victory which the king won over the Libyans in his fifth year (*circa* 1230 B.C.), and by which Egypt was rescued from grave peril.

Men tell of his victories in all lands ; all lands together are made to know, and they are made to see the beauty of his valorous deeds.

King Merneptah, the Strong Bull, that slayeth his foes, beauteous upon the battlefield of valour, when he is assailed. [2]

The sun, that drave away the clouds which were over Egypt, he that caused Timūris to see the rays of the sun.

He that removed an hill of brass from the back of the people, that he might give air to the folk which were in captivity.

He that made Memphis [3] to rejoice over their enemies, and made Ptah-Tenen to exult over his adversaries. He that opened the gates of Memphis which had been shut, and made its temples receive their victuals.

King Merneptah, the Sole One, that strengtheneth the hearts of hundreds of thousands, and breath cometh to their nostrils at the sight of him.

The land of the Temehu [4] was broken in his lifetime, and terror was put for ever in the heart of the Mashawasha.

He hath turned back the Libyans who trod Egypt, and great dread of Timūris is in their hearts ; their march forward *hath come to an end*, and their feet made no stand, but fled.

Their archers cast away their bows, the heart of their fleet ones is wearied with marching. They loosed their water-skins and threw them on the ground ; their sacks were torn (?) and cast away. [5]

[1] Discovered by Petrie in 1896. First translated by SPIEGELBERG, *Zeitschr. für ägypt. Sprache*, xxxiv. pp. 11 ff. See BREASTED, *Ancient Records of Egypt*, iii. pp. 256 ff.

[2] Expressions which are used of bull-fights.

[3] Memphis had been especially hard pressed. But its god Ptah had appeared to the king in a dream and bidden him take courage.

[4] The Temehu, Tehenu, and Mashawasha are Libyan tribes.

[5] In order to make flight easier.

The miserable chieftain, the fallen one [1] of Libya, fled under cover of night, all alone, without the plume upon his head,[2] his feet failed (?).

His wives were taken before his face ; the victuals of his repast were captured ; he had no water in the skin to sustain him.

The countenance of his brethren was fierce to slay him ; one fought against the other among his captains ; their tents were burnt and reduced to ashes ; all his goods were food for the soldiers.

He reached his native country lamenting, and every one that was left over in his land was enraged (?) : ". . . he that is punished (?) by fate, he with the base plume ! " [3]—so say all they of his city concerning him, and : " He is in the power of all the gods of Memphis, the Lord of Egypt hath cursed his name.   Muroayu [4] is an abomination unto Memphis, son to son of his family for ever.   Binerē-Beloved-of-Amūn [5] pursueth his children, and Merenptah-Contented-with-Truth [5] is appointed as his fate."

He hath become a legend (?) for Libya, and one generation telleth another of his victories.   " Will he not be against us again . . . Rē," so saith every old man to his son.   " Alas, for Libya !   They cease to live in (?) the goodly fashion of walking about in the field.   In a single day is an end put to their wandering, and in a single year are the Tehenu consumed.   Sutekh [6] hath turned his back on their chieftain, and their settlements are destroyed with his authority.   There is no work of carrying . . . in these days.[7]   It is good to hide oneself ; in the cave there is safety.

" The great lord of Egypt, might and valour belong unto him. Who will yet fight, knowing how he strideth forward ?

" A witless fool is he that *awaiteth his onslaught, and he knoweth not what the morrow hath in store for him*, that transgresseth his boundary." [8]

Egypt, men say since (the time ?) of the gods, is the only

[1] Regular designation of hostile chieftains.
[2] The distinguishing mark of the Libyans.
[3] See previous note.   [4] The chieftain's name.
[5] The king's name.   [6] See p. 262, note 4.
[7] This will have been the peaceful occupation of the Libyans. They will have furnished the porters for the caravans.
[8] The utterance of the old Libyan extends probably up to this point.

daughter of Rē, and it is his son that sitteth upon the throne of Shu.[1] *None shall undertake to* trespass against her inhabitants ; the eye of every god pursueth him that will plunder her. It will indeed make an end of her enemies, say the . . . of their stars and all the wise men (?), when they look at the wind.[2] A great wonder is come to pass for Timūris. He that assailed her is *given* captive *into his hands* (?) by the counsel of the godlike king, who *was adjudged* triumphant over his enemies in the presence of Rē.[3] Muroayu, the evil-doer, the abomination (?) of every god that is in Memphis, he it is that hath been tried in Heliopolis, and whom the Nine Gods have found guilty of his offence.

The Lord of All [4] hath said : " Give the scimitar [5] to my son, the upright of heart, the kindly, the gentle, Merneptah-Beloved-of-Amūn, who hath cared for Memphis, and pleaded the cause for Heliopolis ; who hath opened the towns which were shut up, that he might set free the many that were confined in every region, that he might give offerings to the temples, and cause incense to enter before the god ; that he might suffer the great ones to keep their possession, and the humble to return to (?) their cities."

This is what the lords of Heliopolis say concerning their son Merneptah-Beloved-of-Amūn : " He shall have a lifetime like Rē, that he may plead the cause of him that is weak against (?) every foreign land. He hath made Egypt over . . . unto him whom he hath appointed to be his representative for ever, that he may strengthen its inhabitants. Behold, one dwelleth (in peace) in the time of the valiant one, and the breath of life cometh from the hand of the mighty one. Riches pour down for him that is righteous, but no sinner keepeth his plunder (?), *and what a man hath of ill-gotten wealth, that falleth to others and not to his children.*"

---

[1] The god of the air, the son of Rē.

[2] The whole passage is probably corrupt ; possibly astrologers and other magicians are meant. How much is to be included in their speech is far from clear.

[3] The entire passage plays with the theme of the law-suit between Horus and Sēth in Heliopolis, when Horus was justified and Sēth found guilty.

[4] Rē, who passes sentence.

[5] *Cf.* the reliefs, which depict a god handing this old sickle-shaped weapon to a king.

This is said : When Muroayu, the miserable fallen one, the fallen one of Libya, was come to invade the Walls [1] of Tenen (?), *who hath caused* his son, King Merneptah, *to mount* his throne, then said Ptah concerning the fallen one of Libya : " Let all his sins be diverted together upon his head. Let him be given into the hand of Merneptah, that he may make him vomit forth that which he hath swallowed like a crocodile. Behold, the fleeter catcheth the fleet, and the Sovereign will ensnare in the net him that is aware of his strength. It is Amūn who shattereth him with his hand, so that he may deliver him over to his ka [2] in Hermonthis, even to King Merneptah."

Great joy hath arisen in Egypt, and jubilation issueth from the towns of Timūris. They tell of the victories which King Merneptah hath won among the Tehenu. How they love him, the victorious Prince ! How they magnify him among the gods ! How fortunate he is, the lord of command ! Ah, it is good to sit down and chatter ! Men walk (again) unhindered upon the road, and there is no fear in men's hearts. The strongholds are left to themselves, the wells lie open,[3] accessible (?) to the messengers. The battlements of the wall *are quiet and only* the sun will awaken their watchmen. The Matoï [4] lie inert and sleep, and the Niau and Tekten [5] are in the fields, wherein they desire to be. The cattle of the field are suffered to go roaming without an herdsman, and to cross the waters of the stream.[6] There is no shouting and calling out in the night of " Halt, halt ! " (?) [7] in the speech of strangers. Men go and come singing, and there is no cry of people that mourn. The towns are yet once more inhabited, and he that hath grown his corn will also eat of it.

Rē hath turned him to Egypt. He is born destined to be her protector, he, King Merneptah.

[1] *I.e.* Memphis, the city of Ptah-Tenen.

[2] The king is conceived of as a part of the divine person. For Hermonthis, see p. 264, note 1.

[3] The fortified well-stations in the desert are meant.

[4] A Nubian tribe, male members of which served as soldiers and policemen.

[5] The N. and T. are light troops in the western desert. The writing of the name suggests runners and scouts. See above, p. 203, note 2.

[6] Which bounds their meadows. On the opposite bank, also, they are not stolen.

[7] The untranslatable words, which I have thus rendered, must have been the cry of the foreign plunderers.

The chieftains lie prostrate and say " Shalôm," [1]
Not one lifteth up his head among the Nine Bows.[2]
Tehenu hath been destroyed,
The land of Khatti is peaceful,
Canaan is captured with (?) every evil,
Askalon is carried away,
Gezer is seized upon.
Yenoam is made as nothing,
Israel is desolated [3] and hath no seed,[4]
Kharu [5] is become a widow for (?) Timūris.
All lands are united in peace,
And whosoever went a-roaming—
He is subdued by the King of Upper and Lower Egypt, Binerē-
    Beloved-of-Amūn,
Son of Rē, Merneptah-Contented-with-Truth,
Who is given life like Rē every day.

6. SHORTER POEMS

(a) [On the accession of Merneptah.] [6]

Rejoice, thou entire land, the goodly time hath come. A
lord is appointed in all countries, and witnesses (?) have come
to his place, he, the king, who reigneth for millions of years,
great of kingship like Horus, Binerē-Beloved-of-Amūn, who
oppresseth (?) Egypt with festivals, son of Rē – – – – Merneptah-Contented-with-Truth.

O all ye righteous, come and behold ! Truth hath repressed
falsehood, the sinners are fallen on their faces, all that are
covetous are turned back.[7]

---

[1] The Canaanite word for " hail ", " peace."
[2] Archaic designation of Egypt's hostile neighbours.
[3] By far the oldest mention of Israel, and the only mention in an
Egyptian text.   In contrast with the others, the name is written here as
that of a people and not of a country.   Israel was thus regarded by the
scribe as a Bedouin tribe.   Since it is inserted among Palestinian place-
names, the tribe must also have been resident in Palestine.
[4] A frequent metaphor for countries that have been laid waste.
[5] Palestine.   The metaphor of the widow is chosen for the sake of the
paronomasia.
[6] *Pap. Sallier*, i. 8. 9.
[7] This sounds as if there had been disputes as to who should succeed
to the throne.

The water standeth and faileth not, and the Nile carrieth a high (flood). The days are long, the nights have hours, and the months come aright.[1] The gods are content and happy of heart, and life is spent in laughter and wonder.

(b) [ON THE ACCESSION OF RAMESSES IV.] [2]

What a happy day! Heaven and earth rejoice, (for) thou art the great lord of Egypt.

They that had fled have come again to their towns, and they that were hidden have again come forth.

They that hungered are satisfied and happy, and they that thirsted are drunken.

They that were naked are clad in fine linen, and they that were dirty have white garments.

They that were in prison are set free, and he that was in bonds is full of joy.

They that were at strife in this land are reconciled. High Niles have come from their sources, that they may refresh the hearts of others.[3]

Widows,[4] their houses stand open, and they suffer travellers to enter.

Maidens rejoice and repeat their songs of gladness (?). They are arrayed in ornaments [5] and say (?): " – – – – he createth generation on generation. Thou ruler, thou wilt endure for ever."

The ships rejoice on the deep – – – –
They come to land with wind or oars,
They are satisfied . . . when it is said:
" King Hekmaatrē-Beloved-of-Amūn again weareth the crown.
The son of Rē, Ramesses, hath received the office of his
        father."
All lands say unto him:

[1] Even a good inundation and the ordered progress of time are ascribed to the new king, perhaps because the gods are so well disposed towards him.

[2] Ostracon in Turin ; see *Rec. de Trav.*, ii. p. 116.

[3] Strangers, or only : the people ?

[4] Possibly also : unmarried women. The meaning, in any case, is that they surrender themselves.

[5] Literally : inlaid (with gold).

" Beautiful is Horus [1] on the throne of Amūn who sendeth
   him forth,
(Amūn) the protector of the Prince, who bringeth every land."

(c) [GOOD WISHES FOR THE KING.] [2]

Life, prosperity, health ! This is written that One [3] may
know it in the Palace, which is beloved of Truth, the Horizon
wherein Rē dwelleth.

Turn thy face unto me, thou rising sun, that illumineth
the Two Lands with its beauty ! Thou sun of mankind, that
banisheth the darkness from Egypt.

Thou art in nature like unto thy father Rē, who ariseth in
the firmament. Thy beams enter (even) into a cavern, and
there is no place that is devoid of thy beauty.

Thou art told how it fareth in every land, whilst thou resteth
in the Palace. Thou hearest the words of all lands, thou hast
myriads of ears.

More bright is thine eye than the stars of heaven, and
thou canst see better than the sun. If one speaketh, and the
mouth is in a cavern, yet cometh it into thine ear. If ought
is done that is hidden, yet will thine eye behold it.

O Binerē-Beloved-of-Amūn, lord of grace, who createth
breath ! [4]

(d) [TO THE KING'S WAR-CHARIOT.] [5]

This poem is a curiosity. Everything appertaining to the
chariot is enumerated, and, as each item is mentioned, a pun is
made upon it in praise of the king's prowess. On this account
the poem is practically untranslatable, and all the more so since
it teems with unknown words. Beginning and end must have been
written on other ostraca.

— — — — knoweth every land ; its ram's head [6] is a wonder
for chief captains.

[1] *I.e.* the king.
[2] *Pap. Anastasi,* ii. 5. 6 ff. ; *ibid.* iv. 5. 6 ff. It stands there as a
model for a letter to the king.
[3] The king.
[4] By speaking thus of the king he hints at the benefits which he himself hopes to receive from him.
[5] Ostracon in Edinburgh, *Zeitschr. für ägypt. Sprache,* xviii. p. 94.
[6] The ram is Amūn's sacred animal, and its head is here, as often,
employed as an ornament.

The . . . of thy chariot—the chieftains are friendly towards thee.

The . . . of thy chariot—every land is . . .

The . . . of thy chariot—it taketh the souls . . . of the warriors.

The . . . of thy chariot—they are Bata lord of Saka, when he was in the arms (?) of Bast, cast away in some strange land.[1]

The . . . weapons of thy chariot—they . . . at the end (?) of the lands.

The spear of thy chariot—terror of thee hath entered in among them.

The sword of thy chariot—it maketh afraid them that are in thine land. It filleth its mouth with the land of Palestine, and it carrieth away the land of Ethiopia.

The knife of thy chariot—thy scimitar heweth in pieces the rebellious hills ; they fall down as boulders.

The . . . of thy chariot—thou breakest (?) their narrow passes.

The . . . of thy chariot—they bend their backs to thee because of (thy) victories.

The . . . of thy chariot—thou art wise like Thōth.

The club of thy chariot—it plundereth the distant lands. It is dashed against one, and a thousand fall ; it leaveth no heir remaining.

The grips (?) of thy chariot—they are Anat and Astarte.[2]

The chain (?) of thy chariot—it enchaineth them that are evil.

The bow – – – –

F. RELIGIOUS POEMS

The old hymns to the gods still continued to be used by the priests all through the New Kingdom, and survived in the ritual as long as there was an Egyptian religion. But side by side with them a new tendency is apparent, that is as alive and multiform as the old was rigid and uniform. In it are to be

[1] See above, p. 150 ; the allusion here presumes an older form of the legend ; the cheerful goddess Bast may correspond to the temptress of the legend, or to the baleful woman, and the foreign land to the Valley of the Cedar.

[2] The two foreign goddesses of war.

seen the effects of the religious revival, for which the New Kingdom affords other evidence,[1]—relationship with God becomes
a personal one,—but there is also to be seen in it the new senti-
ment, which affects us so pleasantly in the other branches
of the lyric poetry : joy in nature and a warmth of human
feeling.

I. THE GREAT HYMN TO AMŪN [2]

My readers will expect to find a hymn to Amunrē, the state
god of the New Kingdom, among the poems of this period, and on
that account I have placed it here. Moreover, individual passages
in the hymn, with their joy in nature and their warmth of feeling,
vividly remind one of hymns which certainly originated at this
time, above all the *Hymn to the Sun* from El-Amarnah. No argument against this view is afforded by the fact that our hymn is
composed in the old language ; for this was still the literary language
in the Eighteenth Dynasty, the period when the papyrus in question
was written.

But the matter is not as simple as all that ; on the contrary,
the hymn is, to a large degree, built up out of older material. For
this speaks the long enumeration of the titles and attributes of the
god, which are only too reminiscent of the old dreary manner of
rendering praise to divinities ; and all kinds of other features also
are to be found, which appear in almost identically the same words
in the older religious poems. Compare, for example, the hymns
to the sun on pp. 138 ff., and the hymn to Min-Horus on pp. 137 f.;
it looks as though hymns to these two gods, who together form
Amunrē, had been amalgamated, and then made to suit the taste
of the period by more recent additions. The way in which the hymn
has been put together has made a complete jumble of it.

It would lead us too far afield, if, in dealing with the hymn, I
were to expatiate upon the details of the cult, to which so many
references are made. Moreover, for us, who are not Egyptian priests,
it is a matter of complete indifference what crowns and titles have
been assigned to the god. I must, however, briefly touch upon
the nature of this composite divinity.

Amūn, the god of Thebes, was originally only a variant form
of the ithyphallic god Min, who was venerated not far off at Koptos.
Like so many other gods, he was later identified with the sun-
god, and henceforth known as Amunrē. During the Eighteenth

---

[1] See BLACKMAN, *The Psalms in the Light of Egyptian Research*, in
SIMPSON, *The Psalmists*, Oxford, 1926.

[2] A papyrus in Cairo, written about the time of Amenōphis II. Often
treated of, and lastly by ROEDER, *Urkunden zur Religion des alten
Ägyptens*, pp. 4 ff. SCHARFF, *Äg. Sonnenlieder*, pp. 61 ff.

Dynasty, when his city became the capital, the veneration in which he was held was immense, and he became the most important of all the gods.

Viewed from another aspect, this union with Rē did Amūn an injury, for as a result not much survives of his original nature—as Min he is still lord of the Eastern countries—and on the whole Amunrē is actually nothing more than the old powerful sun-god, Rē, Harakhti, Atum, Khepre, and whatever else he was called. Like him, he sails over the celestial ocean, and like him wars with the cloud-dragon, Apōphis; and all that Rē possesses in the way of sanctuaries, ships, names, and crowns, becomes his property. Like Rē he has created gods and men, and sustains all that lives. On this last feature, and on the god's loving-kindness and goodness, the hymn lays particular emphasis, as do also the other poems of the New Kingdom (see pp. 307 ff.).

[TITLE.]

Adoration of Amunrē, Bull of Heliopolis, chiefest of all gods, the good god, the beloved, who giveth life to all that is warm,[1] and to every good herd.

[FIRST CANTO.]

Praise to thee, Amunrē, lord of Karnak, who presideth in Thebes ! Bull of his Mother, the first on his field ! [2]

Wide of stride, first in Upper Egypt, lord of the land of the Matoï, prince of Punt.[3]

Greatest of heaven, eldest of earth, lord of what existeth, who abideth in (?) all things.

Unique in his nature . . . among the gods, goodly bull of the Nine Gods,[4] chiefest of all gods.

Lord of Truth, father of the gods, who made mankind, and created beasts.

Lord of what existeth, who createth the fruit-tree, who made the green herb, and sustaineth the cattle.

Beauteous form which Ptah fashioned,[5] the beauteous, beloved boy, he whom the gods praise.

---

[1] *I.e.* probably all that lives. To the god's beneficence described later on, reference is already made here in the title.

[2] The sun is the spouse of the sky-goddess and at the same time her son, in the capacity of sun of the next day. As a bull rules over the field wherein he pastures, so he rules over the sky as its greatest celestial body.

[3] The Matoï are a people in Nubia. Punt is the incense-country.

[4] The leader, the hero of the great gods.

[5] Ptah the craftsman-god, has given Amūn his form.

He who made them that are below and them that are above,[1] he who illumineth the Two Lands. He who traverseth the firmament in peace, King of Upper and Lower Egypt, Rē, the justified.[2]

The chiefest of the Two Lands, great of strength, lord of might, the chiefest, who made the entire earth.

More eminent of nature than any god, over whose beauty the gods rejoice. He to whom praise is given in the Great House, who is crowned in the House of Fire.[3]

He whose sweet savour the gods love, when he cometh from Punt. Richly perfumed, when he cometh down from the land of the Matoï.[4] Fair of face, when he cometh from God's-land.[5]

The gods fawn at his feet, when they know his majesty to be their lord, the fearful, the terrible, great of will and mighty in appearance, who aboundeth in victuals and createth sustenance.

Jubilation to thee who didst create the gods, raise up the sky, and spread out the ground.

[SECOND CANTO.]

He who is in health hath awakened![6] Min, Amūn, the lord of Eternity, who created Everlastingness! Possessor of praise, who presideth in . . . !

Firm of horns,[7] fair of face. Lord of the crown and lofty of plumes, with beauteous diadem and tall white crown. The Mehent-serpent and the two Buto-serpents are above (?) his face, – – – – the double crown, the head-cloth, and the blue crown. Fair of face, when he taketh the atef-crown, beloved of the Upper Egyptian crown and the Lower Egyptian. Lord of the double crown, when he taketh the ames-sceptre, lord of the deeds-case, who holdeth the flail.

The prince, beauteously crowned with the white crown. Lord of rays, who createth light. To whom the gods offer praise.

---

[1] Men and stars.

[2] If the scribe gave it any thought at all, this attribute would designate Rē as a former, and dead, king.

[3] Two sanctuaries in the ancient capitals of Upper and Lower Egypt.

[4] See above, pp. 138, note 3.   [5] The East.

[6] Elsewhere descriptive of the resuscitated Osiris.

[7] What follows describes the god's crown, adorned with horns, feathers, fillets, and serpents; see also BLACKMAN, *Journ. of Egypt. Archæology*, x. p. 194.

He who giveth his hands to him whom he loveth, while he *assigneth* his foe to the fire. It is his eye [1] that overthroweth the enemy ; it thrusteth its spear into him that drinketh up the ocean, and causeth the dragon to vomit forth what he hath swallowed. [2]

Praise to thee, O Rē, lord of Truth. Thou whose chapel is hidden, lord of gods. Khepre in his bark, who gave command and the gods came into being.

Atum, who created mankind, who distinguished their nature and made their life ; who made the colours different, one from the other. [3]

He who heareth the prayer of the prisoner ; kindly of heart when one calleth to him.

He who rescueth the fearful from the oppressor, who judgeth between the miserable and the strong.

Lord of Perception, in whose mouth is Authority. For love of him cometh the Nile, the sweet, the greatly beloved, and when he hath come men live.

He causeth all eyes to open – – – –, his beneficence createth the light. The gods rejoice in his beauty, and their hearts live when they behold him.

[THIRD CANTO.]

O Rē, venerated in Karnak, who appeareth great in the house of the Benben, he of Heliopolis. Lord of the ninth day of the month, in whose honour men keep the sixth and seventh day.

King, lord of all gods ; hawk in the midst of the horizon. Master of mankind . . . His name is hidden from his children —in his name Amūn. [4]

Praise to thee, fortunate . . ., lord of joy, mighty in (his) appearing. Lord of the crown, lofty of feathers ; with beauteous diadem and tall white crown.

The gods love to gaze at thee, when the double crown resteth on thy brow.

[1] The eye of the sun, here conceived of as a warring goddess.

[2] The Apōphis-dragon, which drinks up the celestial ocean, so that the sun's ship may not be able to voyage upon it.

[3] It is the conception, which occurs again more clearly in the El-Amarnah hymn (p. 290), that even the barbarians are God's children, whom He sustains.

[4] Paronomasia. Amūn can **also mean** " the hidden one."

Love of thee is diffused throughout the Two Lands, and thy rays shine in the eyes. (It is) the well-being (?) of mankind when thou arisest ; the beasts wax languid when thou shinest.[1]

Thou art beloved in the southern sky, and art pleasant in the northern sky.[2] Thy beauty captivateth the hearts, and the love of thee maketh languid the arms. Thy fair form maketh feeble the hands ; the heart forgetteth when one looketh upon thee.

Thou art the Sole One, who made all that is, The One and Only, who made what existeth. Men issued from his two eyes, and from his mouth the gods came into being.[3]

He who made herbage for the cattle and the fruit-tree for men. He who made that whereon live the fish in the river, and the birds which (inhabit ?) the firmament. He who giveth breath to him that is in the egg, and sustaineth the son of the worm.

He who made that whereon the gnats live, the worms, and the flies likewise. He who made that which the mice in their holes need, and sustaineth the birds (?) on every tree.

Praise to thee, who didst make all this. Sole One and Only with the many hands.[4] Who passeth the night wakeful, when all men sleep, seeking the best for his cattle.[5]

Amūn, who abideth in (?) all things ! Atum, Harakhti ! Homage to thee in all that they say ! Jubilation to thee, because thou weariest thyself with us ! Reverence to thee, because thou didst create us !

Praise to thee, saith (?) every beast, jubilation to thee, saith (?) every wilderness, as high as is the heaven, as broad as is the earth, and as deep as is the sea.[6]

The gods make obeisance unto thy majesty, and extol the might of their creator. They rejoice when he that begat them draweth nigh, and they say unto thee : " Welcome, in peace !

" Father of the fathers of all gods, who didst raise up the

---

[1] Here, and in the following verse, growing languid seems to be regarded as a pleasant thing.

[2] *I.e.* to the gods dwelling there ?

[3] According to the legend, men originated from the tears of the sungod, and the first divinites, Shu and Tefnet, from his spitting.

[4] Which the god must possess to have created so much for all.

[5] He is a good herdsman, who even by night searches where he may find fodder for his herds.

[6] All created things cry aloud to thee for joy.

sky, and lay low the ground, who madest that which is, and createdst what existeth!

"O king, chiefest of the gods! We revere thy might, because thou createdst us. *We shout for joy to thee*, because thou fashionedst us. We offer thee praise, because thou weariedst thyself with us."

Praise to thee, who madest all that is, lord of Truth,[1] father of the gods, who madest men, and createdst beasts, lord of grain, who makest the sustenance of the wild beasts of the wilderness.

Amūn, bull of goodly countenance, darling in Karnak, great of appearing in the House of the Benben, crowned again in Heliopolis! Who didst judge between the Twain [2] in the Great Hall, chief of the Great Ennead.

Sole One and Only, without peer, who presideth in Thebes, the Heliopolitan, the first of his Ennead, who liveth daily on Truth.[3]

Dweller in the horizon, Horus of the East! [4] The wilderness createth for him silver and gold and real lapis lazuli for love of him, myrrh and incense mixed from the land of the Matoï, and fresh myrrh for thy nose. Fair of face, when he cometh from the land of the Matoï!

Amunrē, lord of Karnak, who presideth in Thebes, Heliopolitan, presiding in his harîm (?) !

[FOURTH CANTO.]

Thou sole king . . . among the gods ; with multitudinous names, whereof the number is not known. Who ariseth in the eastern horizon, and setteth in the western horizon. Who is born early (?) every day, who daily overthroweth his enemies.

Thōth uplifteth his eyes,[5] and delighteth him with his excellence. The gods rejoice over his beauty, and the hetet-apes extol him.[6]

Lord of the ship of evening and of the ship of morning ; [7] they traverse Nun for thee in peace.

[1] Elsewhere this is the designation of Ptah, the craftsman-god, who fashioned everything.

[2] Horus and Sēth.   [3] It is his life-principle.

[4] What follows here applies to him, the patron of the eastern desert and of the countries to which its roads lead.

[5] Meaning ?   [6] The apes which greet the sun at his rising.

[7] The sun-god's two ships. Nun is the celestial ocean.

Thy crew rejoiceth, when they see how the foe [1] is overthrown, and how his limbs are consumed by the knife. The fire hath devoured him, and his soul is punished yet more than his body. That dragon, an end is made of his going. The gods shout for joy and the crew of Rē is content.

Heliopolis exulteth, the foe of Atum is overthrown, Thebes is content, Heliopolis exulteth. The Mistress of Life [2] is glad, the foe of her lord is overthrown. The gods of Babylon [3] are in jubilation and they of Letopolis [3] kiss the earth, when they see him.

Strong in his might, the most mighty (?) of the gods. Just one (?), lord of Thebes, in this thy name of He who created Right.[4]

Lord of victuals, bull of provisions (?), in this thy name of Bull of his Mother.

He who made all men that are, and created all that is, in this thy name of Atum-Khepre.[5]

Great hawk, who maketh festive the body! [6] Fair of face, who maketh festive the breast. With pleasing form and tall plumes, – – – – the two serpents on his brow.

He to whom men's hearts come nestling, who suffereth mankind to come out to him, who gladdeneth the Two Lands with his going forth.[7]

Praise to thee, Amunrē, lord of Karnak, whose arising his city loveth.

2. THE HYMN TO THE SUN FROM EL-AMARNAH [8]

As is well known, Amenōphis IV, the last king of the Eighteenth Dynasty (*circa* 1380 B.C.), attempted to establish a reformed religion, which permitted only the sun to be worshipped. The fullest statement of this faith that we possess is the following beautiful hymn, which is preserved in its entirety in a tomb at El-Amarnah, the heretic king's capital. It appears there as a

---

[1] The serpent Apōphis.
[2] The serpent of the sun. [3] Two cities close to modern Cairo.
[4] It can mean " Truth " as well as " Right."
[5] The two names are puns on " all that are " and " created."
[6] His rays warm the body.
[7] This verse shows that the hymn was intended for one of the festivals in which Amūn was taken in procession out of his temple. The people pour out of their houses to venerate him.
[8] See DAVIES, *The Rock Tombs of El-Amarnah*, vi. pp. 29 ff.

prayer of the deceased, later known as King Ai. Shorter versions
of this hymn are to be found in other tombs at El-Amarnah.

Beautiful is thine appearing in the horizon of heaven, thou
living sun, the first who lived ! [1]

Thou risest in the eastern horizon, and fillest every land
with thy beauty.

Thou art beautiful and great, and glistenest, and art high
above every land. Thy rays, they encompass the lands, so
far as all that thou hast created. Thou art Rē, and thou
reachest unto their end [2] and subduest them for thy dear son.[3]
Thou art afar, yet are thy rays upon earth. Thou art before
their face – – – – thy going.

When thou goest down in the western horizon, the earth is
in darkness, as if it were dead. They sleep in the chamber,
their heads [4] wrapped up, and no eye seeth the other. Though
all their things were taken, while they were under their heads,[5]
yet would they know it not. Every lion cometh forth from
his den, and all worms that bite. Darkness is . . ., the earth
is silent, for he who created it resteth in his horizon.

When it is dawn and thou risest in the horizon and shinest
as the sun in the day, thou dispellest the darkness and sheddest
thy beams. The Two Lands keep festival, awake, and stand
on their feet, for thou hast raised them up. They wash their
bodies, they take their garments, and their hands praise thine
arising.[6] The whole land, it doeth its work.

All beasts are content with their pasture, the trees and
herbs are verdant. The birds fly out of their nests and their
wings praise thy ka.[7] All wild beasts dance on their feet, all
that fly and flutter—they live when thou arisest for them.

The ships voyage down and up stream likewise, and every
way is open, because thou arisest. The fishes in the river leap
up before thy face.[8] Thy rays are in the sea.

Thou who createst (male children ?) in women, and makest
seed in men ! Thou who maintainest the son in the womb of

[1] Other version : " that ordaineth life."

[2] Pun on the name Rē.　　　　[3] The king.

[4] The Egyptian protects his head, before all else, from cold.

[5] The things they thus wish to protect from thieves.

[6] The morning prayer to the sun is an old custom in Egypt.

[7] Thy person, thee. As men raise the arms in praise, so the birds
raise their wings.

[8] In this way they too greet the sun.

his mother, and soothest him so that he weepeth not,[1] thou nurse in the womb. Who giveth breath in order to keep alive all that he hath made.[2] When he cometh forth from the womb unto the earth (?) on the day wherein he is born, thou openest his mouth *when it would speak* (?) and suppliest what it needeth.

The chick in the egg (already) chirpeth in the shell, for thou givest it breath therein to sustain its life. Thou makest for it its strength (?) in the egg in order to break it. It cometh forth from the egg to chirp – – – –; it walketh upon its feet when it cometh forth therefrom.

How much is there that thou hast made, and that is hidden from (me),[3] thou sole god, to whom none is to be likened!

Thou hast fashioned the earth according to thy desire, thou alone, with men, cattle, and all wild beasts, all that is upon the earth and goeth upon feet, and all that soareth above and flieth with its wings.

The lands of Syria and Nubia, and the land of Egypt [4]— thou puttest every man in his place and thou suppliest their needs. Each one hath his provision, and his lifetime is reckoned. Their tongues are diverse in speech, and their form likewise. Their skins are distinguished, (for?) thou distinguishest the peoples.

Thou makest the Nile in the nether world [5] and bringest it whither thou wilt, in order to sustain mankind, even as thou hast made them. Thou art lord of them all, who wearieth himself on their behalf, the lord of every land, who ariseth for them, the sun of the day greatly reverenced.[6]

All far-off peoples, thou makest that whereon they live. Thou hast (also) put the Nile in the sky, that it may come down for them, and may make waves upon the hills like a sea, in order to moisten their fields in their townships. How

---

[1] The babe, which after birth cries when the nurse is not dandling it, would do the same before birth if God did not soothe it.

[2] He lets the embryo breathe.

[3] It is more than can be conceived of, and so I cannot enumerate it.

[4] To put foreign countries on an almost equal footing with Egypt, as is done here and subsequently, is contrary to every tradition. And yet a similar conception already appears in the orthodox *Hymn to Amūn* (p. 282), which is at least a generation older.

[5] That the Nile, or at any rate the inundation, comes from the nether world is an old Egyptian belief.

[6] The passage alludes to the weary evening sun, the morning sun, and the midday sun.

excellently made are all thy designs, O Lord of Eternity ! The Nile in heaven, thou appointest it for the foreign peoples and all the beasts of the wilderness which walk upon feet, and the (real) Nile, it cometh forth from the nether world for Timūris.

Thy rays suckle every field, and, when thou risest, they live and thrive for thee. Thou makest the seasons in order to sustain all that thou hast created, the winter to cool them, and the heat, *that they may taste of thee (?)*.

Thou hast made the sky afar off in order to rise therein, in order to behold all that thou hast made.[1]

Thou art alone, (but) thou arisest in thy forms as living sun, appearing, shining, withdrawing, returning (?) [2] Thou makest millions of forms of thyself alone.

Cities, townships, fields, road and river—all eyes behold thee over against them,[3] as the sun of the day above the earth.

– – – –

Thou art in mine heart, and there is none other that knoweth thee save thy son, Neferkheprurē-Sole-One-of-Rē,[4] whom thou makest to comprehend thy designs and thy might.[5]

The earth came into being at the beckoning of thine hand, for thou hast created them.[6] When thou risest they live, when thou settest they die. Thou thyself art lifetime, and men live in thee. The eyes look on thy beauty until thou settest. All work is laid aside when thou settest on the right.[7] When thou risest, (thou) causest (the) . . . to thrive for the king, – – – – since thou didst found the earth. Thou raisest them up for thy son, the king of Upper and Lower Egypt, who liveth on Truth, lord of the Two Lands, Neferkheprurē-Sole-One-of-Rē, son of Rē, who liveth on Truth, lord of diadems, Ikhenaton, great in his duration, and for the great royal consort whom he loveth, mistress of the Two Lands, Nefernefrurē-Nefretiti, that liveth and is young for ever and ever.

[1] So distant, that thou canst view thine entire creation from it.

[2] Meaning, probably : according to the time of day thou appearest different to us, yet art thou ever the same sun.

[3] Wherever a man may be on the earth, thou appearest to him in the same place.

[4] Name of Amenōphis IV, appearing in Babylonian as Napkhururiya.

[5] The king is thus the founder of the new faith, but not the author of the hymn.

[6] Its inhabitants.

[7] According to the Egyptian view, the west was on the right-hand side.

3. PRAYER FOR THE KING IN EL-AMARNAH [1]

Beautiful is thine arising, O Harakhti-that-rejoiceth-in-the-Horizon-in-his-name-Shu-which-is-the-sun,[2] thou living sun, save whom there is none else ; who strengtheneth the eyes with his rays, who hath created all that existeth.

Thou risest in the horizon of heaven to give life to all that thou hast made, to all men, (all beasts), all that flieth and fluttereth, and to all reptiles that are in the earth. They live when they behold thee ; they sleep when thou settest.

Thou makest thy son Neferkheprurē-Sole-One-of-Rē to live with thee for ever, and (to do what) thine heart (desireth), and behold what thou doest every day. He rejoiceth when he beholdeth thy beauty.

Give him life, joy, and gladness, so that all that thou encirclest may lie under (his feet), while he offereth it to thy ka, he thy son, whom thou thyself hast begotten. – – – – the south as the north, the west and the east, and the isles in the midst of the sea, shout for joy to thy ka. The southern boundary reacheth as far as the wind bloweth, and the northern as far as the sun shineth. All their princes are overthrown and made weak by reason of his might,—the beauteous vital force [3] that maketh festive the Two Lands, and createth what the whole earth needeth. Let him be for ever with thee, in that he loveth to look on thee.

Give him very many jubilees with years of peace.

Give him of that which thine heart desireth, to the extent that there is sand on the shore, that fishes in the stream have scales, and cattle have hair.

Let him sojourn here,[4] until the swan turneth black, until the raven turneth white,[5] until the hills arise to depart, until water floweth up stream, while I continue in attendance on the good god,[6] until he assigneth me the burial that he granteth.

[1] Davies, *El-Amarna*, iii. Pl. xxix. ; translated pp. 31 f.

[2] The official name of the new divinity, in dogmatically exact form.

[3] Therein lies an antithesis to what immediately precedes ; for foreigners it is a constraint, for Egyptians a blessing.

[4] In the newly founded residence.

[5] Swan and raven are only guesses. All that can be seen is that we have to do with two birds.

[6] The king, till my death.

4. POEMS ON THEBES AND ITS GOD [1]

This work, of which the beginning and end are lost, might have once borne the title of *The Thousand Songs*, for, contrary to all precedent, its individual sections bear each a number. Of these numbers, only two are wanting to complete the thousand, and they will have stood in the break at the end of the last page. As a matter of fact, there were not really a thousand songs, for the author only attained this high figure by a strange artifice ; he merely counted the units, tens, and hundreds, so that the thousand is actually only twenty-eight.

That he attached some importance to his numbers can be seen from the fact that he begins and ends every poem with a pun, which is meant to guide the hearer to the number in question. The effort to find puns on the numbers has apparently also influenced the sequence and choice of the subjects treated of. These poems are shown by their contents to be the production of a learned poet, who was not altogether a bad one either. They were written at the beginning of the Nineteenth Dynasty, as the episode of Amenōphis IV was still not forgotten (see p. 288).

CHAPTER SIX.[2]

Every region is in terror of thee – – – – thy name is high and mighty and powerful. The Euphrates and the sea are in fear of thee. *Thy might is heavy upon the earth (?)*, in the islands in the midst of the sea. – – – – The dwellers in Punt come to thee, and God's-Land [3] is verdant for thee from love of thee. *They bring thee perfumes*, to make festive thy temple with festal fragrance. Incense-bearing trees drop myrrh for thee, and the perfume of thine aroma penetrateth into thy nose. – – – –. *All costly oils come to thee.* Cedar trees are grown for thee – – – –, in order to frame thine august barque Userhēt.[4]

The mountains yield thee blocks of stone in order to make great the gateways (of thy temple). Ships are upon the sea and moor (?) beside the strand, load and voyage before thee ; – – – – the river floweth down stream, and the north wind, it bloweth up stream, bringing offerings to thee of all that is – – – –.

---

[1] Papyrus in Leyden, of time of Ramesses II.   Published by GARDINER, *Zeitschr. für ägypt. Sprache*, xlii. pp. 12 ff.

[2] The might of Amūn is felt in all lands.

[3] The East, where spices grow.   [4] See above, p. 174.

CHAPTER SEVEN *begins with :*

The wicked are cast off from Thebes,[1] *and then extols it as the* Mistress of Cities, that is stronger than any city. She gave the land to a single lord by her victories, she that took the bow and grasped the arrow. None can fight near her because her strength is so great. Every city *extolleth* (*herself ?*) in her name,[2] she is their princess, that is mightier than they – – – –.

CHAPTER EIGHT *is destroyed.*

CHAPTER NINE.[3]

The Ennead which came forth from Nun, it assembleth itself, because it beholdeth thee, the great in glory, the lord of lords, who fashioned himself, the lord of the . . ., he is the Lord.[4]

Them that had slept (?), he shineth for them, in order to illumine their faces in another form.[5] His eyes [6] gleam and his [6] ears are opened. All limbs are clad [7] when his brightness hath come (?).

Heaven is of gold, Nun of lapis lazuli, and the earth is o'erspread with malachite, when he ariseth therein.[8]

The gods behold and their temples stand open. Men can see and behold by him (?).

All trees stir at his presence. They turn them towards his eye, and their leaves unfold.

The scaly ones leap in the water – – – –. All cattle frolic before his countenance. All birds dance with their wings ; they know him in his good season. They live [9] because they see him every day. They are in his hand, sealed with his seal, and no god openeth them save his majesty.[10] There is nought that was made without him, the great god, the life of the Ennead.

[1] This might well allude, as do other passages below, to the victory over the heresy.

[2] See p. 295, note 3.

[3] A morning hymn to Amūn as sun-god.

[4] A six-fold paronomasia with *neb*, " lord," and other words.

[5] As the sun of the new day.

[6] Probably not those of the god but those of men.   [7] *Cf.* above, p. 289.

[8] The sky. The earth looks green, the sky gold and blue.

[9] Probably not the birds, but all the previously named creatures.

[10] The sun-god alone provides for them.

CHAPTER TEN.[1]

More orderly (?) is Thebes than any city : The water and the land were in her in the beginning of time, and the sand came to the tillage (?) to create her ground upon the highland, and the land came into being.[2] – – – –

All cities are founded in her real name, and they are named with the name of " City," [3] and they are under the supervision of Thebes, the Eye of Rē !

This is followed by a series of puns on the names of Thebes and its divisions.

CHAPTER TWENTY.[4]

How thou voyagest, Harakhti, and doest daily after thy manner of yesterday ! Thou who makest the years, and marshallest the months ; days and nights are according to his march. Thou art newer to-day than yesterday – – – –.

Alone watchful, whose abomination is slumber. All men sleep, but his eyes are wakeful. – – – – Who voyageth over the firmament, and passeth through the nether world. The sun on all roads, making his circuit before (men's) faces. All men turn their faces towards him, and men and gods say, " Welcome art thou."

CHAPTER THIRTY.

It describes how the enemy of the boat of the sun, the Apophis-dragon, is slain by the god : The spear sticketh in the foe, who hath fallen by its sharp edge. – – – – The ship of millions hath a fair course, the crew shouteth for joy, and their hearts are glad, for the foe of the Lord of All is overthrown. His enemies that were in heaven or on earth are no more. Heaven, Thebes, Heliopolis, and the nether world,[5]—their inhabitants rejoice over their lord, when they see him powerful in his

[1] Thebes is the most ancient city in the world.

[2] Reference to the legend that the hillock, which rose up out of the primæval ocean, was situated in Thebes.

[3] Since in the New Kingdom, Thebes was merely known as " the City,'' other places are supposed to have acquired the designation of " city" from it.

[4] To the sun in the daytime.

[5] Thebes and Heliopolis, as the most sacred places, here represent the earth.

shining forth, furnished with valour and victory, and mighty in his form.

Thou triumphest, O Amunrē! The caitiffs are overthrown, repelled by the spear.

CHAPTER FORTY.

The god hath formed himself and his form is not known. – – – – *He* hath joined his seed with his body, so that his egg existed in his secret self.[1] – – – –

CHAPTER FIFTY.[2]

– – – –. The sun of heaven, whose rays belong (?) to thy countenance. The Nile floweth from his cavern for thy primordial godhead (?), and earth is established for thine image. To thee alone belongeth what Kēb causeth to grow.[3]

Thy name is strong, thy will is heavy. Mountains of ore cannot withstand thy might. Hawk divine, with outspread wings. Speedy one, who carrieth away his assailant in the completion of an instant.

Mysterious lion, loud roaring, he grippeth (?) firm them that come under his claws. A bull for his city, a lion for his people, he who *lasheth with his tail* him that encroacheth upon him. The earth is moved when he sendeth forth his voice, and all beings are afraid of his might. Great of strength, there is none other that is like unto him, – – – –.

CHAPTER SIXTY.[4]

His is Upper Egypt and likewise Lower Egypt ; he hath taken them alone in his might. His boundary is strong . . . upon the earth, as wide as is the whole earth and as high as is the heaven. The gods beg their sustenance from him, and he it is who giveth them bread from his possessions, he, the lord of fields, banks, and plots of ground.[5] His is every land-register – – – –.

His is the royal cubit,[6] which measureth the blocks of stone.

[1] Refers to the legend of how the sun-god begat himself.

[2] The might of Amūn.

[3] All the products of the earth are destined to be offered to him.

[4] Amūn is the wealthiest of all gods.

[5] Amūn possessed under Ramesses III five times as much land as the gods of Heliopolis, and eighty-five times as much as those of Memphis. The preceding verses are thus not merely phrases.

[6] The measure for building purposes.

He who extendeth the cord [1] – – – – ; upon the . . . whereof the Two Lands are founded, the temples and sanctuaries.

Every city is under his shadow, that (?) his heart may walk about where it will. Men sing to him in every chapel, and every place possesseth ever his love.

Beer is brewed for him on the day of the festival, *and the night is spent in wakefulness,* and his name circulateth upon the roofs. His is the singing in the night, when it is dark.[2]

The gods receive bread through him, the rich god, who protecteth what is his (?).

CHAPTER SEVENTY.[3]

He who purgeth away evil and dispelleth sickness, the physician who healeth the eye without remedy, who openeth the eyes and banisheth the squint – – – –. Who rescueth whom he will, though he be in the nether world ; who saveth from Fate to the full of his desire.

He possesseth eyes and ears likewise, wherever he goeth, for him whom he loveth, that he may hear the petitions of him that calleth to him. Coming from afar in the completion of an instant to him that calleth upon him. He prolongeth life and he shorteneth it also. He giveth to him whom he loveth more than is decreed to him.[4]

A water-charm is the name of Amūn upon the flood. No crocodile hath power when his name is pronounced. A wind that turneth back the adverse blast. . . .

With merry countenance, when he . . ., because he is called to mind. With beneficent mouth in the time of turmoil (?). A sweet breeze to him that calleth upon him. Preserving the weary.

The bright (?) god, excellent of counsels. He belongeth to him that leaneth his back upon him, – – – –. He is better than millions to him that trusteth in him. One man is stronger by reason of his name than hundreds of thousands. Good protector in very truth. Perfect, seizing his opportunity, and none repelleth him.

---

[1] At the laying of the foundation-stone ; see p. 52, note 1.

[2] Refers obviously to a night festival, when the people sing in praise of Amūn on the roofs of the houses.

[3] Amūn as physician and helper.

[4] Fate has fixed for every one the duration of his life.

CHAPTER EIGHTY.[1]

The Eight Gods were thy first form, until thou didst complete this,[2] thou alone.

Mysterious was thy body among the great ones, and thou didst conceal thyself as Amūn at the head of the gods. Thou madest thy mode of being as Tenen,[3] in order to fashion (?) the Primordial Gods in thy first origin.

Thy beauty was extolled as Bull of his Mother,[4] and thou withdrewest thyself as the dweller in heaven, abiding as Rē – – – –.

Thou wast the first to be, when as yet there was nought. The land was not void of thee in the first beginning. All gods that came into existence after thee – – – –.

CHAPTER NINETY.[5]

The Ennead was joined in thy limbs, . . . every god was united with thy body. Thou didst emerge first that thou mightest begin the commencement, O Amūn, whose name is hidden from the gods,[6] great aged one, older than these,[7] Tenen, who did shape himself as Ptah. *He then created Shu and Tefnet by spitting, these being the first of the series of actual divinities, and he himself stood forth as ruler of the world,* while he appeared upon his throne, according to the dictates of his heart. He ruled over all that was in his . . ., he set in order the kingdom of eternity unto eternity, abiding as sole lord.

His form shone at the First Occasion, and all that existed was dumbfounded at his glory. He cackled as the Great Cackler – – – – and brake into speech in the midst of the silence.[8] He opened all eyes and caused them to behold. He began to cry aloud, when the land was still dumbfounded. His roaring spread about, and there was none beside him.

[1] Amūn is the first god who came into being. Out of him the other gods came into existence.

[2] The creation of the world out of the chaos of the primordial waters.

[3] Ptah of Memphis, conceived of as a primordial god.

[4] The sun-god.

[5] This, too, is an account of the creation.

[6] Paronomasia. Amūn can mean " Hidden One."

[7] Paronomasia with Tenen.

[8] Into the silent primordial world he brought the first sound, as he flew as a goose over the primæval water, and he also brought the first light.

He fashioned that which is, and made them live. He caused all men to know the way, in order to go. Their hearts live when they see him – – – –.

CHAPTER ONE HUNDRED.[1]

Who came first into being at the First Occasion, Amūn, that came into existence in the beginning, and none knoweth his mysterious nature. No god came into being before him, and no other god was with him, that he might have told him his shape. He had no mother, who might have given him his name, and no father, who might have begotten him and have said : " It is I." [2]

He who shaped his egg himself, the mighty one of mysterious birth, who (himself) created his beauty. The divine god, who came into being of himself ; all gods came into being, after he began to be.

CHAPTER TWO HUNDRED.[3]

Of mysterious form and gleaming shape, the wondrous god with many forms. All gods make their boast in him, in order to magnify themselves with his beauty, for he is so divine.[4]

Rē himself is united with his body, and he is the great one who is in Heliopolis. Tenen is he named, Amūn, who came forth from Nun – – – –. His other form was the Ogdoad.[5]

The begetter of the Primordial Gods, who fashioned Rē ; he completed himself as Atum,[6] being one limb with him.

He is the Lord of All, the first to exist, and it is his soul, men say, which is in heaven.

He it is who is in the nether world and who presideth in the East. His soul is in heaven, his body in the West, and his image is in Hermonthis exalting his brightness (?).

One is Amūn, who concealed himself from them,[7] who hid himself from the gods, and his nature is not known.

He withdrew himself to heaven and raised (?) himself to the Tēi,[8] and no gods know his true shape.

His image is not spread out in books – – – –. He is too mysterious that his glory should be revealed, too great that

---

[1] Amūn fashioned himself. [2] Whereby he recognizes him as his son.
[3] Again the idea that all gods are only parts of Amūn.
[4] They are proud of being a part of him. [5] Paronomasia.
[6] Paronomasia with this name of the sun-god. [7] Paronomasia.
[8] The realm of the dead. Usually the nether world, here conceived of as in heaven ?

men should question concerning him, too powerful that he should be known.

One falleth down dead on the spot for terror, if his mysterious, unknowable name is pronounced. No god can address him by it, him with the soul (?), whose name is hidden, for that he is a mystery.

CHAPTER THREE HUNDRED.[1]

Three are all gods—Amūn, Rē, and Ptah—and there is none like them. Hidden is his name as Amūn, Rē belongeth to him as face (?), and Ptah is his body.

Their cities abide eternally upon earth, Thebes, Heliopolis, and Memphis unto eternity.

A message is sent from heaven, it is heard in Heliopolis, it is repeated in Memphis to the Fair of Face.[2] A letter is composed in the writing of Thōth to the City of Amūn – – – –. The matter is answered in Thebes, and a declaration cometh forth : " It [3] belongeth to the Ennead " – – – –. (Yet another) message is sent : " It [3] shall slay and it shall keep alive. Life and death are in it [3] for all people."

Only he is : Amūn and Rē and Ptah, together three.

CHAPTER FOUR HUNDRED.

Amūn is described as the god of generation, who formed the genitals, the first to impregnate maidens. First he begat himself when he appeared as Rē in Nun, and fashioned that which is and that which is not. Father of fathers, mother of mothers, the bull for those four maidens.[4]

CHAPTER FIVE HUNDRED.[5]

He who throweth his foes upon their faces, and there is none that can assail him – – – – and his adversaries are not found before him.

A glaring lion with raging claws, devouring the might of him that assaileth him in the completion of a moment.

---

[1] There exist actually only three gods, and even they are only one.

[2] Ptah. The message from heaven which is communicated to Thebes is probably as below on p. 301, the promotion of this city to the position of the capital at end of the heretical period.   [4] Reference to an unknown myth.

[3] Thebes.

[5] The god is terrible when confronting his foes. This account naturally calls to our mind the triumph of Amūn over the heretics, which we certainly meet with on p. 301, and in another poem (pp. 309 f.).

A bull firm of back and heavy of hoofs upon the neck of his foe, whose breast he rendeth.

A bird of prey, flying and seizing on him that assaileth him, able to shatter his limbs and his bones. – – – –.

The mountains are moved beneath him at the time of his raging. The earth tottereth when he belloweth (?). All that is trembleth for terror of him – – – –.

CHAPTER SIX HUNDRED.[1]

Perception is his heart, and Command is his lips – – – –. When he entered the two caverns under his feet, the Nile came forth from the grotto beneath his sandals.

His soul is Shu, and his heart is Tefnet.

He is Harakhti, who is in the heaven. His right eye is the day, his left the night.[2] He it is who leadeth mankind to every way.[3]

His belly is Nun, and he who is therein is the Nile, giving birth to all things that are, and making to live what existeth. He bloweth breath into every nose.

Fate and the Harvest-goddess are with him for all people. His wife is the field, and he impregnateth her,[4] and his seed is the fruit tree, his effluence is grain. – – – –

CHAPTER SEVEN HUNDRED.

The poet turns once more to Thebes. From the fragments, we can still learn that the goddess of writing, as scribe of the entire Great Ennead *writes* a testament *for Thebes. For* Atum spake with his mouth and with a loving heart, *and the gods rejoiced thereat. They have* confirmed that which issued from the mouth of Rē. – – – – The enemy of Rē is burnt to ashes *and everything is* given *to Thebes* : Upper Egypt and Lower Egypt, heaven and earth, and the nether world, with banks (?), waters, and mountains, *what ocean produceth and the Nile.* All that groweth upon the earth-god is hers, and all that the sun riseth upon belongeth to her in peace. – – – – Every land payeth her tribute as her subject, for she is the Eye of Rē, whom none repelleth. *The point of all this is quite clear : after the fall of Amenōphis IV, Thebes is again installed as the capital.*

---

[1] The beneficent nature of Amūn.
[2] *I.e.* sun and moon.   [3] By his giving them light.
[4] By the inundation.

CHAPTER EIGHT HUNDRED.

One landeth [1] as a praised one [2] in Thebes, the region of truth, the place of silence.　Impious men (?) enter not into it, the Place of Truth – – – –.　How fortunate is he that landeth in it! He becometh a divine soul – – – –.　*The fragments still surviving also show that the necropolis of Thebes was extolled here as a place where one may rest in fullest bliss.*

5. FROM THE PRAYERS OF ONE UNJUSTLY PERSECUTED [3]

On the ostraca of a teacher, found in the tomb of Ramesses IX (see above, p. 188), are written a number of charming hymns, of which four, at least, possess a common feature, indicative of their being the poems of one and the same person.　They begin with a somewhat long laudation of the god, and at the end entreat his assistance against a powerful personal enemy who has maliciously deprived the writer of his post.　The god is to resist this enemy, he, the " righteous judge, that taketh no bribe " ; thou helpest the needy, but " thou extendest not thine hand to the powerful." " Comfort the wretched, O vizier,[4] let him be in favour with Horus of the Palace." [5]　It might well be supposed that this man, whose verses the schoolboy was set to copy out alongside of poems dating from the time of Ramesses II, was a well-known Egyptian man of letters, a poet who had fallen into disfavour.

[TO THE SUN-GOD.]

Beautiful is thine (awakening), O Horus, who voyageth over the sky – – – –.　The fire-child with glittering rays, dispelling darkness and gloom.　Child increasing in stature (?) and sweet of form, resting within his Eye.[6]　Awakening all men upon their mats, and the creeping things in their (holes).

Thy vessel pursueth its course in the waters of Neserser,[7] and thou voyagest over the firmament with the wind that is favourable to it.　The two daughters of the Nile shatter for thee

---

[1] " Land " is an ordinary euphemism for " die."

[2] Attribute of the blessed dead.

[3] See my article in *Zeitschr. für ägypt. Sprache*, xxxviii. pp. 19 ff.

[4] The god is conceived of as such elsewhere also ; see p. 308.

[5] The king.

[6] What is meant is shown by representations of the sun-god, as a child, sitting in the midst of the solar disk.

[7] See above, p. 6, note 1.

the dragon,[1] the god of Ombos [2] shooteth him with his arrows, Kēb standeth as witness (?) upon his backbone, Selkis . . . on his throat, and the fiery blast of these snakes burneth him up, even of them that are upon the gateway [3] of thine house. The Greater Ennead, it rageth against him, and how it exulteth when he is hewn in pieces. The Children of Horus,[4] they grasp the knife that they may inflict on him many wounds (?). Aha ! thy foe hath fallen, and right standeth firm in front of thee.

When thou changest thyself again into Atum, thou givest thine hand to the lords of the nether world.[5] They that sleep [6] adore thy beauty all in concert, when thy light shineth in their faces. They speak to thee of what they desire, that thou mayest once more vouchsafe them the sight of thee. When thou hast passed them by, the darkness covereth them, and every man is (again) in his coffin.

Thou art a lord in whom men may make their boast, a potent, everlasting god that giveth judgment, that presideth over the Court of Law, that establisheth Truth and assaileth Iniquity. May he be put on trial that hath trespassed against me. Behold he is stronger than I, and hath robbed me of mine office, which he hath taken from me by lying. Give it me again ! Behold, I see it in the hands of (another) – – – –.

[THE SAME.]

Thou lofty one, whose course is not known, how mysterious is thy being ! August mottled one (?), that giveth light with his two divine eyes.[7] When he setteth the Two Lands are blinded. Beauteous disk with shining light, dispelling the darkness. Great hawk – – – – falcon, traversing the two heavens, voyaging (also) over the nether sky to its full length and breadth, and never sleepeth he upon the way. When day dawneth he revealeth himself again in his place, as the shining one, whose course none knoweth. And how mysterious he is, when darkness setteth in, the dark which blotteth out faces ! [8]

---

[1] The Apōphis dragon which threatens the sun. The daughters of the Nile are unknown to us.
[2] Sēth, who is not regarded here as an evil being.
[3] Gateways are often surmounted by a row of protective snakes.
[4] Four beings, whom Horus had created for the protection of Osiris.
[5] The dead, whom the sun visits during the night-time.
[6] The dead. [7] Sun and moon.
[8] When no one can be recognized.

Thou august sun with white light, by whose beams mankind doth see, in whose nose is breath [1] – – – –. Men live and die by his nod. He it is who causeth the closed nostrils to breathe again, and the straightened throats, according as he will. There is none that liveth without him, and we all have issued from his eye.[2] Give me thine hand, help me – – – –, O judge that (taketh) no (bribe ?) – – – –.

[To Osiris.]

(Praise ?) to thee, who stretcheth out his arms,[3] and sleepeth upon his side. Thou who liest upon the sand, the lord of the soil. Mummy with long member ! – – – –

Rē-Khepre shineth upon thy body, when thou sleepest as Sokaris,[4] that he may dispel the darkness which is over thee, and make light for thine eyes. He standeth still (?) when he ariseth over thy corpse, and waileth over thee . . .

The soil is upon thy shoulder, and its corners (?) are upon thee, as far as the four pillars of the sky.[5] If thou movest (?) the earth quaketh – – – –. *The Nile issueth* (?) from the sweat of thine hands. Thou spittest out the air which is in thy throat into men's noses – – – –. Trees and herbs, reeds and . . ., barley, wheat, and fruit tree.[6]

If lakes are digged – – – –, houses and temples are builded, monuments are dragged, the soil cultivated, tombs and burial-places digged,—they are upon thee, and thou it is that makest them. They are upon thy back. There are more of them than can be put in writing, there is no page *that sufficeth for them* (?). They are all placed upon thy back, and thou (sayest not) : " I am too heavily laden."

Thou art the father and mother of mankind. They live on thy breath, and they (eat) of the flesh of thy body. Primordial God is thy name.

I have . . . in that which thou knowest – – – –. [7]

---

[1] The nose is regarded as the place of breath and life.

[2] See above, p. 286, note 3.

[3] The dead god awakes upon the sand, where the dead are buried.

[4] The old mortuary god of Memphis.

[5] From here onwards the conception of Osiris is an unusual one : he is thought of as lying in the earth, indeed as being himself the earth. Even water and air are derived from him.

[6] We owe him thanks for them also.

[7] Again, what followed here bore personal reference to the poet, but it does not appear to be his usual complaint.

6. SHORTER HYMNS AND PRAYERS

These short poems are preserved to us for the most part in the form of school writing-exercises, and many of the cares and aspirations which they lay before the gods are in accord with their origin. I give first place to those which are addressed to the celestial colleague and patron of scribes, Thōth.

[PRAYER TO THŌTH.] [1]

Come to me, Thōth, thou lordly ibis, [2] thou god, for whom yearneth Hermopolis. Letter-writer of the Nine Gods, great one in Unu. [3]

Come to me, that thou mayest lead me, that thou mayest make me cunning in thy calling. Fairer is thy calling than all callings, it maketh (men) great.

It is found that he who is cunning therein becometh a notable. Many deeds (?) there are that thou doest for them, and they are in the Council of the Thirty. [4]

They are strong and mighty through what thou doest. Thou it is who careth for him that hath no . . . Fate and the Harvest-goddess are with thee. [5]

Come to me and care for me. I am a servant of thine house. Let me tell of thy mighty works in whatsoever land I be.

So will the multitude of men say : " Great things are they that Thōth hath done." So will they come with their children, in order to brand [6] them for thine office.

A goodly calling, O strong deliverer (?), and happy is he that followeth it.

[PRAYER TO THŌTH.] [7]

O Thōth, place me in Hermopolis, in thy city, where life is pleasant ! [8] Thou suppliest what I need in bread and beer, and thou keepest watch over my mouth in speaking.

Would that I had Thōth behind me to-morrow ! [9] Come (to

---

[1] *Pap. Anastasi*, v. 9. 2 ff.

[2] Thōth is depicted as an ibis, or more usually with an ibis-head.

[3] This also is Hermopolis, Thōth's city.

[4] The highest officials. [5] *I.e.* thou hast sustenance.

[6] Like cattle or slaves. [7] *Pap. Sallier*, i. 8. 2 ff.

[8] Does he actually wish to go to Hermopolis, or is it meant figuratively : among thy faithful ones, in thy profession ?

[9] *I.e.* may he stand by me at the posthumous judgment !

20

me), when I enter in before the Lords (of Truth), and so shall I come forth justified.

Thou great dôm-palm, that is sixty cubits in height, whereon are fruits. Stones are in the fruits, and water is in the stones.[1]

Thou who bringest water to a place afar off, come, deliver me, the silent one.[2]

Thôth, thou sweet well for one that thirsteth in the wilderness ! It is closed to him that findeth words to say, it is open to him that keepeth silence. The silent one cometh and findeth the well. The hot-headed (cometh) and thou art (choked ?).[3]

[To an image of Thôth.] [4]

The scribe has set up a small statue of Thôth, the patron divinity of the learned, in his house, and now greets this image. It portrays the god, as is often the case, as a squatting ape.

Praise to thee, thou lord of the house ! Ape with white hair and pleasant form, with friendly nature, beloved of all men.

He is of sehret-stone, he, even Thôth, that he may illumine the earth with his beauty. That which is upon his head is of red jasper, and his phallus is of quartz.[5]

His love leapeth (?) on his eyebrows, and he openeth his mouth to bestow life.[6]

Mine house is happy since the god entered it ; it flourisheth, and is (richly) furnished, since my lord did tread it.

Be happy, ye people of my quarter, and rejoice all my kindred. Behold, my lord it is that maketh [7] me ; yea, mine heart longeth after him.

O Thôth, if thou wilt be to me a champion, I will fear not for the eye.[8]

[1] In view of what follows, the meaning must be that some one parched with thirst saves himself by the juice of these stones.

[2] The humble one who has quiet confidence in God.

[3] The water-holes in the desert are often choked up with gravel and sand.

[4] *Pap. Anastasi*, iii. 4. 12 ff.

[5] The figure consists of these semi-precious stones. They were chosen without regard to the natural colours of the animal, otherwise the moon's disk on his head would not have been red.

[6] Here again the god, and not his image, is meant.

[7] *I.e.* gives me prosperity and advancement.

[8] Meaning, perhaps : as thou didst, and dost, heal the eye of Horus (the moon), so too thou wilt show me favour. (Surely the meaning is

[PRAYER TO RĒ.] [1]

Come to me, Rē-Harakhti, that thou mayest care for me.
Thou art he that doeth, and there is none save thee that doeth
aught. Only thou it is that doeth anything.[2]
Come to me, Atum . . . ! Thou art the august god. Mine
heart goeth forward to Heliopolis – – – – mine heart is happy,
and mine heart rejoiceth.
My requests are heard and my daily petitions. My praises
at night and my prayers, which are perpetually in my mouth—
they are heard to-day.

[PENITENTIAL HYMN TO RĒ.] [3]

Thou Sole and Only One, Harakhti, like whom there is here
none other ! Who protecteth millions, and delivereth hundreds
of thousands ! The saviour of him that crieth unto him, the
lord of Heliopolis.
Punish me not for my many sins. i am one that knoweth
not himself (?). I am a witless man. All day long I follow
my mouth,[4] like an ox after fodder, and at eventide . . . I
am one to whom cooling [5] cometh. All day long go I about
in the . . . house, and by night – – – –

[PRAYER TO AMŪN FOR THE ADVANCEMENT OF THE
TEACHER.] [6]

Mayest thou find that Amūn doeth according to thy desire
in his hour of favour, and that thou art praised in the midst of
the great, enduring in the Place of Truth.[7]
O Amūn, thy high Nile leapeth (?) up to the hills, a lord of
fish, abounding in fowl, and all the poor are satisfied.[8]
Put thou great ones in the places of the great, put thou
the scribe of the treasury, Kagabu, in front of Thōth, thy
(scribe ? of) Truth.

that the image of Thōth will protect its possessor from the evil eye
[Translator].) ·
[1] *Pap. Anastasi*, ii. 10. 1 ff.
[2] Meaning, perhaps : all others help only with words.
[3] *Pap. Anastasi*, ii. 10. 5 ff.
[4] Meaning : I only think about my food ?   [5] Thy favour.
[6] *Pap. Anastasi*, iv. 10. 5 ff.   [7] Usual designation of the necropolis.
[8] Meaning : since thou conferrest so many blessings on all, do something likewise for my teacher.

[Prayer to Amūn, as the righteous judge.] [1]

Amunrē, who wast the first to be king! The god of the Beginning! [2] The vizier of the poor! [3] He taketh not unrighteous reward, and he speaketh not to him that bringeth testimony, and looketh not on him that maketh promises (?). Amunrē judgeth the earth with his finger, [4] and speaketh to the heart. [5] He assigneth the sinner to hell, [6] but the righteous to the West.

[Prayer to Amūn in the court of law.] [7]

Amūn, lend thine ear to one that standeth alone in the court, that is poor, and his (adversary) is rich. The court oppresseth him : " Silver and gold for the scribes of accounts ! Clothes for the attendants ! " [8]

But it is found that Amūn changeth himself into the vizier, [9] in order to cause the poor man to overcome. It is found that the poor man is justified, and that the poor (passeth) by the rich.

Thou pilot, who knoweth the water ! Amūn, thou steering-oar ! [10] . . ., who giveth bread to him that hath none, sustaineth also a servant of his house.

I take not unto me a great one as protector in all my . . ., and I have not placed my . . . under the power of a man – – – – my lord is (my) protector.

I know a strong one ; he is a protector with strong arm, and only he alone is strong.

Amūn, who knoweth what is good (?), thou . . . of him that calleth unto him ! Amunrē, king of gods, thou ox with strong arm, who loveth strength !

[1] *Pap. Anastasi,* ii. 6. 5 ff. *Pap. Bologna,* 1094, 2. 3 ff.
[2] Who first came into existence in chaos.
[3] He is better than the earthly officials who oppress the poor.
[4] A movement of his finger is enough.
[5] Or : " his words go to the heart." Meaning, probably : one does not hear them, but one knows them."
[6] Literally : to the " place of ascent " of the sun, where he burns up the wicked.
[7] *Pap. Anastasi,* ii. 8. 5 ff.
[8] These are the bribes they demand.
[9] He is also the chief justice.
[10] The same line below, p. 310.

[PRAYER TO AMŪN.] [1]

Come to me, Amūn, deliver me in this year of misery.
The sun—it hath come to pass that it riseth not. The winter
is come as summer, the months are reversed (?), and the hours
are disordered.[2]

The great cry unto thee, Amūn, and the small seek after
thee. They that are in the arms of their nurses say : " Give
breath, O Amūn."

Then it is found that Amūn cometh in peace with the sweet
wind before him. He causeth me to become a vulture's wing [3]
and as it were – – –, telling of the might for the herdsman in
the field, the fullers upon the river-bank, the Matoï,[4] who come
from the district, and the gazelles in the wilderness (?).[5]

[HYMN TO AMŪN AFTER HIS TRIUMPH.] [6]

*This hymn, which is especially interesting because of its
attack on the El-Amarnah heresy, has suffered so inconceivably
at the hands of the schoolboy who had to write it out, that we can
only guess at the purport of several verses.*

Amūn, thou bull ! Thou calf *of the heavenly cow (?),* he
who sleepeth in the stall of his . . ., – – – – *when he openeth
his eye* the earth is illumined.

Thou findest him that trespasseth against thee . . . Woe
to him that assaileth thee ! Thy city abideth, (but) he that
assailed thee is overthrown.[7] Fie on him that assaileth thee
in any land !

Amunrē, *thou art* a mast of two stems,[8] *that sustaineth* every
wind, whose . . . are of copper, – – – – it is shaken not in
the face of the north wind – – – –.

---

[1] *Pap. Anastasi*, iv. 10. 1 ff.

[2] Probably only an unusual state of weather is meant.

[3] He probably has in mind the vulture's wings with which Isis fanned
breath into Osiris.

[4] See p. 53, note 8.

[5] Meaning, probably : all things existing may tell of the might of
Amūn. *Cf.* the similar passage, p. 311.

[6] *Brit. Mus. Ostracon,* 5656 ; see *Zeitschr. für ägypt. Sprache,* xlii.
p. 106.

[7] Amenōphis IV, who wished to root out the worship of Amūn. See
above, pp. 288, 294, 300 f.

[8] At an earlier date the masts of Egyptian ships did actually consist
of two stems.

Amūn, thou herdsman, who early seeth after the cows, who driveth the patient (?) to the pasture. The herdsman driveth the cattle to the pasture ; O Amūn, so drivest thou the patient (?) to (their) bread. For Amūn is an herdsman, an herdsman *that is not idle.*

Amūn, thou brazen gateway ! [1] He giveth his reward in its season. The sun of him that knew thee not hath set, O Amūn. But he that knoweth thee, he shineth. The forecourt of him that assailed thee is in darkness,[2] while the whole earth is in sunlight. Whoso putteth thee in his heart, O Amūn, lo, his sun hath risen.

Thou pilot, who knoweth the water ! Amūn, thou steering-oar – – – –. Thou experienced one, who knoweth the *shoals,* who is longed after on the water. Amūn is present when one longeth after him upon the water.

Amunrē, thou [3] Fate and Harvest-goddess, in *whose* . . . is all life ! He that knoweth not (thy) name, he hath woe daily.

Amūn, I love (?) thee and I trust in thee – – – –. Thou wilt deliver me from the mouth of man, on the day wherein he speaketh lies. For the lord of gods, he liveth on truth – – – –. I follow not the care (?) in mine heart ; what Amūn *hath said* cometh to pass.

[FROM A MEMORIAL TABLET.] [4]

The author of these short poems was the painter Nebrē, who was employed in the Theban necropolis during the reign of Ramesses II. His son, the painter Nekhtamūn, lay sick unto death,[5] *so Nebrē turned to Amūn and composed* adorations *to him,* because his might is so great, *and addressed* prayers *to him ; whereupon* he found that the lord of gods came as the north-wind, and sweet air went before him, *and he saved the son.*

[PRAISE OF AMŪN.]

I will make him hymns in his name, I will give him praise up to the height of heaven and over the breadth of the earth.

[1] Conceived of as the place of justice, which decides the questions of reward and punishment ?

[2] The buildings of the heretic, in particular El-Amarnah.

[3] See above, p. 305, note 5.

[4] In Berlin ; see *Sitz.-Ber. Berl. Ak.,* 1911, pp. 1088 ff. ; BATTISCOMBE GUNN, *Journ. of Egypt. Archæology,* iii. pp. 83 ff.

[5] The god had inflicted him with sickness because he had laid hands on a cow which belonged to Amūn.

I will declare his might to him that fareth downstream and to him that fareth upstream.[1]

Be ye ware of him! Tell it to son and daughter, to great and small. Declare it to generations and generations that yet exist not.

Declare it to the fishes in the water, to the fowls in the heaven. Tell it to him that knoweth it and him that knoweth it not: Be ye ware of him![2]

Thou, Amūn, art the lord of him that is silent, one who cometh at the voice of the poor. If I call upon thee when I am in distress, thou comest that thou mayest deliver me. Thou givest breath to him that is wretched, and thou deliverest me that am in bondage.

Thou, Amunrē, Lord of Thebes, art he that delivereth him that is in the nether world, for thou art – – – –. If one call unto thee, thou art he who cometh from afar.

Though the servant is disposed (?) to commit sin, yet is the Lord disposed (?) to be merciful. The Lord of Thebes passeth not a whole day wroth. His wrath is finished in a moment, and nought is left. The wind hath turned about to us in mercy, and Amūn hath turned with (?) his wind.

As thy ka endureth, thou wilt be merciful, and that which is turned away will not return again!

To all this Nebrē adds yet the following words : " I will make this memorial in thy name, and establish this hymn upon it in writing, if thou deliverest for me the scribe Nekhtamūn "— so said I, and thou didst hearken unto me. Now behold, I do that which I have said. Thou art the Lord unto him that calleth unto him, contented with truth, O Lord of Thebes.

It should be observed that Nebrē is not really the author of what professes to be his poem, for the same conceptions often occur on other memorials of this date from the Theban necropolis.

On these also the reader is bidden to beware *of the divinity who punishes, the same hope for mercy is expressed, and there is the address to* great and small, *to him that knoweth, and to him that knoweth not, to the fishes in the stream and to the fowls*

---

[1] Those who pass by here on a journey ?

[2] These two strophes invert the sequence of the first : be ye ware— tell—declare.

in the heaven, *etc. etc. It looks, therefore, as though there was living in the holy places, where the necropolis workers erected their memorial tablets, some person who manufactured votive tablets for the sick and for the recovered, and who supplied them with verses suitable to the occasion—a man of defective education, as his wild orthography shows, but not without poetical talent.*

EXPLANATORY NOTES

*on such names and expressions as require elucidation, but
have not in every instance been commented upon in a
footnote. For the royal names, see the outline of the history
on pp.* xix. *ff.—*(Gr.) *following a name denotes Greek
form ;* (Mod.), *the form in use at the present day.*

ABUSIMBEL : a great rock-cut temple in Nubia, founded by
Ramesses II (Mod.).

ABYDOS : the sacred city of Osiris in Middle Egypt (Gr.).

AMŪN, AMUNRĒ : god of Thebes (p. 282).

ANUBIS : jackal-god of the dead, who presides over the burial
rites (Gr.).

APŌPHIS : the cloud-dragon, who threatens the sun.

ARADUS : a city in Phœnicia (Gr.).

ARSA : possibly Cyprus.

ASKALON : a city on the Phœnician coast.

ASTARTE : a Phœnician goddess.

ATEF-CROWN : a form of crown, especially worn by Osiris.

ATHRIBIS : a city in the southern Delta near Benha (Gr.).

ATUM : name of the sun-god of Heliopolis ; especially used of
the sun in the night-time.

BAAL : the Phœnician god.

BABYLON : a city near modern Cairo (Gr.).

BAST, BASTET : cat-headed goddess of pleasure.

BENBEN : sacred stone in the temple of Heliopolis.

BIBÂN EL-MULÛK : Valley of the Tombs of the Kings at Thebes
(Mod.).

BLESSED : the Blessed Dead, who live in the sky as stars.

BOW, PEOPLE OF : the neighbouring peoples, which, according
to ancient tradition, were reckoned nine in number.

BUBASTIS : city of Bast in the Delta, near Zagazig (Gr.).

BULL : designation of the king and certain gods ; Bull-of-his-
Mother = the sun-god.

BUSIRIS : the sacred city of Osiris in the northern Delta (Gr.).
BUTO : the snake-goddess of Lower Egypt (Gr.).
BUTO : city of the above-mentioned goddess ; the capital of the most ancient Lower Egyptian Kingdom (Gr.).
BYBLOS : port for the Lebanon, the modern Gebêl (Gr.).

CARCHEMISH : city on the Euphrates.
CROWNS : white crown of Upper Egypt, red crown of Lower Egypt ; double diadem, the combination of both. Many others besides, especially for divinities.

DEBEN : weight of 91 grammes.
DOUBLE DIADEM : see under Crowns.

EHNAS : the city of Herakleopolis (Mod.).
EIGHT, EIGHT GODS : beings who existed in the primordial waters, before the world emerged out of them.
ELEPHANTINE : island in the first cataract, boundary of Egypt.
EMOR : country in northern Palestine.
EVENING BARK : ship in which the sun voyages during the night.
EYE : 1. sun and moon as eyes of the sky-god ; 2. the sun, as the eye of the sun-god, fights for him.

FAYYÛM : district of Middle Egypt (Mod.).
FOOD, FIELD OF : field in the sky, inhabited by the Blessed Dead.

GAZA : Philistine coast-town.
GOD'S-LAND : the countries of the East.
GOD'S-WORDS : Writing and the ancient writings.

HARAKHTI : name of the sun-god in Heliopolis.
HARDEDEF : the wise son of King Kheops.
HARSAPHES : the god of Herakleopolis.
HARVEST-GODDESS : see Renenutet.
HATHOR : the ancient sky-goddess, goddess of women.
HAWK : sacred animal of Horus ; then used of the sun-god and of the king.
HEAVEN : conceived of as an ocean, a cow, or a woman.
HELIOPOLIS : the sacred city of the sun-god, known to-day as Mâtârîyeh, near Cairo (Gr.).

HERAKLEOPOLIS : city in Middle Egypt (Gr.).[1]
HERMONTHIS : city of the god Month, south of Thebes ; the modern Erment (Gr.).
HERMOPOLIS : city of Thōth in Middle Egypt, the modern Eshmunên (Gr.).
HIERAKONPOLIS : the capital of the ancient Upper Egyptian Kingdom (Gr.).
HIERATIC : see p. xxxivii.
HIN : a measure of capacity of 0·45 litres.
HORIZON : see p. 15, note 2.
HORUS : 1. the ancient sky- and sun-god ; 2. the son of Isis and Osiris, the prototype of the kings ; 3. the king himself (Gr.).

IARU : field of the Blessed Dead in the sky.
IPU : city of Min, in Upper Egypt, the modern Akhmîm.
ISDES : a god.
ISI : Cyprus ?
ISIS : the wife and sister of Osiris and mother of Horus (Gr.).

JOPPA : a Philistine coast-town.
JUDGMENT, POSTHUMOUS : the deeds of the deceased were weighed by Thōth in the hall of Osiris ; on this examination depended the fate of the dead person.

KA : the vital force, personality ; see p. 24, note 2.
EL-KÂB : ancient capital of Upper Egypt (Mod.).
KADESH : city in the Orontes valley in the Lebanon.
KARNAK : the main part of Thebes, with the great temple of Amūn (Mod.).
KĒB : the earth-god, husband of the sky-goddess and father o Osiris.
KEDI : Asiatic country, possibly Cilicia.
KEFTIU : possibly Crete.
KEHEK : a Libyan tribe.
KEMI : a perfume.
KEM-WER : region of the Bitter Lakes in the Isthmus of Suez.
KHARU : Palestine.
KHATTI : people and kingdom in Asia Minor.
KHEPRE : name of the sun-god, particularly the morning sun conceived of as a beetle.

[1] See BLACKMAN, *Luxor and its Temples*, pp. 41 ff.

KHERHEB : learned priest.

KHNUM : the ram-headed god, who fashions all that is.

KHONS : the moon-god of Thebes.

KOPTOS : city of Min, the modern Kuft in Upper Egypt (Gr.).

KYLLESTIS : a kind of bread (Gr.).

LAND : Black Land is Egypt, Red Land the rest of the world ; the Two Lands are Upper and Lower Egypt.

LETOPOLIS : city north-west of Cairo (Gr.).

LIBYANS : the Berbers of North Africa.

LORDS : the Two Lords = Horus and Sēth.

MANUN : a mountain where the sun goes down.

MASHAWASHA : a Libyan tribe.

MATOÏ : a Nubian country, the inhabitants of which served as soldiers and police in Egypt.

MEMPHIS : the city of Ptah, on the west bank, south of Cairo (Gr.).

MESEKHENT : the goddess of birth.

MIN : an ithyphallic god ; also identified with Horus.

MONTH : the hawk-headed god of Hermonthis ; regarded as the war-god.

MORNING BARK : the ship in which the sun voyages by day.

NAHARINA : country on the Upper Euphrates.

NEITH : goddess of Saïs in the Delta (Gr.).

NEPHTHYS : sister of Isis and Osiris.

NESHMET-BOAT : ship of Osiris at Abydos.

NINE : 1. the Nine Gods, the Great Ennead = the sun-god, his children, grandchildren, and great-grandchildren ; there was also a Lesser Ennead of less important divinities ; 2. the Nine Peoples, *i.e.* the hostile neighbouring peoples of Egypt.

NUN : the primordial waters, out of which the world emerged ; the celestial ocean.

NUT : the sky-goddess ; wife of Kēb, and mother of Osiris and Sēth.

OMBOS : city of Sēth, the modern Kom-Ombo, south of Thebes (Gr.).

ONURIS : name of Shu at Abydos.
ORION : the constellation which is identified with Osiris.
ORONTES : river between the Lebanon and the Anti-Lebanon.
OSIRIS : see pp. 141, 304.
OSTRACON : see p. xlii.

PERSEA : a kind of tree.
PTAH : the god of Memphis, the fashioner of all things.
PUNT : name of the spice-bearing countries at the south of the
    Red Sea.

RAMESSES, HOUSE-OF- : see p. 206.
RAMP : made of bricks, and taking the place of our scaffolding.
RĒ : the sun-god.
RENENUTET, RENENET : the Harvest-goddess.
RETENU : Palestine.
ROSETAU : sanctuary of the funerary god Sokaris, at Memphis.

SAKKÂRAH : the necropolis of Memphis (Mod.).
SEKHAIT : sacred cow, which suckles the kings and other super-
    human beings.
SEKHMET : the dreadful lion-headed goddess of war.
SERPENT, ROYAL : the serpent which the sun-god and the king
    wear as a diadem.
SĒTH : the brother and murderer of Osiris ; war-god, and
    storm-god (Gr.).
SHASHOTEP : a city in Middle Egypt.
SHEDEH : a sweet intoxicating drink.
SHMUN : the city of Hermopolis.
SHU : the god of the atmosphere, who supports the sky, son of
    Rē and brother of Tefnet.
SISTRUM : kind of rattle, the instrument of women.
SOBK : the crocodile-god.
SOKARIS : the ancient funerary god of Memphis, identified with
    Osiris.
SOUL : conceived of as a bird with human head.
SOULS : designation of the gods of the prehistoric capitals.
SUPPORTS : four pillars (?), upon which, according to one con-
    ception, the sky is held up.
SUTEKH : another form of the name Sēth.
SYCAMORE : wild fig-tree (Gr.).

Tanis : city in the north-east of the Delta (Gr.).

Tefnet : a lion-goddess and the sister of Shu.

Tehenu : a Libyan people.

Temehu : a Libyan people.

Tenen : a name of Ptah as primordial god.

Thebes : capital of the New Kingdom, the modern Karnak and Luxor in Upper Egypt (Gr.).

Thinis : city of Osiris, near Abydos.

Thoth : the ibis-headed moon-god and god of wisdom, the scribe of the gods. Also conceived of as an ape.

Timūris : a name for Egypt (Gr.).

To-zoser : the necropolis of Abydos.

Trōglodytes : predatory people between the Nile and the Red Sea (Gr.).

Tyre : the Phœnician port-town.

Uræus : see under Serpent, royal.

User-hēt : the sacred ship of Amūn.

Vizier : current rendering of the title of the official at the head of the Egyptian bureaucracy.

Wawat, Wawa : a district in northern Nubia.

Wennofre : name of Osiris.

West, Western Mountain : the realm of the dead.